OSIRIS KHENTI AMENTI, THE GREAT GOD, THE LORD OF ETERNITY. GOVERNOR OF THE GREAT LAND, SEATED ON HIS THRONE IN THE OTHER WORLD RECEIVING THE ADORATIONS OF THE SCRIBE NEKHT AND HIS WIFE.

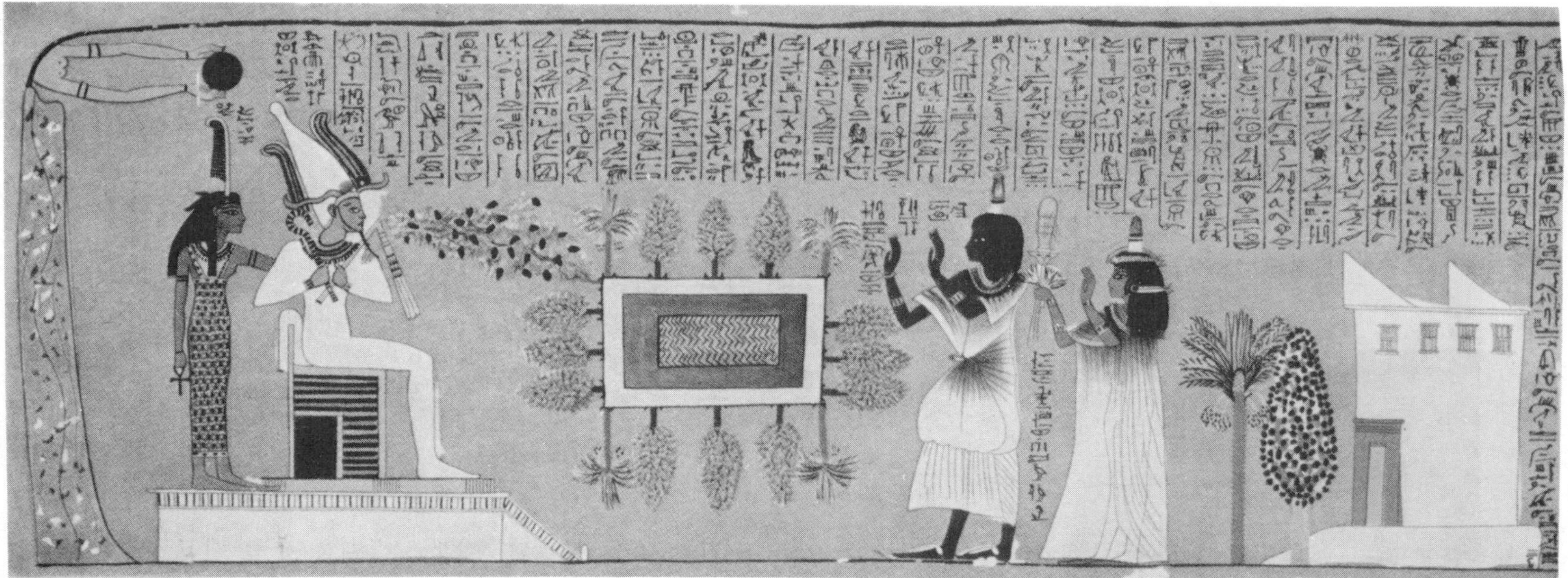

The goddess of the West receiving into her hands the disk of the setting sun.

The goddess Maat, Queen of the Two Lands, (i.e., Upper and Lower Egypt), the daughter of Ra, supporting Osiris.

Osisis, wearing the White Crown with plumes and horns, and holding the symbols of sovereignty and rule, seated on his throne in his Kingdom of Amentet.

The Lake in the Garden of Osiris in the Other World, on the sides of which grow vines, date-palms, fruit trees and spice-bearing shrubs, etc.

The veritable royal scribe and Inspector of soldiers, Nekht.

His beloved sister the singing woman of Amen, Thuau.

Date palm and fruit tree, standing one on each side of the steps leading to the door of the house.

House on a raised platform, with windows high up in the walls, and projections from the flat roof, opening towards the north to admit the wind.

From the Papyrus of Nekht, a royal scribe, in the British Museum (No. 10,471).

OSIRIS AND THE EGYPTIAN RESURRECTION

BY E. A. WALLIS BUDGE

M.A. LITT.D. D.LITT. D.LIT. F.S.A. KEEPER OF THE EGYPTIAN AND ASSYRIAN ANTIQUITIES IN THE BRITISH MUSEUM.

ILLUSTRATED AFTER DRAWINGS FROM EGYPTIAN PAPYRI AND MONUMENTS

From Philip
29 Oct 73
Cairo

In Two Volumes

VOLUME I

DOVER PUBLICATIONS, INC., NEW YORK

This Dover edition, first published in 1973, is an unabridged republication of the work originally published in 1911 by The Medici Society, Ltd.

International Standard Book Number: 0-486-22780-4
Library of Congress Catalog Card Number: 72-81534

Manufactured in the United States of America
Dover Publications, Inc.
180 Varick Street
New York, N. Y. 10014

I

DEDICATE THIS BOOK

ON

THE FUNDAMENTALS OF SÛDÂNÎ AND

EGYPTIAN RELIGION

BY PERMISSION

TO THE HONOURABLE

LIONEL WALTER ROTHSCHILD,

TRUSTEE OF THE BRITISH MUSEUM,

WITH

SINCERE GRATITUDE AND THANKS.

PREFACE.

THE Chapters printed in these volumes are the result of a study undertaken with the object of attempting to discover the source of the fundamental beliefs of the indigenous Religion of Ancient Egypt, to trace their development through a period of some two score centuries, and to ascertain what were the foreign influences which first modified Egyptian beliefs, then checked their growth, and finally overthrew them. There is no doubt that the beliefs examined herein are of indigenous origin, Nilotic or Sûdânî in the broadest signification of the word, and I have endeavoured to explain those which cannot be elucidated in any other way, by the evidence which is afforded by the Religions of the modern peoples who live on the great rivers of East, West, and Central Africa. The central figure of the ancient Egyptian Religion was Osiris, and the chief fundamentals of his cult were the belief in his divinity, death, resurrection, and absolute control of the destinies of the bodies and souls of men. The central point of each Osirian's Religion was his hope of resurrection in a transformed body and of immortality, which could only be realized by him through the death and resurrection of Osiris. I have therefore made Osiris, and the beliefs which grew up under his cult, the central consideration of this enquiry, and have grouped about the history of the god the facts in modern African Religions which are similar and which I consider to be cognate to the old beliefs. The general argument of the book is indicated in the following paragraphs.

The materials now available for the enquiry may be divided roughly into two main classes :—1. The Magical, Religious, and Mythological Texts written by native Egyptians for Egyptians. 2. Accounts of the Magic, Religion, Mythology, and Gods of Ancient Egypt written by Greek and Roman historians and philosophers, *e.g.*, Herodotus, Diodorus, Plutarch, Apuleius, and others, for the use and information of their countrymen. An examination of the statements on the ancient Religion of Egypt found in the works of the above-mentioned and other classical writers, carried on side by side with a study of the Egyptian texts, convinced me that the information supplied by them was wholly unsuitable for the solution of the numerous problems which confront the student of the ancient Egyptian Religion at every turn. The reason of this is not far to seek. The works of classical writers on Egypt and her Religion contain much extremely valuable information, some of which is supported by the native Egyptian texts. On the other hand, there are incorporated with such information many fantastic theories and imaginings which are not only unsupported, but are absolutely contradicted by the facts drawn from the Egyptian monuments; Herodotus and others wrote down, no doubt, accurately enough, so far as they understood it, what they were told by Egyptian priests and by their well-educated friends in Egypt, but it is quite clear, by the construction which they put upon much of the information which they received, that they did not really understand the rudimentary principles of the Egyptian Religion, or its primitive cults, or the nature of their symbolism. There is no evidence in their works that they knew of, or even suspected, the existence in it of the all-embracing beliefs in the power of the great ancestral spirit, and in the resurrection of men in general and their immortality, which are the chief characteristics of the Egyptian Religion. And these writers had no knowledge of the details of the cult of Osiris, and of his history, such as we now possess (thanks to the religious texts of the VIth dynasty), because they could not read the native literature of Egypt. They can hardly be blamed for this, because it is certain that very few of the Egyptian priests took the trouble to read and study it, and to arrange systematically the facts of their Religion which were to be derived from their ancient writings. The confusion and contradictions which appear in the religious texts written under the XXth and following dynasties prove beyond all doubt that the knowledge of the early dynastic Religion of Egypt possessed by the priests in general after, let us say,

1200 B.C., was extremely vague and uncertain. Such being the case, the information which they could impart to cultivated and enquiring foreigners is almost useless of itself for historical investigations. Moreover, the character of the Religion of Egypt changed entirely under the New Empire. Its spiritualities became buried under a mass of beliefs which were purely magical in character, and men in general relied for salvation upon spells, incantations, magical figures, and amulets; only the wise few clung to the beliefs of their ancestors. When Herodotus visited Egypt the knowledge of the Religion of the Ancient and Middle Empires had practically died out.

The general untrustworthiness of the information about the Egyptian Religion supplied by classical writers being thus evident, it is clear that, if we wish to gain exact knowledge about the subject, we must seek for it in the study of the native literature, which is comparatively large and full. A cursory examination of it leads us to hope that we shall find in it all the material we need for the purposes of our enquiry, but a fuller investigation of its contents produces at first a feeling somewhat akin to disappointment. For we find that in no portion of it does there exist a text which is not associated with magic, that no text contains a connected statement of the purely religious beliefs which we know the Egyptians certainly possessed, that on many vital points no text supplies any direct information whatsoever; and finally, that there is in Egyptian no word for "religion" in our sense of the word. After a still further examination, however, the feeling of disappointment vanishes, for if the facts supplied by texts of one period be compared with those afforded by texts of another, it becomes clear that they are all intimately related. The writers of them all assumed the existence of the same beliefs in their readers, and also a knowledge of the essentials of the native Religion of Ancient Egypt, which were understood and were received generally. Thus if we compare the contents of works of the post-Saïte Period, *e.g.*, The Book of Breathings, The Lamentations of Isis and Nephthys, The Festival Songs of Isis and Nephthys, The Book of Making the

Spirit of Osiris, The Book of Traversing Eternity, with those of the works of the New, Middle, and Ancient Empires, *e.g.*, the various Recensions of the Book of the Dead, The Book Ȧm-Ṭuat, The Book of Gates, The Book of Opening the Mouth, The Book of Funerary Ceremonies, and The Book of the Two Ways, we find that the fundamental beliefs in them all are the same, and that the object of one and all was the same, namely, to procure the resurrection and immortality of the persons on whose behalf they were written and recited. In each and all of these a knowledge of the same facts is assumed by the writers to be possessed by the readers, and their acceptance by the readers is regarded as beyond question. In spite of all the popular developments of religious magic which flooded the old Religion of Egypt after the downfall of the New Empire, and the introduction of foreign gods, and the growth of the cults of local tree-gods, phallic gods, etc., the essentials of the indigenous Religion of the country remained unchanged from the time of the early dynasties to the end of the Graeco-Roman Period.

Of the Egyptian works mentioned above the most important for the purpose of an enquiry into the Religion of Ancient Egypt is the Book "Per-em-hru," commonly known as the Book of the Dead. In the oldest form of it with which we are acquainted, namely, that which was in use under the Vth and VIth dynasties, it consists of a long series of spells, and incantations, and rhythmical formulae, etc., which were recited by the priests, probably at regular intervals during the year, for the benefit of the dead. This form is generally known as the "Heliopolitan Recension," because it was the work of the priests of Ȧnu, or Heliopolis, who added to the indigenous sections of it a number of texts in which was promulgated their own particular worship, namely, that of the Sun-god Rā. Each spell and incantation was believed to produce a specific result, but what that result was is not always defined, and the variant titles of some spells prove that the Egyptian priests were not always certain what was the exact result which the recital of the spells would produce. Mixed with these spells are short texts which show that so far back as 3400 B.C. the

Egyptians possessed conceptions of truth, justice, and righteousness. According to these the life everlasting in heaven, in the kingdom of Osiris, could only be attained by those who had lived righteous lives upon earth, and who had been declared to be speakers of the truth in the Judgment Hall of Osiris. The Egyptians set truth-speaking above all other virtues, and in the Great Judgment which took place in the Hall of Osiris the man who had spoken the truth on earth triumphed. Osiris himself was declared by Thoth and by the Great Jury of the gods who tried him to be "TRUTH-SPEAKER," *Maā Kheru*, and the soul of the man after whose name these words could be written with the authority of Osiris was sure of eternal life and bliss.

Under the XIth and XIIth dynasties these spells and texts were copied on to sarcophagi and coffins, *e.g.*, the coffin of Amamu and the coffins from Barshah, and a title was given to each, as, for example, "Chapter of not dying a second time," which generally indicated the object with which the spell was recited. Sometimes a Rubric was added which described the effect which would be produced if the recital of the spell were accompanied by the performance of certain ceremonies. Each spell was complete in itself, and the spells and Chapters taken together composed the Book of the Dead. Under the XVIIIth dynasty an attempt was made to group them together according to their subject matter, and it became the fashion to add to the Chapters vignettes, which were first of all traced in outline in black ink, and were in later times painted in brilliant colours. The idea underlying the addition of the vignettes is not clear, but it seems to have been magical. Under the XVIIIth dynasty it became customary to preface the Chapters and vignettes by a large scene in which was depicted the Weighing of the Heart in the Judgment Hall of Osiris. Such scenes form one of the principal characteristics of the Theban Recension of the Book of the Dead. Down to the end of the XIXth dynasty the Book of the Dead was regarded generally as the final authority on Egyptian psychology and eschatology as understood by the priests of the cult of Osiris. Under the XXth dynasty the priests of

Åmen-Rā succeeded in forcing their god into a position in the Other World which was little inferior to that of Osiris, and this action is reflected in funerary papyri which were written at Thebes under the XXth and XXIst dynasties. With the downfall of the rule of the priests of Åmen-Rā at Thebes Osiris regained his old position of absolute and supreme power in the Other World, and in copies of the Saïte Recension of the Book of the Dead written between 600 B.C. and 100 B.C. the special claim of kingship of all the gods of the Other World put forward by the priests of Åmen-Rā for their god does not appear.

The above facts show that the Book of the Dead existed in an organized and written form during the greater part of the Dynastic Period, and to it we must have recourse if we would understand the Religion of the Egyptians during that time. We might reasonably expect that it would supply us with all the information we require about the Egyptian Religion, and in such a form that there could be no doubt about its meaning. Unfortunately, such is not the case, for however carefully we study the various Recensions, and collate papyri, and arrange the facts available, we find that many gaps still exist in our knowledge, and that our ignorance of the exact meanings of many words makes it impossible to arrive at definite conclusions in many cases. Moreover, we find that such information as we have is not always understood in the same way by all Egyptologists, and that the deductions which they make from the same texts frequently differ in character, and are sometimes wholly contradictory. When, in connection with my official work, I began to enquire into the Religion of Egypt I found that some authorities thought that it was full of the spiritual and metaphysical conceptions which characterize the Religions of some highly civilized modern nations, and was highly philosophical in its nature. Others thought that it consisted of a series of crude and savage beliefs which found expression in disgusting ceremonies, and cannibalistic orgies, and licentious rites, similar to those which are performed at the present day among the Negroes and Negroid peoples in the Southern and Western Sûdân. Others regarded it as a kind of solar cult based upon beliefs which were originally derived from Asia, but which were so corrupted and overlaid with native additions as to be unrecognizable. Others, again, considered it to be wholly phallic in character, and there were yet others who thought that it was nothing but a system of Black Magic, and undeserving of the name of a Religion.

When I had considered these views in detail it seemed to me that their authors must have described the Religion of Egypt from different standpoints, and that their conflicting opinions had been based upon some aspects of it, without due attention having been given to others. It was quite obvious that all these opinions could not be right at the same time, and that the only course left for the enquirer to pursue under the circumstances was to examine them one by one, and to compare them with facts derived exclusively from ancient Egyptian texts. The principal texts available at that time (1883) were the published copies of the papyri of Nebseni, Qenna, Neb-qet and Sutimes, the texts from coffins at Berlin, the Turin Papyrus, the Book of Opening the Mouth, the Book of Gates, and the first portion of the text of Unȧs. In the years which followed editions of many magic, religious, and liturgical papyri appeared, and before the close of last century the material available for an enquiry into the character of the Egyptian Religion was abundant. In fact, the student was then able to compare for the first time the contents of the Heliopolitan, Theban, and Saïte Recensions of the Book of the Dead with those of several other cognate funerary works which, though belonging to a later period, are of great value.

The examination of this material occupied much time, but the more it was worked the clearer it became that many of the theories current as to the Egyptian Religion were wrong. The facts derived from the texts, when arranged, proved beyond all doubt that the indigenous Religion of ancient Egypt was unlike any of the Asiatic Religions with which it had been compared, and that all its fundamentals remained unchanged throughout the Dynastic Period. Moreover, the evidence of the tomb-deposits of the Predynastic, Archaïc, and early Dynastic Periods which, thanks to the excavations of tombs made at Abydos, Naḳadah, Ballâs, and other parts of Upper Egypt, had become available, proved that the religious beliefs of the people who had made these tombs were substantially the same in all three Periods. And it became clear that the general character of the Religion of the dynastic Egyptians was identical with that of the Religion of the primitive Egyptians. In other words, the facts derived from the papyri, sarcophagi, coffins, stelae, etc., were supported in a remarkable manner by the testimony of early tomb-deposits. The evidence derived from the Egyptian texts also supplied information about several beliefs and characteristics of the Religion in all periods. It showed *inter alia* that the Egyptians believed in the existence of God Almighty, and that His behests were performed by a number of "gods," or as we might say, emanations, or angels; that magical rites and ceremonies of all kinds were closely associated with beliefs of a highly spiritual character; that the religion was not phallic, although the importance of the organs of generation, male and female, was greatly emphasized in connection with the worship of such "gods" as Menu and Ȧmen; that birds, beasts, fishes, reptiles, trees, stones, etc., were venerated because they were believed to form the habitations of "gods" and spirits at certain times and under certain circumstances; that amulets of all kinds were worn by the Egyptians, when living, and were laid on the bodies of the dead *because* it was thought that the benevolent, indwelling spirits would protect them from the spirits of evil; that sacrifice was of vital importance, both for the living and the dead, and was regarded as worship of the highest kind; that the natures of material objects were transmuted into spirit entities when they were laid upon consecrated altars, etc. There is no need to refer here to the doctrines of reward and punishment, resurrection and immortality, for the existence of these among the Egyptians was demonstrated by E. de Rougé in 1860, and again by P. Pierret in 1881.

All these characteristics seemed to indicate that the Egyptian Religion was of African rather than Asiatic origin, as many had supposed, but the chief obstacle to the acceptance of this view was the fact that the religious literature of Egypt contains numerous hymns to the Sun-god under his various forms, *e.g.*, Temu, Rā, Horus, and Kheperȧ, and frequent allusions to a heaven in which Rā is the King and Lord of all the Gods. It is well known that the cult of Rā, under one phase or another, was the form of Religion accepted by the Pharaohs, and the priesthood, and a limited aristocracy, from the middle of the Vth dynasty onwards. And as each king, beginning with Ȧssȧ, delighted to call himself "son of Rā," and regarded himself as an incarnation of Rā, this is not to be wondered at. On the other hand, there is no evidence that the great bulk of the people of Egypt adopted the cult of Rā, and many Chapters of the Book of the Dead prove that the Moon-god was their favourite object of worship. Many African peoples, especially those who live in the great forests and on the Nile, Congo, Niger, and other great rivers, not only regard the Sun with indifference, but with positive dislike; on the other hand, the Moon and its spirit are venerated devoutly. Proofs of this fact are found in the writings of many travellers, whose works are quoted in their proper place in this book. Taking into consideration all the information available on the subject, it is tolerably clear that the cult of the Sun-god was introduced into Egypt by the priests of Heliopolis, under the Vth dynasty, when they assumed the rule of the country and began to nominate their favourite warriors to the throne of Egypt. These astute theologians, either by force or persuasion, succeeded in making the official classes and priesthood believe that all the indigenous great gods were forms of Rā, and so secured his supremacy. Meanwhile, the bulk of the people clung to their ancient cult of the Moon, and to their sacred beasts and birds, etc., and worshipped the spirits which dwelt in them, wholly undisturbed by the spread of the foreign and official cult of the Sun-god, which appealed so strongly to the great mixture of peoples in the Eastern Delta, and in the desert to the east and north-east of Egypt. It seems to me, then, that the existence of the cult of Rā in Egypt does not affect the enquiry into the indigenous Religion of Egypt in any way.

During the years 1890–93, I was engaged officially in preparing for publication the volume which the Trustees of the British Museum issued with the second edition of their *Facsimile of the Papyrus of Ani*, and in the three following years I prepared privately the edition of The Theban Recension of the Book of the Dead which appeared, with an English translation and an Egyptian–English Vocabulary, in three volumes in 1897. The writing of the Introductions brought me face to face with the difficulty of explaining the belief in the existence of the Dual Soul, and the extraordinary ideas as to its functions and capabilities which underlie the Chapters of the Heart (XXVI–XXXB), and the Chapters of Transformations (LXXVI ff.), and ancient Egyptian psychology and eschatology in general. None of the existing works on the Egyptian Religion explained the difficulties, but a perusal of the articles which Professor Maspero had contributed to the *Revue des Religions* (tom. XII, p. 123 ff.; tom. XV, p. 159 ff.; and tom. XIX, p. 1 ff.) showed that this eminent Egyptologist had battled with the same difficulties, and that he, like myself, was disposed to explain them by references to the beliefs of modern African peoples in the Sûdân and West Africa. Moreover, the writings of the late E. Lefébure and of Professor Wiedemann, of Bonn, contained evidence that they shared the same view.

Early in the summer of 1897 my official duties led me to Marawi, in the Dongola Province of the Egyptian Sûdân, and I took up my abode in the neighbouring village of Shibbah to be near the excavations which were carried out that year at Gebel Barkal. During the months I lived there I came into contact with shêkhs and "fiḳîs" (*i.e.*, religious teachers) and many kinds of natives, and from them I learned much about Sûdânî beliefs and religion. The information I gained confirmed and supplemented the reports on such matters which I had heard in Egypt on several occasions from Egyptians who had lived in the Sûdân under the rule of Isma'îl Pâshâ, and I found that it explained many of the beliefs which are enshrined in the Book of the Dead.

During subsequent visits to the Sûdân I became convinced that a satisfactory explanation of the ancient Egyptian Religion could only be obtained from the Religions of the Sûdân, more especially those of the peoples who lived in the isolated districts in the south and west of that region, where European influence was limited, and where native beliefs and religious ceremonials still possessed life and meaning. I then began to read systematically the books of all the great travellers in the Sûdân, beginning with the Travels of Ibn Baṭûṭah, and ending with recent publications like Mr. Ward's *Voice from the Congo.* The notes made in the course of this reading formed a large mass of material which seemed to me to be of great value for the comparative study of the Egyptian and Sûdânî Religions, and they illustrated in a remarkable manner the similarity of ancient Egyptian and modern African religious beliefs. It may be objected that the modern beliefs and superstitions of the Sûdân and Congo-land and Dahomey are survivals of ancient Egyptian religious views and opinions, but the objection seems to me to possess no validity. The oldest and best form of the Egyptian Religion died more than 3,000 years ago, and many of the most illuminating facts for comparative and illustrative purposes are derived from the Religions of peoples who live in parts of Africa into which Egyptian influence never penetrated. The power of the Egyptians reached no farther than the northern end of the "Island" of Meroë, and it was not truly effective beyond Napata, the modern Marawi, near the foot of the Fourth Cataract. Modern Sûdânî beliefs are identical with those of ancient Egypt, because the Egyptians were Africans and the modern peoples of the Sûdân are Africans. And making allowance for differences in natural circumstances and geographical position, ancient and modern Nilotic peoples give outward expression to their beliefs in the same way.

Having arranged my notes and extracts from the works of travellers, it became apparent that it was hopeless to expect to print them all as they stood, for the result would be an unwieldy and unreadable notebook. The general evidence derived from the Religion of Ancient Egypt showed that all the great fundamental beliefs centred in Osiris and his cult, and I therefore decided to attempt to write the history of the god and of his principal forms, to describe the salient points of his worship, and to illustrate the beliefs which were crystallized in it with the facts collected in Egypt and the Sûdân, and those derived from narratives of travellers in those countries. With the cult of Osiris was bound up all that was best in the civilization of Egypt during the Dynastic Period. It weaned the primitive Egyptians from cannibalism and from cruel and barbarous customs, it taught them to respect human life and to regard man as the image of God, and his dead body as a sacred thing, it induced them to devote themselves to agricultural labours, and it improved their morality. Above all, it transformed them from nomad hunters and thieves into a settled people with a god, a priesthood, and a worship, and taught them to believe in divine incarnation, and gave them a hope of resurrection and immortality, and of an existence in heaven, which, they were taught, could only be attained by those who had lived righteous lives upon earth, and through the mercy of Osiris.

The Egyptian texts now available enable us to trace the history of the cult of Osiris from the Archaïc to the Roman Period with tolerable completeness, but its beginning is hopelessly lost in obscurity. Osiris was, I believe, an African, though not necessarily a Nilotic, god, and the birthplace of his cult seems to have been Upper Egypt. The exact meaning of his name is uncertain, for that of "Seat-maker," which is suggested by the Pyramid Texts, is hardly convincing; it is better to admit the fact at once and to say that its meaning is unknown. As regards the seat of his worship in Upper Egypt, it is quite certain that a shrine of the god existed at Abydos under the Ist dynasty. At first sight it seems as if he was merely a deified king who had lived and reigned in the immediate neighbourhood of that town. Early in the Dynastic Period his priests cleverly succeeded in incorporating in his worship all that was best in the local cults, and the ideals of morality, justice, and righteousness which they grouped about it appealed quickly to the people all over Egypt. The spread of the cult was rapid, both in Upper Egypt and in the Delta, because no other cult offered to its adherents the hope of the resurrection and immortality. Among the tribes of Egypt in general the cult of Osiris took the place of the cult of ancestral spirits, which was universal in the Nile Valley in primitive times, but the people lost nothing by the exchange, for Osiris became the divine ancestor of them all. His human nature, they thought, enabled him to understand the needs, troubles, and griefs of men, and to listen sympathetically to their prayers, and his divine nature gave him powers to help them in this world and in the next, which no other Ancestor-god ever possessed. Osiris, the divine Ancestor, became the Father of the souls of the Egyptians, and the symbol of their hope of resurrection and immortality.

The early religious texts of Egypt prove beyond all doubt that the Egyptians, in common with many peoples in other parts of the world, when in a primitive state of civilization, were cannibals in the Predynastic Period, and that, like many of the Nilotic tribes of the present day, they ate the bodies of enemies slain in battle as a matter of course. Before the coming of the cult of Osiris they must have eaten their own dead, as many modern tribes do, and there is reason to think that, even after they had learned to know Osiris, the natural liking for human flesh, which is common to most African peoples, asserted itself in times when food was scarce and during famines. The disposal of the bodies of the dead must always have been a matter of difficulty in Egypt, for land suitable for purposes of agriculture was far too valuable to the living to be given up to the dead. The bodies of kings, chiefs, nobles, and rich men were always buried, sometimes in tombs hewn in the rocks, and sometimes in the sandy soil on the edge of the desert, and at one time it must have been thought that they were the only members of the population who would enjoy a future existence. The bodies of the bulk of the people were either laid in extremely shallow graves, from which they would be dragged easily by the dogs, and by the wolves, foxes, and jackals of the desert, or were thrown out boldly into the desert (or into "the bush" as they say in the Southern Sûdân at the present day) to be eaten by the leopards, hyenas, lynxes, etc.

If we assume that during the Dynastic Period, which lasted about four thousand years, the population of Egypt was about four millions, and that the average duration of a generation was twenty-five years, we find that the number of bodies to be disposed of would reach the large total of eight hundred millions. Now it is quite clear that only a very small percentage of these bodies can have been "buried" in such a way that they would be preserved for an indefinitely long period. For the cost of preparing tombs in the hills and of equipping them with funerary furniture even of the most inexpensive kind, or of digging graves and providing them with suitable "deposits," was wholly prohibitive for the greater part of the population. The number of bodies which were made into mummies must have been very small. That very few people were "buried" in Egypt is proved by the comparatively small number of tombs which have been found up to the present time. For, if we were to add together the numbers of all the ancient Egyptian tombs known both to Europeans and natives, it is very doubtful if the total would exceed fifty thousand, if we exclude the Predynastic graves. Many of the rock-hewn tombs were used over and over again, no doubt for many generations, but even so, the proportion of the "buried" bodies to the unburied is very small indeed. Attempts have recently been made to calculate the duration of certain periods of Egyptian history by computing the number of graves found in groups of cemeteries, but it seems to me that all calculations of the kind are worthless, because we do not know what proportion of the population was buried in any century, or even generation.

Now the spread of the cult of Osiris, however great, could never alter the material resources of the country, and make it possible for all persons to be buried in such a way that their bodies would be preserved for an indefinitely long period. Its priests, however, could, and I believe did, lay a *tabû*, or ban, on the eating of the dead, because the bodies of all Osirians belonged to the god. From them, moreover, by means of the ceremonies performed by the priests and the words of their services, were raised up their spirit-bodies, which were to inherit eternity. According to the priests of Osiris immortality could only be attained by belief in their god, and the souls of unbelievers could not enter his kingdom ; they had, to all intents and purposes, no hope of resurrection, and therefore could have no existence in the Other World. What the fate of the body of an Osirian was ultimately mattered very little, provided that the sacred words of the liturgy of the dead had been said over it, for through these the genesis of the spirit-body and its union with its soul in Abydos or Busiris were assured. The costly tombs, and elaborate mummification, and funerary ceremonies, and splendid copies of the Book of the Dead, and inscribed amulets, with which the great and wealthy provided themselves, availed their owners nothing in the Judgment Hall of Osiris, and the true Osirian must have regarded them more as evidences of wealth and power than as effectual means of salvation. For he knew that in that Hall the hearts of kings and peasants alike were weighed in the Balance before a just Judge, and that the sentence pronounced was in accordance with the evidence given by the Warder of the Balance. The pleadings of Thoth, who had acted as advocate for Osiris on a memorable occasion, were heard by Osiris, and his recommendations appear to have been generally adopted by the god. As no man could possibly fulfil the demands of the Law, it was the mercy of Osiris which ultimately decided the fate of a soul in the Other World, and not the splendour of a tomb, or the magnificence of a funeral procession. The king who was declared justified in the Judgment lived presumably with the rank and state of a king in the Other World, the noble as a noble, and the poor man as a poor man ; but for all there was only the same hope, and that hope was Osiris. Osiris the god became this hope because he had lived in a body which had suffered, and died, and had been mutilated, and had, after reconstitution, been raised from the dead by the god incarnate in it, and had passed into heaven.

The texts and monuments also indicate that the

primitive Egyptians were in the habit of burying slaves alive in the graves of great kings and chiefs, so that their spirits might depart to their masters in the Other World, and minister to their souls there as they had ministered to the needs of their bodies upon earth. A vignette in the Book "Am-Ṭuat" even suggests that slaves had been buried alive in the tomb, one at each of the four corners, which held the mortal body of Osiris. Moreover, the presence of the bodies of the women in the tomb of Ȧmen-ḥetep II at Thebes proves that in the XVIIIth dynasty favourite wives were either poisoned or strangled, or allowed to commit suicide, so that their spirits might go to their husband in the Other World and continue their wifely service to him. The bloodthirsty character of this king, which displayed itself in hanging the bodies of seven vanquished chiefs at the bow of his boat, and in exposing them on the walls of Thebes and Napata, suggests that the unfortunate women in his tomb were slain in accordance with his wishes. The absence of bodies of women and slaves from the other royal tombs and from the *mastabahs* of Gîzah, Ṣaḳḳârah, etc., seems to indicate that tomb-murders became less and less frequent as the cult of Osiris spread in Egypt. The custom of burying figures of stone, wood, faïence, etc., with the dead, instead of living slaves with their arms and legs broken at the joints, seems to be as old as the XIth dynasty at least. Other cruel and savage customs also disappeared, and in the sacramental ceremonies of the later period we find the blood of the grape, the bread-cake, and the flesh of newly slaughtered animals, taking the place of the human flesh and blood which played such prominent parts in the older ceremonies.

The sacrificing of prisoners of war to one or other of the gods seems to have gone on to the end of Egyptian history, and the reliefs on the monuments in which kings are seen in the act of "smashing" the heads of living captives are certainly representations of events which actually happened. The importance attached by Africans in all periods to "watering" the statues of gods and divine personages with human blood at frequent intervals, and in all times of war, scarcity, trouble, and distress, is too well known to need mention. And their innate proclivities suggest that portions at least of the bodies of human victims slain to "give life" to the gods were eaten sacramentally. Among the sun-worshippers of Egypt the sacrifice of human victims to the god was held to be of vital importance for the god and themselves, and the festival in which the "smashing of the Ȧntiu" (*i.e.*, the dwellers in the Eastern Desert) was commemorated at Heliopolis was the principal religious event of the year in that city. The festival commemorated a great victory of a decisive character over certain rebel tribes, and the atrocities which triumphant Africans can commit when drunk with slaughter and mad with the smell of blood, readily suggest what was the horrible fate of the Ȧntiu. In the Sun-temples at Abû-Ṣîr of the IVth dynasty, wherein the presence of the god was symbolized by a stone somewhat resembling an obelisk in shape, countless human beings were sacrificed. The size and number of the conduits for carrying away the blood of the victims bear incontrovertible evidence of the magnitude of the slaughterings which took place. And we have it on the authority of Procopius (*De Bello Persico*, I, xix, p. 103) that the Blemmyes at Philae were in the habit of sacrificing men to the sun so late as the reign of Diocletian.

We may now summarize briefly the character of the ancient Religion of Egypt. The Recensions of the Book of the Dead and cognate works prove that, in addition to Osiris, the Egyptians paid divine honours to the Sun-god, Moon-god, Air-god, Water-god, Sky-god, Earth-god, Nile-god, and to a host of spirits, of whom we know the names of about three thousand. What relation all these "gods" and spirits bore to each other and to Osiris is not at first clear, and it is the realization of the existence of these which has induced some writers to declare that the Egyptian Religion was nothing but a polytheistic cult. And yet it was not, for the Egyptians believed in the existence of One Great God, self-produced, self-existent, almighty and eternal, Who created the "gods," the heavens and the sun, moon and stars in them, and the earth and everything on it, including man and beast, bird, fish, and reptile. They believed that

He maintained in being everything which He had created, and that He was the support of the universe and the Lord of it all. Of this God they never attempted to make any figure, form, likeness, or similitude, for they thought that no man could depict or describe Him, and that all His attributes were quite beyond man's comprehension. On the rare occasions in which He is mentioned in their writings He is always called "Neter" 𓊹𓀭, *i.e.*, God, and besides this He has no name. The exact meaning of the word "Neter" is unknown. His behests were carried out in heaven, earth, and the Other World by a number of "great gods" who formed His Council, and who were in turn served by lesser "gods" and spirits. The two eldest of the great gods, Shu and Tefnut, were produced by God from His own Person, and with Him they formed the first Egyptian Trinity. Shu and Tefnut produced Ḳeb and Nut, and they in turn produced Osiris and Isis, and Set and Nephthys, all of whom were born on the earth at the same time, each having a mortal body. Osiris was white and was the personification of good, Set was black (or red) and was the personification of evil. These two gods fought each other continually, and at length Set killed the mortal body of Osiris. Osiris begot by Isis a son called Horus, who avenged his father and slew Set. Osiris rose from the dead and became the king of heaven, the abode of righteous souls, and Set, who took the form of a black pig, became the lord of the region where the souls of the damned congregated.

The management of the physical world and of the lives and affairs of men was deputed by God to the "gods," "goddesses," and spirits, of whom some were supposed to view man and his affairs benevolently, and others malevolently. Little by little the fear of these obtained great power over the minds of men, and at length the worship due to God from men was paid by men to them. No proof of any kind is forthcoming which shows that the Egyptians ever entirely forgot the existence of God, but they certainly seem to have believed that he had altogether ceased to interfere in human affairs, and was content to leave the destinies of men to the care of the "gods" and spirits. Now the Egyptians were not satisfied with this state of affairs, and they craved to know a god who possessed a nature akin to their own, and who because he was of like nature to themselves would be more sympathetic towards them than the Sun-god, or the Earth-god, or any other impersonal nature-god or spirit. To satisfy this craving the primitive theologians of Egypt invented the dogma which declared that Osiris and Set, and Isis and Nephthys, appeared on earth in the forms of human beings, and that their mortal bodies were absolutely similar in every respect to the bodies of men born of women. It is nowhere stated where, or by what means, Osiris and Set obtained their mortal bodies, nor whether they were created from the dust of the earth, or derived from a human mother. The Egyptians do not seem to have troubled themselves about questions of this kind, but were quite satisfied to believe that Osiris became incarnate in a mortal body, which possessed the nature of ordinary man. Other dogmas made Osiris to suffer death at the hands of Set, to beget a son by Isis after his death, to rise from the dead in a transformed body, and to dwell in heaven as the lord of righteous souls. This information is derived from texts which are as old as the VIth dynasty, and thus we see that as early as 3500 B.C. the Egyptians believed that gods became incarnate in man.

Now, if we examine the Religions of modern African peoples, we find that the beliefs underlying them are almost identical with those described above. As they are not derived from the Egyptians, it follows that they are the natural product of the religious mind of the natives of certain parts of Africa, which is the same in all periods. The evidence of the older travellers, De Brosses, Mungo Park, Livingstone, and others, and that of more recent travellers such as Dr. Nassau and Sir Harry Johnston, proves that almost every African people with whom they came in contact possessed a name for God Almighty, in Whose existence and power they firmly believed. Their attitude towards God was, and is, exactly that of the ancient Egyptians. As the view advanced by Mungo Park in the XXIst Chapter of his *Travels in the Interior of Africa* represents the opinion of most travellers, from the days of Andrew Battell to those of Sir Harry Johnston, it must be quoted here. He says: "Some of the religious opinions of the Negroes, though blended with the weakest credulity and superstition, are not unworthy of attention. I have conversed with all ranks and conditions upon the subject of their faith, and can pronounce, without the smallest shadow of doubt, that the belief in one God, and of a future state of reward and punishment, is entire and universal among them. It is remarkable, however, that, except at the appearance of a new moon, as before related, the Pagan natives do not think it necessary to offer up prayers and supplications to the Almighty. They represent the Deity, indeed, as the creator and preserver of things; but, in general, they consider him as a being so remote, and of so exalted a nature, that it is idle to imagine the feeble supplications of wretched mortals can reverse the decrees, and change the purposes of unerring Wisdom. . . . The concerns of this world, they believe, are committed by the Almighty to the direction and superintendence of subordinate spirits, over whom they suppose that certain magical ceremonies have great influence."

This remarkable statement may be supplemented by the opinion of George Grenfell (see *Grenfell and the Congo*, vol. ii, p. 635), who says: "In the east and south-east of Africa the conception of the Deity *may* be gradually attained through steps of ancestor-worship. . . . But in the Congo basin God is rather imagined as the pre-existing Creator, Who has probably called men into existence, however indifferent He may afterwards show Himself to the fate of each human being. . . . In the beliefs of many of these Congo Negroes the Supreme God of the Sky is too far off to care about humanity; He created all things, and left everything but the supreme command to a multitude of petty spirits; or He allowed unchecked the spitefulness of a lesser god, a more or less malignant Devil."

The facts quoted in the preceding paragraphs show that it is wrong to class the Religion of Ancient Egypt with the elaborate theological systems of peoples of Asiatic or European origin, and worse than useless to attempt to find in it systems of theological thought which resemble the Religions of peoples who live on a higher level of civilization than the primitive Egyptians. The fundamental beliefs of the ancient Egyptian belong to a time when he was near to Nature, and when he leaned more upon God than he did upon himself. As he grew more civilized he relied more upon himself, and less upon God, and the forms and ceremonies of religion were then brought into existence by the priests. In its earliest form his religion was not a matter of creed and dogma, but a personal, natural and spontaneous pouring out and uplifting of the emotions from the individual to the Infinite. His religious ceremonials may, it is true, have begun with the worship of the powers of procreation, or of their symbols, the organs of generation, or of spirits of some kind; but the Egyptian's Religion was much older than these, and it must have originated in his sensations, emotions, and instincts. Religion was a reality to him long before he could describe it, and the spirits which he could not see were also realities to him. So real, in fact, were they that the fear of what he thought they could or would do to him became the prime mover of his actions as regards the practical worship of them, or religious ceremonials. In times of difficulty caused by the human beings who lived round about him, and who were always more or less his foes, he appealed for guidance and help as a matter of course to his father and grandfather, so long as they lived, and when they were dead he turned to their spirits for assistance. So long as he was helped out of his troubles, and was successful in all his undertakings, he attributed his good fortune to the power of his father's or grandfather's spirit. But when disaster followed all his efforts he was naturally driven to look for help beyond his father's spirit, to that great, first Spirit, Who had made the first member of his own and of every other tribe, and everything which existed in the world. In this way the Egyptians first found God, the Creator of all. His religion, which was wholly natural and personal, was at all times a mixture of fear of spirits in general, and of hope in the power of ancestral spirits. This power developed later in his mind into the veritable power of

God, Whom he believed to be incarnate in his great ancestor Osiris.

What Major A. G. Leonard says of the religion of the Lower Niger tribes is equally true, in my opinion, of the religion of the ancient Egyptians. Their religion, which was their entire sociology and existence, is nothing from beginning to end but a long chain of ancestral precedents, every single link and rivet of which became a custom and a law from their spiritual fathers unto themselves in the flesh. The fathers of the tribes became first spirit fathers, and when these had developed into ancestral "gods," a system of worship grew up around them, and their propitiation was held to be necessary; out of this worship religious customs arose, a formula of offerings and sacrifices gradually developed, and this finally took the form of ritual.

In setting the facts given in the following pages before the reader I make no claim to have cleared up all the difficulties which surround the history of the origin and development of the Egyptian Religion, but I certainly think that they indicate the means which must be used in explaining fundamental Egyptian beliefs and religious ceremonial. Whether I have succeeded in showing that a general resemblance exists between ancient Egyptian beliefs and the beliefs of modern Sûdânî peoples, the reader will decide. It is important to have the facts collected, and it is high time for the attention of students of comparative African Religion to be directed to them. The plan of this book is simple. I have first of all given the history of Osiris as it is found in the works of Greek and Roman writers. This is followed by a chapter on the death and mutilation of gods, the facts for which are derived from early texts. Next follow a series of chapters in which the various forms of Osiris are described and discussed, and a chapter containing details of the heaven of Osiris and the state of beatified souls and spirit-bodies in the heaven of Osiris. The sources from which the information on these points is drawn are the texts in the corridors and chambers of the royal pyramids at Ṣaḳḳârah. The translations of the passages given in Chapter IV and in the Appendix appear in English for the first time. Other chapters are devoted to describing the principal forms of Osiris, and the cult of Osiris as practised at Abydos, Denderah, etc., and to the history of the decline of the cult of Osiris, and the extraordinary growth of the cult of Sarapis and Isis, not only in Egypt, but in the Islands of the Mediterranean and in Southern Europe. A lengthy chapter containing a series of comparisons between ancient Egyptian and modern Sûdânî Religion and magic is also given. Some important notes, too late for insertion in their proper places, will be found in Vol II, pp. 364–6.

My grateful thanks are due to the Hon. Lionel Walter Rothschild for the kind assistance he has afforded me in all questions relating to the African animals, birds, reptiles, and insects which appear in Egyptian mythology, and for the trouble he has taken in explaining to me the various specimens of them which are preserved in his great collections at Tring Park. To Mr. T. A. Joyce, M.A., of the British Museum, I am also much indebted for information about the manners, customs, and Religion of many West African and Congo-land peoples, and for references to exhibits in the National Collection. I have also derived much information from the invaluable *Annales du Musée du Congo*, and especially from the volume of *Notes Ethnographiques*, by Mr. E. Torday and Mr. Joyce. These works throw great light on the social life and religious customs of the primitive Egyptians. My obligations to the works of the great travellers and missionaries, Mungo Park Burton, Speke, Junker, Stanley, Sir Harry Johnston, Livingstone, Krapf, Nassau, and George Grenfell, to name only a few, are acknowledged throughout in the notes.

I am indebted to Messrs. Harrison and Sons for the skill and care with which they have printed this book and to their Reader, Mr. G. Bishop, for the attention which he has devoted to the reading of the proofs.

E. A. WALLIS BUDGE.

BRITISH MUSEUM,
September 4th, 1911.

CONTENTS OF VOLUME I

		Page
PREFACE		vii
LIST OF ILLUSTRATIONS		xxxiii
CHAPTER	I.—THE HISTORY OF OSIRIS AS TOLD BY CLASSICAL WRITERS	1
,,	II.—THE NAME AND ICONOGRAPHY OF OSIRIS ...	24
,,	III.—THE MUTILATION AND DISMEMBERMENT OF OSIRIS, HIS RECONSTITUTION AND RESURRECTION, HIS ENTRANCE INTO HEAVEN, AND HIS STATE OF BEING THERE...	62
,,	IV.—THE HEAVEN OF OSIRIS UNDER THE VIth DYNASTY, WITH TRANSLATIONS FROM THE PYRAMID TEXTS	100
,,	V.—OSIRIS AND CANNIBALISM	167
,,	VI.—OSIRIS AND HUMAN SACRIFICE, AND FUNERAL MURDERS	197
,,	VII.—OSIRIS AND DANCING	231
,,	VIII.—OSIRIS AND SACRIFICE AND OFFERINGS, THE PROPITIATION OF GOOD AND EVIL SPIRITS BY OFFERINGS, AMULETS, ETC.	247
,,	IX.—OSIRIS, THE ANCESTRAL SPIRIT AND GOD ...	288
,,	X.—OSIRIS AS JUDGE OF THE DEAD	305
,,	XI.—THE AFRICAN BELIEF IN GOD AND THE DOCTRINE OF LAST THINGS	348
,,	XII.—OSIRIS AS A MOON-GOD	384
,,	XIII.—OSIRIS AS A BULL-GOD	397

ILLUSTRATIONS TO VOLUME I

Plates

The Military Scribe Nekht and his Wife adoring Osiris ... *Frontispiece*

Facing page

Osiris seated on his Throne. From the Greenfield Papyrus in the British Museum 43
The lady Ȧnhai in the Elysian Fields. From her papyrus in the British Museum 140
The Princess Nesi-ta-neb-asher in the Elysian Fields. From the Greenfield Papyrus in the British Museum 148
The Weighing of the Heart of the lady Ȧnhai. From her papyrus in the British Museum 330
The Weighing of the Heart of Princess Nesi-ta-neb-asher. From the Greenfield Papyrus in the British Museum 338
Osiris seated in Judgment. From a bas-relief in a Chapel of a pyramid at Meroë 344

Illustrations in Line

Page

Osiris embraced by Isis and Nephthys 3
The Funeral Coffer of Osiris and the Erica tree 5
The Ṭeṭ of Osiris at Abydos 6
Isis, cow-headed, pouring out water for the soul of Osiris ... 8
Thoth bearing life and serenity 10
Thoth writing on his palette 10
Isis addressing the mummy of Osiris 12
Osiris, in the form of a bull, bearing a mummy 13
Nephthys addressing the mummy of Horus of the Ṭuat ... 14
Osiris seated in his shrine 20
Osiris in the Moon 21
Osiris supported by Isis and Nephthys under the Winged Beetle of Rā 29
Scene from the Mace-head of Nārmer 36
Osiris seated in a shrine below clusters of grapes 38
The type-form of Osiris seated 40
The type-form of Osiris standing 41
Osiris seated on top of the steps 42
Ȧmentet in the shrine of Osiris 44
A form of Osiris of Philae 45
Osiris the Riser 46
Osiris-Seker and the Merti-goddesses 47

	Page
Horus and his sons before Osiris and Sarapis	48
The Seven Forms of Osiris worshipped at Abydos	49
Osiris wearing the White Crown	50
Osiris wearing the Atef Crown	50
Osiris wearing the White Crown and plumes	50
Osiris Un-Nefer	50
Osiris, Lord of Eternity	50
The Ṭeṭ as the Ka of Rā	51
Osiris Un-Nefer as Ṭeṭ	51
The Ṭeṭ with the whip and crook of Osiris held in human hands	51
Ṭeṭ with the head of Osiris	52
Priest performing a ceremony on the Ṭeṭ in the presence of Isis	52
Ṭeṭ as an old man (2 forms)	52–3
Osiris-Seker wearing the White Crown	53
Isis setting up the standard of the head-box of Osiris	54
The goddesses of the South and North setting up the standard of the head-box of Osiris	55
Seti I presenting bandlets to the Ṭeṭ	56
Seti I and Isis setting up the Ṭeṭ...	56
Thoth and Anubis setting up the standard of the head-box of Osiris	56
The head-box of Osiris, with plumes and disk	56
Osiris-Seker in his funeral coffer	57
Osiris-Neprȧ with wheat growing from his body	58
Osiris the Moon-god	59
Osiris and Sarapis	61
Horus giving life to Osiris...	83
The Souls of Osiris and Rā meeting in Ṭaṭṭu (Busiris)	87
Horus on a Ka-standard	95
Set on a Ka-standard	95
The Ladder from earth to heaven	124
Hunters and Warriors of the Archaïc Period	170
Egyptian portrait of a Sûdânî man	183
King Nārmer sacrificing a prisoner	199
King Nārmer offering decapitated captives to his gods	201
Decapitated captives with their heads between their feet ...	203
The wicked burning in a pit of fire head downwards	205
Enemies of the god burning in a pit of fire	205
The Heads of Enemies burning in a pit of fire	205
The Souls of Enemies burning in a pit of fire	205
The Shadows of Enemies burning in a pit of fire	205
King Ṭen sacrificing a prisoner	207
King Seneferu sacrificing a prisoner	207
A serpent spitting at the decapitated enemies of Rā	208
King Ȧmen-em-ḥāt sacrificing a prisoner...	209
King Thothmes IV sacrificing a prisoner	209
King Senka-Ȧmen-Seken sacrificing a prisoner	211
Ptolemy VIII spearing a prisoner...	213
Ptolemy XII sacrificing a batch of prisoners	213
A Meroïtic Queen spearing prisoners	215
A Meroïtic Queen spearing prisoners	217

	Page
A Meroïtic Queen sacrificing prisoners	219
A Meroïtic Queen sacrificing prisoners	221
The sacrifice of two Nubians to the Ṭeṭ of Osiris	223
King Semti dancing before Osiris (?)	232
Thothmes III dancing before Hathor	233
Bes, the god of music, playing a harp	235
Primitive shrines in Egypt...	247, 248
Osiris seated in his shrine in Abydos	249
Seti I offering incense to Osiris	249
Horus presenting life to Osiris-Seker	251
Thoth and Horus binding together the two thrones of Egypt ...	251
Seti I pouring out a libation to Osiris	253
A priest pouring out a libation to Osiris	253
Seti I offering incense and a libation to Osiris	253
Seti I offering incense to Osiris (2 scenes)	255
Seti I offering incense to Osiris (2 scenes)	257
Seti I presenting a censer of burning incense to Osiris	259
Seti I presenting a censer of burning incense and pouring out a libation to Osiris	259
Seti I offering unguents to Osiris	261
Seti I anointing the face of Osiris...	261
Seti I offering raiment to Osiris	263
Seti I offering sceptres to Osiris	263
Seti I offering a breastplate to Osiris	265
Seti I offering fruit to Osiris	265
Seti I offering bandlets to Osiris (2 scenes)	267
Seti I opening the door of the shrine of Osiris	269
Seti I addressing Osiris-Seker in his shrine	269
Seti I adoring Osiris, Isis, the Ram-god, and the sacred bull's skin	271
Seti I adoring Osiris-Seker and two Ram-gods in their shrine ...	271
Seti I presenting unguents to Ḥeqet, the Frog-goddess	279
Anubis and the goddess Ḥeqet embalming Osiris	280
The goddess Ḥeqet watching the union of Osiris with Isis ...	280
Ancestor worship in the Sûdân	291
The Birth of Horus in the Papyrus Swamps	301
Nekhebit and Ḥu presenting life to Isis	302
Uatchit and Sa presenting life to Isis	303
Osiris in his closed shrine with Isis and his four grandchildren...	310
The scales of Maāt (Truth)	316
King Munza wearing his crown of state	321
Skin of the pied bull of Osiris	327
Skin of an animal sacred to Osiris	328
Anubis weighing the heart	329
The gorilla of the Book of the Dead	329
A human-headed object (umbilical cord box?)	331
Osiris in the Meroïtic Period	344
The Four Apes of the Lake of Fire	346
Khnemu fashioning a Ptolemy on his potter's wheel	355
The Cow-goddess Hathor	401

OSIRIS AND THE EGYPTIAN RESURRECTION

CHAPTER I.

The History of Osiris as told by Classical Writers.

The religious literature of all the great periods of Egyptian history is filled with allusions to incidents connected with the life, death, and resurrection of Osiris, the god and judge of the Egyptian dead; and from first to last the authors of religious texts took it for granted that their readers were well acquainted with such incidents in all their details. In no text do we find any connected history of the god, and nowhere are stated in detail the reasons why he assumed his exalted position as the judge of souls, or why, for about four thousand years, he remained the great type and symbol of the Resurrection. No funerary inscription exists, however early, in which evidence cannot be found proving that the deceased had set his hope of immortality in Osiris, and at no time in Egypt's long history do we find that the position of Osiris was usurped by any other god. On the contrary, it is Osiris who is made to usurp the attributes and powers of other gods, and in tracing his history in the following pages we shall find that the importance of the cult of this god grew in proportion to the growth of the power and wealth of Egypt, and that finally its influence filled both the national and private life of her inhabitants, from the Mediterranean Sea to the Sixth Cataract at Shablûkah. The fame of Osiris extended to the nations around, and it is to the hands of foreigners that we are indebted for connected, though short, narratives of his history. These, though full of misunderstandings and actual misstatements, are of considerable interest and value, and we must summarize them and set their principal contents before the reader before we attempt to set out the facts concerning the god which are found in the texts of ancient Egypt.

Plutarch, who was born at Chaeroneia, in Boeotia, about the middle of the first century after Christ, in his famous treatise on Isis and Osiris[1] informed the Lady Clea, for whom he wrote the work, that Osiris was the son of Rhea (in Egyptian, Nut, the Sky-goddess) and Chronos (in Egyptian, Ḳeb, the Earth-god). He was born on the first of the five epagomenal days of the Egyptian year, and became king of Egypt; whether he reigned from his birth or was crowned king after he had grown up is not stated. Having become king, he devoted himself to improving the condition of his subjects. He weaned them from their miserable and barbarous manners, he taught them how to till the earth and how to sow and reap crops, he formulated a code of laws for them, and made them to worship the gods and perform service to them. He then left Egypt and travelled over the rest of the world teaching the various nations to do what his own subjects were doing. He forced no man to carry out his instructions, but by means of gentle persuasion and an appeal to their reason, he succeeded in inducing them to practise what he preached. Many of his wise counsels were imparted to his listeners in hymns and songs, which were sung to the accompaniment of instruments of music. During the absence of Osiris his own kingdom was administered by his wife Isis, who performed the duties committed to her charge with great wisdom and prudence. Her task was not easy, for she found it necessary to use all vigilance and to be ever ready to counteract the changes which Typhon,[2] her brother-in-law, was continually endeavouring to introduce.

After Osiris returned from his travels Typhon appears to have made up his mind to get rid of him, and to

[1] *De Iside et Osiride;* see Didot's edition of his *Scripta Moralia*, tom. I, p. 429, where the Greek text is printed side by side with a Latin translation. A most useful English version is that of Squire, published at Cambridge in 1744. The French version, with notes, of Amyot, published at Paris in 1818–1820, contains much interesting information. The German version of Parthey is also useful.

[2] In Egyptian TEBHA .

seize the kingdom, and to take possession of his wife, Isis, with whom he was violently in love. With the view of carrying out his baleful design, he hatched a plot, and persuaded seventy-two persons, as well as a certain queen of Ethiopia, who was called Aso (Ἀσώ), to join in the

Osiris being embraced by Isis and Nephthys. The four mummy figures are the Children of Horus, Åḳeset, Ḥap, Ṭuamutef, and Qebhsenuf. The deities in the circles are Åmen and Rā, Shu and Tefnut, Ḳeb and Nut, Hathor and Maāt. From a bas-relief at Philae.

conspiracy. He caused a very handsome box, or chest, to be made the exact size of the body of Osiris, the measure of which he had caused to be taken by craft, and having richly decorated it, he had it brought into his dining room and left there. He then invited Osiris to a banquet, at which all the fellow-conspirators were present, and whilst the guests were admiring the handsome box, Typhon, speaking as if in jest, declared that he would give it to him that was able to lie down comfortably in it. Thereupon one after the other of the seventy-two conspirators tried to get into the box, but were unable to do so. At length Osiris expressed his willingness to make trial if the box would contain him, and finding that it did he lay down in it. All the conspirators rushed to the box, and dragging the cover quickly over it, they fastened it in position with nails, and then poured lead over it. Thus it became impossible for Osiris to breathe, and he was suffocated. The conspirators, under the direction of Typhon, then dragged the box from the banqueting hall to the bank of the Nile, and cast it into the river, which carried it northwards, and it passed out to sea by the Tanitic mouth of the Nile. The day of the murder of Osiris was the 17th of the month of Hathor,[1] when the sun was in the constellation of Scorpio; according to some Osiris was in the 28th year of his reign, and according to others, in the 28th year of his age. When the report of the murder reached Isis, who was then in the city of Coptos, she immediately cut off one of the locks of her hair, and put on mourning apparel, and wandered about the country in a distraught state searching for the box which contained her husband's body. Certain children who had seen the box thrown into the Nile told her what had been done with it, and how it had floated out to sea by way of the Tanitic mouth of the Nile.

Meanwhile the waves had carried the box to the coast of Syria and cast it up at Byblos,[2] and as soon as it rested on the ground a large Erica tree sprang up, and growing all round the box enclosed it on every side.

[1] November. This day is marked as triply unlucky 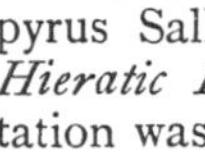 in the Calendar of Lucky and Unlucky Days given in the Papyrus Sallier IV (Brit. Mus. No. 10,184); see also Budge, *Egyptian Hieratic Papyri*, Plates XXXI and XXXII. On this day great lamentation was made by Isis and Nephthys for their brother Osiris, the sounds of which were heard from Saïs in the north to Abydos in the south.

[2] The old town was situated on a tract of high ground between Sidon and the Promontory Theoprosopon. See Strabo, XVI, ii, 18. The modern village of Jebêl is near the site.

The king of Byblos marvelled at the size of this tree, and had it cut down, and caused a pillar for his palace to be made of that portion of the trunk which contained the box. When this news reached Isis she set out at once for Byblos, and when she arrived there she sat down by the side of the fountain of the palace and spoke to no one except the queen's maidens, who soon came to her. These she treated with great courtesy, and talked graciously to them, and caressed them, and tired their

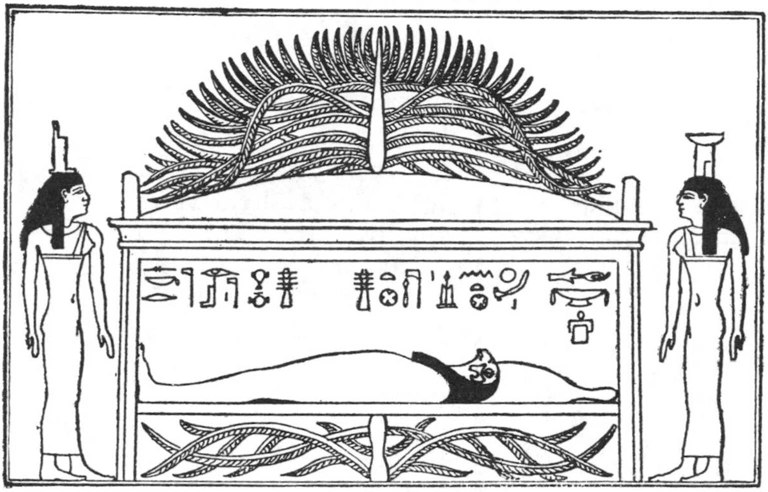

The Funeral Coffer of Osiris and the Erica tree. At the head stands Nephthys and at the foot Isis.
From a bas-relief at Denderah.

heads, and at the same time transferred to them the wonderful odour of her own body. When the maidens returned to the palace the queen perceived the odour which emanated from their hair and bodies, and learning from them that it was due to their contact with Isis, she sent to her and invited her to come to the palace. After a conversation with her she appointed her to be the nurse of one of her children. The name of the king of Byblos was Melkarth[1], and that of his wife Astarte (Ishtar, Ashtoreth). Isis gave the child her finger instead of her breast to suck, and at night she burned away in fire his mortal parts, whilst she herself, in the form of a swallow,

[1] Plutarch calls him Malkandros, but this seems to be a mistake for מלקרת.

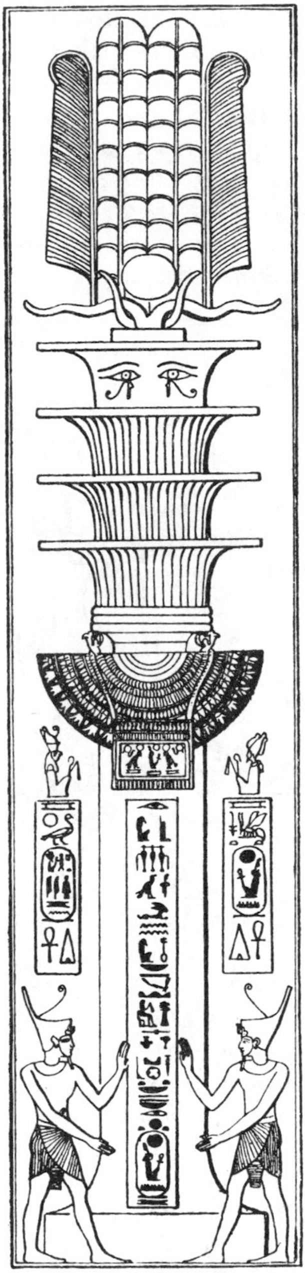

The Ṭeṭ of Osiris, with the plumes, horns, disk, breast-plate and pectoral of the god. From a bas-relief at Abydos.

flew round and round the pillar which contained the body of Osiris, uttering mournful chirpings. After she had treated the child thus for some time, the queen one night saw her son burning in the fire, whereupon she uttered a piercing cry, and so prevented him from obtaining the gift of immortality which was about to be bestowed upon him. Then Isis revealed herself to the queen, and told her her story, and begged that the pillar might be given to her. When this had been done, she removed it and cut out the box, and having wrapped the pillar up in fine linen and anointed it with unguents, she gave it back to the king and queen, who sent it to the temple of Byblos, where it was duly and regularly worshipped by the people of the city. The tree trunk, or pillar, is confused with the Ṭeṭ, the raising up of which to an upright position was one of the most sacred ceremonies of the great festival of Osiris. The illustration shows the Ṭeṭ in the form in which it was worshipped at Abydos. This done, Isis threw herself upon the box and uttered such piercing shrieks and lamentations that the younger of the king's sons was frightened into convulsions and died on the spot. She then placed the box in a boat, and taking the elder son with her, she set sail for Egypt.

Soon after her departure she

opened the box, and laying her face on that of her dead husband, she embraced his body, and wept bitterly. Meanwhile the boy, wondering what was happening, stole up behind and spied upon her; when Isis became aware of this she turned round suddenly, being in a great passion, and in her anger cast so terrible a look upon him that he died of fright. Some, however, say that he did not die through the wrath of the goddess, but that he fell into the sea and was drowned. He is said to be the "Maneros" upon whom the Egyptians call during their feasts.

In due course Isis arrived in Egypt from Byblos, and having placed the box in an out-of-the-way place, she set out to visit her son Horus, who was being reared at Butus.[1] The box was, however, discovered by Typhon, the murderer of Osiris, one night whilst he was hunting by the light of the moon, and knowing whose the body was, he broke it up into fourteen pieces, which he scattered throughout the country. When the news of the dismemberment of Osiris reached Isis, she set out in search of his scattered limbs. This region of the Delta being full of marshes and canals Isis travelled about in a boat made of the papyrus plant, which was sacred to her. No crocodile dared to attack her in her papyrus boat, and unto this day men make their boats of papyrus, because they believe that when in them they are safe from the attacks of crocodiles. Isis was successful in her search, and wherever she found a member of her husband's body she buried it, and built a sepulchre over it; this explains why there are so many tombs of Osiris in Egypt. Some say that Isis only buried figures of Osiris in the various cities and pretended that they were his body, so that she might thereby cause the worship of her husband to be general, and that Typhon, distracted by the number of the tombs of Osiris, might despair of ever being able to find the true one. Isis found all the members of the body of Osiris save one, which was cast by Typhon into the Nile after he had severed it from the body, and had been eaten by the Lepidotus, Phagrus, and Oxyrhynchus fishes, but she made a figure of it which was ever after used in commemorative festivals.

[1] The city Pe-Ṭep of the hieroglyphic texts.

After these things Osiris returned from the Other World and encouraged his son, Horus, to do battle with Typhon. A fight took place between them which lasted for several days, and at length the murderer of Osiris was vanquished and taken prisoner, and handed over to the custody of Isis. Feeling some

The cow-headed Isis pouring out a libation in honour of the soul of Osiris, which rises in the form of a man-headed hawk from the plants growing in a sacred lake.
From a bas-relief at Philae.

compassion for her brother-in-law she cut his bonds, and set him at liberty, an act which enraged Horus so greatly that he tore the royal crown off his mother's head. In its place Thoth gave her a crown made in the shape of an ox's head. Typhon made use of his liberty to accuse Horus of illegitimacy, but the matter was tried before the gods, and by the assistance of Thoth, who acted as his advocate, Horus was enabled to prove to the gods that he was the lawful successor to the throne of his father, Osiris. Subsequently Isis had union with her husband, Osiris, and the result of the god's embrace was the child Harpokrates, who came into the world prematurely, and was lame in his lower limbs in consequence. "Such are the principal facts of "this famous story, the more harsh and shocking parts "of it, such as the dismemberment of Horus, and the "beheading of Isis being omitted."

Diodorus, who was born at Agyrium in Sicily in the latter half of the first century B.C., relates in his famous history the following concerning Osiris and Isis: The early generations of men thought there were two principal gods that were eternal, that is to say, the sun and the moon; the former they called "Osiris," and the latter "Isis." The name Osiris means "many-eyed" (πολυόφθαλμον), and is rightly applied to the sun, which darts his rays everywhere, seeing as it were with many eyes what is on land and sea. The name "Isis" means "ancient," and has been applied to the moon from time immemorial. Osiris and Isis govern the whole world, and they foster and protect everything in it, and they divide the year into three parts, spring, summer, and winter.[1] After Hephaistos, the next king who reigned over Egypt was Kronos (in Egyptian, Ḳeb), who married his sister Rhea (in Egyptian, Nut), and became the father of Osiris and Isis. Others say that Zeus and Hera were the rulers of Egypt, and that from them five gods were born, one upon each of the five epagomenal days, viz., Osiris, Isis, Typhon, Apollo, and Aphrodite. Those who hold this view identify Osiris with Bacchus, and Isis with Ceres. Osiris married Isis, and after he became king he performed many things for the benefit and advantage of mankind generally. He abolished cannibalism, which was common in Egypt, he taught the people to plough and to sow, and to raise crops of wheat and barley, and Isis showed them how to make bread, and was the first to make them acquainted with the use to which wheat and barley could be put. For this reason they offer to Isis the firstfruits of the ears of

[1] Book I, Chap. 11.

corn at harvest, and invoke her powerful assistance with loud cries. It is also said that Isis formulated a code of laws which provided wholesome punishments for wild and violent men.[1]

Osiris was greatly devoted to agriculture. He was brought up in Nysa, a town of Arabia Felix, where he discovered the use of the vine. He was the first to drink wine, and he taught men to plant the vine, and how to make and preserve wine. He held Hermes (in

Thoth, the advocate of Osiris, bearing life and serenity.

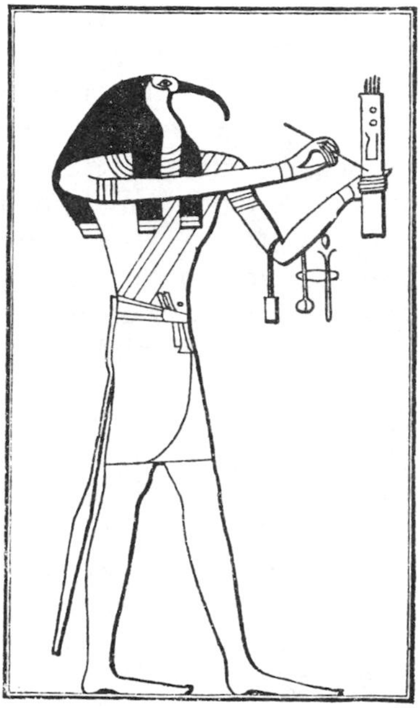

Thoth, the advocate of Osiris, writing on his palette.

From the Papyrus of Hunefer.

Egyptian, Thoth) in high honour, because of his ingenuity and power of quick invention. Hermes taught men to speak distinctly, he gave names to things which possessed none before, he invented letters, and instituted the worship of the gods, he invented arithmetic, music, and sculpture, and formulated a system of astronomy. He was the confidential scribe of Osiris, who invariably accepted his advice upon all matters. Osiris raised

[1] Book I, Chap. 14.

a large army, and he determined to go about the world teaching mankind to plant vines and to sow wheat and barley. Having made all arrangements in Egypt he committed the government of his whole kingdom to Isis, and gave her as an assistant Hermes, his trusted scribe who excelled all others in wisdom and prudence. He appointed to be the chief of the forces in Egypt his kinsman Hercules, a man of great physical strength. Osiris took with him Apollo (in Egyptian, Horus), Anubis who wore a dog's skin, Macedo who wore a wolf's skin, Pan (in Egyptian, Menu), and various skilful husbandmen. As he marched through Ethiopia, a company of satyrs was presented to him; he was fond of music and dancing, and therefore added them to the body of musicians and singers, both male and female, who were in his train. Having taught the Ethiopians the arts of tillage and husbandry, he built several cities in their country, and appointed governors over them, and then continued his journey. On the borders of Ethiopia he raised the river banks, and took precautions to prevent the Nile from overflowing the neighbouring country and turning it into a marsh, and he built canals with flood-gates and regulators. He then travelled by way of the coast of Arabia into India, where he built many cities, including Nysa, in which he planted the ivy plant. He took part in several elephant hunts, and journeying westwards he brought his army through the Hellespont into Europe. In Thrace he killed Lycurgus, a barbarian king, who refused to adopt his system of government. Osiris became a benefactor of the whole world by finding out food which was suitable for mankind, and after his death he gained the reward of immortality, and was honoured as a god.

For some time the priests kept secret the manner of his death, but at length some of them, being unable to keep the knowledge to themselves, divulged the matter. Osiris was, in fact, murdered by his wicked brother, Typhon, who broke his body into twenty-six pieces, and gave a piece to each of his fellow-conspirators, to make them equally guilty with himself, and so to force them to raise him to the throne of Osiris and to defend him when there. Isis, the sister and wife of Osiris, with the assistance of her son Horus, avenged his murder, and took possession of the throne of Egypt. She searched for and found all the pieces of her husband's body save one, and she rejoined them by means of wax and aromatic spices, and made the body to be of the former size of Osiris. She then sent for the priests and told each of them that she was going to entrust to them the body of Osiris for burial, and she assigned to them one-third part of the country to serve as an endowment for his worship. Isis ordered them also to dedicate to Osiris one of the beasts which they bred, and, whilst it was alive, to pay to it the same veneration which they paid

Isis addressing the mummy of Osiris as it lay in her boat ready for removal to the tomb.

to Osiris, and when it was dead, to worship it as sincerely as they did Osiris. This the priests did, and the animal they dedicated to Osiris was the bull, and they renewed their mournings for Osiris over the graves of two bulls in particular, namely, Apis and Mnevis. Isis also ordered that models of the missing part of the body of Osiris should be made, and they were adored in the temples, and were held generally in great veneration.

Isis then made a vow never to marry again, and she spent the rest of her days in administering justice among her subjects, and she excelled all other princes in her works of charity towards her own people. After her death she was numbered among the gods; her tomb, according to some, is at Memphis, and, according to others, at Philae. It is said that Isis discovered many medicines, and that she was greatly skilled in the art of physic. Even as a goddess she interests herself in healing men's bodies, and to all who seek her help she appears in dreams and gives relief. Several people who were sent away by the physicians as incurable have been restored to health by her; and the lame have been

Osiris in the form of a bull, bearing a mummy of one of his worshippers on his back. From a coffin in the British Museum (No. 29,777).

made to walk and the blind to see by her powerful help. They say that she discovered a medicine which would raise the dead to life, and that by means of it she restored to life her son Horus, who had been killed by Titans, and whose body had been thrown into the water; to him she gave this medicine, and he not only came to life again but became immortal. From Isis, Horus learned the arts of physic and divination, which he used for the benefit of mankind.[1]

Julius Firmicus Maternus, who had practised the law, and who flourished in the first half of the fourth century A.D., treats the history of Osiris in a somewhat different manner. In his short treatise *De Errore Profanarum Religionum*,[2] which appears to have been written with a view of exposing the futility of idolatry, and the absurdity of raising men to the rank of gods and then worshipping them, rather than to show the excellence of the Christian religion, he writes of Osiris thus:—Osiris and Isis were brother and sister, and

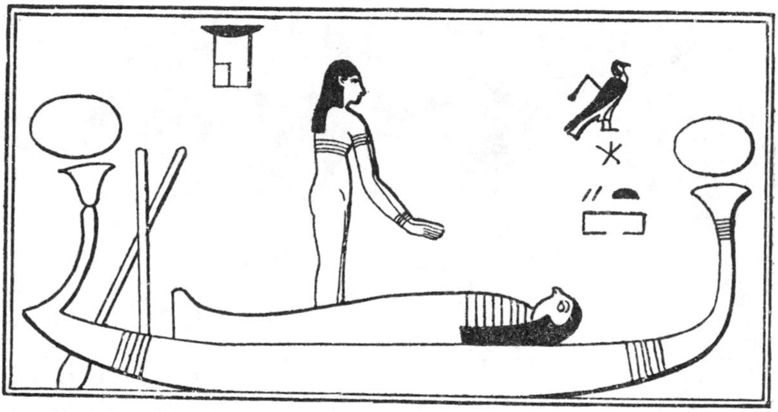

Nephthys addressing the mummy of Horus, who had been slain by Set and his fiends.

Typhon was the husband of Isis. Finding that Isis was overtaken by illicit love for her brother, Typhon slew Osiris in a crafty manner, and having torn the body in pieces, he scattered the quivering limbs along the banks of the Nile. Isis thrust her husband Typhon from her in disgust, and joining to herself her sister Nephthys and the dog-headed Anubis, she determined to search for the limbs of Osiris and bury them. With the help of Anubis she found them, and gave them burial, and Osiris, who had been a just man, was henceforward worshipped in the temples under the form of a figure made to resemble him. Typhon, on the other hand,

[1] Book I, Chap. 25.
[2] See *Mythologicii Latini*, edited by Commelinus, 1599.

being proud, haughty, and arrogant, was held in abomination. In the sanctuaries of Osiris his murder and dismemberment were annually commemorated with weepings, and wailings, and great lamentations. His worshippers shaved their heads, and beat their breasts, and gashed their shoulders, and inflicted wounds on their bodies in imitation of the cuts and gashes which Typhon made in the body of Osiris. Whenever possible they cut into the scars which were left by the gashes of the preceding year, so that the remembrance of the abominable murder of Osiris might be renewed in their minds. When they have done this for a certain number of days, they pretend that the mutilated remains of the god have been found and rejoined, and then they turn from mourning to rejoicing. Those who defend these practices say that grain is the seed of Osiris, that Isis is the earth, and that Typhon is heat.

Another ceremony which connects Osiris with some local tree-god is also described by Firmicus Maternus (*op. cit.*, p. 299). He says that in the mysteries of Isis a pine tree was cut down and hollowed out, and that with the pith of the tree a figure of Osiris was made, which was then buried and, having been kept for a year, was burned.[1] Macrobius, who flourished in the first half of the fifth century A.D., held the view that Osiris was the sun and Isis the earth. In proof of his assertion that Osiris is the sun he says that the Egyptians represent this god in their hieroglyphs under the form of a sceptre with an eye in it, and that they indicate by this the idea of the god surveying the universe from his exalted throne in the sky.[2]

The accounts of Osiris and Isis given by Diodorus,

[1] In Isiacis sacris de pinea arbore caeditur truncus. Hujus trunci media pars subtiliter excavatur. Illis de feminibus factum idolum Osiridis sepelitur. . . . . Sed et illa alia ligna quae dixi, similis flamma consumit, nam etiam post annum ipsorum lignorum rogum flamma depascitur.

[2] Nec in occulto est, neque aliud esse Osirin, quam solem, nec Isin aliud esse, quam terram, ut diximus, naturamve rerum . . . . . hinc Osirin Aegyptii, ut solem esse asserant, quoties hieroglyphicis litteris suis exprimere volunt, insculpunt sceptrum, inque eo speciem oculi exprimunt, et hoc signo Osirin monstrant, significantes hunc deum solem esse, regalique potestate sublimem cuncta despicere. —*Saturnaliorum*, Book I (Panckoncke's edition, tom. I, p. 253).

Plutarch, Firmicus Maternus, and Macrobius, which have been summarized above, are important, and it is clear from the allusions to Osiris and Isis, which are scattered through the works of other authors of the early centuries of the Christian Era that, speaking generally, they represent the views which were current among classical writers at that time. Both Plutarch and Diodorus agree in assigning a divine origin to Osiris, and both state that he reigned in the form of a man upon the earth. This being so it is clear that the Egyptians generally believed that a god made himself incarnate, and that an immediate ancestor of the first Pharaoh of Egypt was a being who possessed two natures, the one human and the other divine. As a man he performed the good works which his divine nature indicated to him, he abolished cannibalism, he improved the manners and morals of men, he taught them to live according to law, to worship the gods, and to practise the arts of agriculture. Filled with love for man he set out to travel over the whole world so that he might teach all non-Egyptians to embrace his beneficent doctrine, and enjoy the blessings which accrue to God-fearing and law-abiding peoples. This god-man was hated by his brother, who by a cunning device inveigled him into a box, which he closed and sealed with lead, and thus killed him. The body of the man-god was thrown into the river, and carried thereby to the sea, whence by some means it was brought to Byblos in Syria.

The events which are stated by Plutarch to have happened to the body in this place are, clearly, interpolations of a comparatively late period, and were, I believe, invented to explain the similarity of the popular worship of Byblos with that of Osiris. Where the box was carried seems beyond doubt to have been the papyrus swamps, or the reedy marshes in the east of the Delta. "Byblos" (Βύβλος) is a well-known word for the papyrus plant, and some copyist, who knew nothing of the fact that the Delta was full of papyrus marshes, concluded that the word in his text referred to the town of Byblos, and so modified the legend considerably. Plutarch tells us that Isis left the box in an out-of-the-way place whilst she went to visit her son Horus at Butus, *i.e.*, the Pe-Ṭep of the Egyptian inscriptions. Now, the well-known legend cut on the Metternich Stele says that Isis brought forth her son Horus among the papyrus swamps, and that she reared him there herself, therefore there must be some confusion in the sources of Plutarch's information. At all events, Isis seems to have left the box for some reason, and during her absence Typhon found it, dragged out the body of Osiris, and tore it into fourteen pieces, which he scattered about the country. Thirteen of these pieces were found by Isis, who buried them, and built sanctuaries over them. Osiris then returned from the Other World, and encouraged Horus to do battle with Typhon, and in the fight which ensued Horus was victorious.

From what Plutarch says we are bound to conclude that the Egyptians did not believe that Osiris perished and came to an end with the dismemberment of his body by Typhon, for if they did Plutarch could not have told us that Osiris returned from the Other World. Unfortunately he does not say whether Osiris came in the form of a spirit, or in his natural body, which he had raised from the dead, but it is clear that he had the power of speech and thought, and that he appeared in a form which Horus could recognize. The divine part of Osiris did not die, it was only the mortal body, which he put on when he came from the abode of the gods to reign upon earth, that suffered death. In the divinity and immortality of the god-man Osiris lay the strength of the power with which he appealed to the minds and hopes of the Egyptians for thousands of years, and we shall see in the course of the following pages that both these conceptions of Osiris are of purely African origin, and that they were in existence long before the Dynastic Period in Egypt. The narratives of Plutarch and Diodorus contain a great many statements about Osiris and Isis which can be substantiated by texts written three thousand years before the Christian Era, but they are arranged in wrong order, and many of them are joined together in such a way that it is certain that neither the classical writers nor their informants understood the original form of the history of Osiris. Thus Firmicus Maternus says that Isis was the wife of Typhon, and that Osiris was murdered because she loved him. It is difficult to believe that so learned a man as Firmicus Maternus was ignorant of what Plutarch and Diodorus had written about Osiris, Isis, and Typhon, and it is equally difficult to explain how such a confounding of persons took place in his mind. Macrobius states, as we have seen, that Osiris was the sun and Isis the earth.

In considering these contradictory statements the only possible conclusion we can arrive at is that none of the classical writers had any exact knowledge of the meaning of the history of Osiris, and that none of them understood the details of his cult. It must, however, be admitted that this is not to be wondered at, for they could not read the Egyptian texts and they did not understand the ancient Egyptian religion. They were only acquainted with the phase of the cult of Osiris which existed in the Ptolemaïc Period, and they were incapable by race and education of appreciating the conceptions and ideas which underlay Egyptian symbolism. We are better off than they because, thanks to the decipherment of the Egyptian hieroglyphs, we are able to read, and often to understand, what the Egyptians thought and wrote about Osiris and Isis. And we can see that in very primitive times Osiris passed through many forms, and that his attributes were changed as the result of the development of the minds of the Egyptians and the natural modification of their religious views. Osiris, as we know him, was a compound of many gods, and his cult represented a blending of numerous nature cults, many of them being very ancient. As his worship spread throughout Egypt in the Dynastic Period he absorbed many of the attributes of local "gods" and "spirits," but so long as his priests gave to the peoples whose own local gods had been dispossessed by Osiris the essentials which their belief demanded, they were content.

The Egyptian texts and the works of classical writers enable us to identify many of the "gods" and "spirits," the attributes of whom were absorbed by Osiris. In the earliest times we find him identified with the spirit of the growing crop and the grain god, and he represented the spirit of vegetation in general. His chief assistant was his wife Isis, who taught men to prepare the grain which her husband had given them, and to make the flour into bread. His connection with the Persea-tree, and the legend which associates him with the Erica-tree, prove that at one time he was a tree-spirit, and that he absorbed the attributes of many tree-spirits both in the north and south of Egypt. Plutarch says that he was the first to drink wine, and to teach men to plant the vine, and this view is supported by vignettes in the Papyrus of Ȧnhai and the Papyrus of Nekht. In the former we see growing near a pool of water a luxuriant vine, the fruit and branches of which extend to the figure of Osiris, who is seated upon a throne.[1] In the latter we see the Lady Ȧnhai entering into the presence of Osiris bearing long branches of vine-leaves. As a great god of agriculture he controls the order of the seasons, and thereby assumes some of the powers of Thoth. His connection with agriculture made it important for him to have the control of the necessary water supply of the country, and he was therefore endowed with the powers of Ḥep, or Ḥeper, the great god of the Nile. In the Papyrus of Hunefer his throne is actually placed by, or above, a lake of water (see illustration). As grain could not be grown without the help of the bull or ox in ploughing, we find him identified with more than one Bull-god, and in the Book of the Dead he is addressed as the "Bull of Ȧmentet," *i.e.*, "Bull of the Other World." The female counterpart of an early Bull-god was the Cow-goddess Hathor, whose attributes were absorbed by Isis before the downfall of the Ancient Empire, probably about the same time that the Bull-god was merged in Osiris.

So far back as the period of the VIth dynasty Osiris was credited with having begotten a child by Isis after his death, and thus he became the symbol of all the gods of virility and reproduction. At one time he must have been the god of the moon, a fact which is proved by

[1] See the Frontispiece to Volume I of this work.

many passages in Egyptian texts, and by the statements of Plutarch that Osiris lived or reigned twenty-eight years, and that Typhon broke his body into fourteen pieces. The Bull Apis was, the texts tell us, the "living soul of Osiris," and was, according to Plutarch, begotten

Osiris seated on his throne by, or above, a lake of water.
From the Papyrus of Hunefer.

not by a bull, but by a "ray of generative light which "appeared from the moon, and rested upon the cow his "mother at a time when she was strongly disposed for "generation."[1] Two of the greatest of the monthly festivals were those which were celebrated on the 1st and

[1] Chap. XLIII.

15th days of each month, *i.e.*, the first day of the period of the waxing moon, and the first day of the period of the waning moon. The fourteen parts into which the body of Osiris was broken refer, beyond doubt, to the fourteen pieces which were assumed to be broken or bitten off from the moon during its period of waning, just as the

Osiris in the character of Menu, the "god of the uplifted arm," and Harpokrates as they sat in the disk of the moon, from the third day of the new moon until the fifteenth day. Below is the Crocodile-god Sebek bearing the mummy of the god on his back. To the left stands Isis.

From a bas-relief at Philae.

twenty-eight years of the reign, or life, of Osiris, refer to the days of the moon's life. Apart from the fact that Osiris is actually called "Åsår Aāḥ," *i.e.*, "Osiris the Moon," there are so many passages which prove beyond all doubt that at one period at least Osiris was the Moon-god, that it is difficult to understand why Diodorus stated that Osiris was the sun and Isis the moon. The Egyptian texts suggest that in late times the Sun-god of night may have been regarded as a form of Osiris, and in the last section of the Book Ȧm-Ṭuat,[1] we see the mummied form in which he passed through the Ṭuat, or Other World; but Osiris the Moon-god and the Sun-god were two entirely distinct beings and the Egyptians never confounded them, whatever the Greeks may have done.

The more the religious texts are examined the more clear does it become that from the XIIth dynasty downwards, there is hardly a local god of any importance with whom, sooner or later, Osiris was not identified. Grain-spirits, tree-spirits, tree-gods, animal-gods, reptile-gods, bird-gods, all were absorbed by Osiris, and additions to his attributes continued to be made until his original form disappeared under a mass of confused and often contradictory descriptions. In religious theorizings the Egyptians never forgot anything which had been imagined and had found expression in the written word, and they discarded no view or belief, however contradictory, fearing lest they should suffer material loss in this world, and spiritual loss in the next. The result of this was to create in their religion a confusion which is practically unbounded, and we need not wonder that ancient Greek and Roman writers produced histories of Egyptian gods and goddesses which border on the ridiculous. They, as well as modern investigators of the Egyptian religion, read into the texts ideas and meanings which were, and still are, wholly foreign to the African mind. The Egyptian was never a profound theologian, and in primitive times his religion was largely a mixture of magic and materialism. The idea of the god-man Osiris was developed naturally from the cult of the ancestor who, having been a man, was supposed to be better able to understand the wants of living men than the great unknowable God, whose existence was dimly imagined. Somehow and somewhere the belief arose that this particular god-man Osiris had risen from the dead, as the result of a series of magical ceremonies which were performed by Horus, his son, under the direction of the great magician-priest Thoth and with the help of the embalmer, or medicine-man, Anubis, and it grew and increased until it filled all Egypt. The fundamental

[1] See Budge, *Egyptian Heaven and Hell*, vol. I, p. 277.

attractions of Osiris worship were the humanity of the god and his immortality, and to these were added later the attributes of a just but merciful judge, who rewarded the righteous and punished the wicked. That these appealed irresistibly to the Egyptians of all periods is proved by the absorption into Osiris of all the other gods of the dead in Egypt.

CHAPTER II.

THE NAME AND ICONOGRAPHY OF OSIRIS.

THE name of the Egyptian god-man, which is commonly known by its Greek form "Osiris," is written in hieroglyphs with the signs , , , , , , , , , , which are read ÅS-ÅR or ÅS-ÅRI. In the Ptolemaïc Period we have , , or , which are to be read US-ÅRI. Other forms are User , Usri , Ausåres , User , , , , , etc.[1] The Coptic and Syriac forms, ⲟⲩⲥⲓⲣⲓ and ܐܘܣܝܪܝܣ *Usiri, Usiris*, show that the *u*-sound predominated at the beginning of the name in the later period, just as Muḥammadans to-day pronounce the name of God "Ullah," instead of "Allah," but this was probably due to the fact that in the later period the Egyptians assigned a meaning to the name Osiris which it had not in the earliest times.

About the meaning of the name Ås-åri or Us-åri many theories have been formed, but none of the meanings proposed is satisfactory. Diodorus[2] and Plutarch[3] thought that Osiris meant "many eyes," but whatever the name means it cannot mean that. Jablonski[4] and, following him, Leemans,[5] connected the name with the Coptic words ⲟϣ and ⲓⲣⲓ, "to do much," and Sharpe derived it from the Coptic words ⲱϣ and ⲓⲣⲓ, "to cry out much."[6] Etymologies have been found for

[1] See Lefébure, *Le Mythe Osirien*, Paris, 1875, p. 131 ; and Erman, *A.Z.*, Bd. 46 (1910), p. 92.
[2] I, 11.
[3] Chap. 10.
[4] *Panthéon*, II, 7.
[5] *Horapollo*, p. 243.
[6] *Egyptian Mythology*, p. 7.

the name in Assyrian and Sanskrit, but they are not acceptable. If we take one of the oldest forms of the name we have the two signs which compose it written thus, 𓊨𓁹 or 𓊨𓁹. The first sign is the hieroglyph for "seat," "throne," "place," and the second as a hieroglyph means "the eye," and with a derived sense it means "to see." However we arrange these meanings it is most improbable that the result can represent the meaning of the name Åsår, or Osiris. The late Dr. H. Brugsch assumed that "Us-iri" was the oldest form of the name Osiris, and stated boldly that these words meant "die Macht, die Kraft des Augapfels," or "Kräftig ist der Augapfel,"[1] but though "apple of the eye" may be a sufficiently good rendering of the second sign 𓁹, "strong" and "mighty" cannot be accepted as meanings for the first sign 𓊨, which means a "seat" or "throne," and nothing else. Even if we take the late form of the name 𓌂𓁹, which is written with the signs for a sceptre and an eye, his meaning "strength, or power, of the apple of the eye," cannot be deduced from them, unless we assume that 𓌂 = 𓄊 *user*, for which there is no justification. Having explained Osiris in this manner, Dr. Brugsch went on to say that the name "Isis," in Egyptian Åst[2] 𓊨𓏏, meant "the strong one," or "the mighty one," a meaning which is impossible. The second sign of the old form of the name Osiris 𓁹, is, however, used as a verb, meaning "to make," "to do," "maker," "doer," etc., and if we apply it to the name we may render it by "he who makes a seat," or "seat maker," *i.e.*, he who takes his seat or throne. That this view was in the mind of the Egyptian scribes at least is proved by the forms 𓁹𓊨𓀭, 𓁹𓂋𓊨𓀭, etc., which Dr. Erman has shrewdly noted in his article.

[1] *Religion und Mythologie*, Leipzig, 1885, p. 81.

[2] Herr Grapow (*Ä.Z.*, Bd. 46, p. 108) calls attention to the reading Åst 𓅐𓊨𓏏𓁐, Isis, which Lacau has published in *Recueil de Travaux*, tom. XXX, p. 192.

If "seat maker," or "he who takes [his] seat" be the meaning of the name Osiris, it is quite certain that his name must commemorate some very important event in the life of the god, and there should exist in the texts some description of it. The words, taking or making a seat or throne, naturally suggest the idea of coronation, but the idea of ascending a throne, or coronation, is always expressed by the word *khā*, , whilst the word used in connection with  in the name of Osiris is . We must therefore find some incident in the life of Osiris which involved "taking a seat" in such a manner that it deserved to be commemorated once for all in the god's name. This, fortunately, is not far to seek. In the text of King Tetȧ it is said: "Hail, "Osiris Tetȧ! Wake up! Horus causes Thoth to "bring to thee thine enemy, he sets thee on his back, he "shall not defile thee. Make thy seat upon him. "Come forth! Sit thou upon him, he shall not commit "an act of paederasty on thee."[1] In another place, in the text of the same king, we read: "Hail, Osiris Tetȧ! "Stand up, rise up! Thy mother Nut gives thee birth, "the god Ḳeb presses thy mouth for thee. The Great "Company of the gods converse with thee. They set "thine enemy beneath thee, they say to him: 'Carry thou "one who is greater than thyself through thy name of "Atfa-ur. Support one who is greater than thyself "through thy name of Ta-Abṭu.'"[2]

From these two passages it is clear that in the

1 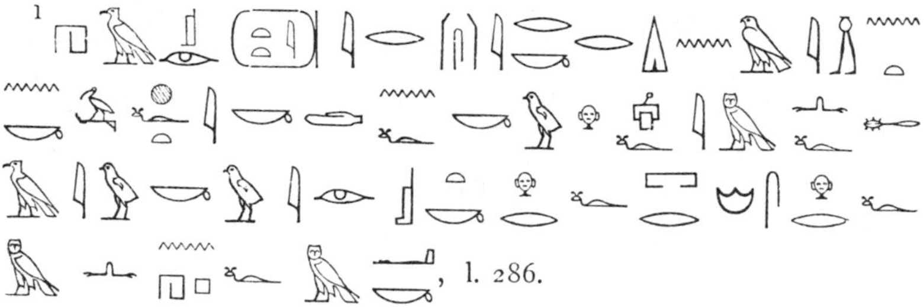, l. 286.

2 

VIth dynasty a belief was current that, after Osiris had been raised from the dead and had entered into heaven, his son, Horus, caused Thoth to bring before him his old enemy Set, so that the murderer of Osiris might see, in a state of glory, the god whom he had killed. When Set appeared the gods threw him down, and Thoth lifted Osiris on to his back, and whilst Osiris sat there triumphant the gods mocked Set, and told him to carry one mightier than himself. At first, Osiris appears to have hesitated, for Thoth exhorted him to "make his seat upon him," and to "come forth and sit upon him." He further promised that Set should not defile him, and that he should not commit an act of paederasty[1] upon him. This passage shows only too plainly that in remote times in Egypt the victors committed nameless acts of abomination on the vanquished, besides frightful mutilations, and evidence is not wanting that such practices were not unknown in the Southern Sûdân a very few years ago. Osiris did as Thoth and Horus had arranged he should do, and "made his seat," or seated himself, upon the body of Set in triumph, and was, presumably, ever after called the "seat-maker," Ȧs-ȧr, or Ȧs-ȧri, which the Greeks turned into Osiris. The crudeness and, it may be added, childishness of the story prove that it is very ancient, and it probably existed in Predynastic times. It may be argued that the story was invented to provide an etymology for the name of Osiris, but even if this were the case it is still very ancient, for the text which contains it was cut upon King Tetȧ's tomb under the VIth dynasty, and it is unlikely that it was new at that time.

, ll. 273, 274.

[1] This view is also held by Maspero, *Les Pyramides*, p. 126, note 2, and by Wiedemann, *Sphinx*, Varia III, tom. XIV, p. 39.

It has already been mentioned in the preceding chapter that Osiris absorbed the attributes of many of the native gods of the dead who were worshipped in Egypt, and that he passed through several phases in which he was respectively a grain-spirit, a tree-spirit, a water-spirit, an animal-spirit, a star-spirit, etc., before he became the god-man, the first of those who rose from the dead. Traces of all these forms survived in his cult long after he became a god-man, just as allusions to his sufferings and death permeated the religious literature of Egypt for thousands of years after he was first alleged to have risen from the dead. Whether forms of the god Osiris were sculptured on the walls of the temples of the Ancient Empire, or similitudes of him were drawn on papyri and leather, or cut on wood under the early dynasties, cannot be said ; certainly no examples of such representations have come down to us. It is, however, well known that the position of Osiris as the god-man was well established in the minds of the Egyptians at the beginning of the Dynastic Period, and that he was even at this remote time regarded as the head of a small company of five gods, each of whom was endued by his worshippers with human attributes. Osiris was a good, benevolent, and just king, who was murdered by his brother Set. Isis, his sister and wife, was a faithful and loving wife, who protected him and his interests with unremitting care during his life, and cherished his memory unceasingly after his death. She endured sorrow, pain, and loneliness in bringing forth his son Horus, and spared herself neither toil nor care in rearing him. As he grew up she taught him that it was his duty to avenge his father's murder, and encouraged a warlike spirit in him. Nephthys, her sister, attached herself to her with loving faithfulness, and assisted Isis by word and deed in all the trouble which she suffered through the murder of her husband, and through the poisoning of her child Horus. Set was the husband of Nephthys, and begat by her Ȧnpu, or Anubis, who acted as embalmer of Osiris. Thus we see that the Egyptians regarded these gods and goddesses as a sort of holy family, all the members whereof were god-men and god-women. These appealed to the Egyptians

Osiris standing between Isis and Nephthys.
From a bas-relief at Philae.

through their affections and, if the word may be used, domestic virtues. Isis was the ideal wife and mother and the perfect woman, and, long before the death of the last native king of Egypt, she held in the hearts of her worshippers a position somewhat similar to that held by the Virgin Mary in the hearts of many Oriental Christians in Egypt, the Sûdân, Abyssinia, and Western Asia. This being so it is not surprising that Osiris, Isis, Horus, and Nephthys always appear in human form, and, though Set and Anubis are given animal heads, the literature of Egypt contains many passages which prove that they possessed human instincts and speech, and that on occasions they did work which men alone can do.

Osiris as the typical god-man who died and rose again is represented in the form of a mummy, or, at all events, in the form of a dead man who has been made ready for burial. This form is a development of an ancient presentment of a dead chief or ancestor, for Osiris took the place of the tutelary ancestor-god who was honoured and worshipped in every village of the Sûdân of any size from time immemorial. This ancestor-god was chosen to be the patron and protector of the village because of either the strength or the wisdom which he had displayed when upon earth, and many modern travellers have put on record that figures of ancestors still occupy prominent positions in African villages and settlements. Often they stand under a rude canopy formed of branches and leaves, which is supported by poles, but sometimes, like the figures of spirits and "gods," they are provided with small huts, or houses. As it has always been the custom to reserve ceremonial burial for the bodies of kings, chiefs, and men of high rank it is clear from the traditional accounts of the burial of Osiris, and of the numerous ceremonies which were performed in connection with it, that he must have been a great and powerful king. Moreover, the figures of the god which appear on sepulchral stelae of the latter part of the Middle Empire, and the reliefs sculptured on walls and pillars of temples of the New Empire, to say nothing of the fine vignettes in papyri of the XVIIIth and XIXth dynasties, all represent him as a great king, and in all essentials and special characteristics of the god they agree.

If we look at the stele of Menthu-ḥetep from Abydos[1] we see sculptured on the upper part the figure of a god in mummied form, wearing the White Crown ; he holds a sceptre in his left hand, and stands on the object , and from the back of his neck hangs a *menȧt* . From the head of his sceptre  proceeds "life" , which he is presenting to his son the king of Egypt, Usertsen I, who appears standing upon the *serekh*[2] in the form of a hawk wearing the crowns of the South and the North. Behind the god are the signs , *i.e.*, "Khenti-Ȧmenti, the Lord of Abydos." Khenti-Ȧmenti was one of the oldest gods of Abydos, and was certainly connected with the dead, being, probably, the ancient local god of the dead of Abydos and its neighbourhood. Now, in the Pyramid Texts, which were written under the VIth dynasty, there are several mentions of Khenti-Ȧmenti, and in a large number of instances the name is preceded by that of Osiris. It is quite clear, therefore, that the chief attributes of the one god must have resembled those of the other, and that Osiris Khenti-Ȧmenti was assumed to have absorbed the powers of Khenti-Ȧmenti. In the representations of the two gods which are found at Abydos there is usually no difference, at least not under the XVIIIth and XIXth dynasties. On some of the stelae and other monuments which belong to the XIIth dynasty,[3] an addition of two feathers is made to the White Crown which Osiris Khenti-Ȧmenti wears,[4] and it is possible that they typify the fusion of the two gods. In papyri of the

[1] Mariette, *Abydos*, tom. II, Plate 25.
[2] See my *Book of the Kings of Egypt*, Vol. I, p. XIII.
[3] See Mariette, *Abydos*, II, Plate 41.
[4] See the shrine of Pa-suten-sa in the British Museum, Egyptian Gallery, No. 174.

XVIIIth dynasty Osiris Khenti-Ȧmenti, or simply Osiris, is seen seated in a sort of shrine under a canopy, and from the XIIth dynasty onwards this is the traditional position of the god on stelae.

Before the XIIth dynasty figures or representations of Osiris, either by himself or with Khenti-Ȧmenti, are very rare, and some doubt if any exist. On a jar-sealing of Per-ȧb-sen, a king of the IInd dynasty, are figures of two male beings, each of which wears the White Crown 𓋑, and holds the sceptre 𓌀 in one hand and the symbol of life ☥ in the other.[1] It can hardly be doubted that these figures represent Osiris. On a second jar-sealing is, undoubtedly, a figure of Set,[2] on a third is a figure of Shu,[3] and on a fourth is a figure of a goddess, who bears the "green" sceptre 𓇅 in one hand, and ☥ in the other, and who must be Isis.[4] If figures of Set were drawn or sculptured under the IInd dynasty, there is no reason why the figure of Osiris should not have been drawn also, and as in succeeding dynasties Osiris was the god *par excellence* of the White Crown, it is nearly certain that the figure on the jar-sealing, with the White Crown and sceptre and ☥, is intended to be that of Osiris. There is, however, a much older representation of a god whom I believe to be Osiris. This is found on an ebony tablet in the British Museum,[5] which records several events that took place in a certain year of the reign of Semti, or Ṭen, who was formerly known as Ḥesepti. Here in the upper register, on the right, is seen the figure of a god seated on a throne, wearing the White Crown and holding a whip, or flail, 𓍱 in his hands. The god is in mummied form. His throne is placed on

1 De Morgan, *Recherches*, II, figs. 816, 819.
2 Petrie, *Royal Tombs*, II, Plate XXII, No. 179.
3 *Ibid.*, Plate XXIII, No. 199.
4 *Ibid.*, Plate XXIII, No. 192.
5 Third Egyptian Room, Table-Case L, No. 124. See the Chapter "Osiris and Dancing," where this tablet is figured.

the top of a flight of steps, and above it is a canopy, supported in front by poles, similar in every respect to the canopy under which Osiris is invariably seen seated in later monuments. Before the canopy is a figure of a king wearing the double crown of the South and North , and holding in one hand a paddle , and in the other a flail , or perhaps . On each side of him are three signs, which represent objects that were associated with dancing. The king, I believe, is dancing, though his back is turned to the god, and this representation appears to be the prototype of all the scenes, down to the Ptolemaïc Period, in which the king dances before his god. Dancing was, and still is, an act of worship in Africa, and Osiris, according to Diodorus,[1] was a patron of dancers and musicians of all classes, both male and female.

The tablet on which the above scene is cut appears to be one of several on which the principal events of the reign of King Semti (Ḥesepti) were recorded, and to contain a list of the chief events of a particular year. (It is probable that the text of the Palermo Stele was compiled from a series of tablets of this kind.) The first event noted of the year was the performance by the king of some ceremony which was connected with the god who sat in a shrine placed on the top of a short flight of steps. The ceremony must have been a very important one, or it would not have been noted in this manner, and, in the light of reliefs and pictures of a later period, it is tolerably certain that it was connected with the founding and dedication of some building to the god, or the presentation of some great offering. About the identity of the king who is dancing before the god there is no doubt. On the left-hand side of the tablet we have his Horus name given, and it reads

"Ṭen," the meaning of which is doubtful. Other objects inscribed with Ṭen's names and titles show that he was called "Semti,"[2] 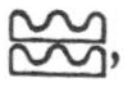, for which the Papyrus of Nu has 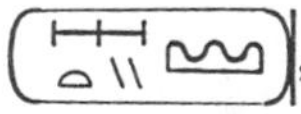, and the King-list of

[1] See above, p. 11.
[2] See Sethe, *A.Z.*, 1897, Band 35, p. 3.

Seti I at Abydos 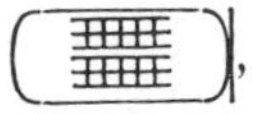, whence the name "Ḥesepti." Now, in the Book of the Dead, certain sections, *e.g.*, Chapter XXXB and Chapter LXIV, are said to have been "found" in the shrine of the god Ḥennu by kings of the Ist and IVth dynasties. Thus, Chapter XXXB was "found" by Khufu's son Ḥeruṭāṭāf during the reign of Men-kau-Rā (Mycerinus).[1] One version of Chapter LXIV was "found" by the same person in the same reign,[2] but the other was "found" by the chief mason in the shrine at Hermopolis during the reign of Semti (Ḥesepti).[3]

There is no need to discuss here the exact meaning that we are to attach to the word "found" in these Rubrics of the Book of the Dead, for that has already been done at great length and with much learning by Professor Naville.[4] All that concerns us here is the fact that in the XIth dynasty the learned men at Thebes believed that in the reign of Semti some work was carried out in connection with the editing, or re-editing, or perhaps even with the composing and writing of certain sections of the Book of the Dead. Now, this work was written for the benefit of the dead, and especially for those who accepted the doctrine of Osiris, therefore in the reign of Semti the cult of Osiris must have been in existence, and also writings which dealt with it and possessed an authoritative character. The scene on the wooden tablet proves beyond a doubt that a development of some religious cult took place in the reign of Semti, and if we connect this with the statements made in the Rubrics of Chapters XXXB,

[1] See the Papyrus of Åmen-ḥetep in Naville, *Todtenbuch*, II, p. 99.

[2] See the Papyrus of Mes-em-neter (ed. Naville), and the Papyrus of Nu (ed. Budge), and Sir Gardner Wilkinson's transcript of the text of a coffin of the XIth dynasty (Budge, *Facsimiles of Hieratic Papyri*, Plate XXXIX ff.

[3] See the Papyrus of Nebseni (ed. Birch), the Papyrus of Nu (ed. Budge), and Budge, *Facsimiles of Hieratic Papyri*, p. xxii. In the Turin Papyrus (ed. Lepsius) Chapter CXXX is also said to have been "found" during the reign of Ḥesepti.

[4] *La Découverte de la Loi sous le Roi Josias*, une interprétation Égyptienne d'un Texte Biblique (in the *Mém. de l'Académie des Inscriptions*, tom. XXXVIII, 2e Partie, Paris, 1910).

LXIV, and CXXX of the Book of the Dead, as I believe we are entitled to do, we arrive at the conclusion that the cult referred to is that of Osiris, and that the god represented on the tablet is Osiris. If he be not Osiris, he must be a god whose form and attributes were absorbed, or usurped, by Osiris, for, from the XIIth dynasty to the end of the Ptolemaïc Period, the representations of Osiris are substantially identical with the representation of the god on the top of the steps on the wooden tablet of Semti.

Among the explanations of the scene which have been put forward is one which takes the view that the figure on the top of the steps is that of a king, but this appears impossible. It is true that on the great mace of Nār-mer, a very early king, we have a scene represented in which what may be perhaps assumed to be the figure of a king is seated on a throne placed on the top of a flight of nine steps. The figure wears the Crown of the North , and holds a whip or flail in his hands, and he sits under a canopy, the front of which is supported by two spears. Above the canopy is a vulture, symbolic of protection, and by the side of the steps are two men holding large fans. The meaning of the whole scene has not yet been satisfactorily explained,[1] but three bearded male figures are dancing, and below, actually on one side of them, are figures of an ox, a goat, and a captive, with his hands tied behind his back. These represent the spoil taken during some expedition, and the numbers given below each figure show that it was very large. The oxen number 400,000, the goats 1,422,000, and the men 120,000. The figure seated on the four-legged frame under a cage or basket may be the captive king of the lands which have been plundered, but on this point more information is required. Now, although the figure under the canopy is probably that of King Nār-mer and not that of a god, the representation, taken together with that on the wooden tablet of Semti, has a direct bearing on the iconography of Osiris. They show that kings and gods were depicted in substantially the same forms, and that the throne of each was placed on the top of a

[1] See Quibell, *Hierakonpolis*, Part I, Plate XXVIb.

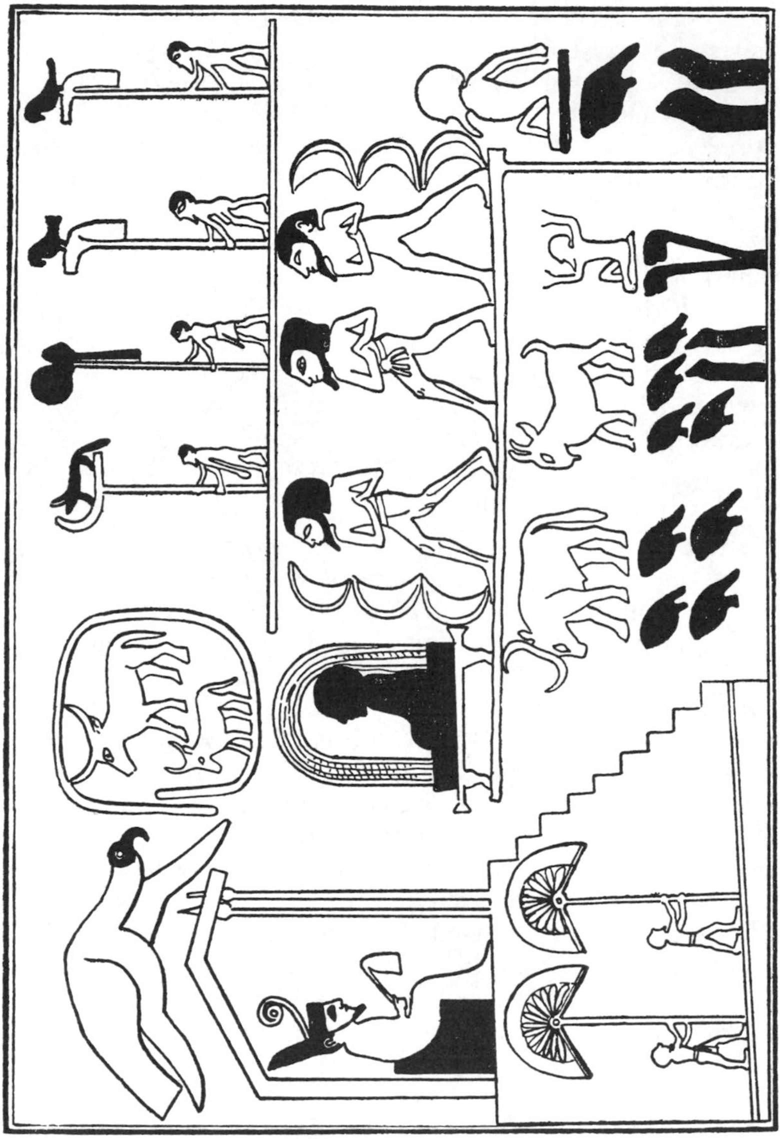

Scene from the mace-head of Nār-mer. From Quibell, *Hierakonpolis*, Part I, Plate XXVIB.

pedestal made with a flight of steps up the front. All tradition makes Osiris a king, and it is certain that he must have lived at an early period. This being so, we should expect him to be represented in the form of an early king, and to occupy the throne of a king, and to sit under a royal canopy. That Osiris should have the form of a mummy is not a matter to wonder at, for he was the god-man-king risen from the dead, but it is difficult to see why Nār-mer should have this form, unless he also is supposed to be dead or risen from the dead.

It is impossible to believe that under the first eleven or twelve dynasties the Egyptians were unable to draw figures of Osiris or to cut them in stone, and the general absence of all representations of the god before the XIIth or XIIIth dynasty only proves that the custom of making similitudes had not yet grown up. The original home of Osiris as god of the North was in the Delta, and the centre of his worship was the temple city Per-Åsår-neb-Ṭeṭu,[1] the Busiris of the Greeks, which was situated in the IXth Nome of Lower Egypt. Here was preserved the backbone of the god, , and here grew the sacred acacia, and persea, and sycamore-fig trees which were associated with it. The oldest symbol of Osiris appears to have been the ṭeṭ , and it is probable that in very early times he was represented by this object alone. and that he had no other form. As his cult extended, Osiris assumed the forms of the gods of the dead of the districts through which it passed, and this is why he is found associated so closely with Ptaḥ and Seker of Memphis, and with Khenti-Åmenti of Abydos. The shrine of Pa-suten-sa in the British Museum[2] supplies proof of this. On the monument we have, in sunk relief, a figure of Osiris in mummied form, holding the crook , or sceptre, in his right hand, and the whip  in the left. He wears the White Crown, with a feather

1 .

2 Northern Egyptian Gallery, No. 174.

on each side of it, and above his forehead is the uraeus, or symbol of sovereignty; on the top of the shrine stands the figure of a hawk. In the inscriptions the deceased prays to Osiris Khenti-Ȧmenti and to Ptaḥ-Seker for sepulchral offerings. This monument dates

Osiris seated in a shrine from the roof of which hang bunches of grapes.
From the Papyrus of Nebseni.

from the reign of Ȧmen-em-ḥāt III, a king of the XIIth dynasty.

With the rise to power of the XVIIIth dynasty, the representations of Osiris become numerous, and as we should expect, the best authorities for them are papyri of the Book of the Dead. One of the oldest of these is the Papyrus of Nebseni, which was written about

1550 B.C.[1] The large figure of Osiris which ornaments the beginning is mutilated, but enough remains of it to show us the god seated on his throne; he holds the sceptre and whip, and wears the White Crown without plumes. He has a long, plaited beard and sits under a canopy made in the form of a funeral coffer, from which the side has been removed. The roof is supported by two pillars with lotus capitals, and from it hang many clusters of grapes. This fact is interesting as proving the connection of the god with the vine, and illustrating the statement of Diodorus[2] that Osiris was the first to plant the vine, and to teach men to make and drink wine. The titles of the god are mutilated, but he is certainly called "Lord of Ȧbydos, great god, Governor of Eternity, Lord of Ȧuḳert, king of Everlastingness." Ȧuḳert[3] is the name of the Other World, or Dead-land, of Heliopolis, and it is important to note that the god is made to claim the sovereignty of this region as well as that of Abydos. Before the god is a table loaded with offerings of all kinds. In Sheet 10 of the same papyrus Osiris appears in the same form and under the same canopy, but his throne rests on a reed mat , which is laid upon a plinth made in the form of a symbol of "law, truth, etc.," . The side of the throne is ornamented with scale work, and in the lower right-hand corner is a panel on which is drawn the symbol of the union of the South and North . The figure of Osiris which ornamented the beginning of the papyrus of Nu (British Museum No. 10,477) is also much mutilated, only the crown of the god being visible; this crown is painted white, and it has two plumes, one on each side. In the Papyrus of Iuȧu, the father-in-law of Ȧmen-ḥetep III,[4] which was written about 1450 B.C., Osiris wears a long white garment, which

[1] British Museum Papyrus No. 9900. See *Photographs of the Papyrus of Nebseni in the British Museum*, London, 1876.

[2] Ed. Didot, Book I, Chap. 15.

[3] .

[4] Naville, *The Funeral Papyrus of Iouiya*, London, 1908, Plate I.

extends from his neck to his ankles; his crown also is white, and has a red feather on each side of it. His plaited beard is unusually long, and round his neck he wears a deep collar. The skin of the god is of an earthy-red colour, and his general appearance is that of the large painted limestone Osirid figure of Àmen-ḥetep I in the British Museum.[1] On Plate XXII of the printed edition we have a standing figure of Osiris, and except for not standing on the object his form is in every respect that of Khenti-Àmenti, or Khenti-Àmentiu, which title is indeed given him in the text.

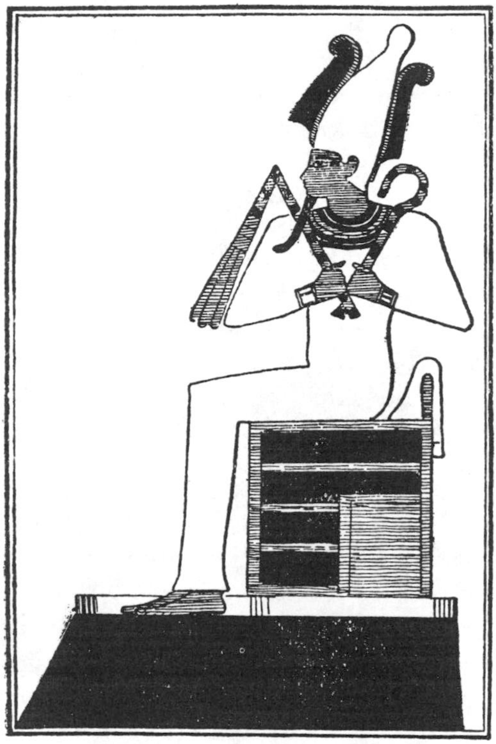

Osiris in the form of a mummified man, seated on his throne, and holding a whip and flail.

In the Papyrus of Ani (Plate 4) the flesh of Osiris is painted a green colour, and his long single white garment is decorated with a design of scale work. In addition to the sceptre and whip he holds in his hands another sceptre. From the back of his neck hangs the *menàt* amulet, which betokens "joy, pleasure, virility," etc. Behind him stand Isis and Nephthys, and before him, standing on a lotus, are the "four children of Horus," who assisted their father in rejoining the members of the god. Below these, hanging to a pole, is the skin of a

[1] Northern Egyptian Gallery, No. 346 (Bay 3).

decapitated bull. The god is seated within a funeral coffer as before, but the raised part of the cover is in the form of a hawk's head, which probably indicates the fusion of Osiris and Seker, the old god of the dead of Memphis. Above the cover rise twelve uraei, and on the cornice is a row of uraei, each of which has a crown on its head; the capitals of the pillars of the coffer are also decorated with uraei. The side of the throne of Osiris is painted to represent the door of a tomb, with a row of uraei wearing disks on the cornice. The coffer rests upon a low pylon-shaped building, and is approached by a flight of steps. The god is called simply "Osiris, Lord of Eternity."

Osiris.
From the Papyrus of Iuáu, Plate XXII.

In the Papyrus of Hunefer (Plate 5), which was written during the reign of Seti I, Osiris is arrayed wholly in white, and his throne is set by the side of a lake of water, out of which grows a lotus plant; on the flower stand the "four children of Horus." The coffer, which has a row of uraei above the cornice, rests on a low pylon-shaped building, as in the Papyrus of Ani, and is approached by a flight of steps. On the sarcophagus of Seti I we have a most interesting figure of Osiris, seated on his throne, which is here in the form of a chair, in his Hall of Judgment. He wears the double crown of the South and North and holds "life" ☥ and a sceptre  in his hands. The throne has nine steps, similar to the throne represented on the mace of Nār-mer, and on each is one of the nine gods who formed the "Company" of Osiris. Osiris is not here seated within a funeral coffer, but in a sort of chamber, and he is dispensing judgment after the manner of an African king.[1]

During the XXth, XXIst, and XXIInd dynasties the

[1] See Budge, *Book of Gates*, p. 159.

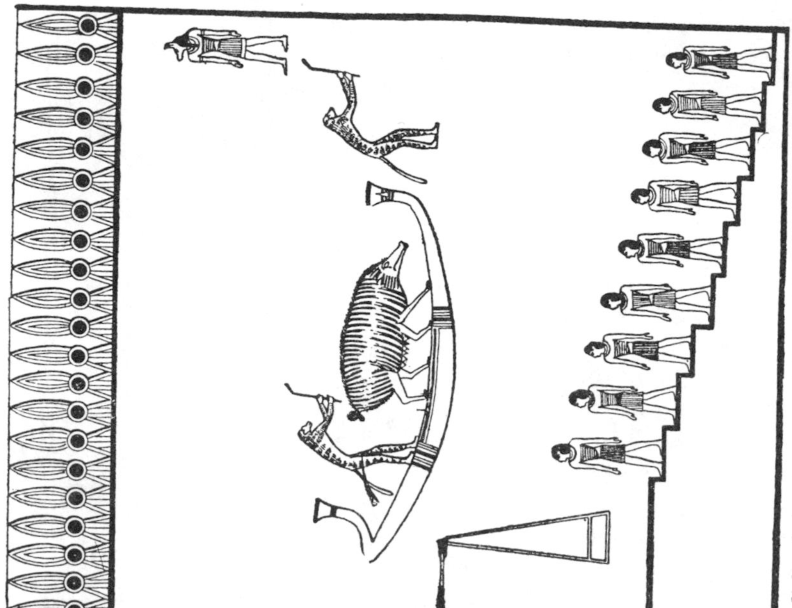

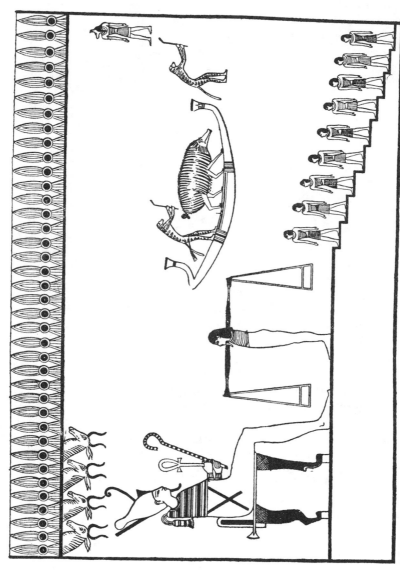

Osiris seated in judgment on a chair placed on the top of a flight of nine steps, on which stand the nine gods of his Company. The pig in the boat represents Set. In the right-hand corner stands Anubis. From a sarcophagus in the Louvre.

OSIRIS SEATED
From the Papyrus

ON HIS THRONE.
of Nesi-ta-neb-ashru.

form of Osiris remains substantially the same, but in some particulars the decoration of his shrine is modified. Thus in the painted leather roll of Nekht,[1] each of the uraei which are above the shrine wears two plumes, and the capitals of the two pillars which support the roof are decorated with the heads of gazelle and geese. Instead of Isis the goddess who is the personification of Ȧmenti stands behind the god in the shrine. In the Papyrus of Nesi-ta-neb-Ȧshru,[2] Osiris is seated upon a throne which has five steps on each side, and wears the Atef crown . He is described as "he who is on his throne, "Lord of Eternity, Maker of Everlastingness, the great "god, chief of Ȧqert."[3] Before him stand "Thoth, dweller in his city, and Horus the Great," behind him are the goddess "Maāt, daughter of Rā, mistress of Ȧmentet," and "Peḥti, the great god."[4] Behind the throne is the Ram-god Shai.[5] On the second of the five blocks which form the throne is the legend, "Throne of Osiris."[6] At the door of the shrine stands a serpent-headed goddess holding a knife in each hand, who appears to be a personification of the huge serpent which lies, with its head upraised, before the throne. The legend which refers to the embracing of the god by Horus may be the name of the serpent.[7] At the door stands the deceased princess seeking admission. From the above it seems that the throne of Osiris was guarded by a monster serpent, which does not appear in the older vignettes in papyri, etc. In late papyri it is tolerably common.[8]

In the Papyrus of Ānkh-f-en-Khensu in Cairo, the

[1] British Museum, No. 10,473.

[2] , British Museum, No. 10,552.

[3] 
. [4] . [5] .

[6] . [7] .

[8] See Lanzone, *Dizionario*, tavv. 208–211.

The goddess Åmentet in the shrine of Osiris. From the leather roll of Nekht.

arms and shoulders of the god are covered with some dark material, and streamers of parti-coloured cloth hang down, one on each side of him. In another papyrus of the same period (XXIInd dynasty) Osiris is seen lying on the slope of a mound of earth, with his right arm extended to the top of it. His hand nearly touches the head of a huge serpent, the body of which passes down the back of the heap, and emerging from under the front of it continues in deep undulations. The legend reads: "Osiris-"Res, Khenti-Åmenti, "great god, dweller in "the Ṭuat, that is to "say, Ta-tchesert, the "Åat of Kheper-Rā."[1] In the papyrus the god is ithyphallic. In the Papyrus of Ånhai[2] (Plate 5), the god wears a different crown, viz., , and a wig with a fillet with two uraei; by his side on the throne stands a hawk wearing a disk; before him is

1 

2 British Museum, No. 10,472.

the bull's skin hanging from a pole, and behind him stand Isis and Nephthys. Before the open door of the shrine stand the Mert-goddess of the South and the Mert-goddess of the North, the former wearing a red, and the latter a green garment. Mert-shemā says: "Come in peace, "protector of the Great Company of "the Gods," and Mert-meḥt says: "Thou risest [in] beauty in the Horizon of Eternity."[1] The presence of these goddesses of vegetation connects Osiris with the inundation and crops of the country. In this picture the god is called Ptaḥ-Sekri-Àsȧr,[2] and thus is regarded as a triad of gods of the dead. The Papyrus of Nekht[3] supplies another interesting picture of Osiris. The god is seated on his throne as usual, and behind him rises the mountain of Àmenti, from the top of which two arms are extended to receive the solar disk. Between the deceased and his wife and the god is a lake, or ornamental piece of water, from the sides of which grow date-palms, etc. From one corner of it a vine springs, and its luxuriant leaves and bunches of grapes extend towards the face of the god. Here again Osiris is specially connected with the vine, and the fact that the Lady Ànhai appears in her papyrus with vine branches about her (see Plate VI) as she stands before him is a further proof of this fact (see the Frontispiece to this volume).

Osiris of Philae.

1 

2 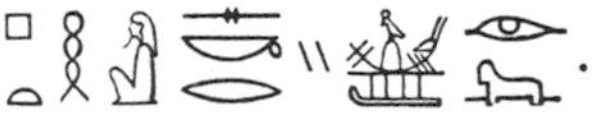

3 British Museum, No. 10,471.

In the Ptolemaïc Period some interesting additions appear in the scenes in which Osiris plays the chief part. Thus, in a relief at Denderah,[1] the god, arrayed in a garment which reaches to his ankles, stands holding his symbols of sovereignty. Before him stands "Horus, son of Isis and Osiris," holding a knife in his left hand. Between the god and his father is the terrible "slave stick" 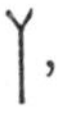, which is stuck in the ground, and to it is tied by the arms an ass-headed man in a kneeling position. Three knives stick in his stomach. This

Osiris-Res, or "Osiris the Riser."

figure, of course, represents Set, who has been vanquished and wounded by Horus and his sons. In another relief Khenti-Åmenti is given the head of the hawk of Seker,[2] and thus Osiris represents the ancient gods of the dead of Busiris, Memphis, and Abydos. In another relief are given the seven forms of Osiris as follows :—

1. Osiris in Ḥet-Ṭeṭet, *i.e.*, the Temple of Busiris.[3] He holds in his hands a sceptre bearing the

[1] Mariette, *Dendérah*, tom. IV, Plate 56.
[2] *Ibid.*, Plate 38.
[3] 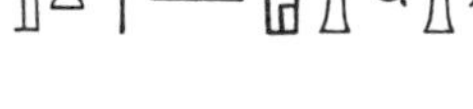, Mariette, *Dendérah*, tom. IV, Plate 89.

symbols of stability and life, and has upon his head the symbol usually worn by the *Meskhenet* goddesses.

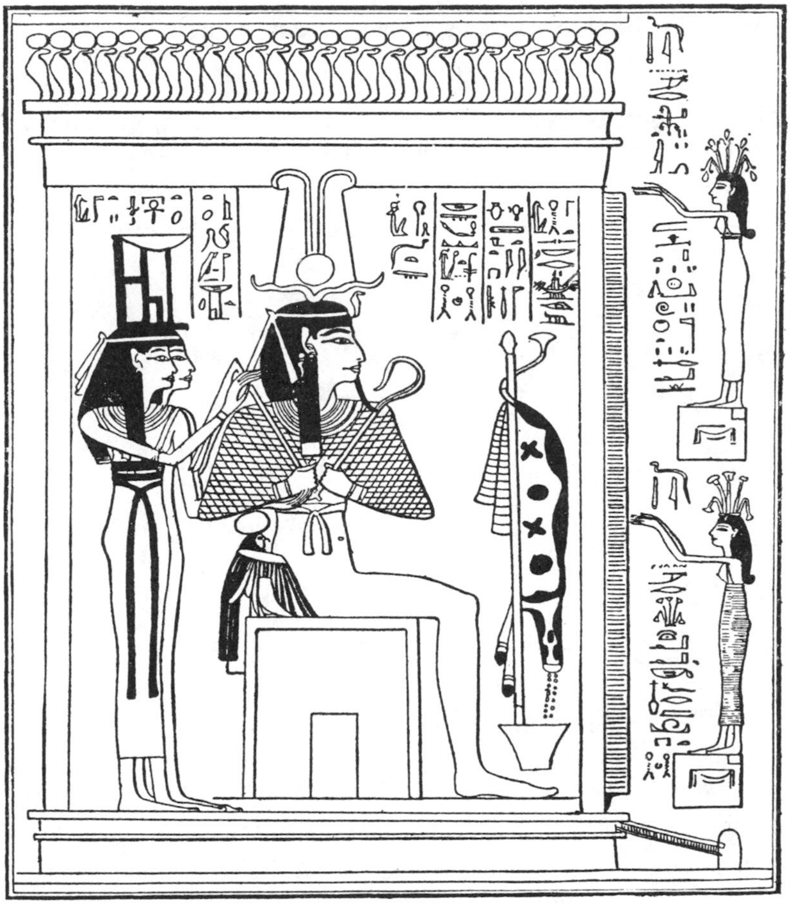

2. Osiris Netcheṭes.[1] He wears the crown and his hands are hidden.
3. Another form of Osiris Khenti-Ȧmenti.[2] He wears the White Crown of the South, and his hands are hidden.

1 

2 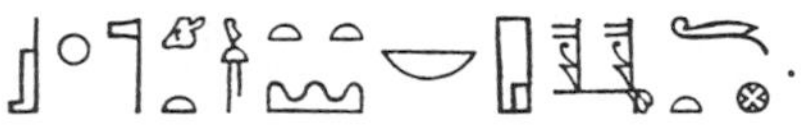

4–7. The four remaining forms of Osiris resemble No. 3. Their names are: Osiris Khenti-Per-sepent (?),[1] Osiris Khenti-Àmenti, Osiris Khenti-Ḥet-Àsàrt,[2] and Osiris, Lord of Mer-Nefert.[3]

One of the earliest things associated with the worship and cult of Osiris was the object which is usually represented by the sign 𓊽, and which is called "Ṭeṭ." Many theories have been formulated about it, and many explanations of it given, but none is satisfactory from all points of view. The object is, in my opinion, the

Horus and his four sons, each armed with a knife, standing before Osiris and Serapis. The animal-headed man, with knives stuck in his body and bound by his arms to a forked stick, represents Set or Typhon, conquered.

sacrum of Osiris, which was confused with a portion of the backbone, and was therefore drawn as 𓊽. This object was in very early times carefully preserved in Ṭeṭ, or Ṭeṭu,[4] the metropolis of the IXth Nome of Lower Egypt (Busirites), to which the Greeks gave the name of

1 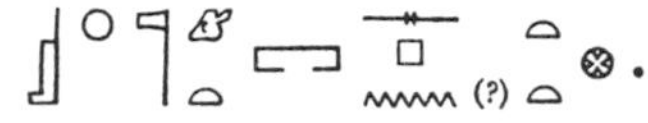 2 

3 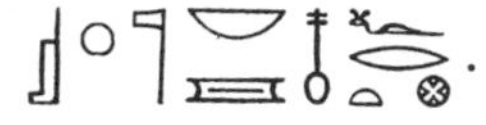

4 

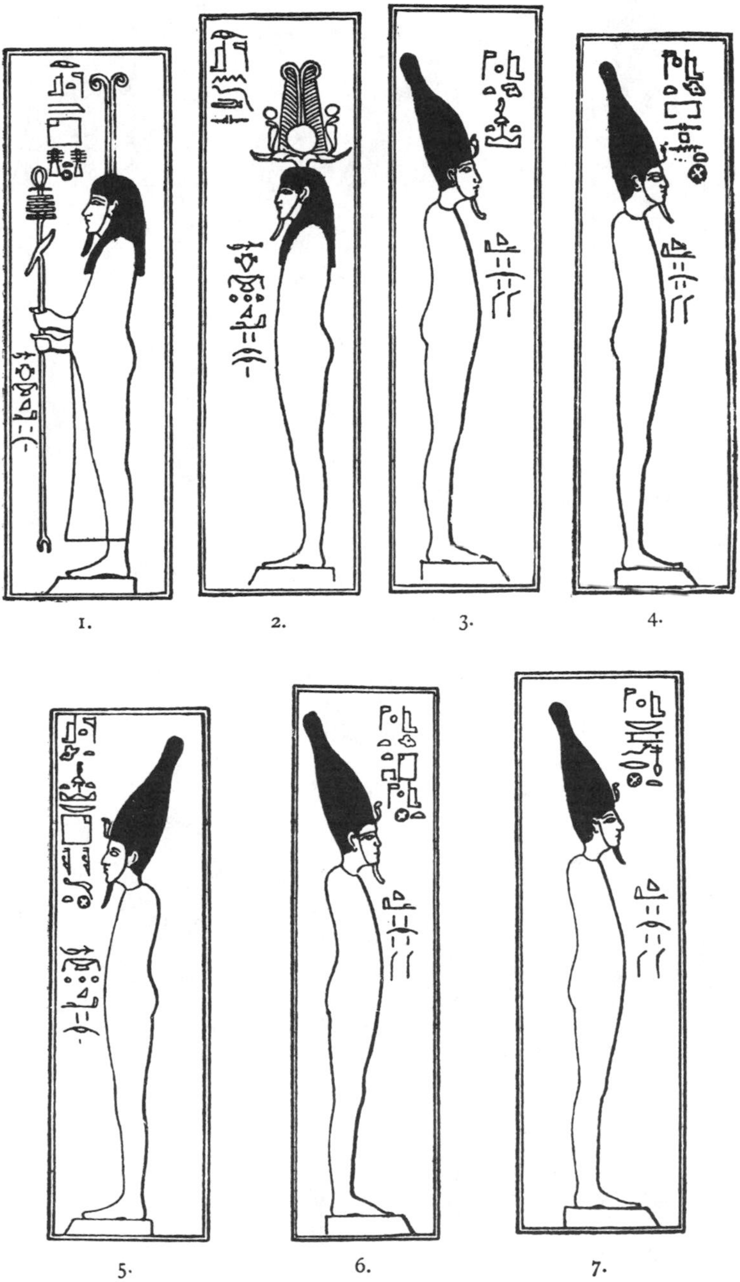

SEVEN FORMS OF OSIRIS WORSHIPPED AT ABYDOS.

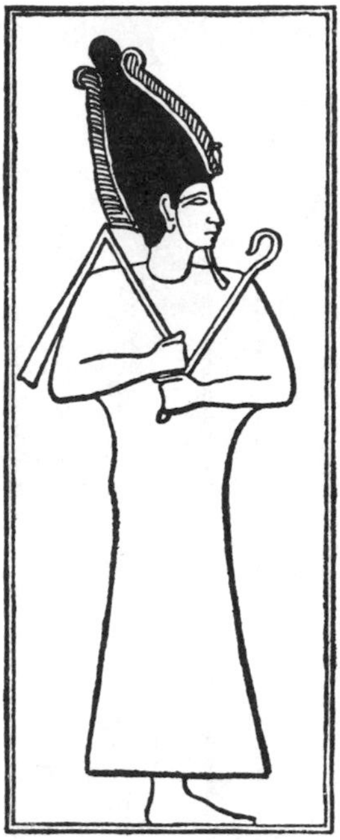

Osiris wearing the White Crown and Plumes.

Osiris wearing the White Crown and Plumes.

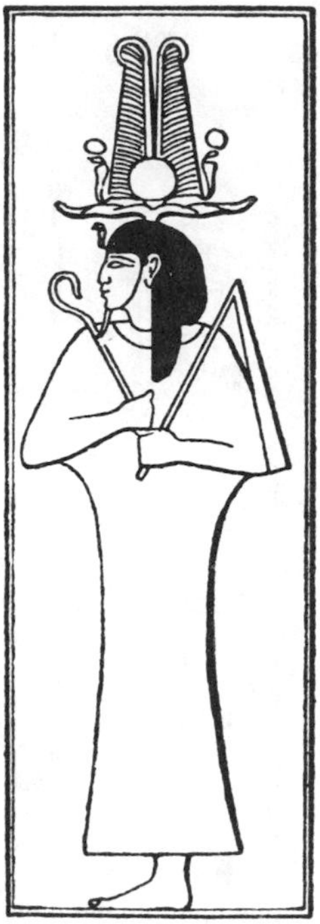

Osiris wearing the Atef Crown.

Osiris Un-Nefer.
From Lanzone, Plate 293.

Osiris, Lord of Eternity.
From Lanzone, Plate 295.

MISCELLANEOUS FORMS OF OSIRIS.

1. The Ṭeṭ, from which proceed "Life" and a pair of arms supporting the solar disk.
From the Papyrus of Ani.

2. Osiris Un-Nefer.
From a bas-relief at Abydos.

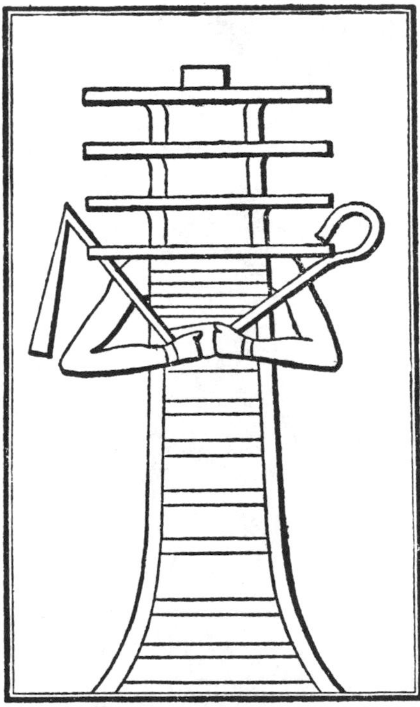

3. The Ṭeṭ, with human arms and hands holding the sceptre and whip of Osiris.
From the Papyrus of Ani.

1. Ṭeṭ with the head of Osiris.

2. A priest supporting Ṭeṭ with the head of Osiris in the presence of Isis.

3. Ṭeṭ as an old man.

"Busiris."[1] The temple, or place, in which the Ṭeṭ was worshipped was, in later times, called "Per-Seḳer," *i.e.*, the "House of Silence."[2] At a very early period Osiris was assimilated to the Ṭeṭ, and the ceremony of "setting up" the Ṭeṭ became the equivalent of the reconstitution of the back-bone and of the body of Osiris generally. The Ṭeṭ can hardly have been a tree with branches, but it may have been confused with a tree trunk, or a sort of coffer or framework made of a tree trunk, in which the relic of Osiris, which was venerated at Busiris, was kept. Quite early in the Dynastic Period the cult of Osiris-Ṭeṭ made its way south-wards, and reached the Nome of This, and became established

[1] From the Egyptian Per-Asȧr

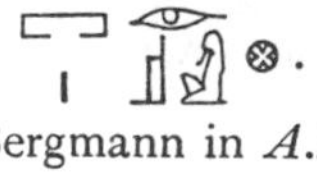

[2] Bergmann in *A.Z.*, 1880, p. 90.

at the capital, Åbṭu, or Abydos. Under the New Empire it was confidently asserted that Abydos possessed the veritable body of Osiris, and the symbol of Osiris-Ṭeṭ is described as the "holy Ṭeṭ in Abydos."[1] The statement of Plutarch as to the rival claims of Busiris and Abydos shows that the tradition had reached the Greeks.[2] Sometimes the Ṭeṭ is surmounted by the horns, feathers, disk, etc., which belong to Osiris, or Osiris Khenti-Åmenti, and sometimes by the head and bust of Osiris, or by his head, with horns and plumes on the top of it. Rarely, Khenti-Åmenti is represented as an old man, whose head forms the base of the Ṭeṭ, on which rest the feathers, horns, etc., which are the attributes of Osiris (see p. 52).

Osiris-Seker.

A very unusual form of Osiris, or Osiris Un-Nefer, is found on a relief at Abydos[3] (see p. 51). On a high pylon-shaped pedestal is a kneeling human figure, on the neck of which stands a Ṭeṭ, within the loop of the symbol of "life," which takes the place of a head and neck. This figure is described as "Osiris Un-Nefer, dweller in the Temple of Men-Maāt-Rā,"[4] and is entreated to give every kind of physical well-being to him (*i.e.*, to the king). The attributes of Un-nefer are not known. It is probable that in his oldest form he was a god of the

4. Ṭeṭ as an old man.

1 Mariette, *Abydos*, tom. I, Plate 16.
2 Plutarch, *De Iside et Osiride*, Chap. XXI.
3 Mariette, *Abydos*, tom. I, Plate 40.
4 .

dead, but in late times he was only a phase, so to speak, of Osiris. The name seems to mean "Beneficent Being," and in the New Empire it had already become a title of Osiris, as we see from the following phrases from the Hymn to Osiris in the Papyrus of Hunefer (Sheet 3):

Isis setting up the standard with box containing the head of Osiris upon it, while a priest anoints it with holy oil.

From a bas-relief at Abydos.

Praise be to Osiris!
Adorations be given to him!
Smelling of the earth to Un-Nefer!
Prostrations to the ground to the Lord of Ta-tchesert![1]

1 

Other forms of Osiris are:

Osiris-Seker [hieroglyphs], in which he appears as a hawk-headed mummy, sometimes standing upright, and at other times sitting. When seated he holds in his

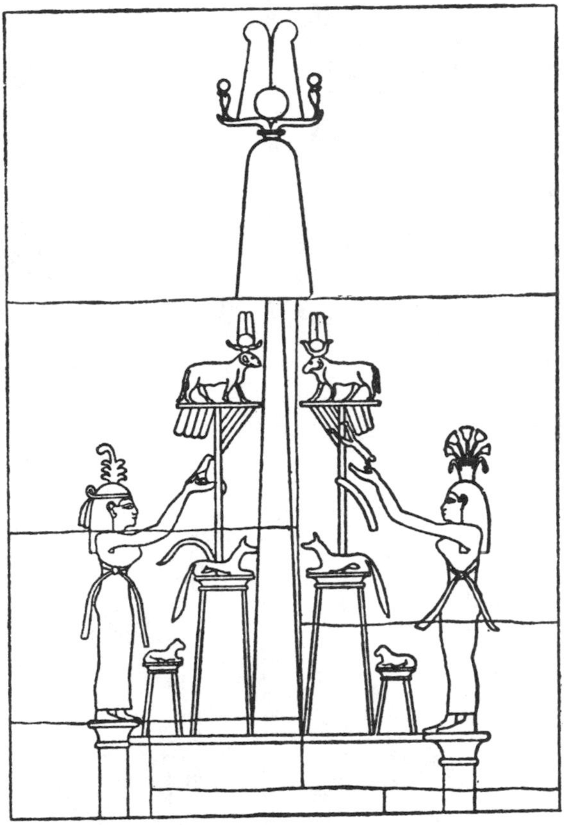

The goddesses of the North and South setting up the standard with the box containing the head of Osiris upon it.
From a bas-relief at Meroë.

hands the whip, sceptre, and crook [hieroglyphs]. The kingdom of Seker was the Ṭuat, or Other World, of Memphis. It was shrouded in thick darkness, and was formed by bare, sandy deserts, which were full of terrifying monsters, some winged, and some many-headed. The prefixing of the name of Osiris to that

Setting up the Ṭeṭ.
From a bas-relief at Abydos.

The king handing the Ṭeṭ to Isis.
From a bas-relief at Abydos.

Thoth and Anubis setting up a standard supporting the box that held the head of Osiris.
From a bas-relief at Meroë.

The box containing the head of Osiris on its standard.
From a bas-relief at Abydos.

Osiris-Seker or Seker-Osiris.
From the Papyrus of Ani.

of Seker indicates that Osiris became the overlord of this very ancient god.

Osiris-Neper. One of the oldest grain-gods[1] of Egypt was Neprȧ 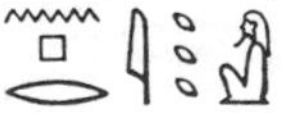, who appears to have been a personification of wheat, barley, dhura, etc., and to have presided over corn-land generally. His

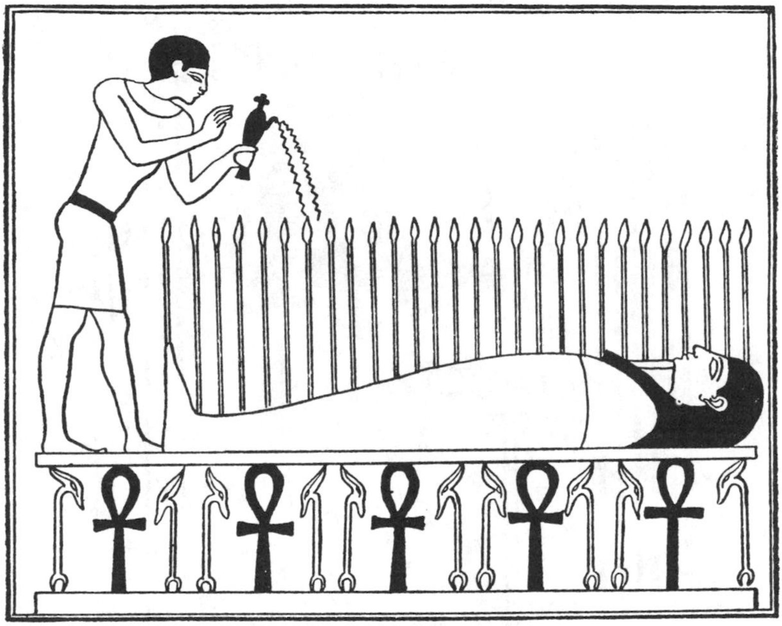

Osiris-Neprȧ, with wheat growing from his body.
From a bas-relief at Philae.

attributes were absorbed by Osiris, the god of agriculture generally. The identification of Osiris as a corn-god is proved by the relief at Philae, in which corn is seen growing out of his mummified body, and by the custom of making a figure of the god in grain on a mat which was placed in the tomb. The germination of the grain typified the germination of the spirit-body of the deceased.

[1] Other grain-gods were Besuā, Pȧn, Ḥetch-ā, Āb, and Nepen. See the Book "Ȧm-Ṭuat," Division II.

OSIRIS-AĀḤ , *i.e.*, Osiris, the Moon-god. He appears in the form of a human-headed mummy, with a crescent moon and full moon on his head. In his hands he holds , *i.e.*, symbols of stability, life, serenity, power, and dominion.

Osiris the Moon-god.

OSIRIS-SAḤ  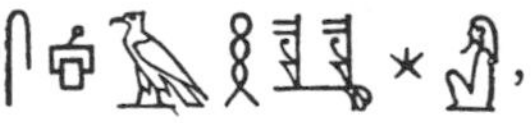, *i.e.*, Osiris-Orion; his female counterpart was Isis-Sepṭ, or Isis-Sothis.

OSIRIS-HORUS, a form of the rising sun.[1]

OSIRIS-HAR-MACHIS-TEMU, a triad representing the evening sun, the night sun, and the morning sun. In late times we have Osiris-Rā, a dual god, who represented the day-sun and the night-sun.

[1] See the list of the forms of Osiris in Chapters CXLI and CXLII of the Book of the Dead according to the Papyrus of Nu (Sheet 15).

OSIRIS-NEB-ḤEḤ ,[1] *i.e.*, Osiris, Lord of Eternity, who appears in the form of a mummy with the head of the Bennu-bird, or phoenix. This name proves that the idea of an existence renewed and prolonged indefinitely was associated with the Bennu-bird at a very early period (see p. 50).

OSIRIS-ḲEB , or Osiris fused with the ancient Goose-god, who produced the cosmic egg.

OSIRIS-BA-NEB-ṬEṬ 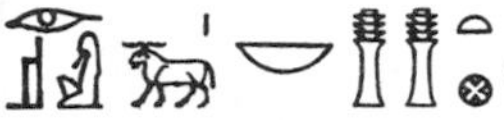, *i.e.*, Osiris, the Ram, Lord of Ṭeṭu, who appeared in the form of the sacred Ram of Mendes.

OSIRIS-TUA , *i.e.*, Osiris the Begetter.

One of the most important forms of Osiris from about 600 B.C. to the Roman Period was Ȧsȧr-Ḥep 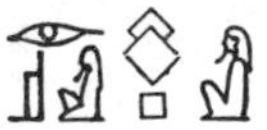, or Sarapis. This form was made by the fusion of the attributes of the old Bull-god Ḥep, the Apis of the Greeks, with those of Osiris. The worship of Apis is very ancient, and, long before the fusion of the gods, the bull of Apis was believed to be an incarnation of Osiris, and to contain his soul ; the appearance of a new Apis Bull was regarded as a new manifestation of Osiris upon earth. To satisfy the priests of the local cult of Apis at Memphis, Apis was declared to be the son of Ptaḥ. Sarapis appears on stelae and in reliefs as a mummified man with the head of a bull ; between the horns he wears a disk which is surmounted by two plumes, and in his hands he holds , , ,  and . On the stele of Th-I-em-ḥetep in the British Museum[2] the deceased is seen worshipping " Seker-Osiris,

[1] Probably the same as  of the Papyrus of Nu.

[2] No. 1027, Bay 29.

Governor of the Ka-House," and Ḥep-Åsår[1] (Sarapis), Isis, Nephthys, Horus and Anubis, and Sarapis is called " Khenti-Åmenti, King of the Gods, Lord of Eternity, Prince of Everlastingness."

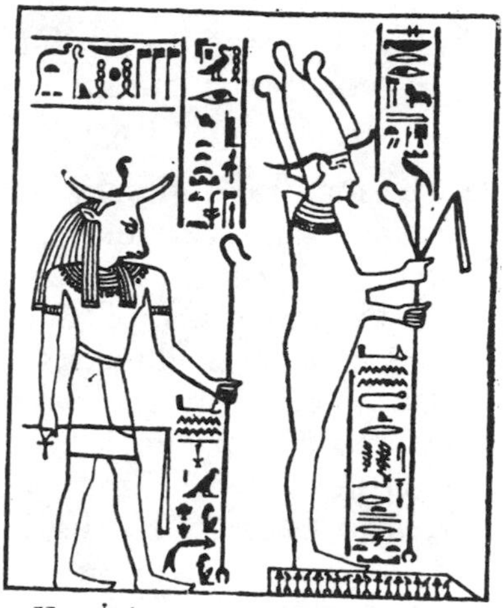

Hep-Åsår, or Sarapis. Seker-Osiris.

In this case Sarapis appears as an unmummified man, with a bull's head, whilst Seker - Osiris has the ordinary form of a mummified man. Thus it seems clear that Osiris of Busiris in the North was fused with Seker, the old god of the dead of Memphis, and that Osiris Khenti-Åmenti from Abydos in the South was fused with the ancient Bull - god of Memphis. Practically Sarapis was the equivalent of the Pluto of the Greeks. For the history of the adoption of the double god by the Greeks in Egypt see Plutarch, *De Iside*, Chapters 27, 28.

1 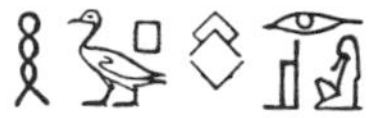

CHAPTER III.

THE MUTILATION AND DISMEMBERMENT OF OSIRIS, HIS RECONSTITUTION AND RESURRECTION, HIS ENTRANCE INTO HEAVEN, AND HIS STATE OF BEING THERE.

IN the magical and religious literature of Ancient Egypt, there are many references to the mutilations which were inflicted on the bodies of the greatest of the beneficent gods by the gods of evil and the powers of darkness, and also several allusions to mutilations which the good gods inflicted on their own bodies under the stress of emotions of various kinds. Thus Set, the Typhon of the Greeks, by means of eclipses blinded temporarily both the eyes of Horus, and tore them out of his head, and under the form of a black pig he swallowed the left eye, which he found one night as he was wandering about the sky. The disappearance of the right eye of Horus, *i.e.*, the sun, from the sky each night, was also caused by Set, and every month, after full moon, the moon was eaten away piecemeal by him. In addition to the eyes the two arms of Horus were removed and destroyed by Set. These facts are made clear by the CXIIth[1] and CXIIIth Chapters of the Book of the Dead. According to the former chapter Horus looked at the black pig into which Set had transformed himself,[2] and at once received a terrible blow of fire in the eye, and through the whirlwind of fire which followed it the eye was destroyed.[3] When Rā had ordered Horus to

[1] The importance of this Chapter has been discussed by Lefébure, *Le Mythe Osirien*, Paris, 1874–5, and by Moret, *Rituel du Culte Divin*, Paris, 1902, p. 40 ff.

[2] 

[3] 

be put to bed, and declared that he would recover, he announced that the "pig was an abomination to Horus," and ever after it was so. The daily restoration of the eye of Horus was effected by means of a ceremony which was performed in the great temple of Ámen-Rā at Karnak. The priest approached the closed shrine which contained the figure of the god, and having broken the seal and untied the cord he said: "The cord is "broken, the seal is undone, I am come to bring thee "the Eye of Horus, thine eye is to thee, O Horus. "The mud of the seal is broken, the celestial ocean is "penetrated, the intestines of Osiris are drawn out "(*i.e.*, fished out of the water). I am not come to "destroy the god on his throne, I am come to set the "god on his throne." The priest next drew the bolt, which symbolized the removal of the finger of Set from the Eye of Horus, and when he had thrown open the doors of the shrine, and the light fell upon the face of the figure of the god, he declared that the "heavens were opened," and the ceremony was complete.[1]

The fishing out of the intestines of Osiris from the celestial ocean is paralleled by the fishing out of certain members of the body of Horus which is mentioned in the CXIIIth Chapter of the Book of the Dead. According to the text, Horus the son of Isis had perished, *i.e.*, he had been mutilated, and some of his members had been cast into the water. Isis invoked the aid of Sebek, the Crocodile-god, an ancient solar deity, who having examined the banks of the swamp with his claws until he found the traces of them, took his net and fished them out with it. The text goes on to say that the arms 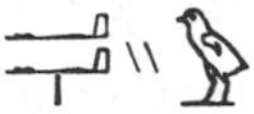 and the hands  of Horus were found by Sebek and the fish which were under his rule. The region was called "Ta-remu," *i.e.*, "Land of fish," a name given to it by Rā, who ordained that the recovery of the hands of Horus should be commemorated at the festival of the "opening of the face,"[2] or "manifestation" of Horus on the first and

[1] See Moret, *op. cit.*, pp. 38–42.

[2] .

fifteenth days of each month. It may be noted in passing that the texts referred to above have confounded two gods of the same name. The Horus who lost his eyes was the old Heaven-god Horus, the eternal victor over Set, whilst the god who lost his arms and hands was Horus, the son of Isis. Such confusions are common in the literature of all periods of Egyptian history, and were due partly to ignorance and partly to carelessness on the part of the scribes.

The texts show that Set did not always work his wicked will on Horus without injury to himself. This we learn from a passage in the Book of Opening the Mouth, where the priest is made to say: "I have "delivered this mine eye from his (*i.e.*, Set's) mouth, "I have cut off his leg." With these words he presented to the statue of the deceased a leg of the animal which had been killed.[1] On one occasion, when Horus and Set, the two Reḥui,[2] were fighting, the latter cast filth in the face of Horus, and the former carried off the genitals of Set.[3] The fight was stopped by Thoth, who pacified the two men, and who spat[4] upon the injured eye of Horus, which was healed at once.

Egyptian legends assert that as Set, or Suti, had waged war against Horus the great Sky-god, and Horus the son of Isis, so he attacked the Sun-god Rā in the form of a monster serpent, or crocodile, called Āpep 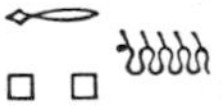, the name of which is perpetuated in the Coptic version of the Bible under the form

[1] See my *Book of Opening the Mouth*, Vol. II, p. 44.

[2] Reḥ, or Reḥu, is an old word for "man";  were the "two men" *par excellence*.

[3]  Book of the Dead, Chapter XVII.

[4] , Chapter XVII, l. 75.

αφωφ (Genesis vi, 4; Psalm xviii, 5). Rā was victorious and thrust his iron lance into him, and Āpep vomited everything which he had eaten.[1] The text does not say what it was that Āpep had swallowed, but in the light of other texts we may assume that it was the left eye of Rā, *i.e.*, the moon.

Turning now to the self-inflicted mutilations of the gods, the well-known instances of Rā and Bata may be quoted. On one occasion "Rā mutilated his own person,"[2] and out of the drops of blood which fell from his phallus the gods Ḥu and Sa came into being, and they associated themselves with Temu, a Sun-god of night. In the case of Bata, the younger brother of Ȧnpu in the Tale of the Two Brothers, the phallus was thrown into the water and devoured by a fish. Though Ȧnpu and Bata are described as men in this tale, it is quite clear that they were originally gods. Osiris, as we learn from Plutarch, was mutilated by Set, and the same fate seems to have overtaken his first-born son Beba ;[3] the phallus of Osiris was never recovered, but that of Beba was "brought" in connection with the magic boat.

The wounds, however, which were inflicted upon the gods by themselves, or by the powers of evil, no matter how many times repeated, were not permanent, for Thoth, the god of knowledge, was always at hand to heal them. Though the right eye of Horus, or Rā, *i.e.*, the sun, was swallowed up one night, it appeared in the eastern sky again on the morrow, and though the moon was devoured one month, it rose in the western sky in

[1] Book of the Dead, Chapter CVIII, 
.

[2] , Book of the Dead, Chapter XVII, l. 62.

[3] Or , or , Book of the Dead, Chapter XCIX, l. 17.

the next. Besides the healing power of Thoth, the gods possessed, in themselves, the wonderful power of renewing their members, and of lengthening their lives indefinitely ; renewed life was their chief characteristic and attribute, and immortality was their inheritance. Because of these qualities, men in all ages in Egypt regarded the gods as being wholly above the nature of man and his spiritual economy, and they felt that it was useless to expect them to concern themselves with human affairs and cares. The experience of primitive man in Egypt told him that when the eyes of men were gouged out, and their shoulders and arms cut off, and their hearts torn out from their breasts, they died, and though he was assured that such men continued their lives in some other place, he never expected them to return to their villages, even for a short visit, with renewed bodies. In fact, he did not believe that a body which had been devoured by a crocodile, or torn to pieces by savage beasts, or dismembered by human foes or masters, could be reconstituted, and in this belief he must have remained for a very considerable time, probably until nearly the end of the Neolithic Period.

With the conquest of Egypt by the early kings of the series which forms the First Dynasty, new views as to the future life appear to have entered the country, and these, having passed through various stages of development, resulted in the belief that a certain man who had lived and died upon earth had, by some means, raised himself up to life again, and that he had succeeded in making himself the god of the dead. The inscriptions of the first three dynasties tell us nothing about this being, and though certain incidents in his life are referred to by the writers of the texts of the IVth dynasty, it is not until we come to the connected religious compositions of the Vth and VIth dynasties that we obtain any definite statements about him. It is, however, quite clear that the cult of this being had been growing and spreading in all Egypt for many centuries, and that even before the close of the Vth dynasty it had profoundly modified the ancient religious views of the people in general. The details of the history of the remarkable being who had risen from the dead were assumed by the scribes to be so well known that they are not described in the great religious compositions which have come down to us. Only by piecing together the information which is given here and there can we arrive at any connected views of what happened to him, and to this day, in spite of the mass of religious and magical literature which is available, we are wholly ignorant of the origin and general history of the first human being in Egypt who rose from the dead, and who was known for thousands of years as "Khenti-Ȧmenti,"  (Tetȧ, l. 286), "Chief of Ȧmenti," or "Khenti Ȧmentiu," , "Chief of those who are in Ȧmenti," *i.e.*, "Chief of those who are in the West, or, Other World."

Of the home of this being who rose from the dead, and of the position which he occupied in this world nothing can be learned from the texts, but late Greek writers[1] assert that he was a king, and they are probably correct. Only kings and chiefs, or men of high rank, are buried in Africa with the pomp and ceremony which must have accompanied the committal to the grave of the man who afterwards rose from the dead. The exact region in Egypt where his kingdom was situated is unknown, but about his burial-place there is no doubt, for all tradition, both Egyptian and Greek, states that his grave was at Abydos ( *Abṭu*), in Upper Egypt. And the name of this man was OSIRIS, in Egyptian *Ȧsȧr* . In the "Pyramid Texts" of the Vth and VIth dynasties, the name of Osiris is frequently prefixed to the names of the deceased kings, *e.g.*, Osiris-Unȧs,[2] Osiris-Tetȧ,[3] etc., and in several passages the deceased is addressed as "Osiris." The identification of the dead king Pepi with Osiris is well illustrated

[1] Plutarch, *De Iside*, § 13; Diodorus I, 15.
[2] See the text of Unȧs, lines 27, 45, 67, 87, etc.
[3] See the text of Tetȧ, l. 153.

by the following: "Horus cometh, Thoth riseth, and "they lift up Osiris (*i.e.*, Pepi) on his place, and they "cause him to stand up among the two Companies of "the Gods."[1]

Since the deceased is identified with Osiris, it is only natural that he should seek the resting-place of this god, and in the text of Pepi I it is said: "Thou "sailest up the river to the Thinite Nome, thou sailest "about Abydos. Thou openest the door in heaven in "the horizon, the gods rejoice at meeting thee. They "draw thee into heaven in thy soul, and thou art "endowed with soul among them. Thou appearest in "the sky as Horus from the womb of the sky, in this "thy form which came forth from the mouth of Rā, "as Horus, the Chief (or First) of the Spirits."[2]

Now this passage is one of considerable importance, for it proves that the door which opened into heaven was at Abydos, that the gods welcomed the deceased when he had passed through it, that they gave him soul-power, and that he appeared afterwards newly-born from the womb of heaven, as Horus, Horus the Chief of the Spirits. These being the views which were current about Abydos under the Vth dynasty, there is no need to

1 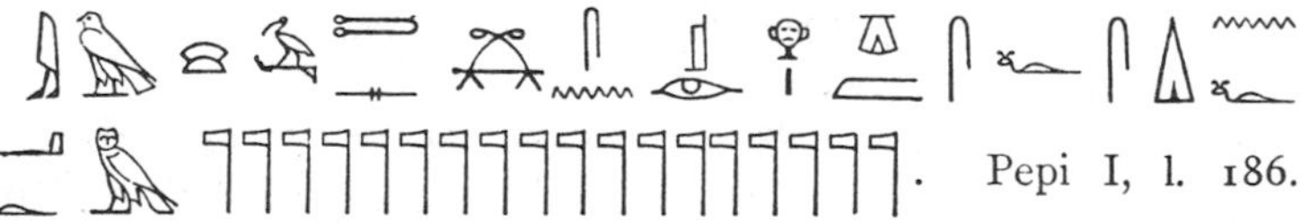
Pepi I, l. 186. See also l. 67.

2 

Pepi I, l. 74 ff.; Mer-en-Rā, l. 104 ff.; Pepi II, l. 15 ff.

wonder why every Egyptian of rank and family wished to be buried there, and they explain the importance of the city in the eyes of all Egyptians.

Returning now to the consideration of the identification of the deceased with Osiris, we shall see by the following extracts from the Pyramid Texts that it is possible to get a tolerably clear idea of much that happened to Osiris. In the text of Unȧs we have :

> " Thy heart is to thee, Osiris, thy feet are to thee,
> " Osiris, thy arms are to thee, Osiris. The heart
> " of Unȧs is to him himself, his feet are to him
> " himself, his arm is to him himself."[1]

From this it is clear that, at some time, the heart, feet, and arm of Osiris were removed from him. In the text of Tetȧ the dead king is addressed thus :

" Hail, hail, rise up, thou Tetȧ ! Thou hast received " thy head, thou hast embraced thy bones, thou hast " gathered together thy flesh. . . . . Rise up, thou " Tetȧ, thou art not a dead thing."[2]

Again, in the text of Pepi I, we have :—

" He who cometh cometh to thee, thou movest not. " Thy mother cometh to thee, thou movest not. [The " goddess] Nut cometh to thee, thou movest not. [The " goddess] Khnemet-urt cometh to thee, thou movest " not. She breatheth (?) on thee, she addresseth thee " with words of power, thou movest. She giveth thee " thy head, she presenteth to thee thy bones, she

1 
Unȧs, l. 476, and compare Pepi II, l. 746.

2 
Tetȧ, l. 287 = Mer-en-Rā, l. 65 = Pepi II, l. 126 ff.

"gathereth together thy flesh, she bringeth to thee thy "heart in thy body. Thou art master of thy utter- "ances, and thou givest words of command to those "who are before thee."[1]

In the same text the gods are called upon "to gather "together the bones of this Pepi, and to unite his flesh "[so that] this Pepi may sit in his house, [that] he may "not suffer corruption, may not be destroyed, may not "be in thrall";[2] and elsewhere it is said: "Pepi hath "collected his bones, hath gathered together his flesh."[3]

Now as the deceased is identified with Osiris, it is clear from the above passages that the head of Osiris was cut off, that his body was broken up and its internal organs separated, and that his bones were scattered. It is equally clear that his head, bones, and organs were reunited, that his body was reconstituted and restored to life, and that he had the power to speak, and to command his followers as he had done when on earth. And by whom was the reconstitution of the body of

1  Pepi I, l. 109 = Mer-en-Rā, l. 75 = Pepi II, l. 77 ff.

2 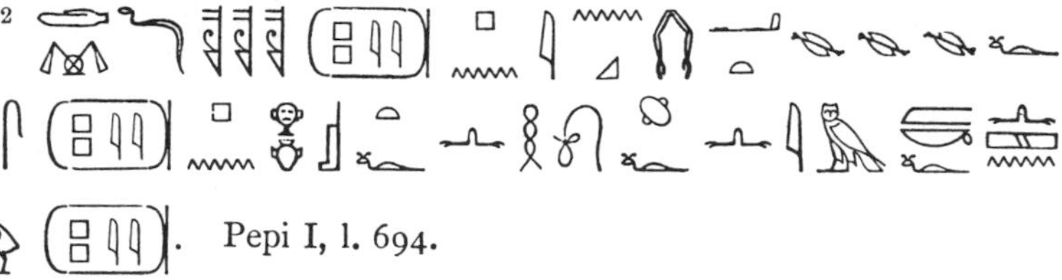 Pepi I, l. 694.

3 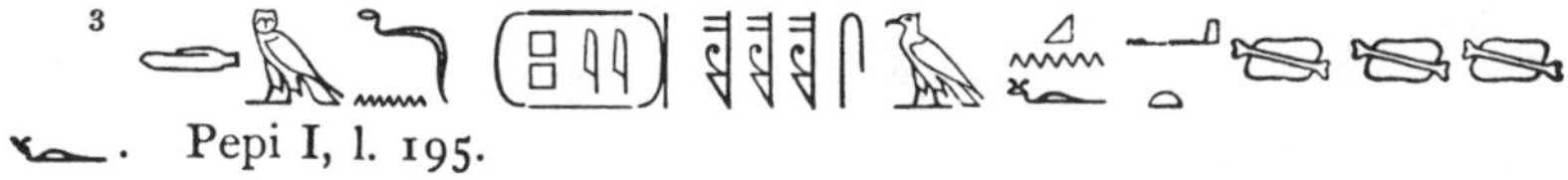 Pepi I, l. 195.

Osiris effected? The texts answer this question, and tell us that it was by Horus, the son of Osiris, who was assisted by his four sons. In the texts of Tetȧ and Mer-en-Rā we have the following important passage:—

"Hail, thou Osiris Tetȧ, stand up! Horus cometh, "he hath counted thee with the gods. Horus loveth "thee. He hath filled thee with his Eye, he hath joined "his Eye to thee. Horus hath opened thine eye that "thou mayest see therewith. The gods have lifted up "thy face, they love thee. [The goddesses] Isis and "Nephthys have made thee strong. Horus departeth "not from thee, behold, his KA (*i.e.*, double). He resteth "on thee, thou livest. Thou hast received the word "of Horus, thou restest upon it. Horus hearkeneth, "never faileth (?) he thee. He maketh the gods to be "thy followers.

"Osiris Tetȧ, rise thou up! Ḳeb hath brought "Horus to thee, he hath reckoned thee up. Horus "hath found thee, he hath performed the ceremonies "for thee. Horus hath brought the gods to thee, he "hath given them unto thee, they illumine thy face. "Horus hath placed thee before the gods, he hath made "thee to take possession of every diadem. Horus hath "bound them on thee, he hath not removed them from "thee. Horus hath given thee life in thy name of "Āntchtȧ (*i.e.*, KING). He hath given thee his Eye "which flourisheth lastingly. He hath given thee thy "weapon, thou hast conquered all thine enemies. Horus "hath filled thee wholly with his Eye in its name of "'Uaḥet.' Horus hath seized for thee the gods, they "shall not depart (?) from thee wheresoever thou goest "by land. Horus hath counted up the gods for thee, "they shall not depart from thee wheresoever thou goest "by water (?). Nephthys hath united for thee all thy "members in her name of 'Seshat, lady of buildings,' "thou shalt be strong thereby. Thy mother Nut is "given [to thee] in her name of 'Qersut,' she uniteth "thee in her name of 'Qersu,' she maketh thee to go "forward in her name of 'Ȧā[r].' Horus presenteth "unto thee thy flesh, he doth not set (or, place) thy "mould (?), he maketh thee to be a complete being, "there is no disorder (or, confusion) in thee. Horus "maketh thee to stand up without support (?).

"Hail, Osiris Tetȧ! Lift up thy heart to him, let "thy heart be great (*i.e.*, bold), open thy mouth. Horus "avengeth thee, he never ceaseth (?) to avenge thee. "Hail, Osiris Tetȧ! Behold, thou art a mighty god, "there is no god like unto thee. Horus hath given thee "his sons, they raise thee up, he hath given unto thee "all the gods, they follow thee, thou hast dominion "over them. Horus hath carried thee (or, raised "thee) in his name of 'Ḥenu,' he hath lifted thee up "in thy name of 'Seker,' living thou passest (or, travellest) "every day. Thou art endowed with a spirit (*khu*) in "thy name of 'Khut,' wherein Rā appeareth, thou art "worshipped, endowed with readiness, soul, [and] "strength, for ever and ever." The hieroglyphic text is as follows :—

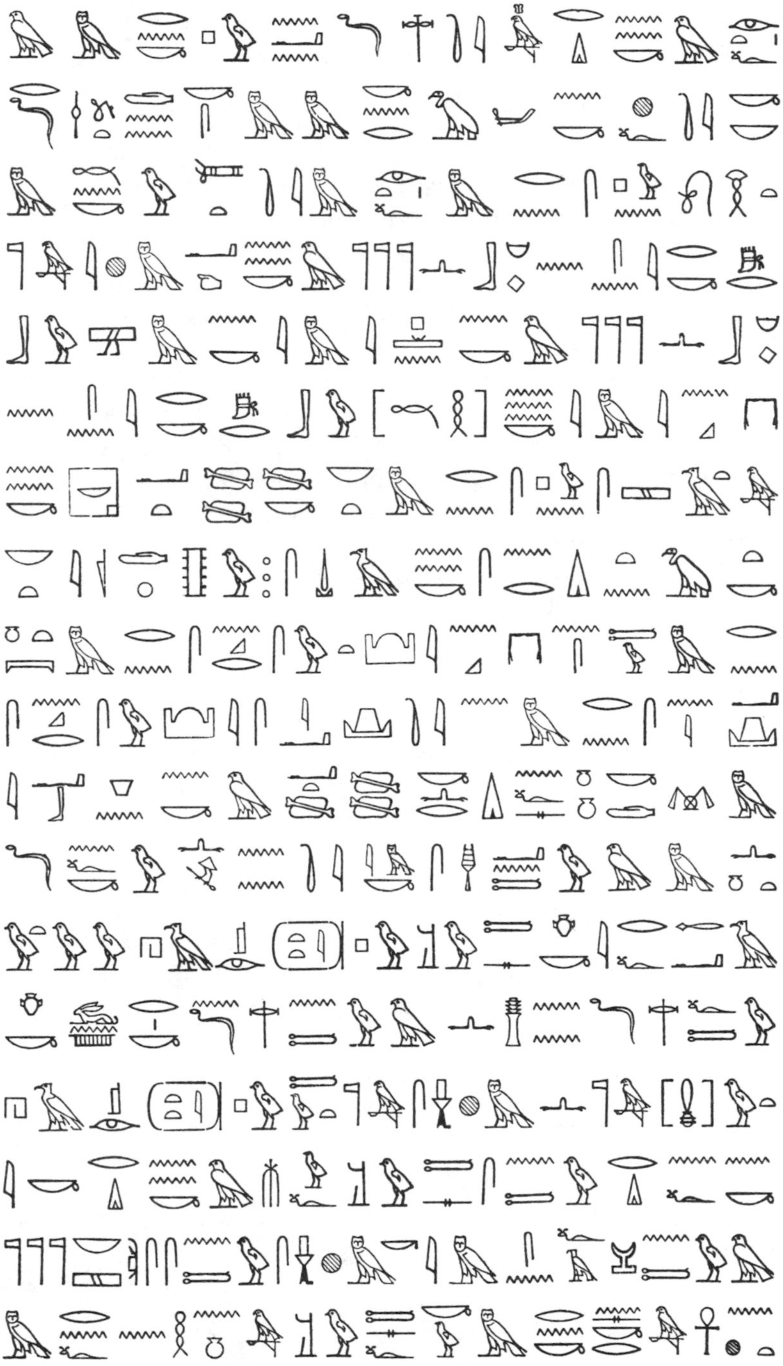

[1]

From the above passage it is clear that Horus did not only collect and reunite the flesh and bones of Osiris, but that he made him once more a complete man, endowed with all his members. Having done this, it was necessary to restore to Osiris the power to breathe, to speak, to see, to walk, and to employ his body in any way he saw fit. To bring about this result Horus performed a number of ceremonies, and made use of several words of power which had the effect of "opening the mouth" of Osiris. There is no detailed and connected description of these ceremonies to be found in the texts of the Vth and VIth dynasties, but several passages indicate their character generally, as may be seen from the following:—

"Horus hath pressed for thee thy mouth, he hath "weighed (or, balanced) thy mouth against thy bones "(*i.e.*, teeth), Horus hath opened for thee thy mouth. "Behold, thy son loveth thee, he hath founded for thee "thy two eyes, Horus doth not permit thy face to be "obliterated in thy name of 'Horus, chief of his "people'" (*rekhit*).[2]

In another passage the mouth of the deceased is said to be opened by Shesa-khent-Shenāt, by Tuȧ-ur in Ḥet-nub, by the two Tetuȧ in Ḥet-Senter, and by Horus, who "did it with his little finger wherewith he

[1] Tetȧ, ll. 264–271 = Mer-en-Rā, ll. 416–437.

[2] 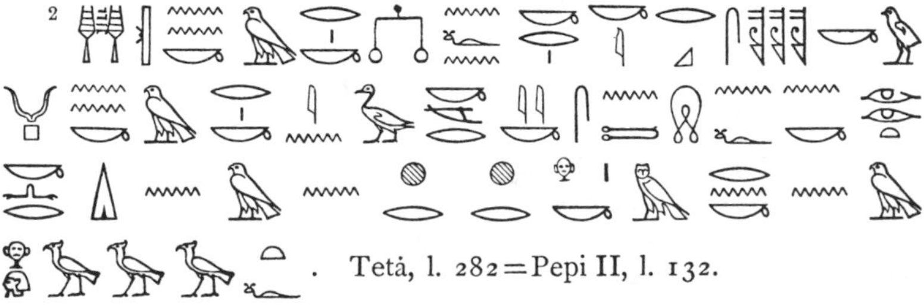

 . Tetȧ, l. 282=Pepi II, l. 132.

opened the mouth of his father Osiris."[1] During the work of reconstituting the body of Osiris, Horus was assisted by the two *tcherti* of Osiris,[2] *i.e.*, the goddesses Isis and Nephthys, and by two nurse-goddesses,[3] who were probably other forms of Isis and Nephthys.

When the body of Osiris was ready to leave this earth for heaven, some difficulty, it seems, arose in raising him up to the sky, and a ladder was found to be necessary. From the text of Pepi II (l. 975 ff.) we learn the tradition that the wooden sides of the ladder were shaped by an adze wielded by the god Sashsa, that the rungs were made of the strong sinews (?) of Ḳasut, the Bull of the Sky, and that they were fastened in their places on the sides of the ladder with knotted thongs made from the hide of the god Utes, the son of Ḥesat.[4] This divine ladder was set up from earth to heaven by Horus and Rā according to one legend, and according to another by Horus and Set. The text of Unȧs says: "Rā setteth up the ladder before Osiris, Horus setteth "up the ladder before his father Osiris in his going to his "spirit. One of them [standeth] on this side, and one of

1 
 Pepi I, l. 590.

2  Tetȧ, l. 260.

3  Tetȧ, l. 261.

4 
 Pepi II, ll. 975, 976.

"them on that side. Unȧs is between them."[1] In the text of Pepi I we find: "Homage to thee, Ladder of "the god! Homage to thee, Ladder of Set! Stand "up, Ladder of the god, stand up, Ladder of Set, stand "up, Ladder of Horus, whereby Osiris made his way "into heaven."[2] Elsewhere it is said: "Lo, Khensu, "lo, Åaḥes, Chief of the South-Land, lo, Ṭeṭun the "Great, Chief of Ta-sti (Nubia), lo, Sepṭ under his "trees. They carry the ladder for this Pepi, they set "up the ladder for this Pepi, they make firm the ladder "for this Pepi."[3] With the assistance of Horus and Set, Osiris stood on the ladder, and with their help he ascended and entered heaven. "Every spirit and every god opened his hand to Pepi when he was on the ladder,"[4]

1 

Unȧs, l. 579 = Pepi II, l. 962.

2  Pepi I, l. 192 = Pepi II, l. 912.

3  Pepi I, l. 200 = Pepi II, l. 936.

4 

Pepi I, l. 195 = Pepi II, l. 926.

and the "Lord of the Ladder," helped him with his two fingers to ascend,[1] and according to a passage in the text of Pepi I, when Osiris ascended the ladder, he "was covered with the covering of Horus, he wore the "apparel of Thoth, Isis was in front of him, Nephthys "was behind him, Ȧp-uat opened the way for him, Shu "bore him up, the Souls of Ȧn drew him up the steps "of the ladder, and Nut gave him her hands."[2]

When Osiris stepped from the ladder into heaven, he entered in among the company of the gods as a "living being," not merely as one about to begin a second state of existence with the limited powers and faculties which he possessed upon earth, but as one who felt that he had the right to rule heaven and the denizens thereof. He possessed a complete body, the nature of which had been changed by ceremonies which Horus, and his sons, and the assistant Tcherti goddesses, had performed for him; the number of his bones was complete and every internal organ and limb were in their place and in a perfect state. Besides these he possessed his forms, or attributes,[3] and his similitude,[4] his heart,[5] his soul,[6] his KA, or double,[7]

1 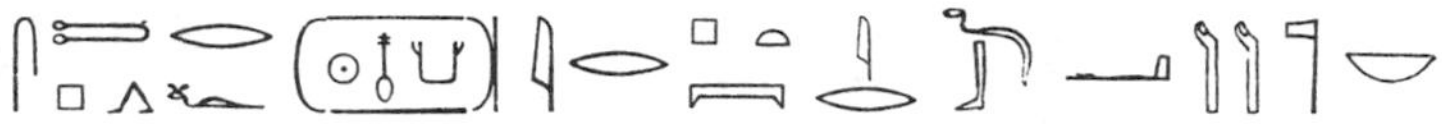
. Pepi II, l. 927.

2 
. Pepi I, l. 256.

3 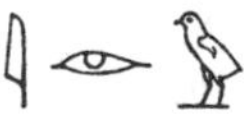. Pepi I, l. 16.

4 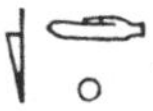. Pepi I, l. 315.

5 . Unȧs, l. 216.

6 . Pepi I, l. 13.

7 . Unȧs, ll. 1–4, Pepi I, l. 108.

his spirit, which was the head of all the spirits,[1] and his power.[2] He had gone to life, and not to death,[3] he was the "Chief of the Living Ones by the command of Rā," and was the "Great God" *par excellence*.[4] He was "Chief of the Powers,"[5] he was "master of heaven,"[6] and he had the power to bestow "life and well-being" upon those in heaven who went to him.[7] He transmitted his own odour to those whom he loved,[8] and his chosen ones sat on his shoulder.[9] He sat upon a throne,[10] holding sceptres emblematic of his various powers in his hands,[11] and he was surrounded by his bodyguard, and nobles, and trusted servants, after the manner of an African king; at the proper moment these cried out, "the god cometh, the god cometh, the god cometh."[12]

1 . Pepi I, l. 108.

2 . Pepi I, l. 4.

3 . Pepi I, l. 108.

4 . Pepi I, l. 17.

5 . Pepi I, l. 166.

6 . Pepi I, l. 188.

7 . Pepi I, l. 188.

8 . Pepi I, l. 695.

9 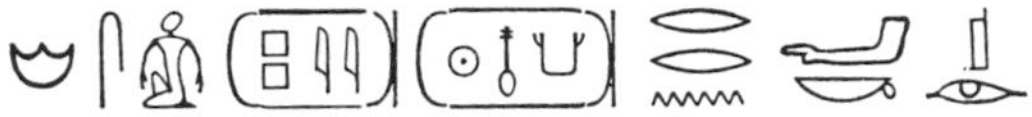. Pepi II, l. 958.

10 Unȧs, l. 206, Pepi I, l. 7. 11 Unȧs, l. 206.

12 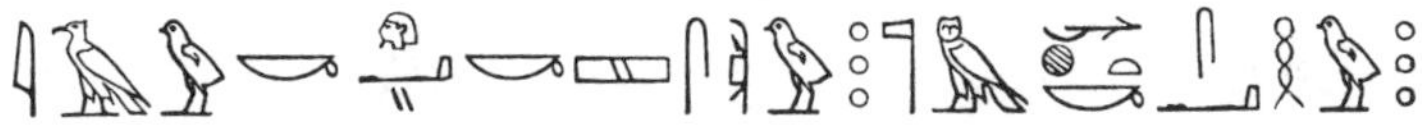 . Pepi I, l. 6.

Near him at all times was his son Horus, who obtained the title "Netch-àt-f,"[1] *i.e.*, "Avenger of his father," because of the labours which he had performed in connection with the reconstitution of his father's body. The hand of Osiris rested upon "life," and his arm was supported by the *uas* sceptre,[2] and the gods of the West, and of the East, and of the South, and of the North, who embrace the Four Pure Lands, devote themselves to his service.[3] "Heaven speaketh, and the earth "trembleth, the Earth-god Ḳeb quaketh, and the two "regions of the god utter a noise,"[4] and as a result the food whereon the gods and the blessed live is created. Osiris was the "great word,"[5] and he gave orders to the Spirits,[6] and he was the "word of what cometh into being and what is not."[7] In other words, Osiris the Word spake the words through which all things in heaven came into being from non-existence.

In origin, however, Osiris, the "Chief of those in Àmenti," or the Other World, was very different from the gods into whose heaven he entered, for he was at one time an inhabitant of the earth. Because he was the first man who had raised himself from the dead,

1 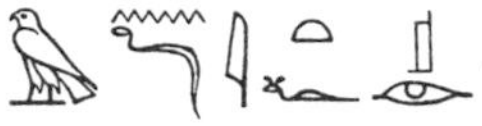. Tetà, l. 167.

2 . Pepi I, l. 190.

3 Unȧs, l. 572 = Pepi II, l. 967.

4 

. Pepi I, l. 304.

5 . Mer-en-Rā, l. 487 = Pepi I, l. 273 = Pepi II, l. 1254.

6 . Unȧs, l. 366.

7 . Pepi I, l. 345 = Mer-en-Rā, . 646.

he became the type and symbol and hope of every dead man, and the older gods in heaven seem to have thought it right to set apart for him a place in the Other World where he could live with all those who died believing in him, and rule over them. In the text of Unȧs the deceased is said to give the word of command to the Domains of Horus, the Domains of Set, and the Domains of Osiris,[1] and from another passage the Domains of Osiris appear to have been also called "Sekhet-Åaru,[2] *i.e.*, "The Fields of Reeds." Among these "fields of reeds" there must have been many fair fields wherein grain of various kinds was grown, for in the text of Pepi II, l. 1316, it is said that Osiris makes Pepi "to plough corn and to reap barley."[3] From this passage we are probably right in assuming that Osiris was, even at this early period, identified with the Grain-god Neprȧ. This view is, moreover, supported by the statement that the deceased drinks the emissions of Osiris and eats what comes forth from him,[4] *i.e.*, he lived on the moisture and meal which formed the Grain-god.

From the extracts from early texts quoted in the preceding paragraphs, it is quite clear that the Egyptians

1 
. Unȧs, l. 298 = Tetȧ, l. 141 = Pepi II, l. 538.

2 . Pepi I, 182 = Pepi II, l. 895. These Fields of Reeds are mentioned with the Domains of Horus, , and the Domains of Set.

3 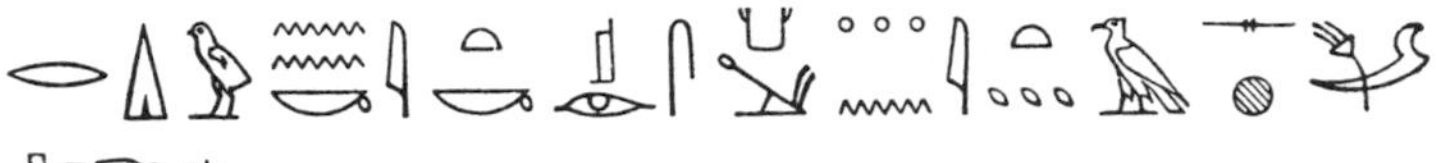
.

4 
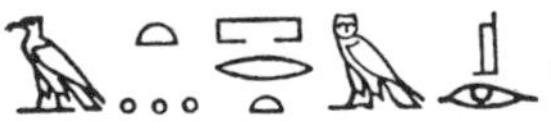. Pepi I, l. 66.

of the Vth and VIth dynasties believed that the body of the first man who rose from the dead, and who afterwards became the god of all the dead, was cut to pieces, and that the head was removed from the body, the bones of which were scattered. The dismemberment of the body was the work of a god called Set, who, curiously enough, appears at one time to be a friend of the dead man, and at another to be his bitter foe. Thus, in one place, Set and Thoth are called his two brothers, and they are mentioned in connection with Isis and Nephthys who weep for him.[1] In another, Set is called upon to give life to Osiris and to make him live,[2] for, continues the text, "if he liveth, this Unȧs liveth; if he "dieth not, this Unȧs dieth not; if he is not destroyed, "this Unȧs is not destroyed; if he begetteth not, this "Unȧs begetteth not; if he begetteth, this Unȧs "begetteth." On the other hand, we have in the text of Tetȧ (l. 170 ff.) definite statements that Set is the arch-enemy of Osiris, as he was of Horus, and the defeat of Set and his followers by Horus is described with great satisfaction.[3]

The texts nowhere say where the dismemberment of Osiris took place, but they prove that at a very early period Abydos in Upper Egypt was believed to be the spot where the reconstitution and revivification of his body were effected, and the box which held his head, surmounted by two feathers , became the symbol of that city. The burial of Osiris, or at least of some very important part of him, certainly took place at Abydos, for a passage in the text of Pepi I (l. 308) says that one of the Anubis gods and Horus buried Osiris at Abydos. The passages already quoted show that the power of

[1]  Unȧs, l. 236 = Pepi II, l. 710.

[2]  Unȧs, l. 246 = Pepi II, 711.

[3] The whole passage is quoted on pp. 26, 27.

Horus was not exhausted when he had reconstructed the body of Osiris, and that what he did for him subsequently was of far greater importance than the gathering together of his bones and flesh, and the rejoining of his head to his body. These acts would have been useless unless Horus had the power to give life to the reconstructed body, and to cause the gods in heaven to regard Osiris as their equal when he arrived there. The Pyramid Texts contain many passages which state that Horus performed a number of ceremonies of a magical character for his father Osiris, and several texts, written in subsequent periods of Egyptian history, describe fairly fully what the ceremonies were. These ceremonies, however, and the words spoken by Horus as he performed them, were only the means to an end, and that end was the restoration of life to the dead body of Osiris.

Reference has been made above to the religious tradition in Egypt which asserted that the Eye of Horus had been carried away from him by Set, and that Horus only succeeded in wresting it from him after a fierce fight in which Set suffered serious injury. Now the Eye of Horus contained his soul, that is to say, his life, and during the period when his Eye was in the hands of Set he was a dead god. When life left Osiris he also was a dead and inert being, and in this respect the condition of Osiris dead was identical with that of Horus dead. Horus, however, was a god, and of himself and by his own power was able to raise himself up to attack Set, and to snatch the Eye from his grasp. The traditions of the VIth dynasty state that it was Thoth, or Rā, the Sun-god of the city of On, who helped Horus to recover his Eye, but in the earliest times it was believed that Horus delivered his Eye by his own power. Be this as it may, the condition of Osiris was very different from that of Horus, for he became, when life left him, an inert dead body, which possessed no inherent power to restore to itself the life which had departed from it. Horus restored life to himself by bringing back his Eye to his body, and he made Osiris to live again by transferring the Eye to him. According to one statement, the god Thoth acted as an intermediary between Horus and Osiris, according to another, Horus himself gave his Eye to Osiris. Thus in the text of Pepi I it is said, "Thoth presenteth to Pepi his life which he hath not, "Thoth giveth to him the Eye of Horus. Horus is in "Osiris Pepi, the Eye of Horus is offered to thee."[1] The passages in which Horus is made to give his Eye

Horus giving life to Osiris.
From a bas-relief at Abydos.

to Osiris are so very important for the right understanding of the Osiris Legend that they are here given in full:—

[1] 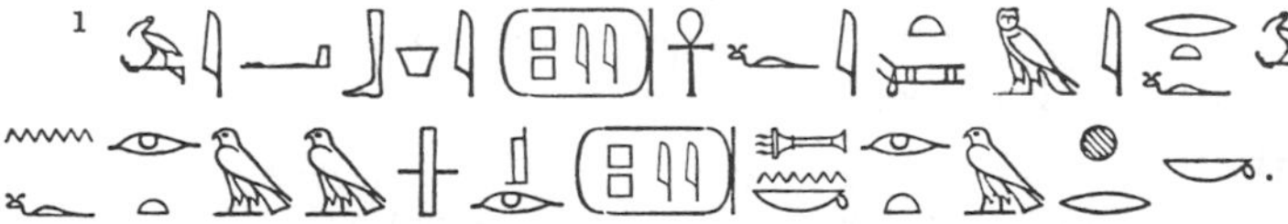 Pepi I, l. 107 = Mer-en-Rā, l. 73 = Pepi II, l. 75.

1. "Hail, thou Osiris Tetȧ, Horus cometh, he "embraceth thee. He causeth Thoth to drive back for "thee the followers of Set, he bringeth them unto thee "[as] prisoners. He hath turned backwards the heart "of Set, [for] behold, he is stronger than he. Thou "comest forth before him (or, in his presence), thy form "is before him (or, in his presence).

"Ḳeb looketh upon thy form, he setteth thee on thy "throne. Ḳeb bringeth thy two sisters to thy side, that "is, Isis and Nephthys.

"Horus hath caused thee to be united to the gods, "they treat thee as a brother in thy name of 'Sent,'[1] "and they do not turn thee back in thy name of "'Ȧtert.'[2] He hath caused the gods to avenge thee.

"Ḳeb hath set his sandal on the head of thine enemy "[saying], Get thee back. Thy son Horus hath smitten "him. He hath delivered (or, snatched away) his eye "from him, he hath given it to thee, thou obtainest a "soul through it, thou gainest the mastery through it at "the head of the Spirits. Horus hath caused thee to "seize thine enemy thereby, and by it he hath crushed "thine enemy. Horus is mightier than he. He hath "counted up his father in thee in thy name of 'Baȧt-er-"pet.' Thy mother Nut hath made thee to be a god to "Set in thy name of 'god.' Thy mother Nut hath "stretched herself over thee in her name of 'Shet-pet.'[3] "Horus hath seized Set, he hath set him under thee, he "lifteth thee up, he is helpless under thee as 'Nurta.' "Thou art more majestic than he in thy name of Ta-"tchesert. Horus hath caused thee to grasp (?) him by "the middle of his body, he shall not escape from thy "hand; Horus hath caused thee to hold him tightly in "the palm of thy hand, he shall not slip out of thy hand. "Hail, Osiris Tetȧ, Horus hath avenged thee. He hath "made his Ka (*i.e.*, double) [to be] in thee; thou restest "in thy name of 'Ka-ḥetep.'

2. "Thou hast eaten the eye, thy body is fortified "through it, thy son Horus seized it for thee, thou livest "thereby." The texts read:—

[1] Here is a play on the words *sen* "brother," and *sent*.

[2] Here is a play on the words *ḥemt-er-tu* "repulse thee," and *Ȧtert*.

[3] Here is a play on the words *peshesh* "stretch out," and *Shet-pet*.

1.

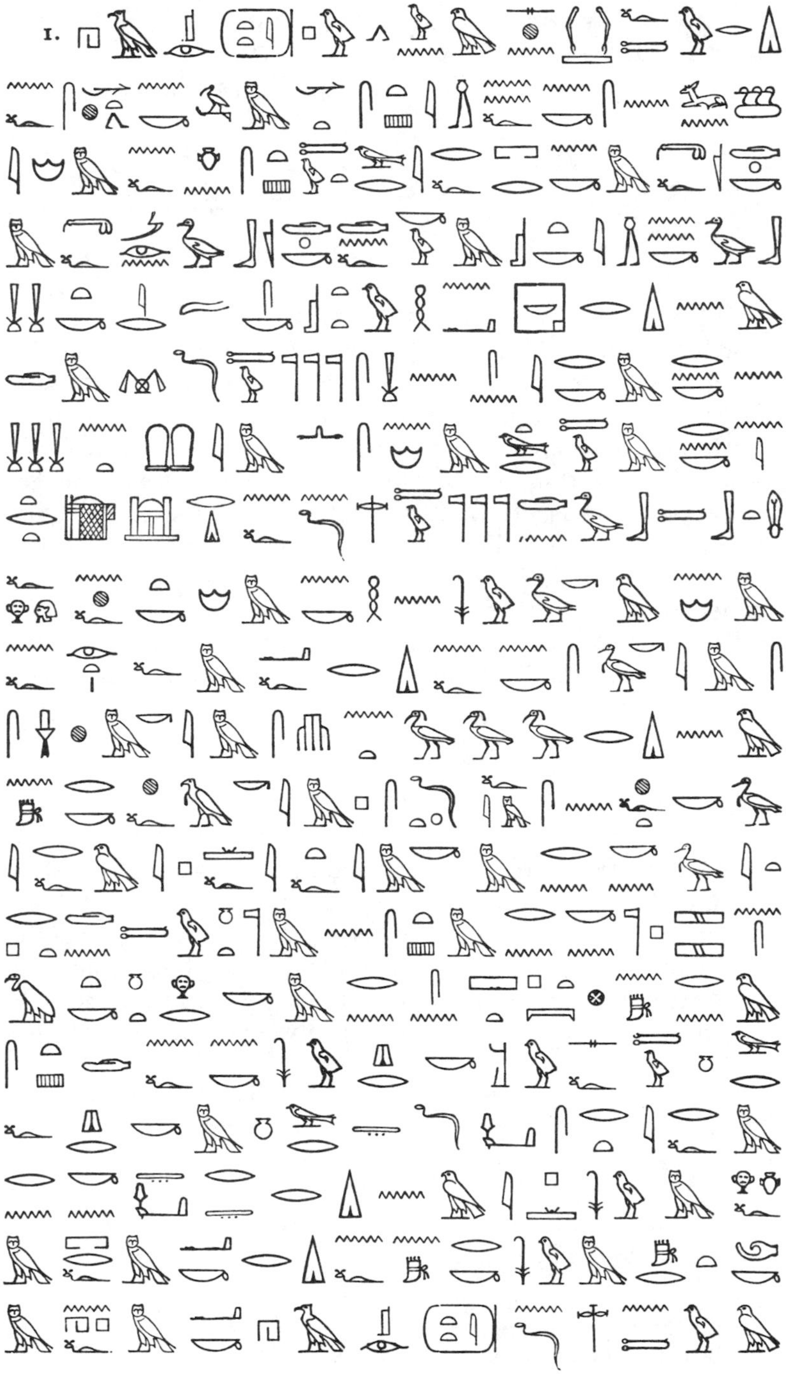

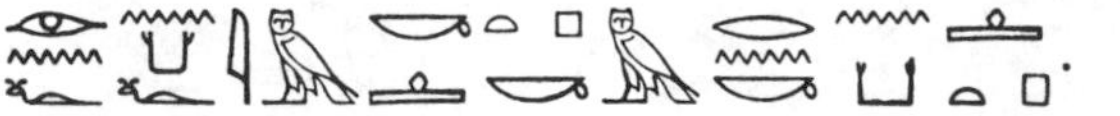 Tetȧ, ll. 170 ff. = Pepi I, ll. 118 ff. = Mer-en-Rā, ll. 150 ff. = Pepi II, ll. 105 ff.

2. 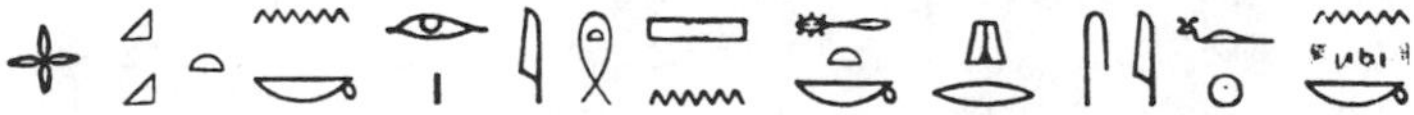
 Unȧs, l. 267.

Thus in the above extracts we have a definite statement about the means employed by Horus to bring his father Osiris to life. Horus first came to Osiris, who was in the state of a dead man, and embraced him. By this embrace he transferred to him either his own KA (double), or a portion of the power which dwelt in it; the embrace was, in fact, an act whereby something of the vital energy of the embracer was transferred to the embraced. When Isis wished to revivify Osiris she gathered together his flesh, and bound up his hands, and embraced him,[1] and Nephthys took in her arms[2] his flesh when she had gathered it together, and was about to build it into a body in her character of the goddess Seshat , who presided over the planning of buildings. Similarly, when Kheperȧ, the primeval Sun-god, had created Shu and Tefnut, and wished to give them life, he took their forms in his arms, and they became living gods.[3] The life of a god could be absorbed by the king's embracing the statue of the god,[4] and in later times, when Osiris had been made to usurp the power of Rā, the souls of Osiris and Rā became one after each god had embraced the other.[5]

1 
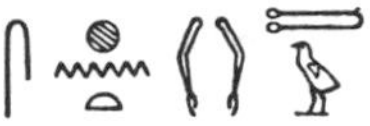 Pepi II, l. 868.

2  Tetȧ, l. 268.

3 Papyrus of Nesi-Ȧmsu, col. XXVII.

4 See Moret, *Rituel*, pp. 80 and 81.

5 See Book of the Dead, Chapter XVII.

The text shows that Osiris is dead, and that Set has killed him, and that the fiends of Set are pressing on to work evil on the body. Thoth, however, intervenes, and drives them back, and, as he is stronger than Set, "he turns backward the heart of Set," that is to say, he destroys his evil will. Thoth, having driven back the fiends of Set, held their master in restraint, and Osiris

The souls of Osiris and Rā meeting to embrace each other in Busiris. From the Papyrus of Ani.

came forth before him in the form in which he had been built up by Horus. Ḳeb, the Earth-god, in whose realm the dead man had been, then looked at Osiris, and, having set him upon his throne, brought to him Isis and Nephthys, his two sisters. It is difficult to know what exactly is meant by the Earth-god "looking at," or "seeing" Osiris, but it is clear that Ḳeb was pleased at the revivification of Osiris, and that, in consequence, he set him upon his throne as king, and brought Isis and Nephthys to him. From this passage we learn that Isis and Nephthys were sisters of Osiris, and that Ḳeb, the Earth-god, bestowed his sovereignty of the earth upon his son Osiris.

We next see from the extract that Horus made his father Osiris known to the gods, that they welcomed him among their number, that they treated him as a brother, because he represented the two *Sent* divisions of the heavens, and that they did not drive him away because he represented the two divisions of earth. Thus the gods "avenged" Osiris, that is, they acknowledged that Osiris had suffered cruel wrong, and they recognized that Horus had made the revivified Dead-man-god to be their equal. We now see Osiris seated as a god in heaven, and the further punishment of Set is described. The Earth-god Ḳeb sets his sandal on his head, *i.e.*, he bruises the head of the monster with his foot, and whilst he is doing this Horus smites Set, and slays him. Thus once and for all the Eye of Horus is delivered, and, having regained possession of it, he gave it to Osiris; when Osiris received it he received into himself a soul, that is new life, or revivification, and it endowed him with such power that he became forthwith the Chief of the Spirits. Thereupon Osiris seized the fiends who were his enemies and the followers of Set through the power which Horus had given him, for Horus was mightier than Set. Horus next dragged Set forward and set him at the feet of Osiris, and lifted up Osiris and seated him upon the back of Set. Set was as inert and helpless under him as the dead earth, which he typified, whilst Osiris himself was the "Sublime Earth," *i.e.*, the land wherein his followers, the blessed dead, were placed. Then Horus made Osiris to grasp Set by the middle of his body, in such a way that he could not escape, and then to hold him in the hollow of his hand. Thus did Horus transfer his Eye, which contained his soul, to Osiris; thus did he make Osiris to crush Set, and thus did Osiris become a "*Ka* at peace." The dead man Osiris was made to live a second time, and a kingdom was given him with the gods.

The shorter of the two passages quoted above supplies a most valuable piece of information. We know that Horus gave Osiris his Eye, but how did he receive it, and by what means did he assimilate it to his own body? The answer is definite: Osiris ate the Eye, and as a result became mighty, and lived. His renewed life was the direct product of the absorption of the Eye of his son Horus, and the strength of his brave avenger entered into him as the Eye was absorbed by his body. When Set stole away the Eye from Horus we know that Horus became as a dead god, but must we assume that when Horus gave his Eye to his father he became a dead god for always? Most certainly not, for the texts are full of allusions to the services which Horus performed for his father after he had revivified him, and many proofs are forthcoming which make it certain that Horus befriended the dead in many ways in his character of a living god.

The texts of the later period contain many references to an attack which the powers of evil made upon Osiris, but unfortunately no details of it are forthcoming. This attack was so serious, and the destruction of Osiris so imminent, that Thoth, who was the spirit and intelligence of the Creator of the world, was obliged to interfere. The instigator of the attack was Set, who apparently stirred up the gods of heaven to resist the entrance of Osiris into their company, and Thoth, the great master-mind of the universe, decided that the matter should be tried in the hall of Ḳeb, the Earth-god, or in some portion of the sky. Under the VIth dynasty it was commonly believed that this trial of Osiris took place in the city of Ȧn (the On of the Bible), as is clear from the passage in the text of Tetȧ (l. 271), in which the deceased is exhorted to go and "sit at the head of the "gods, and to do what Osiris did in the House of the "Prince which is in Ȧn."[1] The same view is taken in the XVIIIth Chapter of the Theban Recension of the Book of the Dead wherein Thoth is thus addressed: "Hail, Thoth, who didst make Osiris to be victorious

1 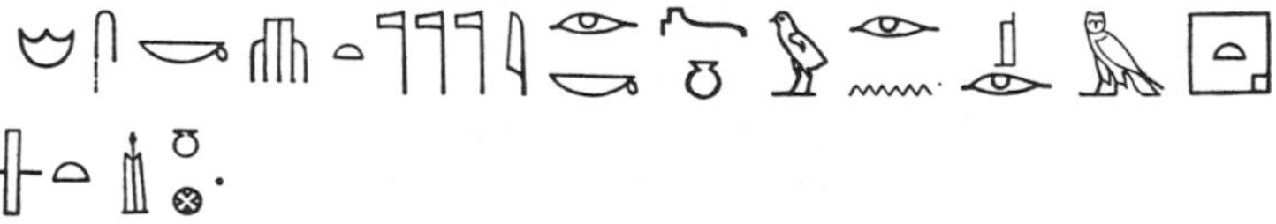

"over his enemies, make thou . . .[1] to be victorious "over his enemies, as thou didst make Osiris to be "victorious over his enemies in the presence of the "Tchatcha[2] who are with Rā and Osiris in Ȧn, on the "night of 'things of the night,' on the night of the "battle, on the night of the shackling of the Sebȧu "fiends, and on the day of the destruction of Neb-er-"tcher."[3] The text goes on to say that the words "shackling of the Sebȧu fiends" signifies the "destruc-"tion of the fiends of Set when he worked evil a second "time."

The night here referred to is undoubtedly the night of the day on which Osiris died. Set, not content with murdering his brother, gathered together the Sebȧu fiends, and prepared to destroy his body by their means, and being foiled in his endeavour by Thoth, made against Osiris a series of charges of such a nature that Thoth determined to investigate them before the gods. The story is nowhere told in a connected form, but it is clear, from many passages in texts of all periods, that the gods assembled in the great hall of the Aged God in Ȧn, and that Set was allowed to make his accusations against Osiris. To these Osiris replied, and when Thoth had heard the evidence he summed up the case, and then declared that Osiris had spoken the truth, in fact that it was not he who was a liar, but Set. Thoth held the word of Osiris to be true, or "made the word true," as the Egyptian text has it. The words actually used are , *smaā kheru*, and they may also be translated "made true the voice." It is possible, too, to understand from these words that Thoth made Osiris to use his voice in such a way that the words which he spoke had exactly the effect which he wished them to have. The words *maā kheru* are written after the name of every dead follower of Osiris, and of all the meanings which have been assigned to them by scholars[4]

[1] Here comes the name of the deceased for whom the papyrus was written.

[2] The "chiefs," or "overseers," or "taskmasters."

[3] *I.e.*, the lord of the universe, or Osiris.

[4] See Maspero, *Études de Myth.*, tom. I, pp. 93–103.

none represents their general meaning better than "victorious" or "triumphant."[1] With what words we translate *maā kheru* matters very little, for the general sense of the words is perfectly plain. When a god, or a man, or a woman, is said to be *maā kheru* (fem. *maāt kheru*) we are to understand that when he or she has spoken, or "uttered words," the words are followed immediately by the effect desired, that is to say, he who is *maā kheru* possessed unlimited power, and there is nothing which he cannot do or obtain.

The trial in the hall at Ȧn was, in reality, a "weighing of words," , the words being the accusations of Set and the defence of Osiris; it was no trial of strength like the fight between Horus and Set, and Rā and Āpep. The matter which Thoth had to decide was, Which witness is true, Set or Osiris? His verdict was in favour of Osiris, and from that time forward the idea of truth was associated with Osiris, who became the god of truth, and of those who spoke the truth. Moreover, Osiris, having been declared true of word, or true of voice, by Thoth, went up into heaven, and reigned there as king. He also became judge of the dead, for all men knew that he had proved Set to be a liar when he was tried by the gods, and that he had the power and the knowledge necessary for "weighing" their words when they should be tried at the last judgment.

Now, the enmity of Set was not directed against Osiris alone, for he attacked Horus, the son of Osiris, and made accusations of a serious character against him. The texts do not say what they were exactly, but it is quite clear from several statements that the object of Set was to discredit Horus, and to prevent him from ruling on the earth in his father's stead. The Greek writer, Plutarch (§ XIX), says that Typhon, *i.e.*, Set, accused Horus of illegitimacy, and the Egyptian texts seem to support this view. Over and over again, in hymns to Osiris, the god is assured that Horus has succeeded

[1] The Copts seem to have preserved the word under the form ⲥⲙⲁⲣⲱⲟⲩⲧ = εὐλογητὸς, or "blessed."

to his father's throne, and the following extract from Hunefer's hymn:[1] "Thy son Horus is triumphant in "the presence of the whole company of the gods, the "sovereignty of the whole world hath been given unto "him, and his dominion is in the uttermost parts of the "earth. The throne of Ḳeb (the earth-god) hath been "adjudged unto him, along with the rank which hath "been established by the god Temu, and also by the "title-deed (or, will), in the House of Books, which hath "been cut upon an iron tablet according to the command "of thy father Ptaḥ-Tanen, [when he sat upon] the "great throne. He hath set his brother over that "which the god Shu beareth up [*i.e.*, heaven], and hath "made him to stretch out the waters over the high "lands, and to cause to grow that which springeth up "on the hills, and the grain which groweth up from the "earth, and to give increase by water and by land. "Gods celestial and gods terrestrial transfer themselves "to the service of thy son Horus, and they follow him "into the hall, where a decree is passed which declareth "that he is their lord, and the gods accept the same "straightway." As in this extract the title-deeds, or will, by which Horus succeeded to his father's property, are mentioned, it is clear that some attempt must have been made by Set to show that Horus was not the lawful heir.

And this brings us to the consideration of the circumstances under which Horus was begotten and brought forth. It has already been seen by the passages quoted from the Pyramid Texts that Isis, the sister, *i.e.*, wife, of Osiris, played a prominent part in the reconstitution of her husband's body, and the texts of the later period are full of allusions to the troubles which she suffered through the enmity of Set, who first murdered her husband, and then caused her son Horus to be stung to death by a scorpion, and finally, after trying to disinherit him, endeavoured to slay him in combat. All the forms of the Osiris Legend agree in representing Isis as being childless when her husband died, and a remarkable passage in the Pyramid Texts explains how

[1] Chapter CLXXXIII of the Theban Recension of the Book of the Dead.

she succeeded in obtaining a child by her dead husband. In the text of Tetȧ it is said :—

"Isis and Nephthys work magic on thee with "knotted cords in the city of Saut, for their lord is in "thee in thy name of 'Neb-Saut' (*i.e.*, 'Lord of Saut'), "for their god is in thee in thy name of 'god' (Neter). "They adore thee; do not depart from them in thy "name of Ṭua-neter (*i.e.*, 'Morning Star'). They "present [themselves] before thee; be not wroth in thy "name of 'Tchenṭeru.'

"Thy sister Isis cometh unto thee rejoicing in her "love for thee. Thou settest her upon thee, thy issue "entereth into her, and she becometh great with child "like the star Sepṭ (the Dog-star). Horus-Sepṭ cometh "forth from thee in the form of 'Horus, dweller in "Sepṭ.' Thou makest him to have a spirit in his "name of 'Spirit, dweller in Tchenṭeru.' He avengeth "thee in his name of 'Ḥeru-sa-netch-ȧtef." The text reads :

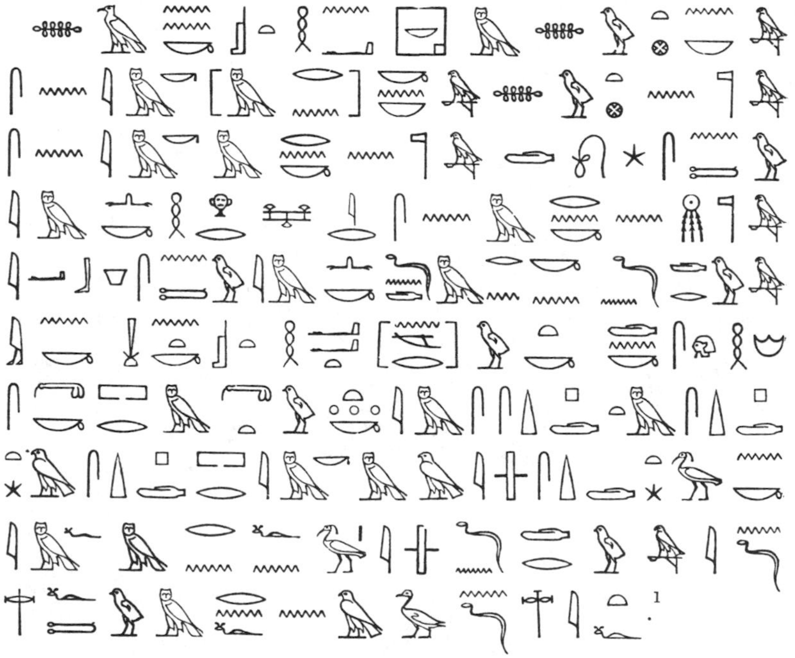

[1] See Tetȧ, l. 275 ff. = Pepi I, l. 28 ff. = Mer-en-Rā, l. 39 ff. = Pepi II, l. 68 ff.

In a hymn to Osiris[1] of a later period the begetting of Horus is described somewhat differently, and we read:—

"Thy sister Isis acted as a protectress to thee. She "drove thine enemies away, she averted seasons [of "calamity], she recited formulae with the magical power "of her mouth, [being] skilled of tongue and never "halting for a word, being perfect in command and "word. Isis the magician avenged her brother. She "went about seeking him untiringly. She flew round "and round over the earth uttering wailing cries of grief, "and she did not alight on the ground until she had "found him. She made light [to appear] from her "feathers, she made air to come into being by means of "her two wings, and she cried out the death cries for "her brother. She made to rise up the helpless "members of him whose heart was at rest, she drew "from him his essence, and she made therefrom an heir. "She suckled the child in solitariness, and none knew "where his place was, and he grew in strength, and his "arm increased in strength in the House of Ḳeb (*i.e.*, "the earth)." The text reads:—

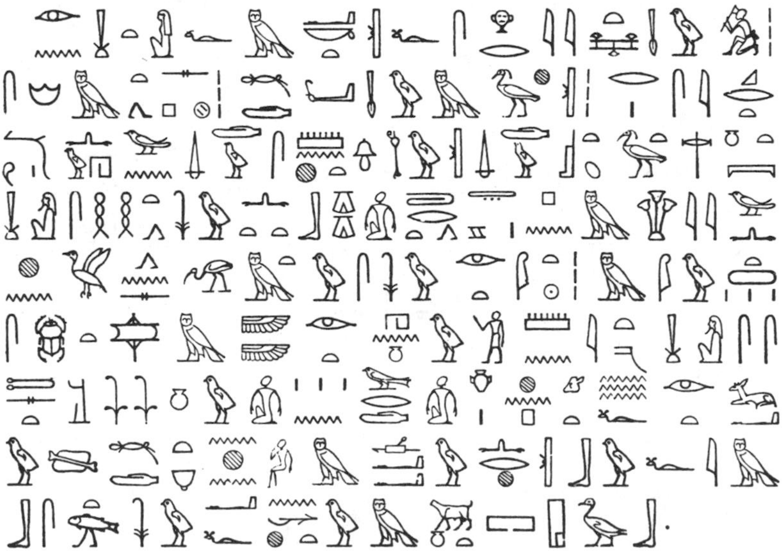

[1] First translated by Chabas, in *Revue Archéologique*, 1857, p. 65; for the text see Ledrain, *Monuments*, Plate XXII ff.

From the Metternich Stele,[1] a monument which was made in the reign of Nektanebês, about 350 B.C., much information is forthcoming about the childhood of Horus,

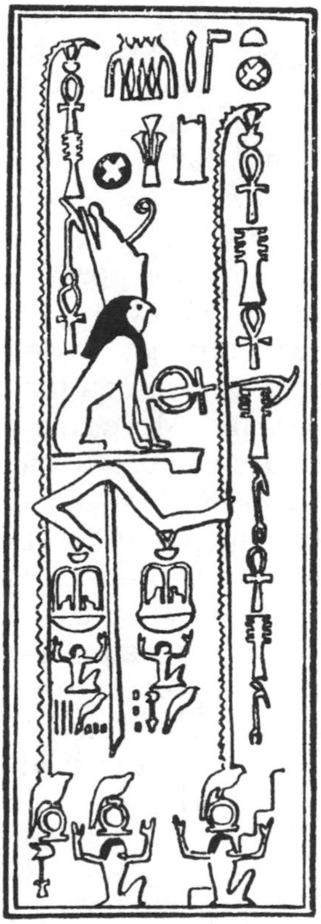

1. 2.

1. Horus, in the form of a hawk-headed lion, seated on a standard, and wearing the Crowns of the South and North.

2. Set, in the form of a lion with the head of the Set animal, seated on a standard, and wearing the Crowns of the South and North.

The two gods are here represented as equals, each having the power to give to the King life for hundreds of thousands of millions of years, stability, and serenity.

From bas-reliefs found by Prof. Petrie at Memphis.

and the troubles which Isis suffered during her wanderings. Set, it seems, had shut her up in some building, but she effected her escape, and fled to the city of Buto,

[1] See the edition of Golénischeff, Leipzig, 1877.

(Pe-Ṭep) in the Delta. There in the papyrus swamps she brought forth Horus, and there she reared him unknown to anyone. During her absence one day a scorpion stung the child, and he died. When Isis returned and found Horus lying dead, she rent the air with her cries of grief, and made bitter lamentation. Her sister Nephthys appeared, and made so fervent an appeal to the god in the Boat of Millions of Years, that the Boat stopped, and Thoth came down and provided Isis with the words of power which restored Horus to life.

With the Egyptian accounts of the begetting of Horus before us, we are right in assuming that Set brought a charge of illegitimacy against Horus, and that his accusations were levelled as much against Isis as against her son. The text of the Metternich Stele suggests that Set had tried to seize his brother's widow for himself, and it states quite clearly that she escaped from the place wherein he had managed to confine her for a time. Defeated in the gratification of his passion for the loving wife of Osiris, and not believing in the possibility of the union of Isis with the dead Osiris, it was only natural, according to African ideas, for Set to accuse Isis of playing the harlot, and her son of illegitimacy. Isis and her sister Nephthys were present at the trial before the gods, the latter presumably as a witness, and Thoth having declared that Osiris had spoken the truth, Isis was by implication also declared "true of word," or "true of voice," and she and her sister were ever after present at the judgment of the dead, and they bore the honourable title of "Ladies (*i.e.*, possessors) of the Truth," and the Hall of Judgment became known as the "Hall of the two Truths."

Several passages in the Pyramid Texts prove that the rule of Osiris in heaven as king and judge of the dead was, even so far back as the period of the VIth dynasty, believed to be a righteous rule, and it seems as if men thought that the god kept a written account of the words and deeds of every man, and a register of the years of his life. In the text of Pepi I two divine scribes are mentioned, and they are said to keep the written roll, and to notch calculations on the two sticks, and to write down the decrees.[1] From another passage we learn that the deceased king wished to identify himself with the god-scribe who decreed the existence of things that are and made to exist the things which had not existed, and also with the cord with which the writings of the god were tied up.[2] From these passages it is clear that the kingdom of Osiris was governed according to laws, and that justice and righteousness were observed by the god in his dealings with his subjects.

We have already seen from a passage quoted above that one of the regions of heaven over which Osiris had special control was called "Sekhet-Åaru"  , a name which, as the determinatives show, means the Field of Reeds; in the text of Unås (l. 193) and elsewhere the region is called simply "Åar"  or "Åal." Within this region was a place called "Sekhet-ḥetep" 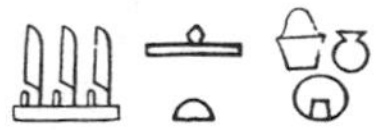, *i.e.*, the "Field of Offerings," where the blessed obtained their supplies of celestial food and drink. The first-named place was the "Elysian Fields" of the Egyptians. Strictly speaking, they were not fields, but islands, intersected by canals filled with running water, which caused them to be always green and fertile. On these grew luxuriant crops of wheat and barley, the like of which were unknown to earth. The Papyrus of Nu (XVIIIth dynasty, Chapter CXLIX) says that the wheat grew to

[1] 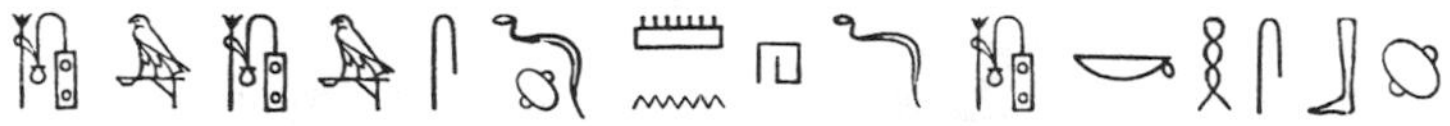 . Pepi I, l. 185 = Mer-en-Rā, l. 300 = Pepi II, l. 899.

[2]  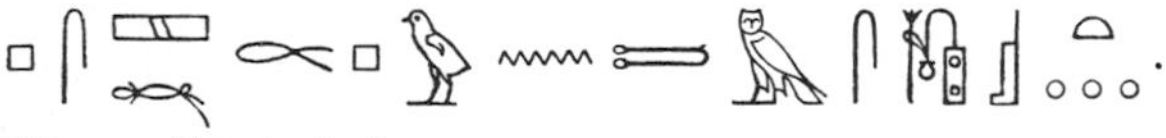. Pepi I, l. 345 = Mer-en-Rā, l. 646.

a height of five cubits, the ears being two cubits long and the stalks three ; the barley grew to a height of seven cubits, the ears being three cubits long and the stalks four. Here lived the spirits of the blessed dead, who were nine cubits high, and the reaping of these crops was, it seems, reserved for them, and for the Souls of the East. In the midst of Sekhet-Ȧaru was a door, with a sycamore of turquoise on each side of it, and through this the Sun-god Rā appeared each day. Some writers would place these Elysian Fields in the Great Oasis (Al-Khârgah), and others in the Delta, and there is much to be said in favour of each view, especially when we look at the pictures of the Sekhet-Ȧaru in the Books of the Dead of the XVIIIth and XIXth dynasties. But it is more probable that the originals from which the idea of the Egyptian Isles of the Blest was taken were the islands in Lake Victoria in Central Africa. Several passages in the Pyramid Texts prove that the abode of the blessed was situated away beyond a large expanse of water, and at one time the Egyptians believed that it could only be reached by means of a boat, or by the personal help of the gods who were thought to transport their favourites thither. Thus we find that more than one view existed as to the position of heaven, some thinking that it could be reached by a ladder set up on the earth, and others that the only sure means of reaching it was a boat. According to another view the abode of the gods was situated among flames of fire, through which Horus led the deceased.[1]

The Pyramid Texts mention a group of three regions, or places which are called respectively the "Ȧat of Horus," the "Ȧat of Set," and the "Ȧat of Osiris," to which the deceased is said to go and to give commands,[2]

1  Unȧs, l. 611.

2  Unȧs, l. 297 = Tetȧ, l. 141 = Mer-en-Rā, l. 198 = Pepi II, l. 537.

or to speak words which shall be beneficial to those who dwell therein. Now the word *Åat*  means "tomb," and thus it seems that there were tombs of Horus, tombs of Set, and tombs of Osiris in the Other World. Of the Aats of Horus and Set nothing is known, but from the Book of the Dead, Chapter CL, we learn that the Åats were fifteen in number, and the text gives their names and describes them, and the vignette depicts their forms. Late tradition asserts that the body of Osiris was cut up into fourteen or fifteen pieces, and that over the place where each was buried Isis caused a sanctuary to be built. These tomb-chapels, or funerary temples of Osiris, which were built in various parts of Egypt, may represent the Åats of Osiris mentioned in the Pyramid Texts, and if this be so we should be justified in assuming that so far back as the VIth dynasty the Egyptians believed that the body of Osiris was divided into fifteen pieces. The tombs of Osiris on earth had their counterparts in heaven, and as the bodies of the faithful journeyed from one to another of them upon the earth on their religious pilgrimages, so would their souls travel from one to another in the Other World that they might partake of the spiritual enjoyments to be found in each.

The extracts from the Pyramid Texts given above make it certain that the principal details of the history of Osiris which the literature of the later periods make known to us, were current and were generally received under the VIth dynasty. In fact, the history of the murder, dismemberment, reconstitution, and resurrection of Osiris can be reconstructed from them. We may now consider what manner of heaven it was into which Osiris passed in his risen form, and what kind of life the blessed lived there under his rule, and what powers they possessed and enjoyed.

CHAPTER IV.

THE HEAVEN OF OSIRIS UNDER THE VITH DYNASTY.

THE oldest source of information concerning Osiris and his kingdom in heaven at present available is the Pyramid Texts, and from these the essential portions of the present chapter are derived. In estimating the value to be attached to facts set forth here in their relation to the history of Osiris, it must be remembered that these Texts were drafted by the priests of Heliopolis, who lost no opportunity of extolling the power and glory of their Sun-god Rā and his various forms, and they naturally made him out to be the supreme power of this and of the Other World. The Pyramid Texts represent in brief the views of the priesthood of Heliopolis, and enshrine their attempt to absorb into the cult of their god the beliefs and traditions of the old gods of Egypt, whom they made to be ministers of Rā. The conception of the heaven which they depict is far older than the cult of Rā, and the heaven over which the Heliopolitan priests made Rā to preside was the heaven of Osiris, the principal characteristics of which had been familiar to the Egyptians for many centuries before the worship of Rā became general in Egypt. There was little left for the priests to invent, but they could alter and modify expressions of belief, and they could make Rā to usurp the functions of older gods; this they did, and in doing so they showed great skill.

The various sections which form the collection of religious works now commonly known as the "Pyramid Texts," appear to have had no recognised order or sequence. Each is a distinct composition, and many repeat phrases and ideas which are found in others. Each was, we may well believe, composed to produce a certain result, but what that result was it is generally impossible to say. At a later period, say the XVIIIth dynasty, several of such compositions were made into chapters, each with its specific title, but it is in many cases impossible to see the connection between the title and the contents of the chapter. It is clear that these compositions are not all the product of one period or of one writer, for the statements in some concerning certain matters contradict those found in others. In many there is obviously confusion of ideas, which is, in some cases, the result of difference in belief on the part of their authors, and in other cases has been produced by the carelessness of scribes. The Pyramid Texts are a mixture of religious writings of many periods, and their contents are an agglomeration of beliefs, legends, and speculations concerning the Other World, which defy systematic arrangement and logical classification. The Egyptian appears never to have relinquished any belief which he once held, and the natural outcome of this characteristic was that ancient texts were copied and recopied indefinitely, even if the beliefs which he held at one period contradicted those which he held at another. His speculations as to a future state he treated in the same way; once written down they were copied by the scribes generation after generation. From all this it follows that the description of the heaven of the Egyptian, depicted in the Pyramid Texts, represents the conceptions of countless generations of theologians, and it is specially interesting to watch how, in process of time, many of the coarser material elements are eliminated, and how ethical conceptions develop in it. In the following pages the order of the descriptions will be chronological, and they will begin with those taken from the text of Unȧs, and continue till the last of the Pyramid Texts, that of Pepi II, is reached.

A large section of the text of Unȧs, about 160 lines at the beginning, is devoted to a Liturgy which deals with the presentation of offerings in connection with the performance of the ceremony of "Opening the Mouth." This ceremony has been described elsewhere[1] in detail, and it is only necessary to state here that during the

[1] See Schiaparelli, *Il Libro dei Funerali*, Rome, 1881–1890; Maspero, *Pyramides de Saqqarah*, Paris, 1894; Dümichen, *Grabpalast*, Leipzig, 1884–5; Maspero, *Revue de l'Histoire des Religions*, XV, pp. 159–188; and my *Liturgy of Funerary Offerings* and *Book of Opening the Mouth*, London, 1910.

ceremony the mouth of the deceased was touched, *i.e.*, "opened" by Horus, who employed for the purpose the two instruments which he had used in "opening" the mouth of his father Osiris. He then pressed the lips into their natural position during life, and "balanced" the mouth, and after this the deceased was able to speak, and breathe, and eat, and think, and his members could perform all their natural functions once more. One instrument was made of the iron which came forth from Set,[1] and was in the form of the forearm of Set;[2] it transferred to the deceased the power of the Eye of Horus . The other instrument was also made of iron, and was associated with Ȧnpu,[3] and transferred to the deceased power to overthrow all his enemies and evil.

The words which follow immediately after the Liturgy are described in later texts as the "Chapter of Supplying the Table (or, Altar) with Food,"[4] and in them the happy labourers who lift up the heart and comfort the body, who have eaten the Eye of Horus, even as did Osiris, and the olive tree in Ȧn (Heliopolis), are called upon to prevent the deceased from suffering thirst, and hunger, and sadness of heart. And it is said that the hands of the god Aḥu, , shall destroy his hunger.[5] Those who preside over the offerings of cakes and beer, and those who guard the celestial abyss, shall give him what they have seized with their hands, that is, wheat and barley, and bread and beer. And Rā shall give him these things also, for the deceased is a great bull, the smiter of Kenset.[6] Next comes the short but interesting prayer: "O Rā, do good to him this day more

1 . Pepi II, l. 215.

2 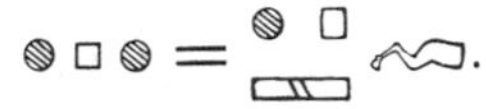. Pepi II, l. 213.

3 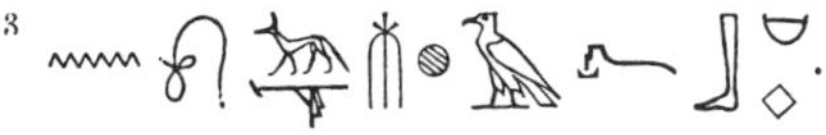.

4 Maspero, *Les Pyramides*, p. 19.

5 Unȧs, ll. 166–173.

6 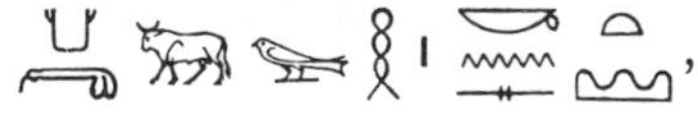, l. 178.

than yesterday,"[1] that is to say, O Rā, increase thy goodness to him as days go on. The deceased then unites with the goddess Mut, or Muit,[2] and "he smelleth the air of Isis";[3] henceforth he is able to enjoy union with a celestial counterpart,[4] and "he sleepeth soundly every day."[5] The messengers of the god Åqa, those who are asleep, those who dwell in Kenset,[6] the ancestors of the Great Terrifier[7] who come forth from Ḥep (the Nile) and Åp-uat, who comes forth from the Åsert tree, are called upon to witness that his mouth is pure, that the two Companies of gods have censed him, and that his tongue has wisdom. As he detests filth of every kind he shall never be obliged to eat it, or to drink filthy water, which he destroys as Set destroyed the issue of the Two Men, *i.e.*, Horus and Set;[8] and he shall sail about heaven. On his behalf this prayer is made to Rā and Thoth: "Make him to feed with you. "Let him eat what ye eat. Let him drink what ye "drink. Let him live as ye live. Let him sit down "(or, dwell) as ye sit down. Let him be strong with "your strength. Let him sail about in your Sektet "boat."[9] He casts nets for the snaring of birds in the reedy marshes of Åaru,[10] his pool of water is in the Field

1 , l. 180.

2 , or , l. 181.

3 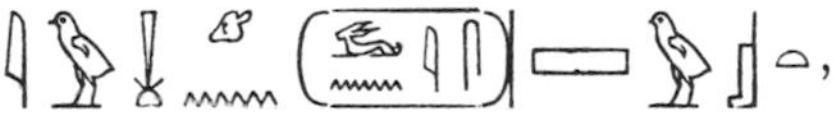, l. 181.

4 , l. 183.

5 . Tetȧ, l. 336=Pepi II, l. 638.

6 A part of the northern Egyptian Sûdân.

7 , l. 187.

8 , l. 190.

9 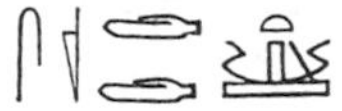, ll. 190–192.

10 .

of Offerings (Sekhet-ḥetep), an oblation is made to him among the oblations made to the gods, and his water is wine, like that of Rā.[1] He circles round heaven like Rā, he travels across the sky like Thoth (the moon). He is conceived in the night and brought forth in the night, and those who follow Rā, the ancestors of the Morning Star, belong to him; he was conceived in Nu, and brought forth in Nu,[2] and he comes and brings to the gods the bread which he finds there, that is, the tears of the Eye of Horus on the foliage of the Tchenu tree,[3] Khenti-Åmenti[4] comes to him and brings him abundance of celestial food, and what the god lives upon he also lives upon, and he partakes of the food and drink, and offerings of the god.[5] Thus we see that the deceased ate and drank with the Being who was the "First in Åmenti," *i.e.*, Osiris.

In the next paragraph of the Unȧs text the deceased is thus addressed: "Hail, Unȧs, thou hast not departed "[as] a dead being, [but] thou hast departed [as] a "living being.[6] Thou sittest upon the throne of Osiris, "thy sceptre is in thy hand, and thou givest commands "to the living. Thy *mekes* and *neḥbet* sceptres are in "thy hand, and thou givest commands to those whose "places are hidden. Thy hand[s], thine arms, thy "shoulders, thy belly, thy back, thy hips, and thy legs "are like those of Temu,[7] thy face is like that of Ånpu "(Anubis), and thou goest round the Domains of Horus "and the Domains of Set.[8] Thy bones are the gods "and goddesses who are in heaven.[9] Thou art by the

[1] , l. 194.

[2] The celestial ocean.

[3] Lines 197 ff.

[4] 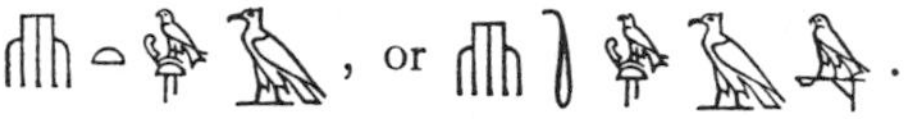

[5] Line 203.

[6] , l. 206.

[7] The Sun-god of night.

[8] Lines 206–208.

[9] , l. 209.

"side of the God, thou art free, thou comest forth to "thy son, thou art purified with the libations of the "stars,[1] thou descendest on the ropes of iron, on the "shoulders of Horus in his name of Dweller in the Ḥen "Boat.[2] The Ḥenmemet beings[3] aid thee, the stars "which never set[4] bear thee up, thou enterest in to the "place where thy father is, where Ḳeb is, he setteth "thee in the breast of Horus, thou becomest a soul "therein, thou becomest strong therein, thou becomest "Khenti Åmenti therein."[5] The last sentence of this paragraph is of peculiar interest, for it proves that the blessed obtained their souls and their vital power by entering into the breast of Horus, and that through him they became one with Khenti-Åmenti, that is to say, with Osiris. It also shows that the power of Horus as a life-giving and soul-giving god was far greater than is commonly thought.

The blessed one was taken by the god Tem into the hollow of his hand,[6] and was led through heaven and into the palace, where he saw those who dwelt therein, Horus and Set. There he spat upon the face of Horus, and did away the injury which it had received, and he bound up the genitals of Set, and made to grow the flesh again.[7] The allusion here is to the great fight between Horus and Set, in which the former lost his eye and the latter his genitals. Rā spat on the eye of Horus and healed it,

1 , l. 210.

2 A very ancient sacred boat, used in connection with the worship of Seker.

3 

4 

5 , l. 212.

6 Line 213.

7 , l. 214.

and presumably Rā or Thoth made the lost members of Set to grow again. The deceased became so greatly identified with the great god of heaven that the text goes on to say: "Thou givest birth to Horus, thou con-"ceivest Set. Thou givest birth to Horus in his name "of He ruleth the earth and terrifieth heaven. Thou "givest birth to Horus for Osiris, thou givest him life, "thou givest him strength; thou conceivest Set for Ḳeb, "thou givest him life, thou givest him strength."[1] Under favour of Rā-Tem his heart is not counted, nor his breast overcome[2] by Osiris and Horus, that is, he escapes the judgment of these gods; to Osiris the great god says: "thou shalt not have power over him, and thy son "shall not have power over him," and to Horus he says: "thou shalt not have power over him, and thy father "shall not have power over him." The text continues: "Thy head is like that of Horus of the Ṭuat, imperish-"able. Thy body is like that of Khent-merti, imperish-"able. Thine ears are the two daughters of Tem, "imperishable. Thine eyes are the two daughters of Tem, "imperishable. Thy nose is like that of Ȧnpu, imperish-"able. Thy teeth are like those of Horus Sepṭ, "imperishable. Thy hands are Ḥep and Ṭuamutef, thou "art strong, thou comest forth into the sky, thou "appearest. Thy feet are Smet and Qebḥ-senuf, thou "art strong, thou enterest Nu, thou advancest. Thy "flesh is the daughters of Temt, imperishable. Thou "shalt never perish, thy KA shall never perish, a KA "established."[3]

Thus being provided with an imperishable spirit-body the deceased goes to Nephthys, and to the Boat of the Morning Sun (Semktet),[4] and to Maāt, and to the goddess who commemorates KAU,[5] or "doubles," and his name is "commemorated," *i.e.*, recorded. From this it seems that a register of the names of doubles was

[1] Line 216.

[2] , ll. 216, 217.

[3] Lines 218–220.

[4] 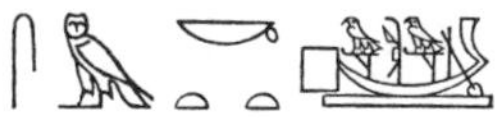.

[5] .

kept in heaven. He then revolves like the sun, leads on the Ṭuat, and is pure of life in the horizon like Saḥu (Orion)[1] and Sepṭ (Sirius, the Dog-star).[2] To these luminaries he gives a spirit, and he refreshes them in the hand of his father, in the hand of Temt.[3] The mention of Orion and Sothis is interesting, for it shows that at one time the primitive Egyptians believed that these stars were the homes of departed souls.

The next paragraphs of the text are a series of addresses to Rā-Tem, who is declared to be the father of the dead king. "Rā-Tem, this Unȧs cometh to thee, a spirit imperishable: thy son cometh to thee, this Unȧs." He has supreme power over the gods and their life for, "if he wisheth you to die, ye shall die; if he wisheth you to live, ye shall live."[4] And he has power over his own life for, "if he wisheth to live, of a certainty he will live; and if he wisheth to die, of a certainty he will die."[5] And he "counteth up hearts, and hath the mastery over breasts,"[6] and he is the "everlasting son" of the body of the god.[7] He counts up hearts, he carries off doubles, and he puts a yoke on doubles wheresoever he pleases; and all those who are in the lands of the West, East, South, and North, and all those who are in the nether sky[8] are his subjects. His existence is bound up with that of the gods and

1 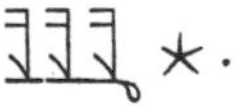

2 

3 Line 222.

4 
, l. 224.

5 
, l. 227.

6 , l. 229.

7 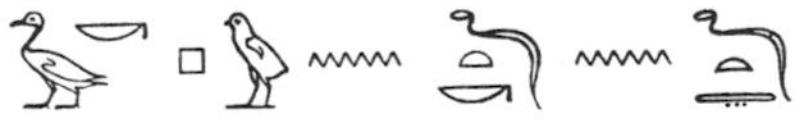, l. 233.

8 , l. 239.

goddesses, for he is Osiris, and he is the son, or relative, of each of them. The gods and goddesses enumerated in the next paragraphs of the texts are Tem, Shu, Tefnut, Ḳeb, Nut, Isis, Set, Nephthys, Thoth, and Horus. He is declared to be the son of the first five of these, the brother of the next four, and the father of the last-named, Horus. These form the Great Company of the gods. He is also the son or relative of the Little Company of the gods, whose names are Rāt, Ȧm-Ȧn, Ȧm-Āntchet, Ȧm-Ḥet-Serq, Ȧm-Seḥ-neter, Ȧm-Ḥetch-pār, Ȧm-Saḥ, Ȧm-Ṭep, Ȧm-Ḥet-ur-Rā, Ȧm-Unu-resu, Ȧm-Unu-meḥt, and Ȧm-Nu-meru (?). Each deity is called upon to give the deceased his support "that he may have life," and we have the following oft-repeated formula :—" He liveth, this Unȧs liveth ; he dieth not, " this Unȧs dieth not ; he perisheth not, this Unȧs " perisheth not; he begetteth not, this Unȧs begetteth not; " he begetteth, this Unȧs begetteth."[1] It is noteworthy that Set is called upon to support his brother,[2] *i.e.*, the deceased, who is identified with Osiris. The deity in Ȧn (Heliopolis) performs some ceremony of importance in connection with his backbone,[3] but the details are not clear. The deity in Orion who makes heaven and earth to be fruitful is reminded that Osiris revolves above him, and he is asked to regard Unȧs as his own offspring by Isis.[4] The body of the god is the body of Unȧs, and his flesh and his bones are the flesh and bones of Unȧs.[5] Before Unȧs the doors of the horizon are opened, and their bolts drawn back, and he advances to the goddesses Net, and Nesert, and Urt, and Urt-ḥekau,[6] and he is

[1] Line 240 ff.

[2] Line 246.

[3] , l. 254.

[4] 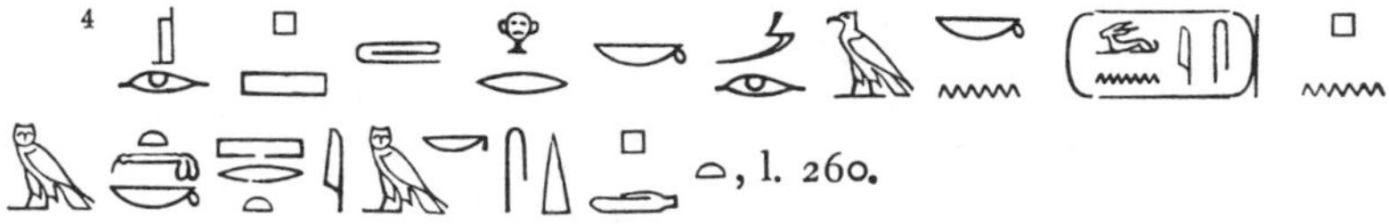, l. 260.

[5] Line 268.

[6] , l. 269.

Horus who revolves in the magical protection of his Eye.[1] These goddesses place his *āb* sceptre at the head of the living ones, and his power at the head of the spirits, and his knife is vigorous against his enemies.[2] He advances to his fathers Rā, Neṭȧ, Penṭen, Ṭenṭen, Sma-ur, Sekhen-ur, Sepṭu, Sepṭ-Ȧbeḥu.[3] He rules the Nine Gods, and he completes in his person the Company of the gods.[4] The North and the South bow their heads before him, and he stands up as chief of the Great Ones in his Lake.[5] "He hath more soul and more strength[6] than the gods of the South and North," he opens up his way through the bones of Shu, he goes about in the hand of his mother Nut, he is purified in the horizon, he bathes naked in the pools of Shu, he appears in the sky and goes down with Rā, he travels with Netȧ, he revolves with Sekhen-ur, he travels with Nephthys and with the Boat of the Morning Sun, he appears and journeys with Isis and the Boat of the Setting Sun,[7] he is strong in his body, and none can resist him.[8]

In this strength he goes about heaven and "utters words" to the Domains of Horus, the Domains of Set, and the Domains of Osiris,[9] and as he is all powerful it seems that such "words" must be of benefit to the denizens of the Domains. The "uttering of words" by

1 Line 271.

2 Line 274.

3 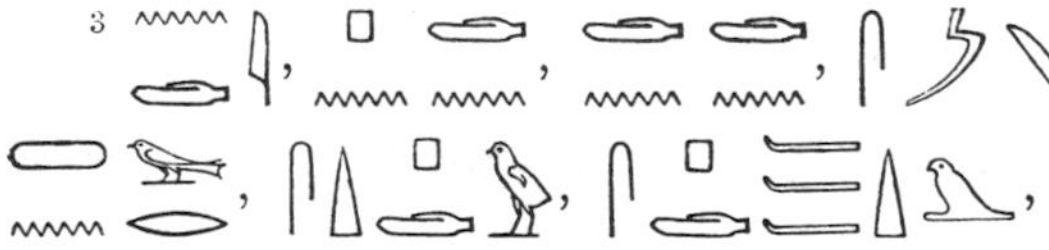 l. 278.

4 , l. 283.

5 , l. 284.

6  ll. 285, 288.

7 .

8 Line 293.

9 Unȧs, l. 297, Pepi II, l. 547.

Rā was a creative act, which was followed by the appearance of the celestial meat and drink whereon the gods lived. On the other hand, the "words" uttered may have been mere salutations or prayers, similar to those which modern pilgrims all over the East make in every shrine which they visit.

The heart-soul of the dead, as we know from many pictures, often took the form of a bird and appeared on earth, and it seems that it moved from place to place in heaven in the form of a bird. Thus in the text of Unȧs the king's soul, provided with its words of power,[1] flew with its wings to heaven, and "opened" its seat there with the stars of the sky,[2] and itself became the morning star,[3] and spake words to the spirits. The Word-god[4] speaks words to the Father-gods, and the deceased himself silences the gods, who lay their hands upon their mouths.[5] His name is mighty among men, and it comes into being before the gods.[6] The gods look at him with his knife in his hand as he comes into the Ṭuat (Other World).[7] He is the Wise-god,[8] created by Ḳeb and brought forth by the gods, he has eyes, he sees,[9] he hears, he hates sleep,[10] he receives his power in Ȧn, and Horus sends [his] Eye to his father, and the lord of

1 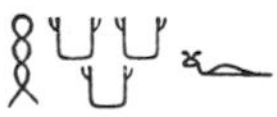, l. 364.

2 , l. 364.

3 , l. 365. See Brugsch, *Thesaurus*.

4 , or .

5 
, l. 373.

6 Line 378.

7 Line 380.

8 , l. 381.

9 , l. 385.

10 , l. 387.

the windstorm makes his voice to travel through heaven and terrify Set.[1]

The blessed one appears in heaven from between the thighs of the gods; Sekhmet conceived him, and Shesti[2] gave him birth. The star Sepṭ (Sothis), with long strides, leads on the celestial path of Rā each day, and the blessed one rises as a star.[3] He is a lily[4] which shoots up in the earth, "he who makes his seat"[5] purifies his hands, and he is "to the nose of the Great Power." Thus we see that the spirit-body in heaven could transform itself into the celestial lily which the great god held to his nose. The Egyptians of all classes loved flowers, and often carried them, and, judging by their descendants of to-day, frequently smelt them as they carried them. The blessed one rises like Nefer-Tem,[6] like a lily, at the nostrils of Rā,[7] he appears on the horizon every day, and the gods are purified by the sight of him.

He next went to the Island of Sȧsȧ,[8] *i.e.*, to the Island of Fire, on which one of the abodes of Osiris was placed. In the Book of Gates[9] this Island appears under the name of "Serser,' and the text makes it clear that it was situated in the kingdom of Osiris. Having arrived he "setteth right in the place of wrong,"[10] a statement which proves that under the VIth dynasty

1 , l. 388.

2 , l. 390.

3 Line 391.

4 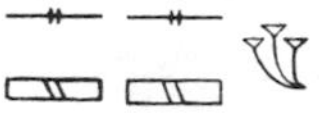, l. 392.

5 , l. 393.

6 The young Tem, the rising sun. He was in later times said to be the son of Ptaḥ and the goddess Sekhet.

7 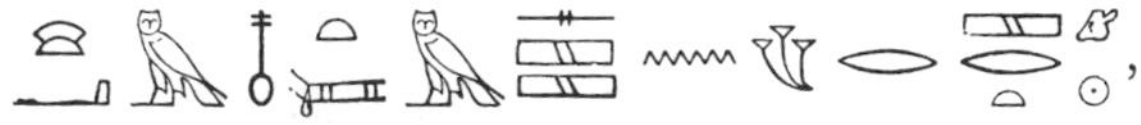, l. 395.

8 , l. 393.

9 See my *Book of Gates*, pp. 227–231.

10 , l. 394.

Osiris was the god of right and law and justice as well as of the resurrection. Like Osiris, the blessed one becomes the "chief of knowledge great,"[1] and he obtains possession of the "book of the god,"[2] and becomes the "learned one of Ȧment."[3] He is the great beloved one in the Festival of the Ȧnes apparel,[4] and the text repeats that he is the "wise one of the Ȧment of Rā." From this passage it is clear that the attribute of wisdom belonged to Osiris, and that the god kept a record in his book, or register, of the words and deeds of those who wished to appear in his kingdom.

From the next section of the text we learn that the newcomer in the kingdom of Osiris was not always cordially welcomed, for we find that the "chiefs of the Hours and the ancestors of Rā" are called upon to make a way for him, and secure for him a passage into the circle of the beings who are "hostile of face."[5] He takes his seat in spite of them, the chief seat, near the god, and being provided with strength and a knife, he subdues the "dwellers in the darkness," and there is none who can resist his power in the horizon.[6] Then to those who are in the Other World it is said: "Lift up "your faces, O ye gods who dwell in the Ṭuat! Unȧs "hath come; look ye at him as he taketh the form of "a great god. He trembleth not, he is equipped. "Observe all of you. He speaketh words to men, he "weigheth the words of the living ones in the Domain of "Rā. He speaketh to that pure Domain; he maketh "his seat there with the messenger of the two gods.[7] "He hath gained the power over his head, he is the

1 .

2 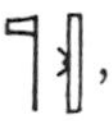, l. 396.

3 , l. 396.

4 , l. 398.

5 , l. 400.

6 Lines 401–403.

7 , l. 408.

" Ames sceptre,[1] he is purified. He sitteth with the " sailors of Rā. He ordereth good, he doeth it, doth this " great god."[2] With words of joy he cries out: " I am pure, I am pure in Sekhet-Åar, [with] the purity of Rā in Sekhet-Åar." His hand is like the hand of Rā, the goddess Nut receives him, and the god Shu gives him air.[3]

" The dew of the great goddess is to you, O Bull of " Nekhen, and the flame of fire of the blessed one " [cometh] to you, O ye who are about the shrine. O " great god, whose name is unknown, let there be " provisions [for him] on the seat of the Lord One! O " lord of the horizon, make thou a seat for him. For if " thou make not a seat for him, he will assuredly make " a place in father Ḳeb. Earth will not speak for him, " Ḳeb will not slay for him; what he findeth on his path " he will eat."[4] The goddess Ḥekenutet[5] makes a spacious seat for him in Tcheṭu, in the shrine,[6] she sets up for him two standards at the head of the great ones, she digs a lake for him in Sekhet-Åaru, and she stablishes for him an estate in Sekhet-ḥetep.[7] He weighs words like the goddess Meḥt-urt between the Two Fighters,[8] for behold, he is powerful with the might of the Eye of the god Tebȧ,[9] and his strength is the strength of the god Tebȧ. He is stronger than those who would seize upon his food and would carry it off from him, and steal the air from his nostrils, and bring his days of life to an end. He rises upon his domain,

1 .

2 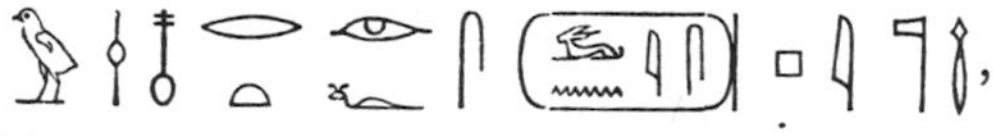, l. 410.

3 Lines 412–415.

4 Lines 416, 417.

5 , l. 425.

6 .

7 , l. 427.

8 , l. 427.

9 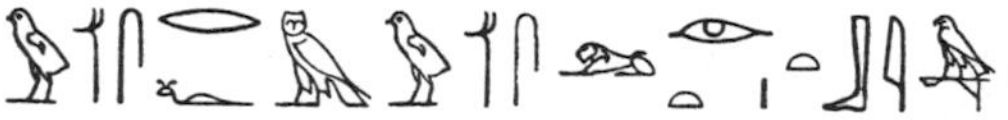, l. 428.

their entrails [are given] to the Guardians of the sky, their blood to the Guardians of the earth, their flesh to the . . . . . , their abodes to the thieves, and their halls to Ḥep-ur. His heart is glad, for he is One, the Bull of heaven, and he has destroyed all his foes, and his father Shu has placed him by the side of Set.[1] His flesh is the gods Ḳeb and Tem, he sits on the throne of Horus the firstborn.[2] His Eye is in his strength, his protection is what it doeth for him. A flame of fire is his goddess Khut,[3] the goddess Rennut is on his head.[4] He sets his conquest in their hearts, and when the gods who are in their *ḥatu* apparel[5] see him they bow down before him with praise.

The next paragraph of the text of Unȧs gives an interesting description of the alarm with which the gods view the arrival of the newcomer in their domain. " There is a commotion in heaven. The old gods[6] say : " We see something new. The Horus gods are in " splendour, the Lords of Forms oppose him." All in vain, for " he courseth round the Two Companies of the " gods, he taketh his seat on every throne of Tem, he " taketh possession of the sky, he cleaveth its substance,[7] " he travelleth over the roads of Kheper, and he sitteth " as a living being in Ȧment. The gods of the Ṭuat[8] " follow him ; he shineth like a new being in the " East, and the Opener of the trouble cometh to him " with bowings."[9] He reduces to subjection the first-born gods, and behold, he is the Power in his seat. He

1 Lines 428–433.

2 , l. 440.

3 

4 , l. 441.

5 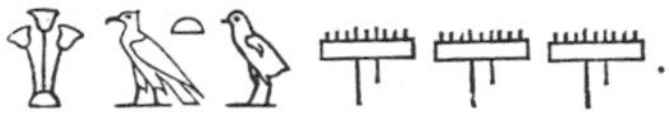

6 , l. 443.

7 , l. 444.

8 , l. 445.

9 , l. 445.

seizes the god Ḥu, eternity[1] is brought to him, the god Sȧa[2] is stablished at his feet, he sets out in a boat, and takes possession of the horizon. His soul (or, son) breaks his sleep in his house upon earth. His bones flourish, his disasters are done away, he is purified by the Eye of Horus, and his disaster is done away by the two Tcherti[3] of Osiris. His sister, the Lady of the city of Pe (Buto), weeps for him. He is in the sky, in the sky, in the air, in the air, and he is not overthrown. He sits not down as an overseer (?) of the god.[4] He is One Face,[5] the firstborn of the gods. His bread-cake is with Rā, his meat and drink are like those of Nu. He goes back, he travels, he comes with Rā. He embraces his temples, he yokes the Kau, he plucks away Kau; he gives disaster, he destroys disaster. His heart is not repulsed.[6] He is Horus, he is the flesh and blood of his father [Osiris].[7] He wills that he shall be triumphant in what he does.[8] He weighs Tefen and Tefent, the Maāti goddesses obey him, Shu bears testimony, and he goes about on the thrones of the Earth-god.[9] He gathers together his members which are in the hidden place,[10] he collects those who dwell in Nu, he causes his word to reach to Ȧn (Heliopolis).[11] "Behold, he cometh

1 , l. 446.

2 , l. 446.

3 Isis and Nephthys, , l. 448.

4 , l. 449.

5 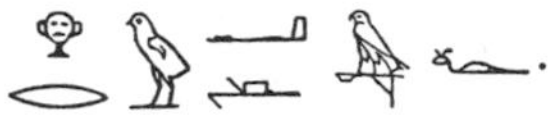.

6 Line 451.

7 , l. 452.

8 , l. 453.

9 , l. 454.

10 , l. 454.

11 .

forth this day in the real form of a living spirit."[1] He sets battle in array, he slays the rebel,[2] his support is in his eye, his protection is in his eye, his strength is in his eye, his power is in his eye.[3] O gods of the South, North, West, and East, protect him, [for] he is afraid; he sits like the hyena (?) of the two houses.[4] He hates to walk in the darkness, for if he cannot see he will fall headlong[5]; let him not be given to your flames, O gods. He travels through Shu, he strides over Aker,[6] he stands up in the eastern part of heaven.[7]

He knows the God, he knows Rā, he knows Thoth, he knows Ḥeru-Sepṭ,[8] he knows the Dweller in the Ṭuat,[9] and he knows the Bull of Heaven.[10] He comes, he comes, behold, he appears, and if he did not come a message of the gods would come to him, and the word of the god, , would bring him in.[11] He sails over the heavens in the Mekhent Boat and lacks not food therein, and the great ones who are in the White House and are over the Mesqet region of heaven do not repulse him.[12]

[1] 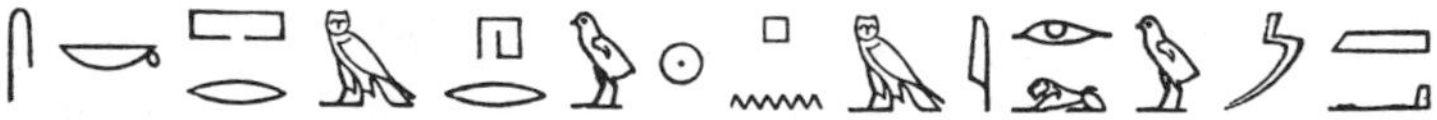
, l. 455.

[2] Line 455.

[3] Line 457.

[4] , l. 457.

[5] 
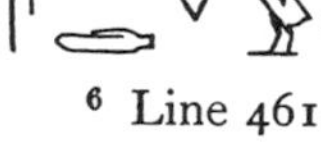, l. 459.

[6] Line 461.

[7] Line 462.

[8] Horus of the East, , l. 465.

[9] 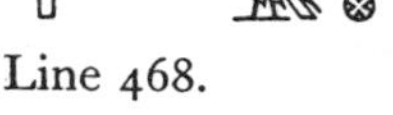, l. 466.

[10] 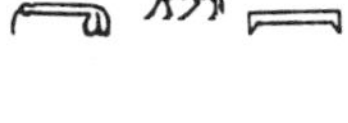, l. 467.

[11] Line 468.

[12] 
, l. 469.

He arrives at the high place of heaven,[1] the Ḥenmemet beings look at him,[2] he sees his body in the Semketet Boat, he works in it; the Uraeus-goddess in the Māntchet Boat recognizes him, and he makes a libation to her. The Ḥenmemet beings bear testimony concerning him (*i.e.*, his identity), and the storm-winds of heaven bear him along and present him to Rā.[3] He sails in the horizon like Rā and Ḥeru-khuti, he is happy with his Ka, he lives with his Ka, he has his tunic on him, and his sceptres in his hands, and the Four Firstborn Spirits with the long tresses[4] of Horus, who stand in the east of heaven, magnificent by reason of their sceptres, proclaim his "fair name" to Rā. He enters to the north of Sekhet-Åar, he sails about the Lake of Kha, he sails to the east of heaven, he sails to the east of the sky,[5] where the gods are born,[6] and he becomes the planet Jupiter.[7]

The next paragraph of the Unås text describes his appearance in the Boat of Rā:—Thy heart is thine, Osiris. Thy legs are thine, Osiris. Thy hands are thine, Osiris. His heart is to himself, his legs are to himself, his hands are to himself. He approaches heaven in his strides, he appears in the sky, he comes forth on the flame of the great dew. He flies as a duck, he hovers over (or, alights) like a scarab on the empty seat in the Boat of Rā.[8] He sits on the seat of Rā, he sails through heaven in the Boat of Rā.[9] He seizes the *urert* crown from the Two Companies of the gods, Isis nourishes him, Nephthys gives him suck. Horus takes him with his two fingers and purifies him in the Lake of the Jackal, he (Horus) withdraws his Ka from the Lake of the Ṭuat, he makes his Ka to come to his body in the

[1] Line 469. [2] Tetå, l. 221. [3] Lines 469–470.

[4] , l. 473.

[5] Lines 473–475. [6] Tetå, l. 228; Pepi I, l. 171.

[7] , Pepi I, l. 488.

[8] Line 477. [9] Line 478.

Great House. Portals are made for him, ropes are plaited for him, the imperishable stars conduct him, he sails to the Fields of Reeds, those who are in the horizon transport him, and those who are in Qebḥu make him to sail.[1] He is with you, O gods, ye are with him, O gods; he lives with you, O gods, ye live with him, O gods. He loves you, O gods, love ye him, O gods. Peq comes. Patch comes, appearing from the thigh of Horus. He who appears comes, he who is weak comes. He appears on the thighs of Isis, he is weak on the thighs of Nephthys. His father Tem grasps his hand, he counts him [among] the gods who are mighty, wise, imperishable. His mother Api[2] gives him her breast, he conveys it to his mouth, he sucks her milk, which is white, splendid, and sweet, he passes through the land, and has neither thirst nor hunger.[3]

In the next paragraph the deceased is supposed to arrive at the place of the god whose face is turned behind him,[4] and who sees what is behind him.[5] This god is provided with a boat in which he transports across the celestial ocean the soul which would make its way to the Elysian Fields. Him the deceased addresses and says: O thou watchest—in peace. O Ḥer-f-ḥa-f—in peace. Maa-ḥa-f—in peace. O Boat of the sky—in peace. O Boat of Nut—in peace. O Boat of the gods—in peace. He (*i.e.*, the deceased) has come to thee. Transport thou him in the boat wherein thou didst transport the gods. He has come to his place as the god came to his place. He has come to his hair (?) as the god came to his place; he has come to his hair (?) as the god came to his hair (?). No living being, no dead being, no bird (?), no quadruped makes him known. If thou wilt not transport him, he will leap up and set himself on the wing of Thoth, and he will transport him to his place in the horizon.[6] He (*i.e*, the deceased) swims to the earth appearing from the lake, and pours moisture on the green [land]. He

1 Lines 481–483.

2 , l. 487.

3 Lines 484–489.

4 Ḥer-f-ḥa-f, .

5 Maa-ḥa-f, .

6 Lines 489–492.

pacifies the Two Lands, he unites the Two Lands. He uniteth with his mother Smat-urt. His mother is Smat, the wife on the mountain, the verdure on the mountain Seḥseḥ. He comes out on the ladder which his father Rā made for him. Set and Horus seize his hand, they draw him to the Ṭuaṭ. He sits on the Great Throne by the side of the Great God.[1] O Qaȧt, who completes not the battlements of Nu, he comes to thee; make thou them open to him. He is a little one there. He is the chief of the Followers of Rā, he is not the chief of the rebel gods.[2]

The next section of the Unȧs text is of the greatest importance. It is assumed that the dead king has succeeded in making his way into heaven, and the section describes the terror of the gods when they see him arriving. They soon discover that he is mightier than they, and the text makes him to hunt them about in the fields of the sky, and when he has lassoed them, he kills them, and cooks and eats them, and thus absorbs into himself all their strength and vital power. The incident is thus described:—The sky dissolves in floods of water. The stars collapse. The bow-bearers[3] run about alarmed, the bones of the Akeru gods[4] tremble, the Ḳenemu[5] whirl, [when] they see him a risen Soul, in the form of a god who lives on his fathers and feeds upon his mothers. He is the lord of sagacity, his mother knows not his name. His riches are in the sky, his strength is in the horizon, [he is] like Tem his father, who gave him birth. He to whom he gave birth is stronger than he is. His doubles are behind him, his . . . .[6] are under his feet. His gods are upon him, his uraei are on his hair.[7]

1 Lines 492–494. 2 Lines 494, 495.

3 , a class of stars (?).

4 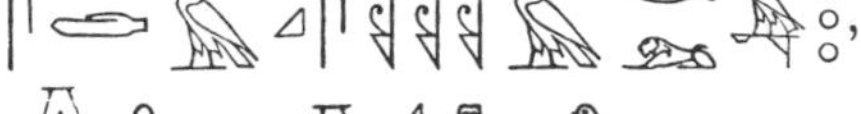, l. 498.

5 , l. 498.

6 , l. 503.

7 , l. 504.

His serpent-guide[1] is in his breast, a soul that sees,[2] an uraeus of fire. His powers protect him. He is the bull of the sky, conquering in his heart, living in the form (or, creation) of every god, eating their flesh (?). What fills their bodies (*i.e.*, intestines) comes by words of power from the Island of Sȧsa.[3] He is a being equipped, his spirits are with him. He rises up in the form of a great god, the lord of the Ȧmu-ȧst-ā beings.[4] He sits down, his back is to Ḳeb. He weighs words with Him of the hidden name[5] [on] the day of the slaughtering of the firstborn.[6] He is the lord of the offering, he plaits the rope,[7] he makes (or provides) his own meat and drink. He eats men, he feeds on the gods, he is the lord to whom tributes are brought, he weighs the gifts. Ȧm-Reḥau,[8] who seizes the hair on top of the head, ropes them together for [him]. Tcheser-tep[9] inspects them and drives them to him. Ḥer-thertu[10] binds them, Khensu cuts their throats, and draws out their entrails, [for] he is the Messenger sent by him to meet him. Shesmu[11] cuts them in pieces, and cooks them in his fiery caldrons.[12]

1 

2 

3 

4 , Tetȧ, l. 322.

5 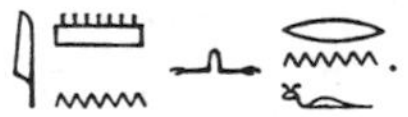

6 

7 The rope which he uses as a lasso.

8 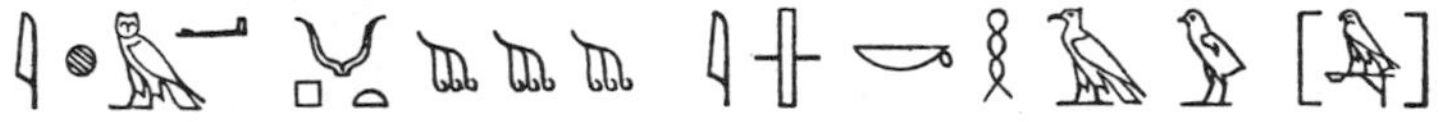 , l. 509.

9 

10 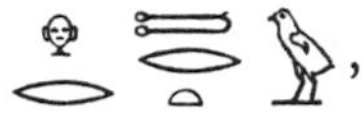, or 

11 

12  , l. 511.

He (the dead king) eats their words of power, he swallows their spirits. The great ones of them are for his food in the morning, their middle [-sized] ones are for his food in the evening, and the small ones are for his food in the night. The old ones, male and female, are for his caldrons. Behold, the Great One in heaven shoots forth fire into their caldrons which contain the thighs of their firstborn. Those who dwell in heaven belong to him, he shoots with the bow at the caldrons with the legs of their women [in them]. He goes round about the two heavens everywhere, he goes round the Two Lands. He is the Great Power,[1] the Power among Powers.[2] He is the Āshem, the Āshem of the Great Āshemu.[3] What he finds on his path he eats eagerly. His protection is in the breasts of all the Sāḥu[4] who dwell in the horizon. He is God, the firstborn of the firstborn. He goes round the thousands, he makes offerings to the hundreds. He is given the arm (power?) as the Great Sekhem, the star Saḥ (Orion), the father of the gods. He renews his risings in the sky, the flesh of the Crown, as Lord of the horizon. He computes the bones and the entrails, he takes possession of the breasts (or, hearts), of the gods. He eats the Red Crown, he swallows the Green Crown. He feeds upon their lungs, he is satisfied to live on breasts (or, hearts), (that is, their magical powers), he devours the things which are in the Red Crown, he flourishes, their magical powers are in his body, the Sāḥu do not retreat from his hand. He eats the wisdom of every god, his period of life is eternity, his limit is everlastingness in this form (sāḥ) of his. What he wills he does, what he hates he does not. He is a dweller in

1 , Tetà, l. 326.

2 , or  .

3 .

4 .

the limit of the horizon for ever and ever. Their soul is in his body, their spirits are with (or, before) him. He has more offerings than the gods. His flame is in their bones. Behold, their soul is before him. Their shadows are with their forms . . . . The seat of his heart is among the living in this earth for ever and ever.[1]

The next section of the text of Unȧs contains a series of about twenty-five adjurations which are addressed to serpent-fiends and other monsters, who were, it seems, supposed to attack the dead in their tombs. Among the beings addressed are Babȧ,[2] Nāi,[3] Hekȧ,[4] Hekert,[5] Setcheḥ,[6] Ȧkenhȧ,[7] Ȧmen,[8] Hȧu,[9] Ȧnṭāf,[10] Tcheser-tep,[11] Thethu,[12] Hemthet,[13] etc. In the following section we find an interesting allusion to the deceased as the son of the goddess Sepṭ (Sothis), and to his heavenly and earthly houses, thus:—" Heaven hath poured out the " life of Sepṭ, and behold the son of Sepṭ lives. The " Two Companies of the gods have purified him in the " imperishable constellation of the Great Bear.[14] His " house is not destroyed in heaven, his throne is not " destroyed upon the earth. Men supplicate him, the " gods fly to him. The goddess Sepṭ hath made him to " fly to heaven to be with his brethren the gods. The " great goddess Nut hath laid bare her shoulders for

1 Lines 496–552.

2 

3 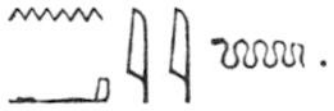

4 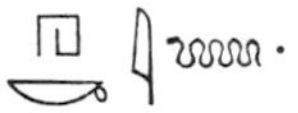

5 

6 

7 

8 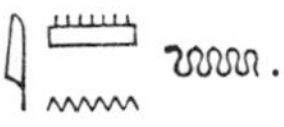

9 

10 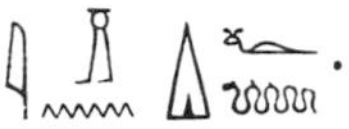

11 

12 

13 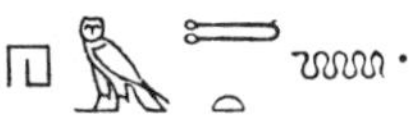

14 , l. 567.

"him, and she hath fashioned Two Divine Souls[1] to be "at the head of the Souls of Ȧn, under the head of Rā. "His throne is before Rā, and they do not give it to any "other, and he appeareth in heaven before Rā. His "face is like the faces of hawks, his wings are like the "wings of geese, his nails are like the claws of the god "Ṭuf (?)."[2]

The blessed one, having been provided with a face (*i.e.*, beak) like a hawk, and the wings of a goose, and the claws of the god Ṭuf, is ready to fly from earth into heaven, but it seems that he was not allowed to start unless the gods who were about to help him were satisfied as to the reality of his moral worth. They demanded that no man should have uttered a word against him on earth, and that no complaint should have been made against him in heaven before the gods. Therefore in the text of Unȧs we read :—"Unȧs hath not been spoken against "on earth before men, he hath not been accused of sin "in heaven before the gods."[3] Thus, even in the period of the VIth dynasty, we find the idea that heaven was reserved for those who had when on earth performed their duty to man and to the Divine Powers.[4] Presumably those who had failed in these respects remained on earth. Unȧs having satisfied all requirements, the god Ȧp-uat made him ascend to heaven among the brethren the gods, and having obtained possession of his arms like the *Smen*[5] goose, he flapped his wings with the strength and vigour of the *Tchert*[6] bird (eagle or hawk ?), and flew from earth to heaven.

1 , l. 569.

2 , l. 570.

3 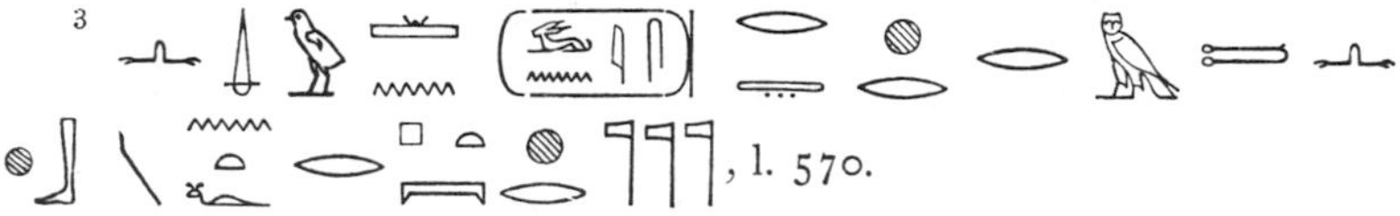, l. 570.

4 Literally "gods," . It is possible that we ought to render  by "God," just as we translate the Hebrew אֱלֹהִים by "Lord," or "God."

5 , l. 571.

6 .

The Ladder by which the deceased ascended from earth to heaven.
From the Papyrus of Ani.

As he flies to heaven the gods of the West and the East, the South and the North, are invoked to receive him when he appears there.[1] Their reception of him is favourable, for he sails about on Qebḥu[2] freely. Being identified with Osiris, Horus, who regards him as his father, comes to his "two fingers," and salutes him, and causes him to rise like the great god on Qebḥu. And the gods say: Assuredly he is Horus, son of Isis, "assuredly he is the firstborn god, the son of Hathor, assuredly he is the seed of Ḳeb." Osiris orders that he is to be crowned as the second of Horus, and the Four Spirits who dwell in Ȧn have written the decree making them the two great gods in Qebḥu.[3]

Two sections of the text of Unȧs deal with the Ladder by which, according to a legend, Osiris ascended from earth to heaven; the first contains a series of addresses to divine powers, and the second refers to the setting up of the ladder. Thus we have: Homage to thee, Set-Ȧmenti,[4] mistress of Peter[5] of heaven, gift (?) of Thoth, mistress of the two sides of the LADDER,[6] open thou the way for

[1] Lines 572, 573.

[2] The celestial ocean.

[3] Lines 572–575.

[4] 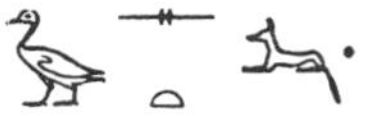

[5] 

[6] 

the deceased, set him on his way. Homage to thee, Nàu,[1] mistress of the marge of the Lake of Kha, open thou the way for the deceased, set him on his way. Homage to thee, O Neḳ, Bull of Rā with the four horns. Thy horn is in the West, thy horn is in the East, thy horn is in the South, thy horn is in the North. The meadow of thy horn is the Ȧment of the deceased, set thou him on his way. Certainly Ȧment is pure, [he] comes forth by thee to Baket. Homage to the Field of the Offering (Sekhet-ḥetep). Homage to the pasture which is in thee. The pasture of the deceased is in thee, pure offerings are in thee. Rā knots the Ladder for Osiris, Horus knots the Ladder for his father Osiris, going to his spirit. The one (Rā) [stands] on this side, and the other (Horus) on that, and the deceased is between them. Behold, he is the god whose seats are pure, he comes forth from a pure place, He stands up Horus, he sits down Set. Rā grasps his hand, a spirit in heaven, a body on earth. The flesh which has not [its] decree is helpless. His decree has the great seal, behold, his decree has not the little seal.[2]

Happy are those who see [the deceased], content be those who behold him, say the gods. Therefore this god comes forth in heaven, therefore the father comes forth in heaven. His souls are on him, his book is by his side, his words of power are in his mouth. . . . The divine Souls of Pe and the divine Souls of Nekhen, and the gods who belong to heaven, and the gods who belong to earth, come to him, and they lift him up on their hands. Come thou therefore to heaven, enter thou therein in its name of "Ladder." Heaven and earth have been given to him by Tem, Ḳeb hath spoken concerning it. The Domains of Horus, the Domains of Set, and the Fields of Reeds praise thee in thy name of Khensu-Sepṭ. The city Ȧnu is as he is, god; thy Ȧnu is as he is, god; Ȧnu is as he is, Rā; thy Ȧnu is as he is, Rā. His mother is Ȧnu, his father is Ȧnu, he himself is Ȧnu, born in Ȧnu.[3]

1 , the Ostrich-god?

2 Lines 579–583.

3 Lines 584–592.

Behold, Rā, Chief of the Two Companies of the gods, Chief of mortals, and Nefer-Tem, who has no second, whose flesh and bone are of the father Ḳeb, and every god put out to him his hand. His face is to thee, he adores thee, he cries to thee. The face of his body is god, the face (front) of his nose is god. His bread and his cake are not among his brethren the gods. He sends not a message, he chooses not a sceptre among his brethren the gods. He opens not the doors in the Semktet Boat, he opens not the doors in the Mātet Boat, he weighs not his word with the dweller in his city, he opens not the doors which are closed (?).[1]

Homage to thee, Horus, in the Domains of Horus! Homage to thee, Set, in the Domains of Set! Homage to thee, Åar, in the Fields of Åarr![2] Homage to you, ye two Tettȧ-ȧb goddesses,[3] ye two daughters of the four gods who are chiefs of the Great House! When his word comes forth unveil. He shall look at you as Horus looks at Isis. He shall look at you as Neḥebu-kau[4] looks at Serqit. He shall look at you as Sebek looks at Neith. He shall look at you as Set looks at Tettȧ-ȧb.[5] O ye gods who are behind the house of Rā, whom Neḥit[6] has brought forth. O ye gods who are in front of the Boat of Rā; he sits before him, he opens his chests, he breaks his decrees (?), he seals his decrees, he sends forth his messengers, who never rest.[7] His foes are the foes of Tem, his dislikes are the dislikes of Tem. His blows are the blows of Tem. What he drives from this path Tem drives away. He is Horus. He comes after his father, he comes after Osiris. His face is before him, his face is behind him.[8] He sees Rā. He knows Rā. Let those who know thee know him. He is not blind that thou shouldst set him in the darkness, he is not

[1] Lines 592–597.

[2] , or, .

[3] .

[4] , l. 599.

[5] Lines 597–600.

[6] , l. 601.

[7] Line 602.

[8] Line 603.

deaf so that he cannot hear thy voice.[1] Take thou him with thee, with thee. He has dispersed for thee the rain-storm, he has driven away for thee the water flood, he has broken for thee the tempests. He utters cries of joy to thee, he acclaims thee. He (*i.e.*, the deceased) opens the doors of heaven by the flames which are about the abode of the gods, he advances through the fire which is about the home of the gods, who make a way for him, who make him pass onwards, for he is Horus.[2]

He comes like the Chief of the Flood of the Celestial Ocean.[3] He is Sebek (the Crocodile-god), with the green feather, watchful of face, exalted of breast. He comes to his lakes in the country of Aḳebȧ in the Great Stream, to the place of offerings, the green place, the fields in the horizon. He makes to flourish the crops on both sides of the horizon. He brings the crystal of the Great Eye in the midst of the Field, he takes his seat in the horizon. He rises like Sebek, the son of Neith.

From the above section it is clear that the deceased is made out to be the lord of the great celestial stream which was supposed to surround the world, but he only becomes so by being identified with Sebek, the Crocodile-god, the son of Neith, who was able to travel about in the stream and land wherever he pleased. The last two lines contain allusions of a most materialistic character, and illustrate the mixed conceptions of the ancient theological writers of Egypt concerning the joys of the departed. The passage reads: He eats with his mouth, he voids water, he unites with women. He is the sower of seed who carries off wives from their husbands to the place which pleases him, according to the inclination of his heart.[4] Now it seems that in these

[1] Line 608. [2] Lines 610–612.

[3] , l. 620.

[4] 

, ll. 628, 629.

lines we have an allusion to a very ancient belief concerning the crocodile, which is extant in the Egyptian Sûdân at the present day. To the crocodile are attributed great powers of vitality and virility, which are coveted by boatmen and others up and down the river. A few years ago the natives between Ad-Damer and Shendî suffered serious losses of cattle and children through the attacks of a huge old crocodile which lived in the Nile, and had succeeded for many years in escaping safely with his prey. A British officer quartered at Ad-Damer had the creature watched, and, after several days' careful observation of his habits, managed to find out the spot to which he retired with his booty. One day he shot him, and with the help of the natives the creature was killed, and his genitals were bought by an enterprising native, who cut them up into small pieces and sold them to his kinsmen, by whom they were eaten as an aphrodisiac. On making enquiries I learned that the genitals of every fine male crocodile were disposed of in this manner. The paragraph (ll. 620–629) in the text of Unȧs suggests that the deceased wished to possess the powers of virility of the Crocodile-god Sebek, and it is clear that its words were intended to make him all-powerful with women.

From the next section we learn that the deceased was identified with Nāu,[1] the Bull of the gods, the master of seven Uraei-goddesses. He is the Bull with the twofold light in his eye, the power among the gods, he makes lapis-lazuli to flourish, he makes the *tun* plant of the South to grow, he raises up the cords (fibres ?) of the *shemshemet* plant, he unites the heavens, he has dominion in the lands of the South and North, he is the god of those who are in the presence, he builds the City of God,[2] and makes it safe. He rules the night and makes the hours revolve, the Powers rise up and he assigns to them their order, like Babi.[3] He is the son of Ȧkhemit, who brought him forth through the embrace of the Lord of

1 , Tetȧ, l. 307.

2 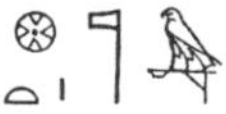, l. 641.

3 .

the Darkness.[1] He is Babi, the Lord of the Darkness, the gracious (or, beautiful) Bull who lives in his death (?).

Finally the god Ḥa-f-em-ḥa-f is called upon to bring the wonderful creature called Sefert, who is in charge of portions of the body of Osiris, and mounted on this he appears in heaven; when he is there he works magic upon, or for, Rā.[2] The Sefert, as we learn from a drawing on a tomb at Beni Hasan, was a creature with the head of a hawk, and the body of a lion, from the back of which grew a pair of wings, but it is possible that in the earliest times the creature was a fabulous bird pure and simple.

With this paragraph we come to an end of the religious texts which were written for King Unȧs. These do not, however, by any means exhaust our sources of information as to the life of the blessed in heaven, for there are still to be considered the texts which were drawn up for Tetȧ and his successors. The texts of Tetȧ and Pepi I are of very great interest, and from these the following statements are obtained.

When Tetȧ leaves the earth he finds heaven opened and earth opened, for Horus has thrown open the doors thereof, and Set has withdrawn the bolts. The ceremonial purity which is so often insisted on in the texts is acquired by the deceased, for he purifies himself with Rā in the Lake of the Country of Reeds,[3] Horus dries his body,[4] Thoth dries his feet, Shu raises him up, and the Heaven-goddess Nut gives him her hand. Horus of the gods opens the gate of heaven and unbolts the doors of Qebḥu at dawn, he appears in the Field of Reeds, and purifies himself therein. Horus of the

1 , l. 645.

2 , l. 649.

3 , l. 6.

4 .

Horizons, Horus of the East,[1] and Horus of Sheståå[2] do likewise, and the deceased does as they have done.[3] He receives bones of a marvellous nature, and a complete and imperishable body is bestowed upon him in the womb of his mother Nut. Rā gives him his hand, and Shu draws him up on his shoulder. He sucks milk at the breasts of the two Cow-nurses[4] of the Souls of Ȧnu, and the three deities Ḥepath, Henen, and Smennu[5] perform service for him. Horus, who loves him, brings him his Eye, Set, who loves him, brings him his testicles,[6] and Thoth, who loves him, brings him his arm and shoulder. The Two Companies of the Gods tremble before him, and bring him offerings.[7] He is the "nose which breathes,"[8] and he appears in the sky from the womb of Ȧmu-ȧpt."[9] He passes through the two heavens,[10] he comes to the two earths, he treads upon the green herbs under the feet of Ḳeb, and he walks over the roads of Nut. He sets up the ladder, being purified, and the Ȧmu-urt[11] grasp his hand.

Homage to thee, O Rā, who dost traverse the sky and sail over Nut, thou dost traverse the Lake of Khaȧ.[12] He (the deceased) grasps thy tail, for behold, he is the god, the son of the god. He is the Uneb-flower appearing from Ka,[13] the gold (?) Uneb appearing from Sentru.

1 

2 

3 Lines 19–21.

4 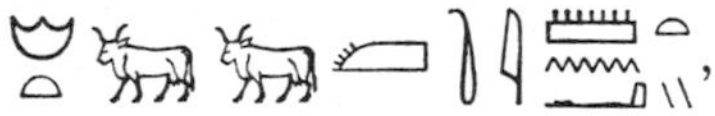, l. 723.

5 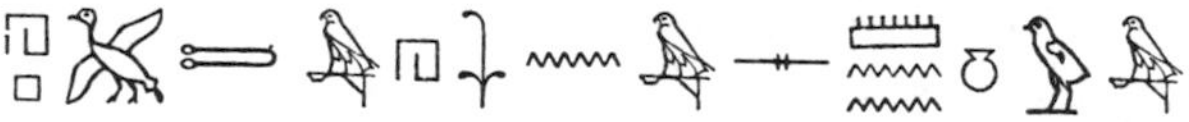, l. 24.

6 Line 27.

7 Line 28.

8 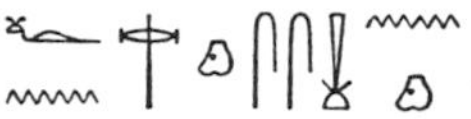, l. 31.

9 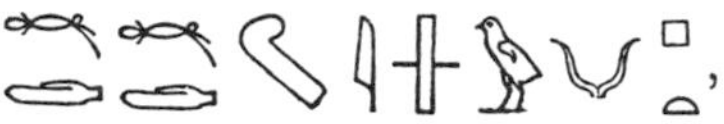, l. 31.

10 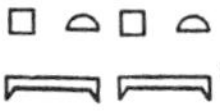, l. 34.

11 , l. 36.

12 , l. 37.

13 , l. 39.

He passes through Pe, he sails over Kenmut like Shesmu, dweller in his boat, beloved of the god.[1] Happy are those who see him tied to the brow of Rā. His tunic is on him like Hathor, his hair is like the plumage of a hawk. He appears in heaven among his brethren.[2] Homage to thee, Bull of bulls! When thou appearest he seizes thy tail, he lays hold of thee by thy . . . .[3] When thou goest forth Urt is behind thee, Urt is by thee.[4] The sky speaks,[5] the earth trembles before thy slaughter (?), O Osiris.[6] Hunger comes not to him (the deceased). He is filled with food. He hungers not, for he eats bread-cakes made of fine flour.[7] The great goddess makes them for him, and he is sated therewith. He thirsts not like Shu, he hungers not like Tefnut, for Ḥep, Ṭuamutf, Qebḥsenuf, and Ȧmset (or Amḳeset)[8] destroy the hunger which is in his belly and the thirst which is on his lips.[9] His hunger is with Shu, his thirst is with Tefnut, he lives on the daily bread[10] which comes in its season. He lives on that whereon Shu lives, he eats what Tefnut eats.[11] He comes to thee, O Nekhekh[12] (Aged One). He drives thee back as the east wind drives back the west wind. Thou comest in his following as the north wind follows the south wind.[13] The god of the great celestial waters, Aḳeb-ur, the fashioner of the gods and the guide of the Ḥenmemet beings, makes gods and men to be at peace with him, and they give him

1 Line 41.

2 Lines 44, 45.

3 , l. 46.

4 Line 47.

5 *I.e.*, there is thunder.

6 Line 50.

7  *qemḥu.* Compare קֶמַח סֹלֶת of Genesis xviii, 6, "fine flour."

8 . Tetá, l. 60; . Mer-en-rā, l. 218; 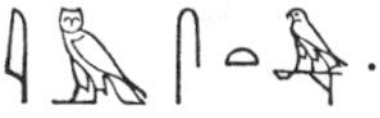. Pepi II, l. 592.

9 Lines 54–61.

10 , l. 63.

11 Lines 62–64.

12 . Pepi II, l. 612.

13 Line 81.

offerings.[1] The god Ur-ka-f,[2] the officer of Horus, the Director of the Hall of Rā, the Firstborn of the workshop of Ptaḥ, also gives him food.

To him one says: Open thou the doors of heaven! Thou hast lifted up thy head on thy bones, thou hast lifted up thy head on thy bones. Thou hast opened the doors of heaven, thou hast drawn back the great bolts, thou hast removed the seal from the great abode. Thy face is that of a jackal, thy tail is that of a lion with a fierce eye. Thou sittest on thy throne, thou utterest commands to the Spirits. Thou comest before Horus, the Advocate of his father Osiris. Stand up, rise up like Osiris.[3] Hail, Horus comes, he embraces thee, he makes Thoth to make to turn back the followers of Set, he brings them to thee prisoners. He drives back the heart of Set, for he is greater than he. Thou goest forth before him, thou turnest about before him. Ḳeb seeth thy going about, he sets thee on thy seat. Ḳeb brings thy two sisters, Isis and Nephthys, to thy side. Horus makes the gods to receive thee, they make friends with thee in thy name of "Sent," and they reject thee not in thy name of "Atert," he makes the gods to be thy advocates. Ḳeb sets his sandal (or, foot) on the head of thine enemy, [as] thou repulsest [him]. Thy son Horus smites him, he snatches away his Eye from him, he gives it to thee, thou gettest a soul thereby, thou gettest strength thereby, at the head of the Spirits. Horus makes thee to seize thine enemies, he is unhurt among them before thee. Strong, then, is Horus; he counts up his father in thee in thy name of Bȧt-erpet. Nut gives thee to be a god unto Set in thy name of god. Thy mother Nut spreads herself out over thee in her name of Shet-pet. Horus seizes Set, he places him under thee; Set bears thee up, he is beneath thee as earth is beneath thee. Rule thou him therefore in thy name of Ta-tcheser. Horus makes thee to grasp (?) him (*i.e.*, Set) by his middle; he shall not go out of thy hand. Horus makes thee to hold him tightly in thy palm; he shall not escape from thy hand. Horus has

[1] Line 86.

[2] , l. 87.

[3] Lines 156–169.

avenged thee, he has made his KA [to be] in thee in thy name of Ka-ḥetep.[1]

Hail, thou Osiris,[2] Ḳeb has given thee thy two eyes, thou restest in the two eyes of this Great One who is in thee. Ḳeb has made Horus to give them to thee that thou mayest rest on them. Isis and Nephthys look on thee, they see thee. Horus has made thee a gift, Horus has made Isis and Nephthys defend thee; they give thee to Horus that he may rest on thee. Horus has recited words before thee in thy name of "Khut" (*i.e.*, Horizon), wherefrom Rā appears in thy hands in thy name of "Khenāḥ." Thou hast seized with thy hands Ḥaf-ḥȧf[3] to strengthen (?) his bones—great is his heart. Horus makes thee to advance, he comes, he examines thee. Thou hast vanquished Set, his KA is fettered. Horus has made thee to drive him back, and assuredly he is greater than thine enemy. He swims under thee, in thee he bears up him that is greater than himself. Those who are in his following see that thy strength is greater than his, and they attack thee not. Horus comes, he counts up his father in thee; thou renewest thy youth in thy name "Water of Youth."[4] Horus opens for thee thy mouth; thou shalt not perish, not decay. Ḳeb brings Horus to thee, and he counts for thee their hearts. He brings to thee all the gods at once, none of them . . . . . from his hand. Horus avenges thee, never ceasing (?) to defend thee. He snatches his Eye from the hand of Set and gives it to thee . . . . The heart of Horus advances before thee in thy name of Khent-Ȧment. Horus defends thee against the work of Set.[5]

The next section of the text of Tetȧ refers to the passage of the deceased across the Lake of Kha on the wing of Thoth, and begins: Horus groans for the loss of his Eye, Set groans for the loss of his testicles. The Eye of Horus passes and falls on the other side of

[1] Lines 169–176.

[2] The name of Osiris is added to that of the king.

[3] , l. 178.

[4] , l. 180.

[5] Lines 176–183.

the Lake of Kha, and it defends its body from the hand of Set; it sees Thoth on the other side of the Lake of Kha. The Eye of Horus passes to the other side of the Lake of Kha, and the wing of Thoth falls on the other side of the Lake of Kha. O ye gods who pass over on the wing of Thoth to the other side of the Lake of Kha, to the eastern side of heaven, if he (the deceased) speaks before Set concerning the Eye of Horus, carry ye him over with you on the wing of Thoth, to the other side of the Lake of Kha, to the eastern side of heaven, if he speaks before Set concerning the Eye of Horus. Watch in peace, O Maa-ḥa-f,[1] in peace. Watch in peace, O Ferryman of heaven, in peace. O Ferryman of the Lake of Kha,[2] speak the name of the deceased to Rā, make mention of him to Rā, let his body be in that celestial palace of the Lords of [their] KAU (*i.e.*, Doubles), who praise Rā in the Domains of Horus, in the Domains of Set.[3]

The divine Ferryman Maa-ḥa-f,[4] who seems to have performed for dead Egyptians what Charon did for dead Greeks, was under the direct control of Rā, who decided which souls were to be ferried over the Lake of Kha, and which were to be left on earth. From the text of Tetà we learn that the deceased did not wait for Rā to give the order for him to be ferried over unto him, but he himself "ordered Maa-ḥa-f, the Ferryman of the Lake "of Kha, to bring the ferry-boat of the Lake of Kha, "wherein he had ferried over the gods to the other side "of the Lake of Kha, to the eastern side of heaven, and "to ferry him over to the other side of the Lake of Kha, "to the eastern side of heaven." And whilst he is in

1 

2 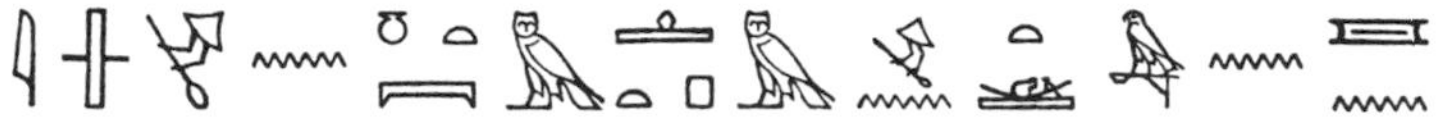

, Tetà, l. 191; Pepi II, l. 1288.

3 Lines 185–192.

4 This name means "he who sees what is behind him," and in a vignette of the Theban Recension of the Book of the Dead we see him seated in a boat with his head turned behind him. See *Papyrus of Ani*, Plate 17 (Chapter XCIII).

the embraces of the Eye of Horus, and his body is between his fingers, the gods, goddesses, and Åmset (Åmḳeset), Ḥep, Ṭuamut-f, and Qebḥsenuf "wash his face."[1] His right side is Horus, his left side is Set.[2]

In the following short sections of the text of Tetå the portal of Nut is informed that the deceased is the Air-god Shu, and that he appears from Tem. The god Nu is called upon to "make open" the bolt thereof to the deceased, who indeed comes as a "divine soul."[3] Nu commits him to Tem, and Peḳa[4] commits him to Shu; he makes to be opened the gate to him before men who have no name. To one of these gods it is said: "Thou graspest his hand, thou drawest him to "heaven. He is not a dead thing on earth among "men."[5]

O thou his father, O thou his father in the darkness, O thou his father Tem in the darkness, bring thou him to thy side. He has lighted for thee the lamp, he has performed the ceremony of transferring the fluid of life[6] upon thee, even as these four goddesses, Isis, Nephthys, Net, and Serqet-ḥetu,[7] performed the ceremony for father Nu on the day when they performed the ceremony on the throne. O road of Horus, cover thou him (the deceased), make thy hands to be [stretched out] to him. Come, Rā, pass thou him over to the other side, even as thy bodyguard Unḳ,[8] who loves thee, passed thee over [to the other side]. Give thou thy hands to the west, give thou thy hands to him; give thou thy hands to the east, give thou thy hands to him, as thou hast done for the . . . of thy firstborn son.[9]

1 , l. 197.

2 Lines 193–198.

3 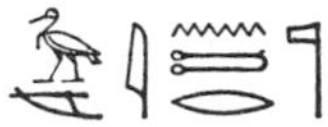, l. 202.

4 , l. 202.

5 Line 204.

6 , l. 206.

7 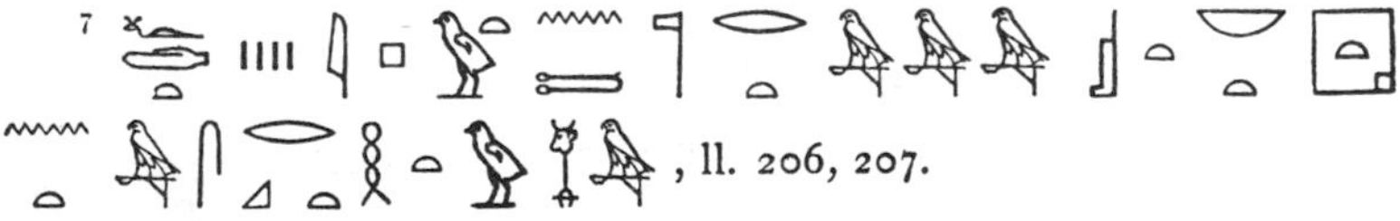, ll. 206, 207.

8 .

9 Lines 204–210.

Hail, Osiris (the deceased), stand up! Horus comes. He counts thee among the gods, Horus loves thee. He fills thee with his Eye, he makes it to complete thee. Horus opens for thee thine eye, thou seest with it. The gods have lifted up thy face, they love thee. Isis and Nephthys make thee to be in a state of well-being. Horus doth not depart from thee—lo, his KA rests upon thee. Thou receivest the word of Horus, thou restest upon it. Horus hears when [as yet] thou hast not entreated him. He makes the gods follow thee. Wake up, Osiris (*i.e.*, the deceased)! Ḳeb brings Horus to thee, he counts thee up. Horus finds thee, he sets a soul in thee. Horus brings the gods to thee, he gives them to thee, they illumine thee. He sets thee in the breast of the gods, he makes thee to take possession of every crown . . . he makes thee to live in thy name of Āntchtȧ.[1] He has given to thee his Eye which flourishes, he has set it in thee, thou terrifiest all thine enemies. He has filled thee wholly with his Eye, in its name of Uaḥet. He has seized for thee the gods. Nephthys embraces all thy members in her name of "Seshat, lady of buildings,"[2] and she makes them to be healthy. Hail, Osiris, lift up thy heart, let thy heart be great, open thy mouth. Horus defends thee, he never ceases to defend thee. Hail, Osiris, thou art a god of strength, there is no god like unto thee. Horus gives thee his children, they lift thee up. He gives to thee all the gods, thou hast dominion over them. Horus bears thee up in his name of Ḥenu,[3] he lifts thee up in thy name of Seker. Thou livest, thou walkest every day, thou hast a soul in thy name of "Khut" (Horizon) wherein Rā appears, thou art adored and art ready, thou hast a soul, thou hast strength for ever and ever.

Rise up, stride with thy legs, O mighty one of strength! Thou sittest at the head of the gods, and thou doest what Osiris did in the House of the Prince

1 , l. 266.

2 , l. 268.

3 , l. 270.

in Ȧnu. Thou hast received thy Sāḥu.[1] Thy foot slips not in heaven, thou art not repulsed on earth. Thou art a spirit (*khu*). Nut gives thee birth, Nephthys gives thee suck, they make thee complete. Thou standest on thy strength. Thou makest thy being, thou makest seed.[2] Thou art more a spirit (*khu*) than the spirits. Thou goest to the city of Pe; thou findest, thou repulsest there. Thou comest to the city of Nekhen; thou findest, thou repulsest there. Thou doest what Osiris did, and behold, thou art on his throne.[3]

O thou Soul most mighty, equipped like Sma-ur, stand up! Thou art not repulsed in any place wherein thou goest, thou art not expelled from any place where thou wishest to be.

Hail, Osiris! Stand up, rise up. Thy mother Nut gives thee birth. Ḳeb fixes (or, slits) thy mouth. The great Company of the gods are thy defenders, they place thine enemy under thee, and they say unto him: "Bear thou up one who is mightier than thou art, in thy "name of Ȧtfa-ur.[4] Pay honour to one who is greater "than thou in thy name of Ta-Abṭ."[5] Thy two sisters Isis and Nephthys come to thee, they make thee to journey—Kamt-urt in thy name of "Kam-ur,"[6] Uatchet-urt in thy name of "Uatch-ur."[7] Verily thou art Urt-shent in Shen-ur.[8] Verily thou circlest in the circle of Rā, going round the Ḥau-nebu.[9] Verily thou art the

1 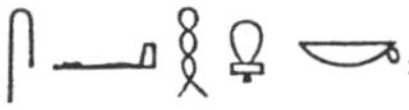, l. 271. The *form* which he had upon earth.

2 , l. 272.

3 Line 272.

4 , l. 274.

5 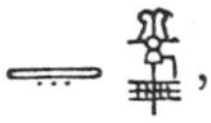, l. 274.

6 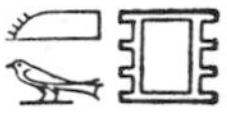.

7 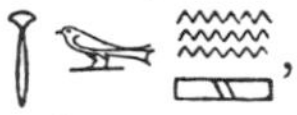, *i.e.*, "Great Green Sea" = Mediterranean.

8 , l. 275.

9 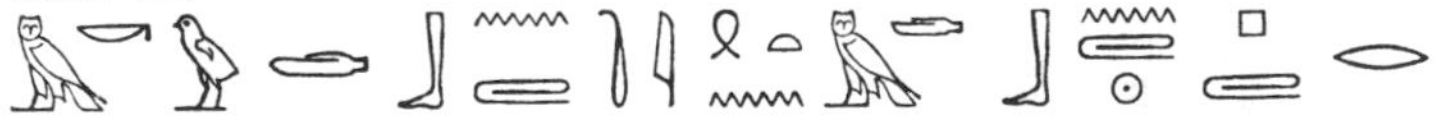

, l. 275. The Ḥau-nebu were the dwellers in the extreme north of the Delta, and at a later time the term included the people of the sea coasts and islands of the Eastern Mediterranean.

great circler in the circle which is a mighty stream. Isis and Nephthys bestow upon thee the fluid of life[1] in the city of Saut; behold, their lord is in thee in thy name of "Lord of Saut." Behold, their god is in thee in thy name of "god." They adore thee; depart not thou from them in thy name of "Ṭua-neter" (Morning Star).[2] They present offerings to thee; be not wroth (?) in thy name of Tchenṭeru.[3] Isis thy sister comes to thee rejoicing because of her love for thee, etc.[4]

Hail, Osiris (the deceased). Ḳeb hath brought Horus to thee; he defends thee. He brings to thee the hearts of the gods; thou failest not, thou lackest nothing (?). Horus has given to thee his Eye, thou takest possession through it of the Ureret Crown, at the head of the gods. Horus presents to thee thy flesh and bones, he makes thee to be complete, and there is no disorder in thee. Thoth seizes thine enemy for thee, and he slays him and those who are in his following, and he escapes not from him.[5] Ḥa-f-ḥa-f grasps thy hands, Horus sets thine enemy under thy feet. Thou livest. He gives to thee his sons, they place themselves under thee, none of them turning back, and they carry thee. Thy mother Nut makes thee to be like the God, thine enemy existing not, in thy name of "God." She withdraws thee from every evil thing in her name of "Khnemet-urt."[6] Thou art the great one (Chief) among her sons.[7] Thou hast pacified Ḳeb, he loves thee, he protects (?) thee, he gives thee thy head, he makes Thoth to present unto thee what thou lackest.

Hail, Osiris (the deceased), stand up! Horus gives thy rising up, Ḳeb makes Horus to see his father [Osiris] in thee in thy name of "Ḥet-Åtu." Horus gives thee the gods, he makes them come to thee, they illumine thy face. He gives thee his Eye, thou seest

[1] , l. 275.

[2] , l. 276.

[3] , l. 276.

[4] See above, p. 93.

[5] Line 278.

[6] 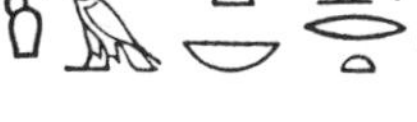, l. 280.

[7] 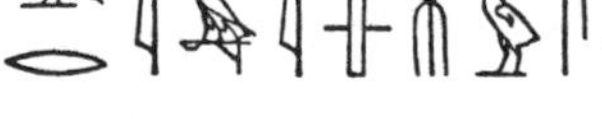, l. 280.

with it. He sets thine enemy under thee, he (the enemy) lifts thee up, thou art not dropped by him. Thou comest to thy form,[1] the gods knit together for thee thy face. Horus opens for thee thy eye, thou seest with it in thy name of "Åpt-uat."[2] The sons of Horus smite thine enemy, they make his smiting red,[3] they drive him away, dissipating the evilness of his smell. Horus presses for thee thy mouth, and he makes thy mouth to be in its true position in respect of thy teeth. Horus opens for thee thy mouth. Behold, thy son who loves thee finds for thee thy two eyes, Horus permits not thy face to be awry, in thy name of "Horus, Chief of his Rekhit."[4]

Hail, Osiris (the deceased), Horus makes thee to be joined to the gods, they make friends with thee in thy name of "Sent." Horus makes thee approach. Depart not from him in thy name of "Ḥert." Receive thou his word, rest upon it. He hears thee [though] thou hast not entreated him. He brings to thee the gods in a body. None among them escapes (?) from his hand. Horus loves thee more than his own offspring, he unites thee to those of his own body, they love thee. Horus makes his KA to be in thee, thou art content in thy name of "Ka-Ḥetep." Horus finds thee, he makes a spirit to be in thee. Thou comest forth against thine enemy, thou art mightier than he in thy name of "Per-ur."[5] Horus makes him to raise thee up in thy name of "Utes-ur."[6] He delivers thee from the hand of thine enemy. He avenges thee as the Avenger in his season. Ḳeb sees thy form, he sets thee on thy throne. Horus makes thine enemy to bow beneath thee. When

[1] , literally, thy building, or construction, *i.e.*, thy fabric.

[2] *I.e.*, "Opener of the ways," , l. 281.

[3] *I.e.*, they smite him with such severe blows that his body becomes covered with blood, ll. 281, 282.

[4] Lines 280–282.

[5] , l. 285. This name means "Great House."

[6] *I.e.*, "Great Lifter."

he would have union with thee,[1] thou escapest his member. Thou art the father of Horus, thou didst beget him in thy name of "Utet-khu."[2] The heart of Horus comes forward before thee in thy name of "Khent-Åmenti."[3]

Hail, Osiris (the deceased), wake up! Horus has made Thoth to bring thine enemy to thee. He places thee on his back, he cannot throw thee off. Thou makest thy seat upon him. Come forth, sit upon him, he escapes not from thy hand. Hail, be thou master of him, Horus chooses the thighs of thine enemies, he brings them to thee when cut off, he drives away their KAU (*i.e.*, doubles) from them, thy heart feeds on them according to its desire in thy name of "Neser-meresh."[4]

Ho, ho, thou art raised up! Thou hast received thy head, thou hast embraced thy bones, thou hast collected thy flesh, thou hast searched the earth for thy body. Thou receivest thy bread which decays not, and thy beer which perishes not. Thou standest at the doors, repulsing the Rekhit. Khent-ment-f[5] comes forth to thee; he grasps thy hand, and leads thee to heaven before thy father Ḳeb, who rejoices to meet thee and gives thee his two hands. He kisses thee, he fondles thee, he pushes thee forward at the head of the indestructible spirits. Those whose seats are hidden adore thee. Thou givest offerings to the Great Ones, thou standest up [before] the Watchers.[6] Thou smitest (threshest) grain, thou reapest barley, thou keepest the festivals of the first day of the month, and the festivals of the fifteenth day of the month, according to the decree

[1] 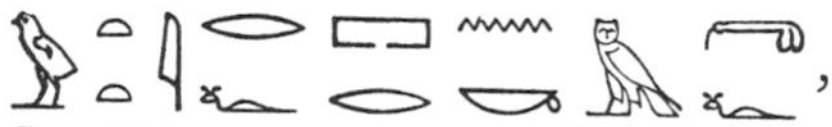, l. 285.

[2] *I.e.*, "Begetter of a spirit"?

[3] *I.e.*, "First one of Åmenti," l. 286.

[4] The forms of this name are ,  , , l. 287.

[5] 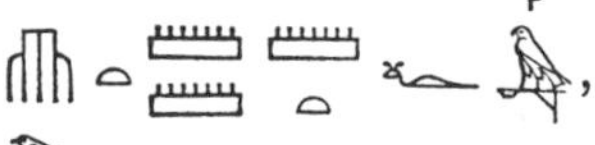, l. 288.

[6] , l. 289.

THE ELYSIAN FIELDS OF THE EGYPTIANS.

(1). THE LADY ANHAI PAYING HOMAGE TO HER FATHER AND MOTHER IN THE OTHER WORLD.

(2). ANHAI BINDING WHEAT IN BUNDLES. (3). ANHAI PLOUGHING.
(4). THE ABODE OF THE GODS, CELESTIAL BOAT, ETC.

From the Papyrus of Anhai, in the British Museum. (No. 10,472)

which thy father Ḳeb made for thee. Thou art raised up, thou art not dead.[1]

O thou great one, O thou who sailest, Osiris raises up thy name. Thy leg is great, thy leg is mighty, it strides to the great throne.[2] The Aker god seizes thee not, the *seḥṭu* stars[3] oppose thee not, the gates of heaven are open to thee, thou appearest in them. . . . Thy father brings thee not forth among men, thy mother brings thee not forth among men.[4]

The next two paragraphs of the text of Tetȧ, though short, are difficult. The first appears to refer to some revenue and offerings which are brought by Teshi,[5] and to contain a petition to the "son of the Great One" not to come against the deceased.[6] In the second paragraph the "rising one" and Untȧ[7] are mentioned, and the sails of the Māntchet Boat are said to be filled with wind. The text continues: Thou art stable in thy name of "Menu,"[8] thou art capsized in thy name of 'Ȧḳaȧ."[9] Thou art the serpent Hepȧu[10] on his belly, thou livest on the hearts of the gods who dwell in Ȧnu.

The body to heaven, the empty case of Horus to the earth. The sandal (*i.e.*, foot) of Horus treads on the serpent Nekhȧ.[11] The Nekhȧ serpent of Horus the Child,[12] the babe [with] his finger in his mouth. He (*i.e.*, the deceased) is Horus the Child, the babe [with] his finger in his mouth. Though thou hast no feet [O Osiris, *i.e.*, the deceased], though thou hast no arms,

1 Line 290.

2 , l. 290.

3 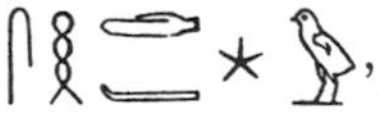, l. 291.

4 Lines 290, 291.

5 .

6 The epithets  (or ) and  are unintelligible.

7 , l. 292.

8 Stable One.

9 , l. 293.

10 , l. 293.

11 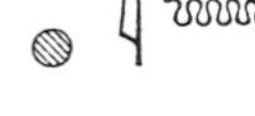, l. 301.

12 Ḥeru-p-kherṭ, the later Harpokrates.

thou shalt travel among them in the following of thy brothers, the gods.[1] Thy water is in heaven, thy solid parts are on earth ; thou art fashioned, thou art satisfied. Thy foot is behind thee. The god Urur gives thee the fluid of life.[2]

The next three paragraphs refer chiefly to serpents. Mention is made of Sepa-ur,[3] who descends and circles about the Two Houses, and of Åqeru, Åqert, Neni, and Thethu.[4] Horus goes round following his Eye, and the serpent Neni ploughs the earth. Next comes the curious passage: "The hand of the deceased comes to "thee. The hand fetters the great one who is in the "House of Life (Ḥet-ānkh). It grasps, he lives not ; it "seizes, his head is not fastened [to his body]. Fall "down, turn back."[5]

The next paragraph contains a spell which was used against the serpent Tcheser-ṭeṭȧ, to whom several names are given. It begins: Rā rises on thee. Horus has stretched his nine bows against this spirit which comes forth from the earth. The head is cut, the tail is severed, Tcheser-ṭeṭȧ, son of Serqet-ḥetu.[6] Thou circlest, thou art overturned, thou art destroyed by him, Ḥefen, Ḥefnent. He hears, the earth hears, thy father Ḳeb hears. If thou hearest not him thou hearest his . . . in thy head. Serȧu,[7] lie down! If the hand of the deceased seizes thee thou diest, if his hand touches thee thou dost not live. Shu stands on thy fetters; thou circlest, thou art overturned. The fingers of the deceased are on thee, the fingers of the Lynx[8] which dwells in the House of Life. Thou spittest, fall down,

[1] Lines 301–302.

[2] , l. 304.

[3] , l. 304.

[4] 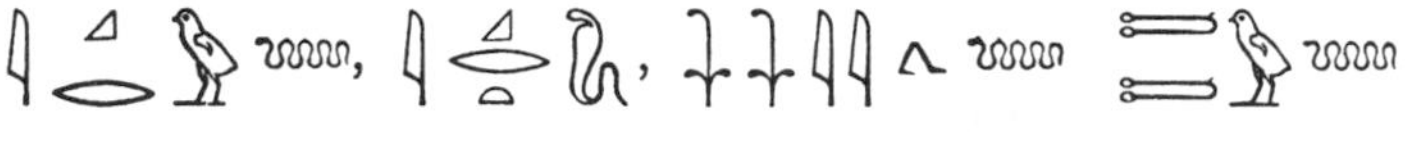.

[5] Line 308.

[6] 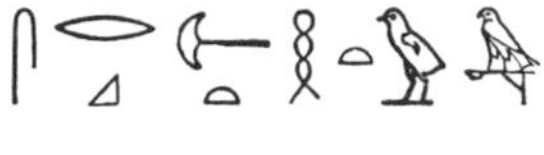, l. 309.

[7] , l. 309.

[8] , l. 310.

retreat, be overturned! Horus tramples on thee, thou livest not; Set hacks at thee, thou standest not up.[1]

Several of the paragraphs which follow in the text are spells which were used against serpents. In l. 311 Tcheser-tep, the dweller in the bushes,[2] is adjured to fall down and retreat, and in l. 312 Horus is said to kick another serpent in the mouth with his foot. In l. 313 Seràu is adjured to retreat, and his overthrow is decreed. In the following paragraph we read: "He is pure, his KA is pure. He is sound, he is sound, Horus has made sound his body. He is sound, he is sound, Set has made sound his body. His body is sound among you. He is bound up like Horus, he is drawn with a cord like Osiris. Horus drags along the serpent which falls headlong; Set drags him along and the monster falls on his face. The foot of the deceased and the foot of Mafṭet trample upon him, and the hand of the deceased and the hand of Mafṭet are laid upon him. He (the deceased) seizes him by the face. Sàu[3] serpent, lie down! Nāu[4] serpent, retreat!

In the paragraph which begins with l. 331 it is said, "The Eye of Horus sheds moisture on the leaves of the Tchenu tree;"[5] and the two Horus-gods who are at the head of the houses [and] the lord of food, the great god in Ȧnu, are entreated to give bread, and beer, and abundance to the deceased, to supply his altars with offerings, and to fill his slaughter house with victims for sacrifice. If he hungers the two Lion-gods[6] hunger; if he thirsts Nekhebit thirsts.[7] The *heṭenth*[8] incense is brought to him in bags by the god Heṭenut.[9]

He sees the Great Crown (?), he receives the Great

[1] Lines 308–311.

[2] 

[3] 

[4] , l. 315.

[5] 

[6] *I.e.*, Shu and Tefnut, 

[7] Lines 331, 332.

[8] 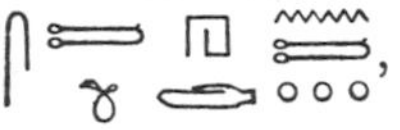, l. 332.

[9] , l. 332.

Crown (?), his face has fallen on the Great Crown (?).[1] The god Ḥu places his hair[2] on him, he (the deceased) sails on his lake, his body is in his following.

In the next paragraph we see that the deceased is identified wholly with the Earth-god and with Rā: He makes broad his seat with Ḳeb, he makes high the starry firmament with Rā, he walks about in the Fields of Offerings,[3] he is the Eye of Rā, which lies down, and conceives, and gives birth each day. Next we have an appeal to the Four Bulls of Tem, who are asked to provide the deceased with food:—O Uatch-āab-f,[4] the chief of thy field, O Uba-ukhikh,[5] the chief of thy sycamore tree, O 'Theḥen-āṭebu,[6] the chief of thy date palm, O Lord of the Green Fields,[7] he is with you, let him live upon what ye live. O ye Four Bulls of Tem, make ye him to flourish, (or, have abundance), let him have the Net Crown upon his head and water for his legs and dates in his hand.[8]

O Rā, O Uakhtȧ, O Uakhtȧ, O Pentȧ, O Pentȧ! He (*i.e.*, the deceased) is thou, thou art he. He cries with joy, his Ka cries with joy. Thou lightest him, he lights thee. He is sound, he makes thee sound. He flourishes, he makes thee flourish. He is thine eye on the brow of Hathor. The years turn back, turn back, on him, he lies down, he is conceived, he is born every day.[9] Homage to thee, Rā, in thy beauty, in thy beauties, in

1 

2 , l. 332.

3 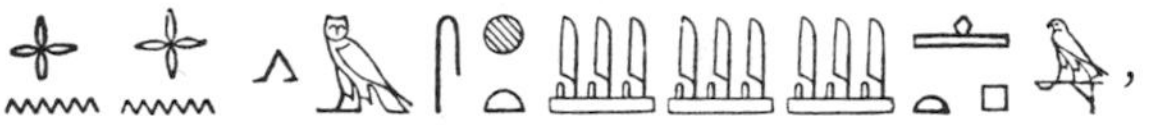, l. 333.

4 

5 

6 

7 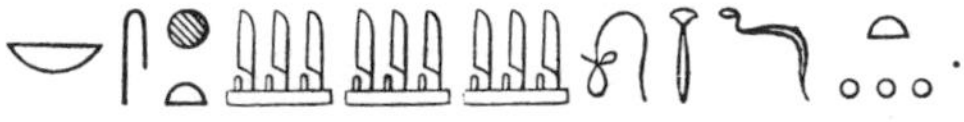

8 Lines 333–336.

9 Lines 336–338.

thy seats, in thy properties (?). Thou bringest the milk of Isis to him, and the water-flood of Nephthys. He goes round about the lake [and on] the flood of the Great Green Sea.[1] Life, strength, health, gladness of heart, bread, beer, apparel and provisions of all kinds, whereon he lives! He hears the Āfa-gods,[2] he rejoices during the days,[3] he is content during the nights. He collects the offerings which they have offered on their tables of offerings. He sees thee when thou comest forth as Thoth working forward the Boat of Rā to his field in Ȧasu,[4] when thou goest at the head of those who rejoice.[5]

He (*i.e.*, the deceased) is purified, and he takes his pure seat in heaven. He makes firm, he makes firm his beautiful seat. He takes his pure seat on the front of the Boat of Rā. When the rowers transport Rā they transport him also; when the rowers make Rā to travel about the horizon, they make him also to travel about the horizon. He opens his mouth, he makes a passage through his nostrils, and a way into his ears, he weighs the word, he judges the Two Brothers, and he gives commands to him that is greater than himself. Rā purifies him, and Rā protects him from the hand of him that would work evil against him. The Great God falls by his side. The dweller in Neṭȧt[6] goes about, Rā lifts up his head,[7] he abominates sleep, he hates weakness. O flesh of the deceased, decay not, perish not and have no foul smell. Thy foot shall not go from thee, thy stride shall not slip, thou shalt not step upon filth, O Osiris. Thou traversest the sky like Orion, thy soul is provided like the star Sepṭet (Sothis). Possess thy soul being strong, have strength being strong. Thy soul

1 , l. 338.

2 , l. 339.

3 .

4 , or , ll. 338–340.

5 Lines 340–342.

6 , l. 346.

7 *I.e.*, the head of the deceased.

stands up among the gods, like Horus, the dweller in Åru.[1] Thy book (?) comes to the heart of the gods, like the Net Crown  upon the Båt Crown , like the Måsut Crown[2] on the king, like the beard on the Mentu folk. Thou seizest the hand of the imperishable stars, thy bones are not destroyed, thy flesh wastes not, thy members rot not away from thee, for behold, thou art one of the gods. Thou sailest to the city Pe, thou sailest to the city Nekhen, Smentet . . . . thee, thou art arrayed like the men of the south (?). Thy father comes to thee in peace, Rā comes to thee in peace. The doors of heaven are opened to thee, the doors of the firmament are unbolted for thee. He (*i.e.*, the deceased) comes like a jackal of the south, the jackal which is on his belly, the Messenger-god,[3] who is at the head of Ȧnu. The great goddess Ḥunt[4] who dwells in Ȧnu gives her hands to thee. Thou hadst no mother among men to give thee birth, thou hadst no father among men to give thee birth. Thy mother was Samt-urt, who dwells in Nekheb, with the White Crown, and the wig, and the two full feathers, and the two full, hanging breasts. She suckled thee, and she did not let thee lack [milk]. Thou didst lean on thy left side, thou didst sit on thy right side. The seats are hidden among the gods. Rā lifts up thy face on his shoulder. The odour of thee is as their odour, thy sweat is the sweat of the Two Companies of the Gods. Rise with thy wig on thee, make the palm of thy hand grasp the Mas[5] sceptre and whip, make thy fist to hold firmly the club. Stand up at the head of the Ȧterti,[6] judge (or, weigh the words of) the gods, the aged ones who revolve round Rā, the ancestors of the Morning Star (Venus). Give birth to thyself month by month like the moon, lift up thy face in the horizon. The imperishable stars

1 , l. 351.

2 .

3 , l. 357.

4 .

5 , l. 363.

6 The two halves of the sky, or, the North and the South.

follow and minister unto thee. Thou presentest (?) thyself to Rā at his coming. Thou art pure. Thou appearest for Rā, heaven shall never be empty of thee.[1]

Rise up, father! Thy water is to thee, thy flood is to thee, thy milk is to thee in the breasts of thy mother Isis. Rise up, O Son of Horus, who art born of the dweller in the city of Tchebā-kherut. Behold, Set is the dweller in Ḥent (?). This great one lies down, he sleeps. Wake up, rise up, thou hast received thy head, thou hast collected thy bones for thyself, thou hast searched out thy effluxes. Sit thou, then, on thy throne of iron (?). Thou eatest the thigh, thou hast gone through flesh and bone, thou feedest upon thy food in heaven with the gods.[2] Hail, thou hast received thy robe of honour, thou hast arrayed thyself in the Ḥatȧ garment. Thou art clothed with the Eye of Horus, the dweller in the city of Taȧt, which gives thee thy apparel before the gods. Through it thou takest possession of the Urert Crown before Horus, the Lord of men. Hail to thee, Tait,[3] mistress of the lips (?) of the great nestling. The divine one kisses his brother. Touch the head of the deceased, which is not fastened [to his body], gather thou together his bones which are not tied together. Let love for him be in the body of every god who shall see him.[4] This is the swathing which Horus made for his father Osiris.

O great one, who liest on thy mother Nut, thy mother Taȧt clothes thee, she lifts thee up to heaven in her name of "Tchert."[5] She finds her Horus. This is thy Horus, O Isis. Make thou his hand to pass to Rā in the horizon. Homage to thee, O Ḥātet Oil! Homage to thee, dweller on the breast of Horus, which Horus placed on the brow (or, skull) of his father Osiris. He (*i.e.*, the deceased) sets you on his brow as Horus set you on the brow of his father Osiris.

Homage to thee on this thy day! Thou standest before Rā [when] he appears from the East. Thou art

[1] Lines 346–367.

[2] Lines 368–372.

[3] 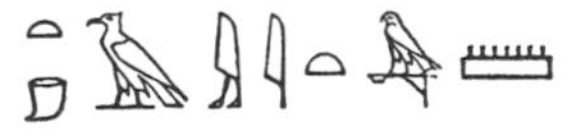, l. 376.

[4] Lines 373–378.

[5] , l. 381.

provided with thy form,[1] O dweller among the spirits. Thou swingest thine arms, thou stridest with thy legs, thou wavest joyfully thy hands. Isis grasps thee by the hand, she brings thee in among the *menȧu*,[2] the earth is rewarded, those who watch for thee rejoice. Ȧnpu Khenti-Ȧmenti gives an offering! Thy thousands of loaves of bread, thy thousands of pots of beer, thy thousands of vessels of oil, thy thousands of linen garments, thy thousands of suits of apparel, and thy thousands of bulls. The *Smen*-goose is slain for thee, the *Terp*-goose is killed for thee. Horus destroys the evil appertaining to thee by means of his Four [sons], Set forgets what he would do to thee by means of his Eight [fiends]. The doors are opened for those whose seats are hidden. Stand up! Turn to thy earth, seek out thy effluxes, rise up. Thou sailest among the Spirits. Thy wings are like those of a hawk, thy movement (?) is like that of a star. No ruin falls on thee. Thy heart is not vanquished, thy breast is not taken possession of, thou art a great one, safe with the Urert Crown. Thou art complete in thy members of crystal (?). Thou walkest across heaven to Sekhet-Ȧaru, thou makest thy stay permanent in Sekhet-ḥetepet, among the imperishable stars who follow Osiris. Hail, thou pure one, Rā censes thee. Beautiful is thy purity, and made abiding. Established, thou art established among the gods, established. Established, thou art established among the beings of the Hall of the God, established. Thou movest, thou travellest, a shining being, thou art a god of light above the thigh[3] (or passage) of heaven.[4]

From the text of Pepi I a very considerable number of facts may be gleaned as to the state in which the blessed were believed to dwell in the Other World. The paragraphs are longer and fuller than those of the texts of Unȧs and Tetȧ, the language is clearer, and the sentences are less disjointed and abrupt. The following translations illustrate their contents:—

1 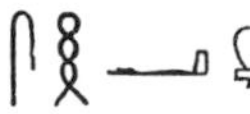, l. 385. 2 , l. 387.

3 Perhaps the passage which led from earth to heaven.

4 Lines 382–399.

The Princess Nesi-ta-neb-asher in the Elysian Fields.

From the Greenfield Papyrus, in the British Museum (No. 10,554).

Hail, thou Pepi! Thou journeyest, thou shinest, thou art strong like the god, and hast thy seat like Osiris. Thy soul is to thee within thee, thy power (*sekhem*) is to thee about thee. Thy Ureret Crown is on thy head, thy Mȧsut Crown is to thee, above thy shoulders. Thy face is before thee, those who praise thee are on both sides of thee, the Followers of the God are behind thee, the Forms of the God are on both sides of thee. They shout:—The god comes, the god comes, Pepi comes on the throne of Osiris. This spirit comes, the dweller in Neṭȧt, the Chief dwelling in Ȧbṭu (Abydos). Isis speaks to thee, Nephthys addresses thee. The Spirits come to thee with bowings, they smell (*i.e.*, kiss) the ground at thy feet. Thy slaughter is in the towns of the god Sȧa. Then thou comest forth before thy mother Nut. She grasps thy hand, she makes for thee a way into the horizon, to that place where Rā is. The doors of heaven are open to thee, the doors of the sky are unbolted for thee. Thou findest Rā, standing up he guards thee. He grasps thee by the hand, he conducts thee through the Ȧterti of heaven, he sets thee on the throne of Osiris.

Hail, Pepi! The Eye of Horus comes to thee, it speaks to thee. Thy soul, the dweller among the gods, comes to thee; thy power, the dweller among the spirits, comes to thee. As a son defends his father, as Horus defends Osiris, so Horus defends Pepi from his enemies. Thou standest up, being protected, thou art wholly like the god, thou art provided with the form[1] of Osiris on the throne of Khent-Ȧmenti. Thou doest what he does among the imperishable Spirits. Thy son stands on thy throne endowed with thy form, he does what thou doest at the head of the living, according to the command of Rā, the great god. He ploughs [the land for] grain and for barley, he makes an offering to thee thereof.

Hail, Pepi, Rā hath given unto thee all life and serenity (or, well-being) for ever; thy word, thy body, thou hast received the form of the God. Thou art great there before the gods who are at the head of the Lake.

Hail, Pepi, thy soul stands up among the gods, among the spirits. Thy fear is in their breasts.

[1] , l. 16.

Hail, Pepi! Thou standest up on thy throne at the head of the living ones. Thy slaughter is in their breasts, Thy name lives upon the earth, thy name grows old upon the earth, thou perishest not, thou comest not to an end.[1]

Hail, Osiris Pepi! This libation is presented to thee, thou art refreshed before Horus in thy name of "Comer forth from Qebḥu." Incense is presented unto thee, thou becomest God. Thy mother Nut makes thee to be as God to thine enemy in thy name of "God." The effluxes which came forth from thee are presented unto thee. Horus has made the gods to hold thee up to the uttermost limit of every place where thou journeyest. The effluxes which came forth from thee are presented unto thee. Horus has made his sons to count thee up to the uttermost limit of the place of which thou takest possession. Horus counts for thee two years,[2] thou renewest thy youth in thy name of "Mu-Renpu."[3] A soul is to Horus, he discerns his father in thee in his name of "Ḥeru-Bȧt."[4]

Hail, Pepi! Thy journeying and the journeying of these thy Mothers are [like] the journeying of Horus when he journeyed with these [same] Mothers. Those who form his bodyguard follow his steps, and they convey him as Director into the East. Hail, thou Pepi, thy shoulders are like the divine messengers[5] (Upȧu), thy face is like Up-uat. Hail, thou Pepi. SUTEN ḤETEP TĀ![6] Thou sittest in thy Domains of Horus, thou walkest about in thy Domains of Set. Thou sittest on thy throne of iron. Thou weighest their words at the head of the Great Company of the Gods who dwell in Ȧnu. Hail, Pepi! The god

1 Lines 1–21. 2 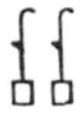, or, perhaps, a second season of youth.

3 , *i.e.*, "water of youth."

4 , ll. 31–34. 5 , l. 42.

6 These words mean "King, give an offering," and in very early times the king, no doubt, did send a gift of funerary food to each of his favoured servants when he was about to be buried. The use of them here shows that so far back as the VIth dynasty these words had become a mere formula, for Pepi was himself king.

Khent-n-Merti[1] protects thee as thou herdest thy calves. Hail, Pepi! Ār . . .[2] protects thee against the Spirits. Hail, Pepi! Know that thou receivest this divine offering, which is offered to thee each day, a thousand bread-cakes, a thousand pots of beer, a thousand bulls, a thousand geese, a thousand of every pleasant thing, a thousand garments of every kind. Hail, Pepi! Thy water is to thee, thy flood is to thee, thy *besen* grains are to thee, brought to thee before thy divine brother Nekhekh. Osiris Pepi, thou art defended. All the gods give thee their flesh and their food, and all their possessions. Thou shalt not die.[3] Osiris Pepi, thou art crowned king of the South and king of the North. Thy strength is from the gods and their Doubles (KAU). O goddess Nut, spread thyself over thy son Osiris Pepi. Protect him from the hand of Set, guard him, O Nut. Come, protect thy son. Come, protect this great one. O Nut, bend over thy son Osiris Pepi, guard thou him, O great guardian. Let this great one be among thy children. O Nut, through Ḳeb thou didst become a spirit (?), thou hadst power in the womb of thy mother Tefnet before thou wast brought forth. Guard thou Pepi in life and well-being, and let him not die![4] Thou hadst strength of heart, thou didst move in the womb of thy mother in thy name of "Nut." O mighty daughter who hadst power in thy mother, who wast crowned Queen of the North,[5] make thou Pepi to be glorious (or, mighty?) within thee, and let him not die![6] O Mighty Lady who art in heaven, thou hast power (or, dominion). Thou goest about, thou makest every place to be full of thy beauty. All the earth is under thee, thou hast taken possession of it. Thou encirclest the earth, everything is in thy two hands. Make thou this Pepi to be an imperishable star in thee.[7] Thou art mistress (?) in Ḳeb in thy name of "Pet," thou hast united the whole earth in every place. O Exalted One

1 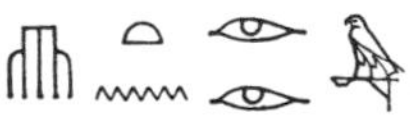, or Khent-merti 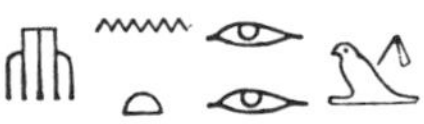, l. 44.

2 , l. 45.

3 Lines 40–58.

4 Line 62.

5 .

6 Lines 62, 63.

7 Line 63.

over the earth, thou art the head of thy father Shu, thou hast dominion over him. He loves thee, placing himself and all things under thee.[1] Thou hast taken possession of every god [bringing him] before thee with his boat,[2] thou hast appointed them to be stars in the form of the Dekans,[3] and assuredly they shall not cease from thee as stars. Do not thou cause Pepi to depart from thee in thy name of "Ḥert."

Curiously enough, the next paragraph (ll. 64, 65) supplies us with the royal names of Osiris Pepi on earth. He, the child of Nut, is called as Horus, "Meri-taui"; as king of the South and North, "Pepi"; his Nebti[4] name is "Meri khat Pepi," and as the triple hawk of gold he is also called Pepi. As the heir of Ḳeb, who loved him, and as the beloved of all the gods, he is called "Pepi," "to whom are given life, stability, well-being, and joy of heart, like Rā, living for ever." The text continues :—

Thy water is to thee, thy flood is to thee, the effluxes[5] coming forth from the god, the matter which cometh forth from Osiris. Thy two hands are washed, thine ears have a passage through them, this Power makes glorious his soul (?). Thy two hands are washed, thy KA is washed, thy KA sits and eats bread with thee for ever and ever. This thy journeying makes thee to be on thy throne. Thy face is before thee, those who praise thee are close to thee. Thy nostrils are gratified with the odour of the goddess Åkhet-utet.[6] Behold, thy legs walk round at thy festival, thy teeth and thy

[1] The allusion is to the old legend in which Shu is made to place himself between the Earth-god Ḳeb and the Sky-goddess Nut, whom he raised up to her place above the earth on his two hands.

[2] , l. 64.

[3] , l. 64.

[4] See Moret, *Royauté Pharaonique*, p. 30; my *Book of Kings*, Vol. I, p. xv f.

[5] , or , l. 66.

[6] , l. 68.

nails count (?) thy pools. Thou sailest like a great bull [through] An-uatchet (?) to the Fields of Rā, which he loves. Rise up, thou Pepi, thou shalt not die.[1]

Horus wakes up, standing up to Set. Rise thou up, like Osiris, as a spirit, the son of Ḳeb, upon him. Stand thou up like Anpu upon the . . . The Nine tremble before thee, making to thee [bowings of] heads. Thou art pure with the incense of Horus, thou risest up (or, art crowned) on the first day of the month. Menȧt-urt[2] addresses thee, as En-urtch-nef[3] stands up in the city of Abydos, hearing the things which the gods say. Rā speaks, he makes this Pepi glorious. He receives his spirit at the head of the gods, even Horus, the son of Osiris. He gives to him his spirit among the Watchers of the city of Pu,[4] he gives him the form[5] of a god among the Watchers of Nekhenu. The earth speaks, the doors of Aker are open to thee, the doors of Ḳeb are unbolted for thee. Thou comest forth at the word (or, voice) of Ȧnpu, he makes thee to be glorious like Thoth. Thou judgest the gods, thou settest a limit (?) for the Petchet,[6] between the Two Powers[7] when thou art made glorious by the decree of Ȧnpu. Thy stride is the stride of Horus. Thy word is the word of Set. Thou journeyest to the Lake, thou advancest to the nome of Teni (Thinis). Thou sailest through the city of Ȧbṭu (Abydos). Thou openest the gate in heaven [leading] to the horizon, and the hearts of the gods rejoice at meeting thee. They draw thee to the sky with thy soul, and thou becomest a soul among them. Thou comest forth to heaven, like Horus in the womb of the sky,[8] in this thy

1 Lines 66–69.

2 , l. 70.

3 , l. 70.

4 , l. 71.

5 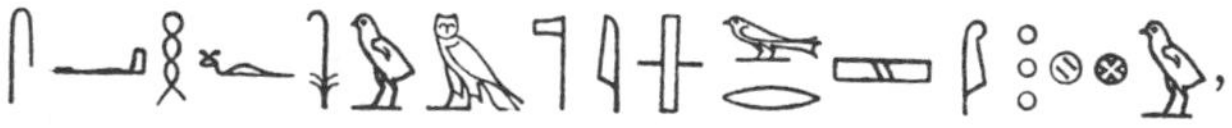, l. 72.

6 , l. 73.

7 , l. 73.

8 , l. 75.

form which comes forth from the mouth of Rā, like Horus at the head of the Spirits. Thou art seated on thy throne of crystal (?), thou art more crystal (?) than heaven. Thou directest the roads of the Petchet, Horus brings thee in, the heart of Set, the great one of Ȧnu makes friends with thee. Thou sailest over the Lake of Kha, in the north of heaven, like a star passing over the Great Green Sea with the constellation Khat-Nut, thy hand grasps the Ṭuat of heaven (?) as far as the place where is the star Seḥ (Orion). The Bull of heaven gives thee his hand. Thou hast thy meat and drink from the meat and drink of the gods which they eat and drink. The odour of Ṭeṭun the Great, the Child of the South,[1] who comes forth from Ta-sti, is upon thee, he gives to thee the incense wherewith the gods are censed there. The Two Daughters of the king of the North[2] give birth to thee, the great ladies of his head. Rā hails thee from the . . . of heaven, like Horus Khent-ment-f, thou art filled, the Lord of Sebut, like the Jackal, Chief of the Lake of the Petchet, like the Jackal, the Chief of the Pure Land. He places thee like the Morning Star in the Field of Reeds (Sekhet-Ȧaru). Thou sittest on thy throne, Sekhmet,[3] the Lord of the Petchet lifts up thy knife. Thou hast in great abundance in the Field of the gods the meat and drink which the gods live upon therein. Thou hast thy state of glory, thy ministrants bring offerings to thee. Thou hast thy faculty of knowledge, thou hast with thee those who adored thee on earth (?).

SUTEN ṬĀ ḤETEP. Anubis gives an offering, thy thousand of gazelles and antelopes, for the desert lands come to thee with bowed heads. SUTEN ṬĀ ḤETEP. Anubis gives an offering. Thy thousand bread-cakes, thy thousand pots of beer, thy thousand grains of purification which come forth from the Hall, thy thousand pleasant offerings of all kinds of things, thy thousand bulls, thy thousand offerings of all kinds.

1 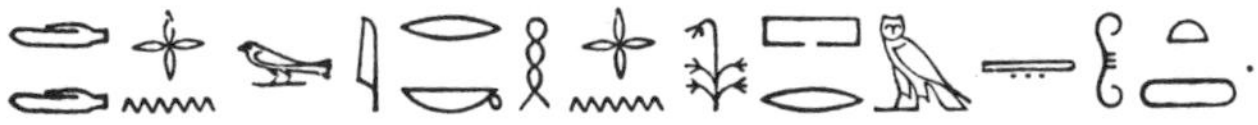.

2 , l. 79.

3 , l. 81.

Thou eatest them at the dictates of thy heart. The palm tree follows thee, the mulberry tree bows its head to thee, through what Ȧnpu does for thee.[1]

Ihȧ, Ihȧ, thou hast made him, this Ihȧ, my father. Thy fathers were not men, thy mothers were not women. Thy father is Sma-ur, thy mother[s] are the Four young women. Live the life; behold thou shalt not die death, even as lives Horus Khent-Sekḥem. He has opened the Great Chamber in Ȧnu, the great director of the tomb, the very great one of the funerary chest, Khent-Menti. She gives thee water on every first and every fifteenth days of the month. Thou givest to the Great Ones, thou guidest the little ones, thy meat is to thee in the slaughter-house of Khent-Menti, the lords of loyal service give thee thy reward.[2] Pepi is the country (or, the god) Setet, the conqueror of the Two Lands, whose flame receives its two portions. Pepi comes forth to heaven. He finds Rā, standing up he meets him. He sits upon his shoulders, Rā permits him not to rest upon the ground, [for] he knows that Pepi is greater than he. Pepi is more a Spirit than the Spirits, more perfect than the Perfect Ones,[3] more stable than the Stable Ones.[4] The festival of Pepi is abundant in offerings. Pepi stands up at the north of heaven with him, he takes possession of the Two Lands like a king of his gods.[5]

Thou lovest thy life, Horus, chief of his veritable amulet of "life."[6] Thou sealest (or, closest) the two doors of heaven, thou pushest away those who close the doors thereof, as thou drawest the Ka of Pepi into this heaven to know the nobles of the god,[7] the lovers of the god, who are raised up on their sceptres, who watch the country of the South, who are arrayed in garments like those of . . . . , who live upon figs, who drink wine, who are anointed with ointment of the

[1] Lines 79–84. [2] Lines 84–87. [3] .

[4] , or . [5] Lines 90–92.

[6] , l. 93. [7] , l. 94.

finest quality, the Chief speaks [for] Pepi before the Great God, he introduces him to the Great God.[1]

Thou ploughest the earth, thou hast gotten the offering on thy two hands. Thou journeyest on the road whereon the gods journeyed. Thou goest round about, thou seest these offerings about thee, which the king makes to thee, which Khent-Åmenti makes to thee, and thou journeyest towards these imperishable gods of the North.[2]

This Great One falls on his side, the dweller in Neṭȧt holds him up. Rā takes thy hand, the Two Companies of the Gods lift up thy head. Behold, he comes as the star Seḥ (Orion); behold, Osiris comes as the star Seḥ (Orion), the lord of wine in the Uaḳ festival. Assuredly his mother says: "Heir,"[3] [and] his father says: "Heaven conceives, the Ṭuat brings forth." Hail, Pepi, heaven has conceived thee with the star Seḥ, the Ṭuat has brought thee forth with the star Seḥ. Life, life, by the command of the gods, thou livest! Thou comest forth (risest) with the star Seḥ in the eastern part of heaven; thou settest with the star Seḥ in the western part of the heaven. Thy third is the star Sepṭet (Sothis, the Dog-Star), whose seats are pure, she guides thee over the beautiful roads in heaven into the Field of Reeds.[4]

O goddess Nut, in whose head appear two eyes, who hast taken possession of Horus and art his great one of words of power, who hast taken possession of Set and art his great one of words of power, Nut, who hast decreed thy birth in thy name of "Repit-Ȧnu,"[5] decree thou this Pepi for life, and that he shall not perish. O Nut, who hast risen as the Queen of the North, who hast dominion over the gods, and over their KAU (Doubles), and their flesh and bones, and their food, and all their possessions. O Nut, grant that this Pepi shall subsist and live. O Nut, thou livest, Pepi shall live.[6]

[1] Lines 93–95.

[2] Lines 95, 96.

[3] , or 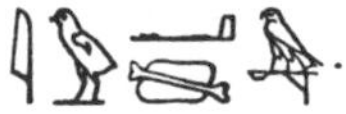.

[4] Lines 97–100.

[5] 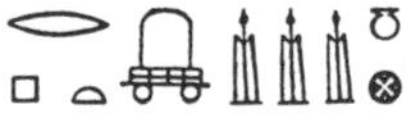, l. 101.

[6] Lines 100–192.

Osiris Pepi, thy mother Nut spreads herself over thee, and she protects thee from every evil thing. Nut draws thee away from every evil thing, thou art the Great One among her children. Whosoever passes passes with his KA. Osiris passes with his KA. Set passes with his KA. Khent-Merti (?) passes with his KA. Thy word passes with thy KA. Hail, thou Pepi, the comer comes, thou movest (?) not. Thy mother comes, thou movest not. Nut, thou movest not; Khnemt-urt, thou movest not; the terrible Khnemt, thou movest not. She fashions thee, she gives thee a spirit, she gives thee thy head, she presents to thee thy bones, she joins together thy flesh, she brings to thee thy heart into thy body. Thou art master of thy speech, thou issuest commands to those who are in thy following, thou makest to flourish thy house after thee, thou protectest thy children from grief, thou art pure with the purity of the gods, who journey unceasingly (?).[1]

Thoth presents to Pepi his life which was not to him, Thoth has given to him the Eye of Horus. Horus is in Osiris Pepi, the Eye of Horus has been presented before thee.[2]

Hail, thou Pepi! Thou goest, thou livest, for behold, if thou didst not go, thou wouldst die. Thou goest, thou art made glorious at the head of the Spirits, thou art strong at the head of the living. A soul hath been made in thee, thou livest as a soul; thou willest, thou usest thy will. The comer comes, thou movest not. Thy mother comes, thou movest not. Nut comes to thee, thou movest not. Khenemet-Urt comes to thee, thou movest not. She fashions thee, she gives thee a spirit, she gives thee thy head, she presents to thee thy bones, she makes complete for thee thy flesh, she brings to thee thy heart in thy body. Thou art master of thy speech, thou issuest commands to those who are before thee. Thou protectest thy children from grief. Thou art pure with the purity of the gods, the lords of things, who journey with their KAU.[3]

Hail, thou Pepi! Wake up! Rise up! Stand up. Thou art pure. Thy KA is pure. Thy soul is pure. Thy power is pure. Thy mother comes to thee. Nut,

[1] Lines 103–106. [2] Line 107. [3] Lines 107–111.

Shenmet-Urt, comes to thee. She purifies thee, O Pepi. She fashions thee, O Pepi. She protects thee. Hail, thou Pepi! Thou art pure. Thy KA is pure. Thy power is pure among the spirits, thy soul is pure among the gods. Hail, thou Pepi! Thy bones are presented to thee. Thou hast received thy head before Ḳeb; he destroys the evil which appertains to thee, O Pepi, before Tem. Hail, thou Pepi! Stand up. Thou art pure. Thy KA is pure. Horus purifies thee in the celestial ocean.[1] Thou art pure with the purity of Shu, thou art pure with the purity of Tefnet. Thou art pure with the purity of the four Spirit Houses,[2] who acclaim (?) [thee] in Pe. Therefore art thou pure. Thy mother Nut, Khenemet-urt, purifies thee, she fashions thee. Thou hast received thy head. Thy bones are presented to thee before Ḳeb. The evil which appertains to this Pepi is destroyed, the evil which appertains to him before Tem is destroyed.[3] Hail, thou Pepi! Stand up! Thou art arrayed in the Eye of Horus, thou hast taken it upon thee; join it to thee, join it to thy flesh. Thou comest forth in it, the gods see thee dressed therein. Thou hast taken possession of the Great Ureret Crown before the Great Company of the Gods in Ȧnu. Hail, thou Pepi! Life to thee. The Eye of Horus is brought to thee, it shall never, never depart from thee.[4]

Osiris Pepi, thou hast encircled every god with thine arms, and their lands and also all their possessions. Osiris Pepi, great one, thou goest round the whole circuit of the Ḥa-nebut.[5]

O Filler of the Lakes, who makest to blossom the watercourses of the pure lake which comes forth from Osiris, the Erpā[6] of the Ten Great Ones of Memphis, and of the Ten Great Ones of Ȧnu, and of the Great Company of the Gods, seat thyself and look at this pure one, at this Osiris Pepi. He is censed with the *smen* incense and with *beṭ* incense, [which are] the saliva that

1 , l. 115.

2 .

3 Lines 114–116.

4 Lines 117, 118.

5 , or , l. 122.

6 *I.e.*, Chief.

comes forth from the mouth of Horus, and the spittle that comes forth from the mouth of Set, wherewith Horus was purified, whereby the evil which appertained to him was cast to the earth when Set performed [the censing] for him; wherewith Set was purified, whereby the evil which appertained to him was cast to the earth when Horus performed [the censing] for him. This Pepi is purified thereby, [and] the evil which appertains to him is cast to the earth . . . .[1]

The doors of heaven are opened for thee, the doors of the sky are unbolted for thee, which are shut against the Rekhit. Menȧt[2] addresses thee, the Ḥenmemet[3] beings hold converse with thee, the imperishable stars stand up [before] thee, thy winds are incense, thy north wind[4] is warm. Thou art the Great One in Abydos, thou art the Morning Star which appears in the eastern part of heaven, to which Horus of the Ṭuat has given his body. O great and exalted one among the imperishable stars, thou shalt never perish.[5]

O ye gods of the horizon, who dwell in heaven to its uttermost limit, if ye love the life of Tem anoint ye yourselves with unguents, array ye yourselves in your apparel, take ye your bread (?), and take ye by the hand this Pepi, place ye him in Sekhet-ḥetep, place ye his spirit among the Spirits, place ye his Power among the gods. He makes to you a large offering, a great oblation. He sails over heaven, those who dwell in the regions[6] thereof conduct him. There Pepi takes possession of the Urert Crown like Horus, the son of Tem.[7] Hail, thou Pepi! Thou art the Great Star. Orion beareth thee on his shoulder. Thou traversest heaven with Orion, thou sailest through the Ṭuat with Osiris. This Pepi appears in the eastern part of the sky. Thou art renewed in thy season, thou becomest young again at thine appointed time. Nut brings forth this Pepi with the constellation of Orion. The year

1 Lines 123–128.

2 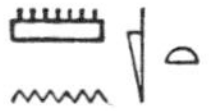, l. 155.

3 .

4 Usually a cool, pleasant wind.

5 Lines 153–159.

6 .

7 Lines 161, 162.

binds thee with Osiris. Are given to thee thy two arms. Thou descendest under protection (?), are given to thee bread, wine, and cake which are set before thee. Menanet-urt calls to thee, behold Osiris . . . . his two hands. Hail, thou Pepi, thou sailest, thou arrivest protected by the Great Lake[1] . . . . Thou art endowed with a soul, with power, and with will. [Thy] two hands are brought [to thee], the stride of this Pepi is long. This Pepi shines in the east like Rā, he travels in the west like Khepren.[2] This Pepi lives on what Horus, the Lord of heaven, lives on, by the command of Horus, the Lord of heaven. Rā purifies this Pepi. He descends on his throne. He takes his paddle, he ferries Rā about in the wide space of heaven, a star of gold, the tiara of the Bull that gives light, a brother (?) of gold in the vault of heaven. He flies, flies, flies from you, O men. He belongs not to the earth, he belongs to heaven. O god of the double city, his Ka is in thy two fingers. He pounces upon heaven like the āḥāu bird, he kisses heaven like the hawk. He goes round about heaven like Ḥeru-Khuti[3] . . . . He is not turned back (?), a king. He suffers not, Bastet. He makes not . . . . like Ur-ā.[4] If he be the son of Rā he will make his seat; Pepi has made a seat. If he be the son of Rā he will be safe; Pepi is safe. If [Rā] hungers Pepi hungers.[5]

This great one watches before his Ka, this great one opens his mouth before his Ka, and this Pepi watches before his Ka, he opens his mouth before his Ka. This great one keeps watch, this Pepi keeps watch, the gods keep watch, the Powers wake up. Hail, thou Pepi, rise up, stand up. The Great Company of the gods who are in Ȧnu have adjudged thee to thy great seat. Thou sittest at the head of the gods and art Chief of Ḳeb, the hereditary Chief of the gods, and Osiris, the Chief of the Powers, and Horus, Lord of men[6] and of the gods.

[1] Line 163.

[2] 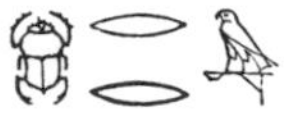, l. 163.

[3] Var., "like a grasshopper," , Pepi II, l. 860.

[4] , l 165.

[5] Lines 162–165.

[6] *Pāt*, , l. 166.

Hail, thou Pepi, who hidest thy form in that of Ȧnpu, thou hast received thy face, which is like that of a jackal. Thou standest up to guard the shrine, Chief of the Aterti, and also Ȧnpu, Chief of the Hall of the god. Thou propitiatest the Followers of Horus.[1] Horus defends thee. Horus propitiates thee. [As] Osiris lives, as the Spirit lives in Neṭȧt, [so] Pepi lives. Hail, Pepi! Thy name lives at the head of the living. Thou art a spirit at the head of the Spirits, thou art a power at the head of the Powers. Hail, Pepi, thy book (?)[2] is the Eye of Horus, which is whole, the White Crown,[3] the Uraeus-goddess dwelling in Nekheb. It (the Eye of Horus) places thy book (?), O Pepi, before the eyes of all the gods, before the eyes of the imperishable spirits, whose seats are hidden, and before the eyes of all the beings who see thee, and also those who hear thy name. Hail, Pepi! Thou art filled with the Eye of Horus, the great one[4] of souls, of manifold existences. It protects thee, Pepi, as it protected Horus. It places thy souls at the head of the Two Companies of the Gods, in the form of the Two Uraei-goddesses who are on thy forehead. They raise thee up, they lead thee before thy mother Nut, she grasps thy hand, thou movest not, thou slippest not, thou stumblest not. Horus makes thee to be a spirit at the head of the Spirits, and sets thy Power at the head of the Powers. Horus does good things for this Pepi, for this spirit, the son of a god, the son of two gods. Hail, Pepi, thy soul is the Souls of Ȧnu, thy soul is the Souls of Nekhen, thy soul is the Souls of Pe. Thy soul is a living star at the head of his brethren. Hail, thou Pepi! I am Thoth. SUTEN ṬĀ ḤETEP.[5] Thy bread shall be given to thee, thy beer shall

[1] *Shemsu Ḥeru* .

[2] , l. 166. Var. .

[3] .

[4] *I.e.*, possessing many souls.

[5] This is another proof that the words *Suten ṭā ḥetep* had become a mere pious formula. In ordinary cases the friends of the deceased spoke them, and they were cut on stelae and tombs, painted on coffins, etc., that they might be pronounced for the benefit of the dead by those who saw them. Here it is Thoth who speaks them, and the bread,

be given to thee, and thy cakes which appear before Horus in the Hall. He shall satisfy with offerings thy heart there, O Pepi, for ever and ever![1]

This Pepi is pure. He takes his paddle, he provides himself with his seat, he sits in the bows of the boat of the Two Companies of the Gods. Rā ferries him to Ȧment. He stablishes the seat of this Pepi at the head of the seats of the Lords of Doubles, he writes down [his name] at the head of the living ones. The two doors Peḥ-ka (?) in the sky are open to him, the two doors of crystal (?) in the firmament are unbolted for him, and he passes through them. His tunic is on him, his *ames* sceptre is in the hollow of his hand, he is sound with his flesh, he is happy with his name, Pepi lives with his KA. Driven away is the evil which is before him, scattered abroad is the evil which is behind him, as by the clubs (?) of him that is Chief of Sekhem. Scattered abroad is the evil which is before him, driven away is the evil which is behind him. He sees the work of the Nekhkhu,[2] the great one of goodness at their side. Pepi is good (or, happy) with them; they are good (or, happy). I am Nekhekh, the beard of Nekhekh. This Pepi shall become aged, this Pepi shall never come to an end.[3]

This Pepi has knowledge of his mother, he is not ignorant of his mother, the White Crown which conceives, the begetter, the dweller in the city of Nekheb, the lady of Per-ur, the lady of the Semȧ-land, the lady of the Hidden Land, the lady of the Field of the Fishers (?), the lady of the Lake (or, Valley) of the Ḥeteptiu beings, who registers (?) the Red Crown, lady of the lands of the city of Ṭepu. The mother of this Pepi calls, she gives her breast to him, and he sucks thereat. Son Pepi of the father, the breast is presented to thee which the father sucked. Thou livest, O father, thou wast little, father. Thou comest forth to heaven like hawks, thy feathers are like those of geese, father. The god Hetchhetch[4] brings this to this Pepi. O Sma-ur,

and beer, and cakes, which appear as a result of using the formula in the great hall of the tomb, shall never be lacking for Pepi.

[1] Lines 166–169.

[2] The aged ones (?), l. 170.

[3] Lines 169, 170.

[4] .

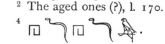

bull of offerings turn aside thy horn, make this Pepi to pass on his way, let him come. Let him journey as a being of distinction, let him journey to the heaven of life and all well-being. This Pepi sees his father, this Pepi sees Rā. Thou comest to the exalted Domains, to the Domains of Set. Are given to him the exalted Domains of the Domains of Set. The high sycamore [in] the east of heaven bows down, the gods sit on it. Pepi is the life of Horus, making a way into the sky (Qebḥ). Pepi is the great paddler who ferries [himself to] the two *khata* of heaven. Pepi is the great sandal long in [his] stride. Pure is this Pepi in Sekhet-Åaru, he dresses [himself] in the Field of the Beetle-god.[1] He finds Rā there, Rā comes forth from the East, he finds Pepi in the horizon; Rā comes forth to the West, he finds Pepi there, living and stable. Assuredly in every place whereto Rā goeth he finds Pepi there.[2]

Pepi is the god Un of the god [the son of the god], the envoy of the god. He comes, he is pure in Sekhet-Åaru. He descends (or, enters) into the Field of Kenset. The Followers of Horus[3] purify him. They purify him, they cleanse him. They recite for him the Chapter of those who are true, they recite for him the Chapter of those who come forth to life and well-being. He comes forth to heaven in life and well-being. This Pepi of life and well-being embarks in the Boat of Rā, he directs for him the rowing of the gods who row him. Every god shouts with joy when he meets this Pepi, even as he shouts for joy when [he meets Rā]. He comes forth in the east side of heaven being content, being content.[4]

Heaven cries out and earth quakes before this Pepi; he is the words[5] of power, he has the word of power. He comes, he makes the star Saḥ (Orion) to shine, he makes Osiris to advance, he sets the gods on their thrones, O Ma-ḥa-f, Bull of the gods, bring these things to him,

1 , l. 174.

2 Lines 172–174.

3 , Pepi II, l. 947.

4 Lines 175, 176.

5 , l. 176.

and place thou this Pepi in his place of life and well-being.

Make the two regions of heaven to embrace for the Mātchet Boat of Rā so that Rā may sail over them with Ḥeru-khuti to the horizon. Make the two regions of heaven to embrace for the Semktet Boat of Ḥeru-khuti, so that Ḥeru-khuti may sail over them with Rā to the horizon.

Pepi makes the two regions of heaven to come and embrace for the Māntchet Boat, and he comes forth on them with Rā to the horizon. Pepi makes the two regions of heaven to come and embrace for the Semktet Boat, and he comes forth on them with Ḥeru-khuti [to the horizon]. This Pepi comes forth on the east side of heaven where the gods are born, and he is born [there] with Horus and Khuti. This Pepi is triumphant, the KA of Pepi is triumphant.[1] His sister is Sepṭ (Sothis), he is born as the Morning Star (Venus). He finds the Spirits with their mouths provided seated on the two sides (or lips) of the Lake of Seḥseḥ,[2] the place where drinks every spirit whose mouth is provided. He is a spirit whose mouth is provided, he comes to the seat which is the most majestic of all.[3] He comes[4] with you, he makes his way onward with you in Sekhet-Ȧaru, he stops as ye stop in Sekhet-Mafkat.[5] He eats what ye eat there, he lives upon what ye live upon there, he clothes himself as ye clothe yourselves there, he anoints himself with what ye anoint yourselves there. He receives water with you from the Lake Menā at the drinking place of every spirit whose mouth is provided. He sits in front of the Great Temple (Atert), he issues commands to every spirit whose mouth is provided. He sits on the sides of the Lake of Seḥseḥ, and issues commands to every spirit whose mouth is provided.[6]

Happy are those who see the father, says Isis; content are those who see the father, says Nephthys, the father, this Osiris Pepi. He cometh forth into heaven among the

1 , l. 178.

2 .

3 Line 178.

4 Line 180.

5 , "Field of turquoise."

6 Line 181.

stars, among the imperishable stars. His headdress is on him, his knife is at his sides,[1] his words of power are at his feet. He journeys there with his mother Nut, he enters in on her in her name of "Maqet."[2] They bring to thee the gods of heaven, they gather together to thee the gods of earth. Thou art with them, thou journeyest on their hands. One brings to thee the Spirits of Pe, thou art joined to the Spirits of Nekhen. Thou art Tem. Ḳeb spake the word concerning it to Tem, who performed it. The Field of Reeds, the Domains which are above, and the Domains of Set, are to this Pepi-Tem. Ḳeb spake the word concerning it to Tem, who performed it: One comes to him, he says, "Slay him"; thou art not slain, nay, Pepi slays his enemy, and makes him to be the offering of the day. Pepi is stablished in life and well-being.[3]

Hail, thou Ferry-god![4] Carry thou this to Horus—carry his Eye. Carry thou this to Set—carry his testicles. The Eye of Horus goes and alights in the eastern part of heaven; Pepi goes with it and travels in the eastern part of heaven. He journeys, he works magic upon Rā in the place of the gods whose KAU pass, who live in the Domains of Horus, who live in the Domains of Set. Verily this Pepi comes, verily he comes forth to life and well-being. He traverses the zenith[5] of heaven, the Great Ones of the White House do not drive him away to the Mesqet of the firmament.[6] The Māntchet Boat calls to him, he makes a libation (?) thereto, and Rā makes him a lord of life and well-being.

Pure is the heaven of Rā, pure is the earth of Horus, and every god who is in them purifies this Pepi, who worships the God. Hail, thou road of this Pepi to the great hall, bear witness concerning this Pepi before

1 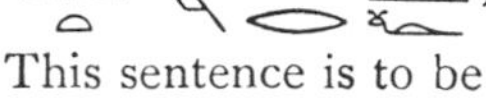, l. 182. 2 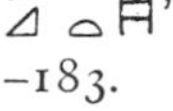, l. 182.

3 This sentence is to be said four times, ll. 181–183.

4 , Pepi II, l. 896.

5 , l. 184.

6 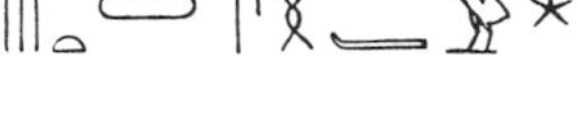, l. 184.

these two very great gods, that he is Unḳ,[1] the son of Rā, who bears heaven upon his shoulders, who is the guide of the land of the gods. Pepi takes his seat among you, O ye star-gods of the Ṭuat. Bear ye up on your shoulders this Pepi like Rā. Follow ye him like Horus. Exalt ye him like Åp-uat. Love ye him like Menu, O ye two Scribe-gods, reckon up your registers, make calculations on your number-sticks, search (?) your rolls. O Rā, who placest thyself on thy throne, set this Pepi on his throne and let him live for ever . . . with his *ābut* staff, this Pepi is for life.[2]

Heaven is strong, the earth . . . Horus comes, Thoth rises (or, makes an appearance), they lift up Osiris on his place, they make him to stand at the head of the Two Companies of the Gods. Remember, O Set, and place in thy heart the word which Ḳeb spake, and the condemnation (?) which the gods passed on thee in the House of the Prince in Ånu (Heliopolis) at thy casting down Osiris to the earth. At thy saying, Set, "I have not done this to him," thou wast mastered there, carried away, and Horus gained the mastery over thee. When thou didst say, Set, " . . . those who acclaim," his name became that of Åku-ta. When thou didst say, Set, " . . those who journey," his name became that of "Saḥ" (Orion) of the long stride and extended step, Chief of the Land of the South.[3]

[1] , l. 185.

[2] Lines 185, 186.

[3] Translations of many other important passages from the texts of Pepi I and Pepi II, all bearing on the lives of the beatified in the heaven of Osiris, will be found in the APPENDIX.

CHAPTER V.

Osiris and Cannibalism.

Diodorus, who was a keen student of the religions and mythologies of the peoples with whom he came in contact, tells us (I. 14) that Osiris forbade men to eat each other. Isis had found out how to make bread from wheat and barley, which had hitherto grown wild with the other herbs of the field, and men, having learned the arts of agriculture, adopted the use of the new food willingly, and were thereby enabled to cease from the habit they had of killing and eating one another. Every student of African customs, ancient and modern, knows that the tradition recorded by Diodorus rests on fact, and that, under certain circumstances, most of the peoples of Africa, especially those of the Sûdân, have dropped into the habit of cannibalism with readiness and satisfaction. We have now to consider the part which Osiris is alleged to have played in connection with the suppression of cannibalism in Egypt, and how the doctrine of this great god of the dead influenced the custom of his subjects in this respect. Speaking generally, the Africans have always had three ways of disposing of the bodies of the dead: (1) Kings and great chiefs were always buried with ceremonies more or less elaborate, because the living wished to enjoy the protection of their spirits, and to feel that they had friends and helpers in Spirit-land, or Dead-land. (2) Common people, *i.e.*, all those who did not belong to ruling families, were not buried, but their bodies, after death, were thrown out into the "bush" to rot, or to be devoured by hyenas and other wild beasts. (3) Among several peoples it has been the custom to eat the bodies of the dead, as well as to kill systematically the old and infirm, and slaves, and prisoners of war, and strangers, and to eat them.[1]

[1] "Im Anfang werden sicherlich Menschen geopfert worden sein, und zwar noch spät, denn das Opfer gehörte ja auch zum Kult des Pharao von Bigge."—Junker, *A.Z.*, 1910, Vol. 48, p. 69.

Now tradition, as reported by Plutarch, Diodorus, and others, aserts that Osiris once lived upon the earth and reigned as a king, and the Egyptian inscriptions not only support this tradition, but prove, by the descriptions which they give of the elaborate ceremonies performed in connection with his burial, that he was a very great king, and that he was buried with true African pomp, but not according to the African custom of the period in which he lived. The earliest texts state repeatedly that his head, and flesh, and bones, and heart, and other organs of his body were collected and rejoined, and that his reconstituted body was swathed in linen smeared with sweet-smelling unguents, and sprinkled with preservative spices. It is clear from the frequency of the repetition of these statements that, before his time, it was not customary to treat the bodies of the dead in this fashion, and that the rejoining of the limbs of the dead before burial was unusual. The graves of the predynastic inhabitants of Egypt contain bodies which have been buried whole, a fact proved by the remains of the muscles and tendons which M. de Morgan found still attached to the bones.[1] On the other hand, many graves contain bones from which the flesh has been removed by some means, and frequently the bones themselves are strewn about the graves in the greatest disorder. Often the head is entirely separated from the body, but sometimes it remains attached to the vertebrae of the neck, though it is not in its normal position in respect of them. In other graves the disposition of the human remains suggests that the bodies were roughly hacked in pieces, so that they might be huddled together in a small space. The older graves are probably those in which the bodies were buried whole, and, if this be so, we are right in assuming that the primitive, indigenous Egyptians neither dismembered the dead, nor stripped the flesh off their bones, and that those who treated the dead in either manner were foreigners, or, at all events, not Egyptians. The cult of Osiris demanded that the dead body should be neither mutilated nor dismembered permanently, and every

[1] *Recherches sur les Origines de L'Égypte*, Paris, 1897, p. 134.

worshipper of Osiris wished and hoped to enter into eternal life with his tale of members complete. Every Egyptian knew that Osiris was himself dismembered, and that Set had scattered the pieces of his body all over Egypt; but, in breaking up the body of Osiris, Set only seems to have conformed to the custom common in the country at the time.

The head of the dead man was treated quite differently from the other portions of his body, even in the earliest times, and it was often placed upon a brick, or upon a small heap of stones by itself. Special care seems to have been taken also with the hands and feet, which are often found together, and this custom survived till the Graeco-Roman Period. At many places in Upper Egypt models of the head and hands and feet in painted plaster were laid upon the plain rectangular wooden coffins in the early centuries of the Christian Era, and several examples of them may be seen in the Second Egyptian Room in the British Museum. It seems, as has already been pointed out,[1] as if the cutting off of the head was not fatal to the attainment of eternal life, and that, in the earliest times, the Egyptians practised decapitation on the dead in order to extract the brain and to fill the skull with preservative spices and unguents.[2] At a later period they discovered how to extract the brain through the nose, and by the same opening they inserted the myrrh and unguents. It was foreseen that in the process of embalming, the head might be mislaid, and that the head of one man might be joined to the body of another. To avoid this terrible possibility, the priests at the time when decapitation of the dead was general drew up the following formula: "I am the Great One, son of the "Great One, I am Fire, the son of Fire, to whom was "given his head after it had been cut off. The head of "Osiris was not taken away, let not the head of so-and-so "be taken away from him. I have knit (or, arranged) "myself together; I have made myself whole and "complete; I have renewed my youth; I am Osiris, Lord "of Eternity." This formula forms the XLIIIrd

[1] Wiedemann, in de Morgan, *Recherches*, p. 207.

[2] Fouquet, *Sur les Squelettes d'El'Amrah*, in de Morgan, *Origines* p. 267.

Chapter of the Book of the Dead, and is found in papyri of the XVIIIth dynasty, *e.g.*, in the Papyrus of Nu, Sheet 5, which was written about 1500 B.C. At

1.

2.

3.

EGYPTIAN HUNTERS AND WARRIORS OF THE ARCHAÏC PERIOD.

1. Egyptian wearing a feather and a loin-cloth with a tail, and armed with a bow and arrow.
2. Egyptian wearing two feathers and a loin-cloth, and armed with a bow and mace.
3. Egyptian holding the symbol of his Hawk-god in his right hand, and a double-headed axe in his left.

From a green stone object in the British Museum.

this time the custom of decapitating the dead had ceased to exist in Egypt, but the scribes included the formula against it in the Theban Recension because they never willingly omitted any ancient text from this great collection of religious compositions which was believed to be of the least value to the dead.[1] There was always the chance that owing to some untoward event the head of a man might be lost so far as he was concerned, and in such vital matters the priests thought it best to provide against every contingency.[2]

Now, since it is certain from the evidence of one class of tombs of the Predynastic Period that the flesh was stripped from the bones of dead men before their burial, the question naturally arises: "What became of the flesh?" When these tombs were discovered it was stated that among the bones were several which were broken, and that portions of them bore the marks of teeth. From this statement it was deduced that the marks on the bones were those of human teeth, and that the men who had buried the bones had eaten the flesh, in fact it was concluded that the Egyptians of the period were cannibals. This view, however, was not generally accepted, for many reasons. In the first place it was found, when attempts were made to reconstruct the skeletons from several of these graves, that in each case many of the bones were missing. Thus, of the graves at Gebel Silsilah, some contained skulls and no other bones, and some contained bones and no skulls.[3] Assuming that the Egyptians ate the flesh of their dead there is, as Wiedemann has pointed out,[4] no reason why they should not have thrown all the bones into the grave for it cannot be seriously suggested that they ate any of them. Besides this, another more rational explanation is possible:—The bodies were buried for a time, in fact long enough for the flesh to rot off the bones, and then the bones were dug up, and carried to their final resting place. If the bones of several men were dug up and taken together to the cemetery, it would be easy for them to become mixed, and a little carelessness would account

[1] In West Africa the heads of the dead, who when alive were supposed to possess witch power, or to be able to rise in an altered form from their graves, were cut off and thrown into the sea or burnt. —Nassau, *Fetichism in West Africa*, p. 220.

[2] Professor Naville has shown that the Egyptians sometimes placed a head made of stone in the grave, which was intended to take the place of that of the deceased if necessary.

[3] Fouquet, *Recherches sur les Crânes*, in de Morgan, *Recherches*, p. 271.

[4] In de Morgan, *Recherches*, p. 211.

for one grave containing too few, and another too many. This explanation is illustrated by facts recorded by modern travellers.

Mr. J. F. Cunningham tells us that among the Kavirondo a chief is buried in his hut in a sitting position, with his head above the ground. His wives keep watch in the hut till the flesh on the head is rotten, and then they take it away and bury it in its final resting place.[1] Captain Barlow relates[2] that among the Latuka, in 1903, the dead man was buried in front of the door of his house. After twelve months the remains were exhumed and placed in an earthenware jar, which was put under a tree if there happened to be one near. Sir Harry Johnston found that all the Bantu Kavirondo buried a chief in a sitting position in the floor of his own hut with his head above ground. The head was covered with an earthenware pot, which was removed from time to time by the elder relations, to see how the cleaning of the skull by the ants was proceeding. When cleaned the skull was removed from the body and buried close to the hut. Later all the bones were dug up and buried with great ceremony in one of the sacred places, which were usually situated on the tops of hills where there were trees.[3] Among the Masai, the eldest son or successor of a buried chief one year after the burial removes the skull of the deceased, making at the same time a sacrifice and a libation with the blood of a goat, some milk and some honey. The skull is then carefully secreted by the son, whose possession of it is understood to confirm him in power, and to impart to him some of the wisdom of his predecessor.[4] In Usoga, a state tributary to Uganda, when a dead chief has been buried for some time his bones are dug up again. Anyone who happens to pass by the place when this work is going on must die. The skull and the larger bones are put aside, while the smaller ones are taken away to be used as drumsticks. When the chief's bones have been disinterred they are laid in a hut built specially for the purpose, upon a bed, and

[1] *Uganda and its Peoples*, London, 1905, p. 275.
[2] In Cunningham's *Uganda*, p. 369.
[3] *Uganda Protectorate*, Vol. II, p. 749.
[4] Johnston, *Uganda Protectorate*, Vol. II, p. 828.

covered with fine bark-cloth; then the drums are beaten with the small bones, and all the people chant that their chief has come back again.[1]

Miss Kingsley notes that the Bubis bury their dead in the forest with their heads just above the ground, but does not say if they dig the bones up after a time.[2] The Calabar people cut off the head of a dead chief and bury it somewhere with great secrecy, and the Adûmas and other Upper Ogowé tribes beat the flesh of the body into unrecognisable pulp. The destruction of the body by beating, or by cutting it up into pieces, is a widely diffused custom in West Africa.[3] In Taveta a dead chief is buried in a sitting position, with the left arm resting on the knee, and the head supported by the hand; the wife is buried in a similar position, but with the right arm resting on her knee, and her head supported by the hand. When they have been buried long enough for the flesh to have disappeared, the skulls of the man and wife are dug up and placed in oval-shaped pots. These are laid on their sides at the bases of dracoena trees in the centre of the plantation, where as good spirits they guard the crops. "A more queer and "ghastly thing cannot be imagined than the sight of these "skulls grinning inside the dark pots."[4]

The quotations given above make it quite clear that many African peoples have been accustomed to burying their dead twice, the first time to allow the ants to eat the flesh, or the earth to make it rot off the bones, and the second time to dispose of their bones finally. This custom is too widespread to be considered a peculiarity of a tribe or people here and there, and it must be regarded as one of the recognized ways in Africa of disposing of the flesh of the dead. For those who were anxious to preserve all the bones of a dead person it had many disadvantages; for in digging up the bones for the second burial it was easy to overlook some of the smaller ones, and in carrying them to their final resting place it was equally easy to drop

[1] Decle, *Three Years in Savage Africa*, London, 1898, p. 461.
[2] *Travels in West Africa*, p. 70.
[3] *Ibid.*, pp. 479, 480.
[4] Thomson, *Through Masai Land*, p. 110.

some of them and lose them. The cult of Osiris which prescribed the burial of the body in an intact state was a protest against the system of two burials, and we can readily understand how promptly the new system of burial, which was associated with the worship of Osiris, would be adopted by all who disliked the decapitation or dismemberment of their dead in any form. Religion was called in by the primitive Egyptians to carry out a reform which, though generally desired, could not be effected by public opinion without the aid of the priests. Underneath the new system there lay, as under nearly all the religious ceremonies of the Africans, strong common sense, and the reform established a custom which the experience of the people generally made them feel was a necessity.

Now, although there is no evidence to be obtained from the remains in the graves of the early Egyptians which would prove them to have been eaters of the dead, or cannibals, it is futile to pretend that the Egyptians or their indigenous ancestors, whoever they may have been, were not eaters of human flesh at some time or other in their history, or that they did not offer up human sacrifices. Everything that we know of them proves that they possessed all the characteristics of the African race, and especially of that portion of it which lived in that great tract of country which extends from ocean to ocean, right across Africa, and is commonly known as the Sûdân, *i.e.*, the country *par excellence* of the Blacks. One of these characteristics is the love of uncooked meat, and another is cannibalism. According to Professor Westermarck,[1] the practice of cannibalism may be traced to many different sources :—1. Scarcity or lack of animal food. 2. Revenge or hatred. 3. The wish to absorb the qualities of the person eaten. 4. The belief in the supernatural effect of human flesh and blood when eaten. Mr. Crawley asserts that the origin and chief meaning of cannibalism is the "belief that properties such as "strength, courage, swiftness, and the like, can be "transmitted by contact with those possessing them, "or by assimilating separable parts of such persons. "The flesh and blood of a man are, by a natural fallacy,

[1] *Origin and Development of the Moral Ideas*, Vol. II, p. 555.

"regarded as the best means for transmission of his "properties."[1] It has been argued that a nation which possessed such a comparatively high civilization as the Egyptians would not have retained the practice of cannibalism, but Professor Westermarck states, as a result of his general study of cannibalism, that it is much less prevalent among the lowest savages than among races somewhat more advanced in culture.[2] In America it was practised to a greater extent and with more horrible rites among the most civilized, and, says Mr. Dorman: "Its religious inception was the cause of this."[3] The same is exactly the case in the Sûdân at the present time, for, as we shall see presently, notorious cannibals like the A-Zande, or Niam-Niam, are superior both mentally and physically to all the other peoples who live round about them.

One of the strongest proofs that the Egyptians in the Dynastic Period had no horror of cannibalism is proved by a chapter in the text cut on a wall inside the pyramid of King Unȧs, a king of the Vth or VIth dynasty, at Ṣaḳḳârah.[4] In this the dead king is supposed to feed upon his fathers and his mothers, and, not content with this, he hunts the gods in the meadows of the sky, and his helpers snare them, stab them, disembowel them, cut them up, and cook them for him. He then eats three full meals a day, at morning, noon, and night, and devours their hearts and entrails till he can eat no longer. By gorging himself in this manner, he absorbs all the magical powers and mental characteristics of the gods, as well as their spirits, his object being to live for ever. This text was so popular that another copy of it was cut on a wall inside the pyramid of Tetȧ, a king of the VIth dynasty, who wished, apparently, to emulate the exploits of Unȧs.

That the Egyptian ate raw meat is proved by the

[1] *The Mystic Rose*, p. 101.

[2] *Op. cit.*, II, p. 578.

[3] *The Origin of Primitive Superstitions*, p. 152.

[4] See the text in the editions of Maspero and Sethe, l. 496 ff.; the text and an English rendering will be found in my *Gods of the Egyptians*, vol. I, p. 33 ff.

ceremonies which were performed at the "Opening of the Mouth" of the dead. The bull to be sacrificed was brought close to the tomb and thrown down, and his feet tied together. The "butcher" then stabbed him in the chest and put in his hand and dragged out the heart, which was presented in the earliest times to the deceased, and at a later period to a statue of him. A leg of the beast was then cut off and presented to the deceased, and then the kinsfolk of the dead man ate both the heart and the leg. The Egyptian was in all periods, under certain circumstances, an eater of raw meat, and the taste and smell of blood were dear to him. He shared this characteristic with the African in general, and it remained with him to the end, in fact, as long as he was able to celebrate the mysteries of his religion. His brother Africans continue to eat human flesh, and to drink human blood, and to eat raw and freshly killed meat, to the present day. The proofs of this statement are given below. These I have collected from a series of authoritative narratives written by serious travellers whose statements are trustworthy. Their evidence, it seems to me, proves beyond a doubt that the liking for raw meat and human flesh is, and always has been, a natural instinct of all Sûdânî peoples, and that Diodorus was correct in describing the primitive Egyptians as cannibals. The cult of Osiris no doubt made human flesh tabû, but there is no evidence that it prohibited the eating of raw meat or the drinking of blood.

One of the chief reasons for cannibalism in Egypt in all periods has been the lack of food caused by a series of low Niles, such as are described in the inscription on the Island of Sâhal in the First Cataract.[1] Of a few of the famines which have devastated Egypt during the Christian Era records are extant, and the atrocities which they describe are truly terrible. In 1069, owing to the low Niles of several years preceding, food was so scarce that the people began to eat each other. Passengers were caught in the streets by hooks let down from the windows, drawn up, killed, and cooked.

[1] Published by Brugsch, *Die Biblischen Sieben Jahre des Hungersnoth*, Leipzig, 1891.

Human flesh was sold in public.[1] Again, in the terrible famine which happened in 1201–2, the people in Cairo were driven to eat dead bodies, carcases of dogs and other animals, filth, etc., and at length they began to eat children roasted or boiled. 'Abd al-Laṭîf, who was an eye-witness of the terrible scenes that were enacted,[2] saw the roasted body of a child in a basket one day, and two days later that of a youth who had been roasted and partly eaten. The Government burnt those who did these things, when they could be caught, but even the bodies of those who were burnt were devoured by the mob! The greater number of the lower classes were killed and eaten. Men of wealth and position waylaid unwary passengers, and, having taken them home, killed them, cut them up, and kept them in pots in brine! In one house 400 skulls of human beings who had been killed and eaten were counted. The authorities, in trying to search out and punish the offenders, found cooking pots containing two or three children cut up, ten hands, etc. A woman was found eating her husband's body, and parents ate their own children; this was the case throughout Egypt, from Syene to the Mediterranean. In this case the Egyptians were made cannibals by want, but they sometimes ate men through hatred or revenge. Thus in 1148, when Ruḍwân had escaped from prison, he was struck down in front of the Khalîfah's palace, and his head was thrown into his wife's lap. His body was cut into little pieces and devoured by the young soldiers, in the belief that they would thus assimilate his pith and courage.[3]

Ibn Baṭûtah, a Muslim who flourished in the first half of the fourteenth century of our era, tells a story of the Sulṭân Mensa Sulêmân, who was once visited by a company of man-eating negroes in the Sûdân. The Sulṭân paid them honour, and sent them a servant to wait upon them. The negroes promptly cut his throat and ate him, and, having smeared their faces and hands with his blood, they waited upon the king to offer him

[1] Stanley Lane-Poole, *A History of Egypt in the Middle Ages*, p. 146.

[2] De Sacy, *Relation de L'Égypte*, p. 360 ff.

[3] Lane-Poole, *Middle Ages*, p. 169.

their thanks. These negroes stated that the daintiest portions of the human body are the hands and breasts of a woman. Ibn Baṭûtah also relates that Mensa Mûsa banished a certain judge to the country of the cannibals, presumably expecting that he would be eaten there. At the end of four years he was sent back, the natives refusing to eat him because he was white.[1]

Coming now to the testimony of European travellers in Africa, we find that Andrew Battell, who journeyed thither in the latter half of the sixteenth century, states that the Gagas were in the habit of bringing the bodies of their enemies from the battle-field to be eaten. And he goes on to say that although their country is filled with cattle, they "feed chiefly upon man's flesh."[2] Further, the great Gaga Calandola was anointed each day with human fat.[3] Battell found that the Angicas[4] and the elephant-hunting pygmies also lived upon human flesh; the latter killed with bows and arrows the men they ate. The local name of the pygmies was "Matimbas," and he describes them as being "no bigger than boys twelve years old."[5] Among travellers in Africa in the last century may be quoted Dr. Schweinfurth, who says that near the dwellings of the Niam-Niam[6] were many posts on which rested the skulls of animals and men. Close to the huts were human bones, which bore marks of the hatchet or knife, and all around hanging on the branches of the trees were human hands and feet.[7] This people are undoubtedly cannibalistic, and they make no secret of their craving for meat of all kinds, and especially for

[1] *Voyages d'Ibn Batoutah*, ed. Defrémery and Sanguinetti, tom. IV, pp. 428, 429.

[2] *Strange Adventures*, London, 1901 (Hakluyt Society), p. 21.

[3] *Ibid.*, p. 31.

[4] *Ibid.*, p. 101 (Knivet's narrative).

[5] *Ibid.*, p. 59.

[6] The plural of this Dinka name is Niamah-Niam; the name means "Great Eater," or cannibal. The Bongos call them "Mundo," or "Manzanza"; the Dyvor, "O Madyaka"; the Mittu, "Makkarakka," or "Kakkarakka"; the Golos, "Kunda"; the Mañbattu, "Babungera." The men are of a chocolate colour, and the women copper colour; they tattoo their bodies, wear skins, and file the incisor teeth to a point for the purpose of getting a firm grip on the arm of an enemy.

[7] *Heart of Africa*, Vol. I, p. 517.

human meat,[1] and they "ostentatiously string the teeth of their victims round their necks. They even eat newly born babes. Human fat is universally sold, and when eaten in a considerable quantity is said to have an intoxicating effect." On the other hand, many of the Niam-Niam turn with loathing from the eating of human flesh, and would refuse to eat out of the same dish with a cannibal. They breed a peculiar dog which they eat and regard as a great delicacy. Akin to the Niam-Niam are the Fân who barter their dead among themselves, and dig up to eat the dead who have been already buried.[2] Among the Mañbattu the bodies of all who fall in battle are distributed on the field, and are prepared by drying for transport to the homes of the conquerors, where also are driven their prisoners like sheep to the shambles, to be killed as needed. Whilst Dr. Schweinfurth was at Munza's Court a child was slain daily for his meal. On two occasions Dr. Schweinfurth saw human flesh being prepared for food. He found some young women scalding the hair off the lower half of a human body, and saw in a hut an arm being smoke-dried over a fire.[3] The cannibalism of the Mañbattu is unsurpassed by any nation in the world. Yet they are a noble race of men, and they display a certain national pride, and have intellect and judgment such as few Africans possess. The Nubians praise their faithfulness, and the order and stability of their national life.[4] In the Southern Sûdân soldiers are addicted to the eating of human livers, which they tear out of the bodies of their neighbours.[5]

Near Mundo, Petherick found that the heart, lungs, and intestines were taken out of the dead body, and given to the women to eat. And the Abarambo sold the dead body to the highest bidder, who paid for his purchase in lances. Having cut off what he wanted

[1] On one occasion they captured a number of female slaves, whom they disposed of thus : the youngest went to their houses, the middle-aged were sent to till the fields, and the oldest to the cooking-pots.—*Heart of Africa*, Vol. II, p. 222.

[2] *Ibid.*, Vol. II, pp. 18, 19, 224.

[3] *Ibid.*, Vol. II, p. 93.

[4] *Ibid.*, Vol. II, p. 94.

[5] *Ibid.*, Vol. II, p. 322.

himself he sold the remainder. The family of the deceased showed their respect for him by not partaking of his body.[1] In 1904, Mr. Cunningham found among the Sese Islanders of Lake Victoria a secret society called the Bachichi, the sole object of which was to continue the custom of eating the dead.[2] In Busoga the medicine-men make a most deadly poison from dead bodies, and spears and arrows which have been dipped in a decoction of it are greatly feared.[3] The Manzema always eat their dead, sometimes roasted and sometimes boiled with bananas. The dead are never eaten by their fellow villagers, but by the people of the next village whither they are carried on a wooden frame borne by four men.[4] Dr. Junker reports that the A-Kahle are worse cannibals than the southern peoples, and tells the story of a wretched negress who had been lynched because the local oracle had pronounced her guilty of witchcraft. Her body had been ripped up and her murderers had dragged out the gall bladder, which was then burnt, as it was supposed to contain the magic charm. They cooked the body, and a cooked foot, wrapped up in banana leaves was brought to Dr. Junker by his servant Dsumbe, and he saw that the flesh was discoloured, and that the nails had fallen off in cooking. He adds: "human flesh is always cooked with the skin after the hair is singed off."[5] The Niaanos eat their enemies who are killed in battle, and also all those who die a natural death.[6]

Dr. Nassau states that the practice of digging up dead bodies to feast on their flesh existed largely among the natives in the region of Lake Nyassa, and he is of opinion that cannibalism has some connection with the religion of the negro. He thinks this form of cannibalism different from that of the Congo tribes, who merely kill and eat people as we eat game. Though cannibalism is practised, it is not universal with the tribes among which

[1] Petherick, *Travels in Central Africa*, pp. 274, 275.
[2] *Uganda and its Peoples*, p. 73.
[3] *Ibid.*, p. 124.
[4] *Ibid.*, p. 316.
[5] *Travels in Africa*, Vol. III, pp. 101, 283.
[6] Gleichen, *Anglo-Egyptian Sûdân*, p. 161.

it is found, and is condemned by the public opinion of those who do not practise it. "The real public opinion is witchcraft, and real public opinion tends to shield the perpetrators, because they are reported to be sorcerers of high quality."[1] Dr. Trumbull also regards cannibalism as possessing a religious significance. This will explain why the African cannibal, after conquering his enemy, eats him; why the heart is especially desired at such feasts; and why the body of anyone of distinguished characteristics is prized for the cannibal feast. His strength or skill or bravery or power is to be absorbed with his flesh. Uncivilized peoples, and even some civilized, regard the heart as the epitome of the individual, his soul in some sense, so that to appropriate his heart is to appropriate his whole being. The Ashanti fetichmen of West Africa make a mixture of the hearts of their enemies soaked with blood and consecrated (*i.e.*, magic) herbs, for the vivifying of the conquerors.[2]

Stanley, whose experience of the tribes in Central Africa is probably unique, says, on the authority of Emin Pasha, that the Dinkas rarely kill their cattle for meat, and that they keep them solely for their milk and blood. The latter they mix with sesamune oil, and then eat as a delicacy.[3] The Bangala, Wyyanzi, Batomba, Basoka, Baburu, Bakumu, and Balessé all eat the flesh of their enemies.[4] Among the Baima a man would shoot an arrow into a cow's neck and, when he had pulled the arrow out, the owner of the animal would put his mouth to the wound and suck the blood; which gave him strength and boldness.[5] The Aliab tribe bleed their cattle and boil the blood.[6]

Stanley further relates that, when the great magic doctor Vinyata presented him with a fine fat ox, he made the request that the heart of the animal should be returned to him.[7]

[1] *Fetichism in West Africa*, London, 1904, p. 246 ff.
[2] Trumbull, *Blood Covenant*, pp. 107, 115, 129.
[3] *In Darkest Africa*, Vol. I, p. 424.
[4] *Ibid.*, Vol. II, p. 90.
[5] Broadwood Johnson, *Tramps round the Mountains of the Moon*, London, 1909, p. 187.
[6] Baker, *Albert N'yanza*, p. 53.
[7] *Through the Dark Continent*, Vol. I, p. 123.

Baker describes, on the authority of Ibrahimawa, a native of Bornu, the habits of the slave traders in his day. In their razzias they frequently took with them a number of the Makkarikas, but complained that they were poor partners, as they insisted upon killing and eating the children whom the party wished to secure as slaves. Their custom was to catch a child by its ankles and to dash its head against the ground; thus killed, they opened the abdomen, extracted the stomach and intestines, and, tying the two ankles to the neck, they carried the body by slinging it over the shoulder, and thus returned to camp, where they divided it by quartering, and boiled it in a large pot. On one occasion, after the arrival of a number of slaves, one of the girls among them tried to escape; her master fired at her, and the ball struck her in the side, and she fell wounded. The girl was remarkably fat, and from the wound a large lump of yellow fat protruded. No sooner had she fallen than the Makkarikas rushed upon her in a crowd and, seizing the fat, they tore it from the wound in handfuls, the girl being still alive while the crowd were quarrelling for the disgusting prize. Others killed her with a lance, and at once divided her by cutting off her head and splitting the body with their lances, used as knives, cutting longitudinally from between the legs along the spine to the neck. Many slave women and their children fled and took refuge in the trees, but the children were dragged from the branches and many were killed, and in a short time a great feast was prepared for the whole party.[1] Whenever Sir Samuel Baker shot an animal, the Shoa natives would invariably cut its throat and drink the blood as it gushed from the artery.[2] On one occasion, Baker's "Forty Thieves" shot an Unyoro, whereupon they cut out his liver and divided it among them and ate it raw.[3]

Speke mentions the Wilyanwantu, who disdained all food but human flesh, and Rŭmanika confirmed the statement of the man from Rûanda from whom he obtained the information, though he was a little

[1] *Albert N'yanza*, p. 187.
[2] *Ibid.*, p. 420.
[3] *Ismaïlïa*, p. 393.

sceptical about it. He states as a fact that the Wahûma mixed blood with milk for their dinners.[1]

The Fân ate the gorilla, but carefully preserved the brain of the animal, from which they made two charms; the one gave the wearer success in hunting and the other gave him success with women. Du Chaillu saw a woman in one of their villages carrying a piece of a human thigh just as we carry a joint from the market. He found some of the Fân quarrelling over the division of a human body because there was not enough for all; the head was saved for the king as his royalty. Ribs, leg-bones, arm-bones and skulls were piled up by each house, and there were signs of cannibalism everywhere.[2] The Fân buy the dead of the Osheba tribe, who, in return, buy theirs. They also buy the dead of other families in their own tribes, and besides this, get the bodies of a good many slaves from the Mbichos and Mbondemos, for which they readily give ivory, at the rate of a small tusk for a body. A party of Fân who came down to the seashore actually stole a freshly-buried body from the cemetery, and cooked it and ate it; and on another occasion a party took a body into the woods, cut it up, and smoked the flesh, which they carried away with them. These stories are vouched for by the Rev. Mr. Walker of the Gaboon Mission. The Fân practise cannibalism unblushingly, and in open day, and are unashamed. Du Chaillu saw knives with handles covered with human skin, which their owners valued highly; he

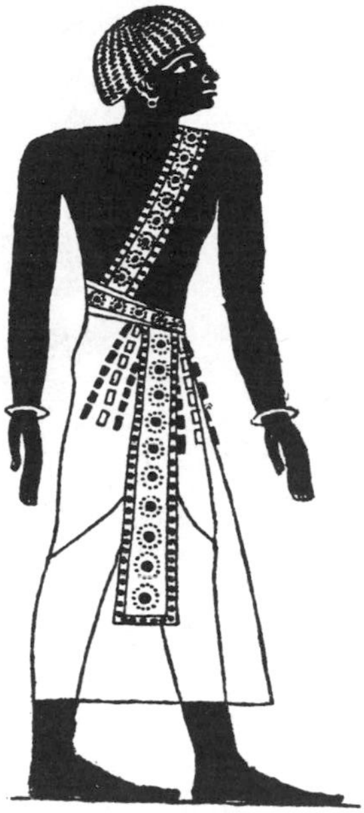

Egyptian portrait of a Sûdânî man.
From a wall-painting at Thebes.

[1] *Journal of the Discovery of the Source of the Nile* (Dent's reprint), pp. 191, 199.

[2] *Explorations and Adventures in Equatorial Africa*, pp. 71, 74–76.

describes them as the "bravest-looking set of negroes" he had ever seen in the interior.[1]

In West Africa human eyeballs are much prized as charms or amulets, and Dr. Nassau has known graves to be rifled for them. This is, of course, to secure the "man that lives in your eyes" for the service of the village.[2] It is interesting to note in connection with this fact that so far back as the VIth dynasty in Egypt an offering which symbolized the "child which is in the Eye of Horus" , was presented to the dead king Unȧs.[3]

At Gabun Mr. Alldridge was told by a Beri chief that there was no one in his country over three years of age who had not eaten human flesh.[4] Mr. Hutchinson says that cannibalism exists in the Omun country up to the Cross River. The Boola tribe comes to the Mooney River to get sea-shore folk for "chop" as they have a saltish flavour, and in 1859 human flesh was exposed for sale at Duketown in Old Calabar. The Pangwes exhume and eat the dead, and when a man was executed boys and girls walked away with pieces of bleeding flesh in their hands. A Juju-man refused to eat a human head because his cook had "spoiled" it by not putting enough pepper in it, and cannibalism is almost as rampant on the West Coast of Africa as it has ever been.[5] The tribes of the Lower Niger eat all their prisoners of war. During the period of these feasts the orgies which take place are positively disgusting and repulsive, men and women rushing, dancing, or reeling through the town, carrying in their hands pieces of cooked or smoked human flesh, which they eat and revel in with absolute pleasure and enjoyment from a sheer sense of satisfaction in the solid and substantial. Brutal and loathsome as it all is, there is in this hideous carnival of the carnal lusts and passions a spiritual significance, a satisfying sacrifice to the ancestral spirits who have given them the victory

[1] *Ibid.*, pp. 88, 89.

[2] Kingsley, *Travels in West Africa*, p. 449.

[3] See Budge, *Liturgy of Funerary Offerings*, pp. 136, 188.

[4] *The Sherbro and its Hinterland*, p. 238.

[5] *Ten Years' Wanderings among the Ethiopians*, pp. 58, 60, 61, 62, 73, 76.

and delivered the enemy into their hands.[1] When charms were needed by the chief of Matiamvo a man was slaughtered for some part of his body.[2] In the "Kasendi" ceremony which is performed to make blood-brotherhood, the hands of the parties are joined together. Small incisions are made on the clasped hands, on the pit of the stomach of each, and on the right cheeks and foreheads. A small quantity of blood is taken off from these points in both parties by means of a stalk of grass. The blood from one person is put in one pot of beer, and that of the second into another; each then drinks the other's blood.[3]

In and about Bambarré there are no graves; all the dead are eaten. A quarrel with a wife often ends in the husband killing her and eating her heart, mixed up in a huge mess of goat's flesh. The body of Moenékuss was eaten, and the flesh removed from his head and eaten too; his head is preserved in a pot in his house, and all public matters are gravely communicated to it.[4] Commenting on the reason for cannibalism in the country Dr. Livingstone says: "It is not want that has led to the custom, for the country is full of food; nobody is starved of farinaceous food; they have maize, dura, pennisetum, cassava, and sweet potatoes, and for fatty ingredients of diet, the palm-oil, ground nuts, sessamum, and a tree whose fruit yields fine fresh oil; the saccharine materials needed are found in the sugar-cane, bananas, and plantains. Goats, sheep, fowls, dogs, pigs, abound in the villages, whilst the forest affords elephants, zebras, buffaloes, antelopes, and in the streams there are many varieties of fish. The nitrogenous ingredients are abundant, and they have dainties in palm-toddy, and tobacco or Bangé; so that the reason for cannibalism does not lie in starvation or in want of animal matter. The only feasible reason I can discover is a depraved appetite, giving an extraordinary craving for meat which we call 'high.' They are said to bury a dead body for a couple of days in the soil in a forest,

[1] A. G. Leonard, *The Lower Niger and its Tribes*, p. 179.
[2] Livingstone, *Missionary Travels*, p. 317.
[3] *Ibid.*, p. 488.
[4] Livingstone, *Last Journals*, Vol. II, p. 49.

and in that time, owing to the climate, it soon becomes putrid enough for the strongest stomach."[1]

Decle states that a great deal of "unsuspected cannibalism" still exists in Africa, *e.g.*, in Nyassa-land, where the dead are secretly dug up and eaten. This practice is, however, strongly condemned by local public opinion, and those found guilty of it are condemned to be burned alive. Decle himself ate a curry made of human ribs without knowing it, but thought the flesh had a fine flavour of venison with a salty taste, one of the reasons why cannibals greatly relish human flesh.[2] Winwood Reade describes cannibalism of two kinds: the first is sacrificial, or priestly, and the other is simply an action of *gourmandise*. On questioning a veteran cannibal this man told him that they all ate men, and that he ate men himself. Being asked if man was good, he replied with a rapturous gesture, that it was "like monkey, all fat." Reade investigated the story told by Du Chaillu, which was generally disbelieved, in which he stated as a fact that on one occasion a clan of the Fân on their road to the sea came by night to the burying-ground, opened all the graves, robbed them of their treasures, and filled two canoes ready to carry away, when they found a freshly buried corpse in one of the graves. This they also took possession of, and having come to a convenient place, under the shelter of some mangrove trees, they lighted fires, boiled the body in the pots which they had just disinterred, and ate it on the very spot where Winwood Reade was first told this story.[3]

According to Skertchley the cannibalism of Dahomey is of a ceremonial character. In describing the Attoh Custom he says: Then four men, the Menduton, or Cannibals, stationed themselves before the platform, each being furnished with a sharpened stick, by way of a fork, and a knife. In their left hand they carried a small calabash filled with salt and pepper, and they at once commenced to cry out to the king to give them meat to eat, for they were hungry. These were the "blood drinkers" mentioned by Duncan, who are

[1] *Last Journals*, Vol. II, pp. 148, 149.
[2] *Three Years in Savage Africa*, p. 311.
[3] *Savage Africa*, pp. 156–161.

supposed to devour the flesh of the victims of the Customs. When the captives are beheaded they take one of the bodies and cut off pieces of flesh, which they rub with palm oil, and roast over a fire kindled in the square before the platform. The human flesh is then skewered on the pointed sticks, and carried round the market-place, after which the Menduton parade before the State prisoners, and go through the action of eating the flesh. They chew the human meat before the terrified captives, but do not swallow it, and when they have worked upon the fears of the poor wretches for a sufficient time, they retire, and spitting out the chewed flesh, take strong medicines which act as an emetic. This is the nearest approach to anthropophagy in Dahomey.[1]

The works of Bentley, George Grenfell of Congo fame, and Sir Harry Johnston prove beyond all doubt that cannibalism was common over a very large region in Africa as recently as 1907. The last states that the Bantu negroes have been peculiarly prone to eating human flesh, and that the Nile negroes are almost free from this failing, though the immunity may not go back many centuries. Cannibalism lingers in Uganda, parts of German East Africa, Nyassaland, Portuguese South-East Africa, in the hinterland of the Gaboon and Cameroons, it rages in the Niger delta, and elsewhere westwards, and crops up in the French Ivory Coast, in Eastern and Central Liberia, and perhaps in Portuguese Guinea and along Kwango. In 1907 as a raging vice cannibalism was almost limited to the innermost Congo basin. Bentley says that the whole wide country from the Mubangi to Stanley Falls, for 600 miles on both sides of the main river, and up the Mubangi as well, is given up to cannibalism. The natives of the upper river begged Grenfell to sell them some of his Luango or Kruboys from off the steamer, because they must be very "sweet," very appetising. When the son of Mata Bwiki was asked if he had ever eaten human flesh, he replied, "Ah! I wish I could eat everybody on earth"![2] There was a much greater demand for human

[1] *Dahomey as It is*, London, 1874, p. 367.
[2] Sir Harry Johnston, *George Grenfell and the Congo*, Vol. I, p. 401.

flesh than the local markets could supply. The people did not, as a rule, eat their own townsfolk and relatives, but they kept and fattened slaves for the butcher, just as we keep cattle and poultry. There used to be a constant traffic in slaves for that purpose between the Lulongo River and the Mubangi. The people on the Lulongo organized raids on the upper reaches of their river, or landed at some branch to raid the inland towns. They fought the unsuspecting and unprepared people, killed many in the process, and brought the rest home with them. They divided up their human booty and kept them in their towns, tied up and starving, until they were fortunate enough to catch or buy some more, and so make up a cargo worth taking to the Mubangi. When times were bad these poor starving wretches might often be seen tied up in the towns, just kept alive with a minimum of food. A party would be made up, and would fill two or three canoes with these human cattle; they would paddle down the Lulongo, cross the main river when the wind was not blowing, make up the Mubangi, and barter their freight in some of the towns for ivory. The purchasers would then feed up their starvelings until fat enough for the market, then butcher them, and sell the meat in small joints. What was left over, if there was much on the market, would be dried on a rack over a fire, or spitted, and the end of the spit stuck in the ground by a slow fire, until it could be kept for weeks and sold at leisure.

Sometimes a section of the town would club together to buy a large piece of the body wholesale, to be retailed; or a family would buy a whole leg to divide up amongst wives, children, and slaves. Dear little bright-eyed boys and girls grew up accustomed to these scenes from day to day. They ate their own morsels from time to time in the haphazard way they have, and carried the rest of their portion in their hand, on a skewer, or in a leaf, lest anyone should steal and eat it. That is how cannibals are made.[1]

One of the Bangala chiefs visited by Bentley in 1887 had already killed and eaten seven of his wives—

[1] Bentley's Report to the Baptist Mission in *Pioneering on the Congo*, and in Sir Harry Johnston's *George Grenfell*, Vol. I, pp. 399–401.

not selfishly, because he had bidden the relations to each feast in turn, so that there should be no family unpleasantness. In Bangala, Ibuti's country, when a woman bears a child her husband buys a slave, kills him, and has the meat dried as food for his wife, who during the early period of lactation may not go outside the house. The Bopoto people do not refuse to supply with meat their cannibal neighbours in the interior. In February, 1890, they killed a woman at Bopoto, and cut off her head and kept it, but they exchanged the body with the Ngombe people at the back for the price of a couple of boys. The Mubangi women were not admitted to cannibal feasts, but they were greatly valued as the material of the banquet, the Buaka and Banziri men preferring the flesh of women and infants, without, however, despising that of prisoners of war and male slaves. Along the Ruki-Juapa River a favourite dish was a paste made of human blood and manioc flour.

The Ngombe tribes of Bwela, Buja, and other districts behind Bopoto cut up and retail the bodies of their victims with the skill of a perfect butcher. It often happens that the poor creature destined for the knife is exposed for sale in the market. He walks to and fro and epicures come to examine him. They describe the parts they prefer, one the arm, one the leg, breast, or head. The portions which are purchased are marked off with lines of coloured ochre. When the entire body is sold the wretch, who stoically submits to his fate, is slain.[1]

The Basoko eat the dead as well as those who are specially killed for the feast. Only the chiefs are allowed to rest in their graves; all other persons who are free from skin diseases are cooked and eaten, not buried. They prefer the flesh of the thighs and breast. They cut this off in strips and eat small pieces raw, threading the longer strips on skewers and drying and smoking the jerked meat before a fire. They also pickle human meat in jars with salt, or blend it and cover it with a grease resembling lard and used for the same purpose. They usually confine themselves to young girls or elderly matrons who have ceased child-bearing.

[1] Torday, in *George Grenfell*, Vol. I, p. 403.

The Manyema practise a still more repulsive form of cannibalism, for they eat diseased bodies, and only like them "high." They soak them in running water till the flesh is macerated and almost putrid, and then eat this disgusting carrion without further preparation, not even cooking it.[1] After describing a fight at Mampoko the Rev. W. Holman Bentley says: Whilst this was proceeding, as a kind of introduction to what would follow, two men passed, one carrying a human neck poised aloft upon a spear, the other an arm; both had been lopped off an unfortunate man who had been killed and left on the field. Later on we were horrified by a more ghastly sight. A party of warriors returned, who had joined somewhat late in the chase. They marched in single file past our house. In the middle of the line three men bore the remaining parts of the mutilated body. One carried the still bleeding trunk; he had slung the other arm through a large wound in the abdomen, and suspended on this the ghastly burden swung at his side; two others shouldered the legs. In the evening a few of the young men from the town went down to the feast for a share, but were too late, the flesh had all been eaten. However, they were generously invited to partake of the vegetables still remaining in the water in which it had been boiled. Two days after, a lad walked into the station carrying in a plantain leaf some of the flesh that had been roasted, and one of our workmen eagerly joined him in disposing of the dainty morsels. This cooked flesh we saw.[2]

Mr. Torday's account of the Bakanzanzi sect, compiled from the writings of Roman Catholic missionaries, is as follows:—When the Bakanzanzi have succeeded in getting possession of a human corpse, they gather together at the confines of the village, or, by preference, on the banks of the neighbouring river, and there, without avoiding the gaze of the onlookers, they divest the body of its skin, which they throw on the fire with the clots of blood. They next cut the body down the middle to the loins and take off the head. The legs and thighs are given to the old men, the breast and arms to the

[1] Torday, in *George Grenfell*, Vol. I, p. 404.
[2] *Pioneering on the Congo*, Vol. II, p. 256.

young recruits, and the head and feet to the chief of the band. Each group makes an equal division among its members, who string their portions on sticks and put them to smoke over slow fires, preserving a part for the feast of the day. This last is cooked in a large earthen pot. When all is ready, each comes in turn to take his portion quickly and swallow it, running and imitating the cry of the hyena, before returning to his place. The chief of the band is seated apart. While, with the utmost unconcern, he is boiling in a pot the victim's head, he divests of their skin the two feet which have been given him, cooks and eats them with deliberation. All this time the drums beat furiously, and the brotherhood, now satiated, give themselves up to a frenzied dance. After this they burn part of the bones, and catch the cinders in a small pot, on which they set a larger pot upside down. A pin attached to the inside of the under one is fastened by a cord to a branch fixed in the ground and bent in a bow ; in this way the victim's soul is supposed to be imprisoned. Meantime the chief has removed the flesh from the head, has carefully rubbed oil into it, burnt the brain, and slaughtered a white hen to appease the dead man's soul. The hollow of the skull is carried away to be used for magic remedies. There are various ways in which the Bakanzanzi obtain human flesh. Enemies slain in battle or useless prisoners, such as old men and village chiefs, victims of the trial by poison, are generally made over to them, either gratis or for some service. When there is a deficiency of these, they proceed to violate graves, to rob them of their dead. This is frequently done, and particularly in the case of slaves and persons of small standing. When a cannibal has succeeded in following the track of a funeral procession, or if he has discovered by chance a new grave, he hastens to inform some of the brotherhood. They all go by stealth to disinter the corpse, fill up the ditch with earth, branches, and grass, and arrange everything in such a way that no trace is visible. They at once hasten to wash the body at the river, and assemble for the feast.[1]

Elsewhere, speaking of the fight for the Congo

[1] Johnston, *George Grenfell*, Vol. I, p. 406.

between the Belgian and the Arab, Sir Harry Johnston says that it was marked by horrors scarcely recorded of the worst days of the Spaniards in Central America, or the Englishman or Dutchman in Southern Asia. Men were shot, speared, knifed, drowned, and invariably eaten. Prisoners seem to have been issued as rations by the native commanders of both armies; indeed, Grenfell, writing from hearsay of this warfare from the west, and Hinde, from closer knowledge, allude to instances of men and women being handed over to these wild soldiers for their food allowance that were cut to pieces as they stood, and devoured as soon as their flesh could be cooked. Nothing but a few bones were left of the killed on the morning after every fight.[1]

Hitherto the extracts from the works of travellers which have been quoted to show the universality of cannibalism in the Sûdân have dwelt only with the peoples of Central and West Africa. That the peoples of East Africa also are sometimes cannibals, and that they revel in drinking blood and eating raw meat, is proved by the following extracts from the works of trustworthy travellers. First comes the extract from Bruce's "Travels," in which he states that he saw three Abyssinian soldiers driving a cow before them. Soon after he arrived at the "hithermost" bank of the river, the drivers threw the cow on the ground. One sat on her neck, another twisted a halter about her fore-feet, and the third got astride upon her belly before her hind-legs, and gave her a very deep wound in the upper part of her rump. He then cut out of the top of the rump two pieces of meat, which were thicker and longer than our ordinary beef steaks. The men then drew the skin which had covered the flesh that had been taken away, over the wound, and fastened it to the other part of the hide with small skewers or pins, and then they covered it with a layer of clay from the river bank. They next forced the animal to rise, and then drove it on before them.[2] This story, which was generally discredited when it was first published in England, is no doubt perfectly

[1] *Ibid.*, p. 429.
[2] *Travels to Discover the Source of the Nile*, Vol. IV, p. 332 f.

true, for Mr. Pearce saw a cow treated in exactly the same way. According to Henry Salt,[1] the natives threw the beast on the ground and proceeded to cut out two pieces of flesh from the rump, near the tail, which together might weigh a pound. As soon as they had taken these away, they sewed up the wounds, plastered them over with cow-dung, and drove the animal forwards, while they divided among the party the still reeking steaks. The animal, after this barbarous operation, walked somewhat lame, but nevertheless managed to reach the camp without any apparent injury, and immediately after their arrival it was killed by the Worari and consumed for their supper. Mr. Salt says that the pieces cut from the animal were called *shulada*, and that they were parts of the two "glutei maximi," or larger muscles of the thigh."[2]

Bruce, in describing a native dinner, says that a cow, or bull, is brought close to the door, and his feet strongly tied. The skin that hangs down under his chin and throat is cut only so deep as to arrive at the fat of which it totally consists, and, by the separation of a few small blood vessels, six or seven drops of blood only fall to the ground. Having satisfied the Mosaical law, according to native views, by pouring these six or seven drops upon the ground, two or more of them fall to work; on the back of the beast, and on each side of the spine, they cut skin deep: then, putting their fingers between the flesh and the skin, they begin to strip the hide of the animal halfway down his ribs, and so on to the buttock, cutting the skin wherever it hinders them commodiously to strip the poor animal bare. All the flesh on the buttocks is cut off then, and in solid, square pieces, without bones, or much effusion of blood; and the prodigious noise the animal makes is a signal for the company to sit down. Whilst the guests eat the flesh wrapped in bread cakes, the victim stands bleeding at

[1] *A Voyage to Abyssinia*, London, 1814, p. 295.

[2] In Amharic ሹላዳ ፡ which D'Abbadie explains by "moëlle de la cuisse." The savage customs of the Gallas are well illustrated by the remarks of Salt on pp. 292, 293, and by his confirmatory extract from De Bry: "Victores, victis, caesis et captis pudenda excidunt, quae exsiccata regi in reliquorum procerum presentia offerunt."

the door. At length they attack the thighs where the great arteries are, and soon after the animal bleeds to death.[1]

The eminent missionary, Dr. Krapf, describes how a husband was asked to kill his wife, and to take a piece of her flesh to the king of Senjero[2]; and he says that the Wadoe cook and eat the dead, and drink out of their skulls.[3] He himself had a supper of raw meat, with pepper-soup, etc., and confirms Bruce and Salt in their statements about the love of the Abyssinians for the *shulada* muscle of the cow. He speaks of the habit of the people of eating *brundo*,[4] or raw meat, and mentions how the soldiers of Shoa would cut off the feet of live sheep and eat them.[5] According to Salt,[6] the Woldutchi and Assubo draw off the warm blood from animals and drink it, and the *Bondas* claim to have the power of changing themselves into hyenas, cows, cats, stones, etc., and of drinking the blood of friends at a distance, and of so causing their deaths.[7] The daughter of Râs Gûgsa was said to be a cannibal lady and to eat children, and Gobat was inclined to believe the story.[8] The Shoans used to kill people and cut off strips of flesh from their bodies, and eat them, sometimes doing this as a religious ceremony.[9] The Kormoso Gallas and the Kankano Gallas eat the livers of the dead, and one of their proverbs says that they bury the dead in bellies and not in tombs.[10]

The extracts given above prove, beyond all doubt, that the eating of raw meat, the drinking of blood,

[1] Bruce, *Travels*, IV, p. 486 ff. Mr. Salt seems to have doubted the truth of this story, and an Abyssinian of some position to whom he narrated it, declared that he had never witnessed any such cruel practice, and expressed great abhorrence at the thought.

[2] *Travels, Researches, and Missionary Labours*, 1869, p. 69.

[3] *Ibid.*, p. 392.

[4] In Amharic ብሩንዶ፡ *brûndô*.

[5] *Op. cit.*, p. 463.

[6] *Voyage*, p. 301.

[7] Gobat, *Journal of a Three Years' Residence in Abyssinia*, London, 1847, p. 178.

[8] *Ibid.*, p. 63.

[9] Bottego, *Il Giuba esplorata*, p. 172; the *Athenaeum*, 1845, p. 243.

[10] Paulitschke, *Ethnographie*, 1896, tom. II, p. 49.

and cannibalism, are characteristics of a large number of African tribes, and that they have been so from the earliest times of which we have any record. The priests of Osiris made a strong protest against cannibalism, but the fact remains that the Africans like, and have always liked, raw meat, and that, even when highly civilized, they readily slip back into cannibalistic habits. Thus 'Abd al-Laṭîf says: "When the poor began to eat human flesh, the horror and astonishment caused by such extraordinary food were so great that these crimes became the subject of every conversation, and people never tired of talking about them. At length they became so much accustomed to them, and conceived such a taste for this detestable dish, that one saw men making it their ordinary food, and feasting gladly on it, and even laying in a stock of it. Moreover, various different ways of preparing it were thought out, and once the habit of eating human flesh was introduced it spread in the provinces to such an extent, that examples of cannibalism were to be seen all over Egypt. This caused no surprise, for the horror of human flesh as food had completely disappeared, and one spoke, and heard others speak of it, as quite a commonplace matter."[1] This took place in the thirteenth century of our era, and we may assume that the Copts, or Christians, of Cairo, as well as the Muslims, are included in 'Abd al-Laṭîf's description. Cannibalism was not confined to the negro tribes of the Sûdân and North-East Africa, and it is quite certain that the indigenous Egyptians, like the Baganda and A-Zande, or Niam-Niams, and other superior African peoples, never wholly relinquished the habit of eating human flesh. The modern tribes of Africa cannot have learned cannibalism from the Egyptians, any more than they adopted the custom of human sacrifice from them, or any other custom which they observe in common with them. This being so, it is clear that, whereas in Egypt cannibalism has to all intents and purposes disappeared, it still survives and flourishes in many districts, and even in some which are not remote from the eye of the British Administrator. The Egyptians were Africans, and their

[1] De Sacy, *Relation*, p. 361.

manners and customs can therefore be illustrated and explained by those of other African peoples.[1]

[1] Among the works of quite recent travellers the reader is referred to E. Foà, *Résultats Scientifiques des Voyages en Afrique*, Paris, 1908. Here on pp. 262–268 the author discusses the cannibals of the Congo, and he shows that even during the last ten years cannibalism has been rampant among them. He claims to have understated facts, and says that after all he is not completely informed as to all the atrocities which were undoubtedly committed. He thinks it will need much time and patience before the tribes of whom he speaks will be brought to consider their cannibalistic customs reprehensible.

CHAPTER VI.

Osiris and Human Sacrifice, and Funeral Murders.

The facts set out in the preceding chapter prove that the dynastic Egyptians and their descendants, even in Christian times, had a strong inclination towards cannibalism which they indulged whenever the opportunity offered itself, and that many modern peoples throughout the Sûdân were, and still are, professed cannibals, often naked and always unashamed. The cult of Osiris set a curb on the cannibalistic tendencies of the Egyptians, but it did not eradicate them, any more than it put a stop to human sacrifice and funeral murders. As far as the evidence goes it seems to show that, although the Egyptians ceased to eat each other generally, they ate their enemies on occasions, and that they certainly slew their enemies, especially those whom they regarded as belonging to inferior races, and offered them up as sacrifices to their gods. Such sacrifices were commonest after successful raids and wars, and it can be proved that they were the almost necessary concomitants of every battle and raid. The cut on p. 207 depicts such a sacrifice. It is taken from an ivory plaque found at Abydos, and now in the possession of the Rev. M. MacGregor.[1]

Here Ṭen, a king of the Ist dynasty, better known as Ḥesepti, or Semti, in whose reign certain Chapters of the Book of the Dead were "found," is seen in the act of sacrificing a conquered enemy. He grasps the hair of the enemy's head with his left hand, in which he also holds a bow, and is about to smash the skull with the mace which he holds uplifted in his right hand. Immediately behind the captive is a standard surmounted by a figure of a jackal, which represents a god, either Anubis or Åpuat, and thus it is clear that the sacrifice is being made to a god by the king. This scene occurs over and over again in

[1] See Amélineau, *Les Nouvelles Fouilles d'Abydos*, 1895–6, Paris, 1899, Plate XXXIII.

reliefs of all periods of Egyptian history, and as we find it in the temples and on reliefs of the tomb chapels of the Meroïtic kingdom of the Egyptian Sûdân, it is certain that the sacrificing of prisoners to the gods went on in Egypt from the Ist dynasty to the early centuries of our era. The terrible massacres of prisoners which have gone on among the modern inhabitants of the Sûdân are too well known to need detailed descriptions, and they prove that from time immemorial the Africans have systematically offered up their prisoners in one form or other as sacrifices to the gods.

Seneferu, a king of the IIIrd or IVth dynasty, according to the statement on the Palermo Stele,[1] brought back from the Sûdân 7,000 men, *i.e.*, slaves, and 200,000 animals, *i.e.*, oxen, cows, goats, and we can imagine the awful destruction of human life which attended his footsteps through the Sûdân. One of his reliefs at Wâdî Maghârah in Sinai shows that he slaughtered his prisoners in that region in exactly the same way as Semti did in Egypt. Passing to the times of the XVIIIth dynasty, when the civilization of Egypt became very highly developed, we read on a stele of Åmen-ḥetep II at Amâda that the king "slew seven "chiefs with his own club when they were living in the "country of Thekhsi, and that he hung their bodies, "head downwards, at the bows of his boat." When he returned to Thebes he hung six of these opposite the pylon of the temple of Åmen, and the seventh he sent to Napata, in Nubia, to be hung on the wall of the city to terrify rebels. The records of the wars of the Thothmes kings, Seti I, Rameses II, Mer-en-Ptaḥ, and many other kings make it quite clear that they sacrificed prisoners in large numbers to the gods. The annals of the Nubian kings Ḥeru-sa-åtef and Nåstasen record a number of expeditions against tribes in various parts of the Egyptian Sûdân, and these kings boast that wherever they conquered they made a massacre, and depopulated the country. Both Nubians and Egyptians made raids for the sake of loot, *i.e.*, for living slaves and

[1] Pellegrini, *Archivio Storico*, N.S., anno XX, Palermo, 1896; Naville, *Les plus Anciens Monuments* (*Recueil*, tom. XXI); Schäfer, *Ein Bruchstück altägyptischer Annalen*, Berlin, 1902.

cattle, and when they had collected these, they filled in the wells, reaped the crops, burnt the houses, with

King Nārmer smashing the head of a prisoner of war. Ist dynasty.
From the cast in the British Museum.

everything in them, and then marched back to their homes, leaving the wild animals in possession of districts which until their arrival had been populous, and often well cultivated.

The Egyptians, however, did not always confine themselves to the sacrifice of prisoners on the battle-field, and proof exists that they were in the habit of putting Nubians and Blacks to death systematically. This only can be the meaning of the festival which is mentioned on the Palermo Stele under the name of "smashing of the Ȧntiu."[1] The Ȧntiu were the dwellers in the Eastern Desert and Sinai, with whom the early kings of Egypt waged war continually. It seems that one of them must have won some decisive battle, which was held to be of such importance that an annual festival was established to commemorate it. It goes without saying that at such festivals many human lives would be sacrificed. All these facts show that the Egyptians had no horror of human sacrifice as such, and that the cult of Osiris did not effect the abolition of the custom, but only caused the choice of victims to be made from among foreigners and from among vanquished peoples, especially those whose homes were in the Egyptian Sûdân.

The Egyptian texts contain many proofs that the overthrow of the original enemies of Osiris by Horus was accompanied by great slaughter, that their bodies were presented to him as sacrifices, and that, at the burial of the god-man Osiris, human beings were slain, and their bodies placed in his tomb. Thus, in Chapter XVIII of the Book of the Dead, we read of the great battle which took place at night, when all the Sebȧu fiends were taken prisoners, and then butchered by order of Osiris. The Sebȧu fiends were the associates of Set, and in primitive times they were living men, and not the animals and birds which were substituted for them in official ceremonies and customs of ritual. On another terrible night, another paragraph (E) informs us, Osiris sat in judgment on the dead, and the wicked were separated from the good, and the sentences of doom were forthwith carried out by the ministrants of the Great Judge. Another paragraph (G) refers to the ceremony called "Digging up the

1 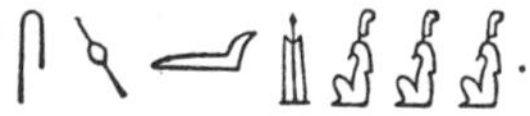.

earth in Ṭeṭu."[1] In late times this ceremony was a very harmless matter, for all that was done was to break up

Scene from the stone "shield" of Nārmer, a king of the Ist dynasty, on which is represented the offering of ten decapitated captives to the emblems of the gods. From the cast in the British Museum.

the ground with great ceremony, by means of the implement , and then sow the corn, which was the

1

earnest of next year's harvest. Originally, that is to say, when Osiris was buried, the earth was broken up with the implement, but it was then turned over and over and mixed with the blood[1] of the victims who had been sacrificed to Osiris, as the text definitely states. A later version of the Chapter[2] goes into fuller details about the slaughter of these enemies, and says: "their "heads were cut off, their necks were broken, their "thighs were chopped off by the 'Great Destroyer' in "the Valley at the Block of the East."[3] In Chapter XVII[4] we read of another great fight, which took place in Ȧnu (Heliopolis), near the Persea Tree, and this was followed by the "burning of the defeated, and the dragging to the block of the fettered rebels"[5] by night. This block is described as the "slayer of souls," and he who presided over it was Shesmu, , the executioner of Osiris. The functions of Shesmu are well known from the text in the pyramid of King Unȧs (l. 496 f.), where it is said that he slaughtered the gods and boiled their flesh in his fiery caldrons. Associated with Osiris, too, even in a text written under the XVIIIth dynasty, were the "Watchers, who brought the "god along, and the butchers,[6] who were equipped with "deadly claws, ever ready to slay" (l. 30). The idea of their pits of slaughter terrified the minds of the Egyptians in all periods. In another section of the same Chapter mention is made of a god with the face of a dog, and the brow of a man who "feeds on the slain, "who keeps guard at the corner of the Lake of Fire,

1 

2 Or, Chapter XIX.

3 

4 Papyrus of Nebseni, Sheet 14, l. 16 ff.

5 

6 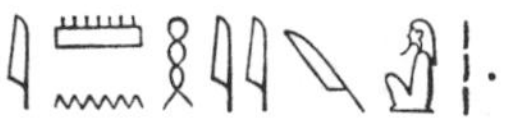

"who devours the bodies of the dead, who tears out "hearts, and who is at the same time invisible." The commentary on the passage asks who this being is, and then goes on to suggest various names, among them being that of Baba, the first-born son of Osiris. The text next speaks of a certain "victorious lord, prince of

Enlarged view of ten decapitated captives with their arms bound to their sides and their heads placed between their feet.

From the "shield" of Nārmer.

Egypt," who supplies the blocks of slaughter, and lives on intestines,[1] and keeps watch over the circuit of Åmenti. In answer to the question: "Who is this?" we are told that it is the "heart of Osiris which devours every slaughtered being"[2] (l. 46). The terror reflected

1 

2 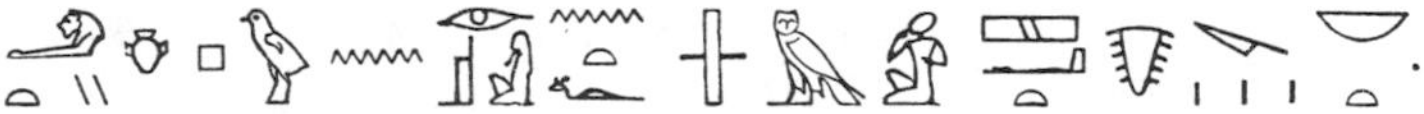

in the prayer (l. 117 ff.) to be delivered from the judges appointed by Osiris, who superintended the fettering of those doomed to slaughter, and stabbed their bodies with their daggers, and smashed in their skulls in their slaughter-houses, proves beyond all doubt that the sacrifices to Osiris were, in primitive times, human beings, and little else. In the Papyrus of Ani (Sheet 12) there is a picture of the block of slaughter over which Shesmu presided; the head was placed between two uprights set in a solid pedestal, and then lopped off, probably with a flint knife. The text refers to the rejoining of the bones of the neck and back.

The Book Ȧm-Ṭuat (Division XI) shows that, after the enemies of Osiris were beheaded and mutilated, the remains of many of them were disposed of by burning. The bodies were cut into pieces, their spirits and souls were severed from them, their shadows were driven away, their skulls were battered in, and the pieces were cast down into a pit, or pits, of fire. The pictures which accompany the texts leave no doubt on this point, for in them the pits are shown clearly, and we see the bodies, souls, shadows, and heads being consumed. Each pit is under the charge of a goddess, who vomits fire into it, in order to keep the flames renewed, and the knife which each goddess holds in her hand indicates what her functions were.

The scenes in the Book of Gates also afford indications concerning the tortures which were inflicted upon the original enemies of Osiris. It was impossible for Osiris to slay all his enemies at once, even though they were in his power, and, whilst various batches of them were awaiting their turn at the block, they were kept tightly fettered and bound. One terrible instrument of torture was the , the modern equivalent of which is known as the "goree stick."[1] It is a branch of a tree, forked at one end, by which, with the help of a strip of leather, it is fastened round the neck of a man, and it hangs down in front of the wretched creature who is

[1] Livingstone, *Expedition to the Zambesi*, p. 125; Thomson, *To the Central African Lakes*, p. 130.

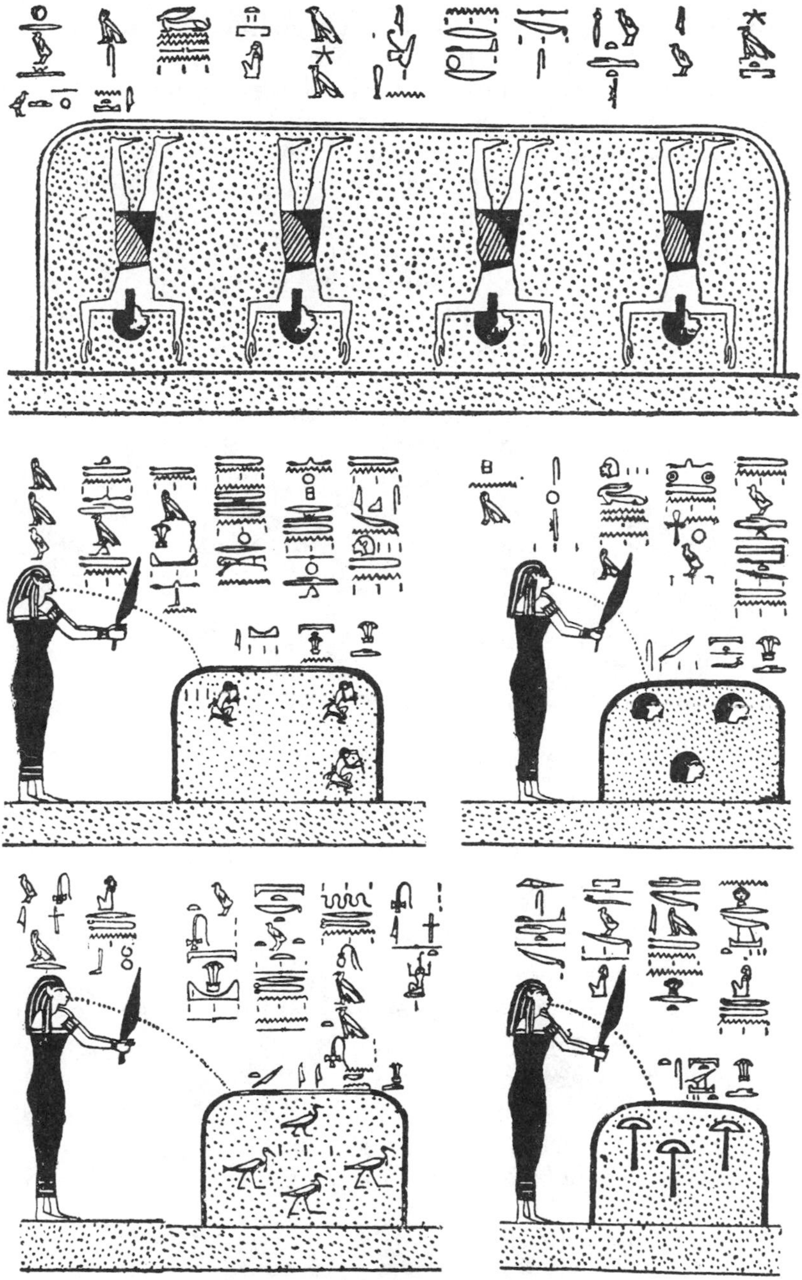

1. 2. 3. 4. 5.

1. The wicked cast head downwards into a pit of fire.
2. Enemies being burnt in a pit of fire.
3. The heads of the damned being burnt in a pit of fire.
4. The souls of the damned being burnt in a pit of fire.
5. The shadows of the damned being burnt in a pit of fire.

From the Book Åm-Tuat.

doomed to carry it. If the branch be thick the weight is considerable, and if to the end near the ground a block of stone weighing about 20 lb. be fastened, its efficiency as an instrument of torture can well be imagined. The captives of Osiris had to march with such "sticks" suspended from their necks, and their hands probably fastened to them, like modern captives, or slaves in the Sûdân. Lepsius, who saw them used, writes: "Each "captive carried before him the stem of a tree as thick "as a man's arm, about five or six feet long, which "terminated in a fork, into which the neck was fixed. "The prongs of the fork were bound together by a "cross-piece of wood, fastened with a strap. Some of "their hands, also, were tied fast to the handle of the "fork, and in this condition they remained day and "night."[1] For a captive to make his escape with such a "stick" attached to his neck is impossible. There is yet another use to which the "stick" can be put, *i.e.*, it can be driven into the ground firmly, and then prisoners can be tied to it;[2] with the arms tied in this position to the "stick" the pain is said to be almost unendurable. The hieroglyphs also cast light on the use of the "stick." In  we see a captive with his arms tied behind him to the "stick." In  we see a captive tied to the stick by the neck, and his arms tied behind his back; in this attitude his head was cut off, as we see from the hieroglyph . Another form of torture which was applied to the enemies of Osiris is also given in the Book of Gates (Division VIII). Here we see a group of captives who are called "Kheftiu Àsàr butchiu,"[3] *i.e.*, the "enemies of Osiris who are to be burnt." Their arms are tied across their bodies and behind their backs in positions which cause intense pain, and they are doomed to stand and receive in their faces the fire which the serpent Kheti

[1] Lepsius, *Letters*, p. 200.

[2] The sculptor has made the top of the stick in the form of the head of Anubis.

[3] 

King Ṭen smashing the head of a prisoner of war.
Ist dynasty.

Seneferu smashing the head of a prisoner of war. IIIrd or IVth dynasty.

is about to spit at them, and then to be hacked to pieces and burnt. Horus commands the serpent, saying: "Open thy mouth, distend thy jaws, and belch forth thy "flames against my father's enemies; burn up their "bodies, consume their souls by the fire which issueth "from thy mouth, and by the flames which are in thy "body."

From the Book Åm-Ṭuat yet other scenes of torture of the enemies of Osiris may be taken. In the first of these we see three kneeling foes, with their arms tied behind their backs, and it is clear that they have been decapitated by the animal-headed executioner who stands flourishing his knife behind them. In the extracts given

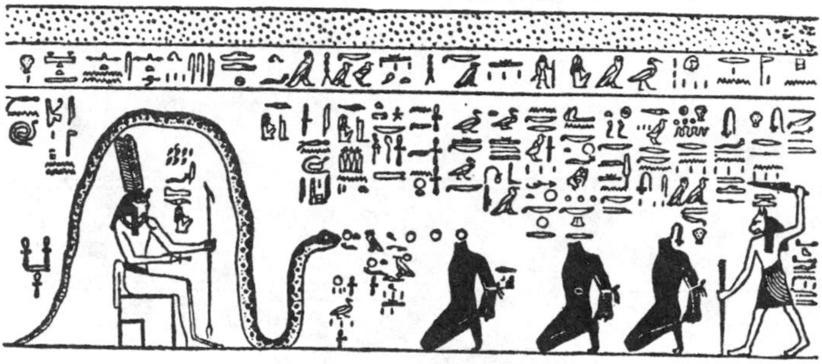

Decapitated enemies of Osiris.

further on from the works of Burton and others, it will be seen that this method of decapitation was employed in Dahomey until a very few years ago. In the next scene three male figures are lying bound in positions of excruciating agony. The arms of each are tied together at the elbows, behind his back, and the whole weight of his body is resting upon them. Their necks have been twisted round until their faces are turned towards the ground. A fiend holds ropes which are attached to the arms of each, and the least movement of these must have produced terrible agony in the wretched captives.

We have already seen that Osiris had a chief executioner called Shesmu, and we learn from the Book Am-Ṭuat that Rā was accompanied by a bodyguard of nine attendants, whose duty it was to chop off the heads of his enemies. Six of these are represented in the "Book of Gates." Here we see the hieroglyph

Åmen-eru-ḥāt III smashing the heads of prisoners of war. XIIth dynasty.

Thothmes IV smashing the head of a prisoner of war. XVIIIth dynasty.

in a modified form, but it is quite clear that it means *shems*, "servant, minister," etc. Hanging to the curved part of each hieroglyph is a human head, and in front is, I believe, the block of slaughter over which each presides. The accompanying text leaves no doubt as to the duties of these servants, for it reads: "Their "work is [to seize] the enemies of Rā everywhere in "this district (the Eighth Division of the Ṭuat), and "to make their heads to pass under their swords after "this god hath passed them by."

From what has been said above, it will be seen that there is abundant proof for the statement that the Egyptians offered up sacrifices of human beings, and that, in common with many African tribes at the present day, their customs in dealing with vanquished enemies were bloodthirsty and savage. Now the men sacrificed to the gods after a battle were strangers, or foreigners, and it was only natural for the conquerors to kill to the uttermost, if merely to terrify the vanquished foe as much as possible. We have also to consider whether the Egyptians were in the habit of sacrificing human beings to the gods in times of peace, and if so, to what degree. There is, unfortunately, little evidence in the texts which will help us to decide this point, but the writings of some classical authorities afford us very useful information. Thus, Diodorus says that in former times the kings of Egypt were in the habit of sacrificing on the tomb of Osiris men who were of the colour of Typhon.[1] Now the tomb of Osiris, *par excellence*, was at Busiris, and red was the colour typical of Typhon, or Set; therefore Diodorus says, in effect, that the kings of Egypt used to sacrifice red, or fair, men to Osiris in Busiris. Apollodorus also knew of this tradition, and he states that a stranger was offered up each year, not at Busiris, but by a king called Busiris, until the arrival of Hercules, who put Busiris to death on the very altar on which he had been in the habit of sacrificing strangers.[2] The custom of sacrificing strangers

[1] Book I, Chaps. 45 and 88.

[2] This point has been well discussed by Lefébure in *Sphinx*, tom. III, p. 133. See *Fragmenta Hist. Graec.*, ed. Didot, Frag. 33, pp. 78 and 79.

arose during a famine, owing to low Niles for nine successive years. Phrasious came to Busiris, and told

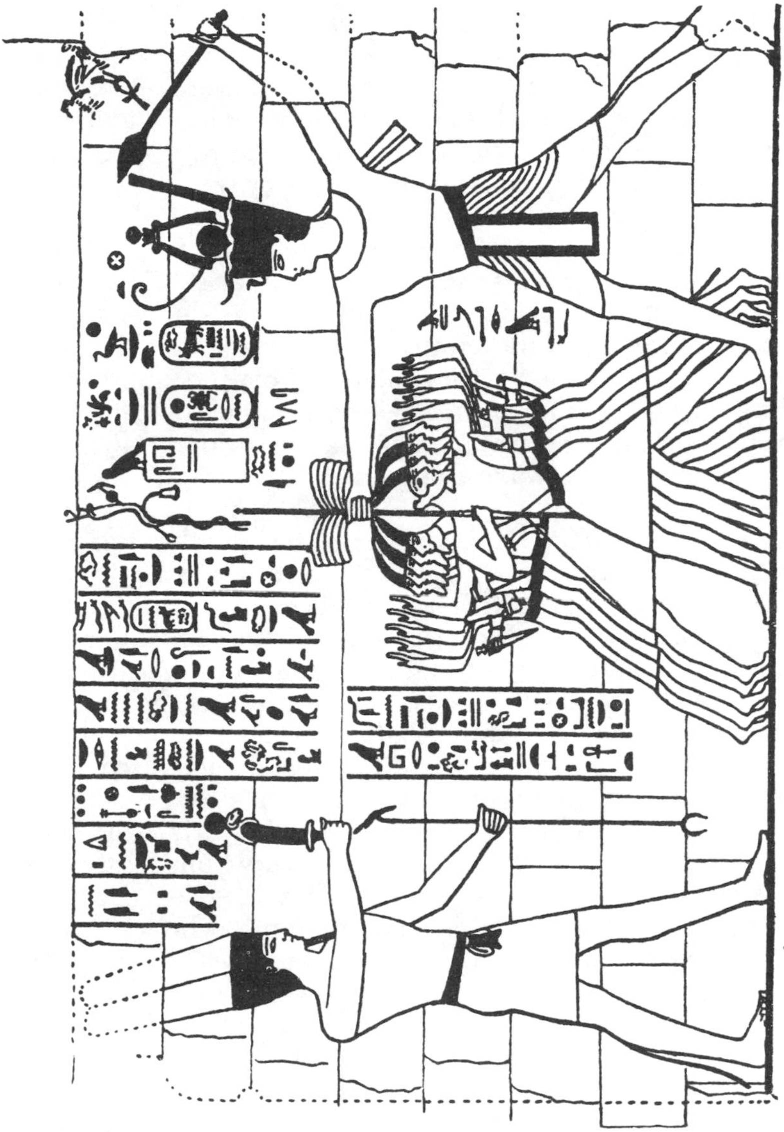

Senka-Åmen-seken slaughtering prisoners of war in the presence of Åmen-Rā. VIth century B.C. (?)

him that if he sacrificed a stranger each year, the country would enjoy water in abundance.[1] There is, of course, a

[1] See also Ovid, *Ars Amator.*, I, 647.

misunderstanding on the part of the Greek writers, for there never was a king of Egypt called Busiris; and they have made the name of the city, or temple-city, Per-Åsår, or Pa-Åsår,[1] into the name of a king.

The passages from Egyptian works quoted earlier in this Chapter prove that human sacrifices were offered up at Heliopolis as well as at Ṭeṭu, or Busiris, and the rumour of such sacrifices has found expression in the works of Greek writers. Thus, Porphyry says: "Amosis "abolished the law of sacrificing men in the Egyptian "city Heliopolis; the truth of which is testified by "Manetho in his treatise on Antiquity and Piety. But "the sacrifice was made to Juno, and an investigation "took place, as if they were endeavouring to find pure "calves, and such as were marked by the impression "of a seal. Three men also were appointed for this "purpose, in the place of whom Amosis ordered them to "substitute three waxen images."[2] If human sacrifices were common at Busiris and Heliopolis in the North of Egypt, it is perfectly certain that men would be sacrificed to the gods in the large cities of the South, *e.g.*, in Abydos and Thebes. The ceremonies connected with the cult of Osiris which were performed at Busiris were duplicated at Abydos, and the "setting up of the Ṭeṭ" was carried out with the greatest possible attention to ceremonial and ritualistic detail on the part of the priests. At Busiris the Ṭeṭ, or backbone of Osiris, which had been discovered at Mendes and brought to Busiris, was the permanent symbol of the Great Sacrifice, *i.e.*, of Osiris, who was slain and hacked to pieces by Set. Every human sacrifice offered up there was regarded as a successful effort to avenge the death of Osiris, and every one who took part in the ceremony was believed to receive benefit. At Abydos precisely similar views were held and the sanctuary of the god in that city was believed to be holier, if possible, than that of Busiris, because the head of Osiris was buried there. Now the head is the most treasured relic among all African peoples. The religious symbol of the city of Abydos was the coffer containing the head of Osiris, surmounted by two

1 .

2 *De Abstinentia*, Lib. II, Chap. 55.

Horus and Ptolemy VIII slaughtering a prisoner of war.

Ptolemy XII slaughtering prisoners of war in the presence of Isis.

plumes, and mounted on a staff , just as , the backbone of Osiris, was the religious symbol of the city of Busiris ; each was the symbol of slaughter, or sacrifice, and to each, or before each, sacrifice had to be made. Details of the early history of Busiris and Abydos are not forthcoming, but it is tolerably certain that the worship of Osiris was the most important feature in the life of these cities at all periods of their existence, and that among all the observances connected with his cult, the sacrificing of human beings was not the least frequent, and not the least important.

We have now to consider some of the proofs found in Egyptian texts that human sacrifice was regarded as a necessary concomitant of burials of the followers of Osiris, and the evidence on the same point which is deduced from Egyptian archaeology. Every one is familiar with the little figures, found in such large numbers in our museums, which are made in the form of a mummy and are commonly called "Shabtiu," or "Ushabtiu."[1] The Shabti, or Shauabti,[2] is a figure made of stone, alabaster, wood, faïence, etc., and is found in tombs from the VIth dynasty to the Roman Period. In the VIth dynasty the Shabti appears to have been uninscribed ; in the XIIth it frequently bears the name and titles of the person for whom it was made, and with whom it was buried ; and in the XVIIIth and following dynasties, in addition to the name and titles of the deceased, it bears a text which is identical with the VIth Chapter of the Book of the Dead. Its earliest form is that of a mummy with no hands showing, later it has its hands crossed over the breast,[3] later each hand holds the emblem of life,[4] still later each hand holds a hoe ,[5] and

[1] 

[2] 

[3] See the Shabti figure of Amasis I in the British Museum (No. 32,191).

[4] See the Shabti figure of Åmen-ḥetep II in the British Museum (No. 35,365).

[5] See the Shabti figure of Seti I in the British Museum No. 22,818).

A Meroïtic queen spearing captives.
From a pyramid chapel at Meroë.

last of all a basket is thrown over the shoulder.[1] The text, which is cut or written on figures from the XIIth dynasty onwards, explains quite clearly the purpose which the figures were intended to serve, for in it the figure is called upon, in the name of the deceased person written upon it, to perform whatsoever labours he might be adjudged to do in the Other World. These labours consisted in tilling and planting and watering the fields, and in bringing sand from the East to the West, and in doing whatsoever had to be done in connection with agriculture in the Other World.

Now, the earliest figures of this class are uninscribed, and the custom of burying mummy-figures of this kind with the dead seems to be senseless unless we accept the view which we owe first of all to Professor Maspero, viz., that they represent the slaves who were buried, alive or dead, with their masters, in order that their spirits might serve the spirits of their masters in the Other World, just as their bodies had ministered to their masters' bodies in this world. This view is undoubtedly correct, and agrees with all that we know about African funeral murders. When, however, we come to apply this view to the *ushabtiu* figures which have names and a formula cut upon them, certain difficulties appear in the way, for it seems as if they were made for an entirely different purpose. The early uninscribed figures were intended to do work of every kind for their master, in fact, to make themselves generally useful in the Other World. The inscribed figures were intended, as we learn from the formula, to do agricultural work chiefly, and it is clear that they were destined to perform celestial *corvée* work in the kingdom of Osiris. The purposes of all of these figures was to do work for the dead, but why particular kinds of work are specified on those which have names cut upon them it is hard to say. Some think that the early and late figures represent two distinct beliefs, *i.e.*, in the first case, that whatsoever a man needed to have done in the Other World would be done as a matter of course by servants, or slaves, and in the second case, that whatsoever he needed to have done

[1] See the figures of the XXVIth dynasty.

A Meroïtic queen spearing captives.
From a pyramid at Meroë.

would have to be done by himself.[1] To avoid this unpleasant possibility, *ushabtiu* figures were invented. This view does not, it seems to me, explain the difficulty, for it was obvious to the Egyptian of all periods that if he had no one to do work for him in the Other World he would have to do it himself; and, believing this, he took steps to provide *ushabtiu* figures, which in the early times were without inscriptions, and in the later times had names and a formula cut or written on them. The explanation of the appearance of the name and the formula is, I believe, to be sought for in connection with the development of the cult of Osiris during and after the XIIth dynasty. It is possible that men began to think that the spirit of an unprincipled chief or king in the Other World might lay claim to, or annex, the services of the spirit-slaves belonging to other people, and do this to such a degree that certain spirits would have no spirit-slaves left to minister to their wants. Whether *ushabtiu* bore names or not makes no difference to the fact that they represented slaves, but if an Egyptian gave a figure his own name, a spirit-slave so represented would bear that name, and no spirit-chief could then annex the services of that spirit-slave and plead ignorance of his identity and of his master's name if called upon to explain. It appears to be certain that the naming of the figure in some way assured the services of a spirit-slave to the man whose name it bore.

The application of the formula, or VIth Chapter of the Book of the Dead, to the shabti figure represents, I believe, the adoption of the old African custom of funeral murder into the cult of Osiris. This cult, as we have already seen, abolished cannibalism, or at least the eating of Egyptian human flesh by the Egyptians, and as Osiris introduced the eating of grain and cereals in its stead, it was meet that his followers should be proficient in the arts of agriculture. But no Egyptian ever loved digging or top-dressing the ground, or the toil of the *shâdûf*, for its own sake, and if the shabti figure could be made to serve in the capacity of a farm-labourer, by cutting upon it the magical formula, the

[1] *A.Z.*, Band XXXII, p. 116. On the so-called "servant figures," see *A.Z.*, Band XXXV, p. 119.

A Meroïtic queen slaughtering prisoners of war.
From a bas-relief at Nagaa.

demands of the cult of Osiris would be fulfilled, and the high-class Egyptian might reasonably hope to enjoy absolute idleness in the Other World, as his fathers had done before him. A pious follower of Osiris like Seti I took great care to provide himself with a large *corvée* party, for seven hundred ushabtiu, at least, inscribed with the VIth Chapter of the Book of the Dead, were found in his tomb. In later times, when the ushabtiu were placed in boxes, it seems that some people had buried with them one shabti figure for each day in the year. This was probably the case with the officials Åmen-ḥetep and Ānkh-f-en-Khensu, for of the former 149 ushabtiu, and of the latter 171 ushabtiu are preserved in the British Museum.[1] When the boxes were first found each was full, and each contained very many more figures.

Another proof that human beings were sacrificed at funerals of the followers of Osiris is furnished by Chapter LII of the Book of the Dead. In this Chapter, which was written with the view of providing the deceased with food, he is made to say: "Let me direct "my fields in Ṭeṭu (Busiris), and my crops in Ånu "(Heliopolis), let me live on bread made of white grain, "and beer made of red grain (barley), may there be given "to me the victims of my father and mother as guardians "of my door." The word I have here rendered "victims" is *abtu* . Formerly I translated it by "ancestors," and compared it with the Hebrew word for "fathers,"[2] but it seems that it is rather to be connected with the idea of "smiting," "slaughtering," etc., an idea which is suggested by the determinative . The word, no doubt, means sacrifices,[3] and the other determinatives, , indicate clearly that they were men and women, and the deceased

[1] See Third Egyptian Room (Wall-case 115), Nos. 35,289, 35,290.

[2] אָבוֹת.

[3] Compare , "slaughters" (Papyrus of Nu, Chapter CXLVI, § XVI).

A Meroïtic queen slaughtering prisoners of war.
From a bas-relief at Nagaa.

seems to wish that victims may be sacrificed to him, even as they were for his father and mother.

A tradition extant in the XIXth dynasty, and illustrated in the Book Åm-Ṭuat (Division VII), also proves that the Egyptians believed human sacrifices to have been made when Osiris himself was buried. The illustrations on the tomb of Seti I represent the tombs of Tem, Kheperå, Rā, and Osiris. At each end we see a human head, and these, as Professor Maspero suggested many years ago, represent those of the victims who were buried in the foundations of the grave. The custom of resting the coffin, where a coffin is used at all, on human heads, is common in many parts of the Sûdân.[1]

In Ashanti several persons are invariably put to death after an earthquake, as a sacrifice to Sasabonsum, and houses which are rebuilt or repaired after an earthquake are sprinkled or moistened with human blood. In 1881 an earthquake shock threw down a portion of the wall of the king's residence in Coomassie, and the priests declared it to be the act of Sasabonsum. Fifty girls were slain, and the wall was rebuilt of mud moistened with the blood of these virgins. Slaves often are sacrificed when a building is begun, to make it stable, and the foundations are sprinkled with their blood. The idea that human blood is necessary to make a foundation secure is very widespread.[2]

A direct proof that human sacrifices were offered to Osiris under the New Empire is afforded by the tomb of Mentu-ḥer-khepesh-f,[3] from which the following illustrations are taken. Here, in the first cut, we see three men drawing a sledge, on which, kneeling with his face downwards, is a man, who is described as the "Tekenu," . In the second cut we see a "kher-ḥeb" priest,

[1] Compare, "The heads of the victims slain are usually placed at the bottom of the grave, and on them the coffin rests."—Ellis, *Tshi-speaking Peoples*, p. 164.

[2] *Ibid.*, p. 36.

[3] . See Maspero, *Mémoires Miss. Archéologique*, tom. V, Paris, 1894, p. 435 ff.

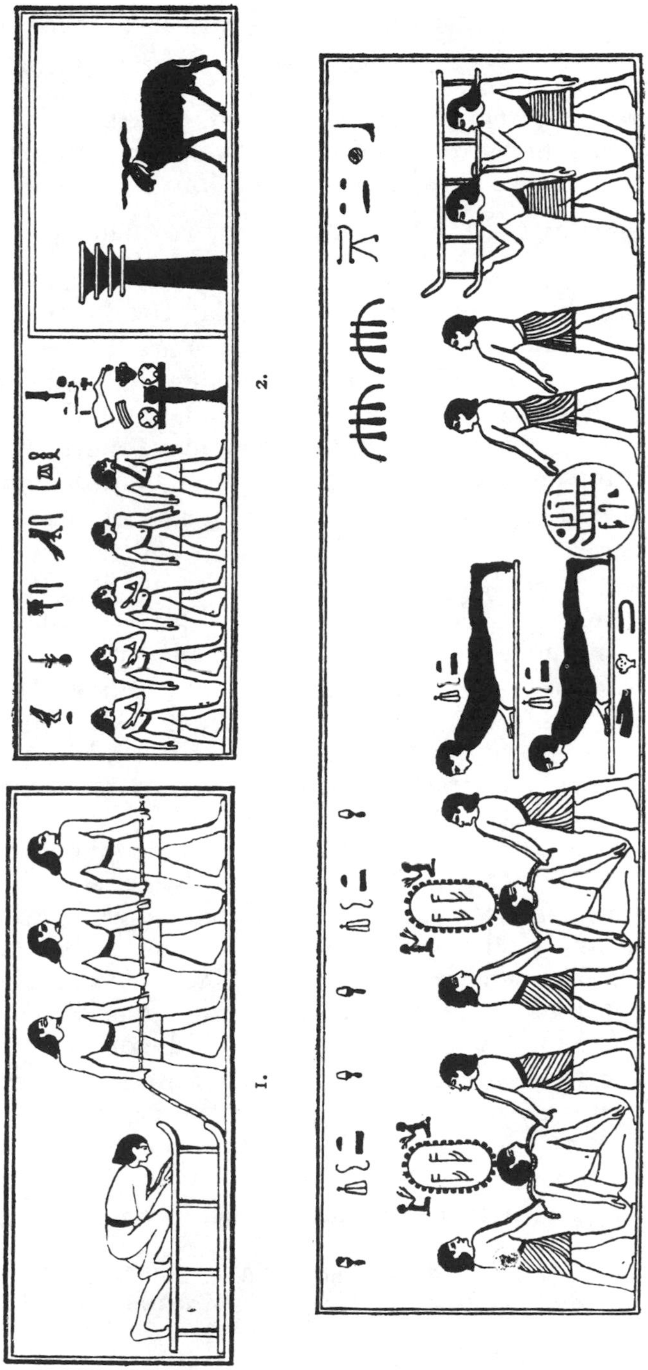

1. 2. 3.

a "smer" priest, a "sem" priest, a "royal kinsman," and an Ut official, presenting a table of offerings to the Ṭeṭ, symbol of Osiris, and the Ram of Mendes, where the backbone (ṭeṭ) of Osiris was found. In the third cut we see, beginning on the right, two men bringing a sledge. Next we see the sledge cast into a grave-pit, or pit of slaughter, *kheb* 𓐍𓃀, and then two men, who are arrayed as mummies, lying flat supported on their hands, which are free from the bandages, and on their toes. The inscription shows that they are "Ȧnti, from the land of Sti," *i.e.*, Nubians, or Sûdânî folk. We next see each of these seated on the ground, with his grave garment stripped from him, and two men, one on each side of him, engaged in strangling him. It is, of course, possible to argue that the strangling of two of the Ȧnu, or Ȧnti, folk here represented is only a symbolic act, and that these men did not lose their lives at all. When, however, we remember that the festival of sacrificing the Ȧnu began under the Ancient Empire, and that sacrifices of the Ȧnu, or Ȧnti, were offered up by Usertsen III in the XIIth dynasty, and by Thothmes III in the XVIIIth dynasty, and that other kings religiously followed their example, we can only conclude that the sacrifice of the two Ȧnti represented in these cuts actually took place. Apart from the political importance of the ceremony of sacrificing the Ȧnti, which has been well described elsewhere,[1] the Egyptians were accustomed to strangle human victims at funerals, and of this fact there is abundant evidence. Thus in the XIth dynasty tombs of the priestesses at Dêr al-Baḥarî Mr. H. R. Hall, in 1905, found the body of a woman who had been strangled, and the priestess Ȧmenit, whose body may now be seen in the Egyptian Museum in Cairo, was also strangled.[2] And the women who are now lying on the floor of the sarcophagus chamber of Ȧmen-ḥetep II either committed suicide on the death

[1] Naville, *Les Anu* (in *Recueil*, tom. XXXII); and Capart, *La Fête de Frapper les Anou* (in *Revue de l'Histoire des Religions*, tom. XLIII, 1901).

[2] King and Hall, *Egypt and Western Asia*, p. 329.

of their lord, or were strangled, so that their spirits might be united with his in the Other World.

The putting to death of human beings at funerals does not appear to be the result of bloodthirstiness and cruelty on the part of those who sacrifice them ; on the contrary, it arises from feelings of fear or respect, or feelings of love and affection for the dead, and the wish to pay them honour. It would be a disgrace to the whole community for a king to arrive in the Other World without a proper retinue of wives, slaves, and attendants, for, as it is certain that the king will live again, or rather continue his existence which death interrupted temporarily, he will need everything which he needed in this world. Moreover, sacrifices must be offered up at intervals at his grave, so that additions may be made to his retinue, and his state maintained. Among the Africans of all periods the belief in immortality has always been implicit and absolute, and there can be no question that human sacrifices and "funeral murders" are the logical outcome of this belief in immortality, and of the fear and honour in which they have always held the gods and the dead.

We may now illustrate the custom of "funeral murders" during the Middle Ages and in modern times from the writings of travellers. Ibn Baṭûṭah, writing in the first half of the fourteenth century of our era, learned from credible witnesses that in the Sûdân they buried the king in a large grave, in which they placed thirty men and thirty women, who were selected from among the chief families of the State, after their hands and feet had been broken. In this subterranean tomb they also placed vases full of drink.[1] On the Island of Biṣsao nine kings ruled in 1697, and, when one of these died, thirty persons were strangled and buried with him.[2] Writing about 1820, John M'Leod says that the royal graves of Dahomey are deluged with human blood yearly.[3] And whenever a king wants to inform his

[1] *Voyages d'Ibn Batoutah*, ed. Defrémery and Sanguinetti, Paris, 1879, p. 302.

[2] Claude Jannequin, *Voyage to Lybia* (in *Collection of Voyages*, Vol. II, p. 118) (Brit. Mus. Press-mark No. 2058*d*). See also the funeral of a chief described in Moore, *Travels*, pp. 129–134.

[3] *A Voyage to Africa*, p. 57.

forefathers of any remarkable event, he sends a courier to the Shades by having his head chopped off. Sometimes a second follows with the postscript![1] Along the Gold Coast at that time it was customary to bury a woman alive with the body of a great man.[2] Among the Mundu, Abukâya, and Abâka peoples it is customary to bury from five to fifteen female slaves alive with a departed chief, and these go to their fate voluntarily, in the firm belief that he will continue to provide for them in the grave.[3] Among the Kalikâ people a chief is buried with his cattle, and all his effects, and all his nearest relatives.[4] Vangele, with his own eyes, saw beheaded fourteen slaves, whose spirits were required to go to the Other World to attend a chief of the By-yanzi and Bakuti tribes, who had departed thither. The skulls, having been boiled clean, were placed on poles over the grave, the bodies were thrown into the Congo, and the blood-saturated earth was gathered up and buried with the dead chief.[5] In Benin the greatest favourites of the king were buried with him,[6] and the Bonny men were in the habit of sacrificing men annually to their Ju-Jus.[7] Among the Barotse a man will kill himself on the tomb of his chief, thinking that he hears him calling upon him to bring water.[8] When King Pass-all died, one hundred slaves were killed, and their bodies laid round about his coffin, and chests of goods also surrounded it on the ground. The Oronugou kings, it seems, were not laid in the earth at all.[9] In the inland Gold Coast the widows mourn for several months, and then a selection of them, and a number of slaves, and one or two free men, are killed to escort the dead man to Srahmandazi (the Other World). And, besides these, to provide him with means, quantities of gold dust, rolls of rich velvets, silks, satins, etc., are

1 *Ibid.*, p. 64.
2 *Ibid.*, p. 133.
3 Junker, *Travels in Africa*, Vol. I, p. 296.
4 *Ibid.*, 358.
5 Stanley, *The Congo*, Vol. II, p. 181.
6 Kingsley, *West African Studies*, p. 452.
7 *Ibid.*, p. 513.
8 Decle, *Three Years in Savage Africa*, p. 74.
9 Du Chaillu, *Adventures*, p. 183.

thrown into the grave.[1] In 1808 the king of Dahomey sacrificed three thousand slaves on his mother's grave, and Badahung, king of Dahomey, sacrificed two thousand. At festivals in Abomey it was usual to sacrifice one thousand slaves, and this was done when De Souza visited the king, and also when General Verheer visited him. Badahung, it is said, filled a lake large enough to float a canoe with the blood of his victims. In Ashanti, the young slave who was supposed to contain the ruler's soul was slain at his death.[2]

On the Niger human sacrifice was an "indispensable feature" of the second burial, and everywhere the number of persons sacrificed varied from one to one hundred, or more, twelve being considered the ordinary number for a chief of some standing, or a king. These persons were slaves who were purchased from neighbouring localities, and were generally killed, but they were buried promiscuously whether alive or dead. Formerly, less than fifty years ago, hundreds were sacrificed in this way, among them being free-born men. At the present day the Aro sacrifice one hundred slaves and a horse or two on the death of an elder.[3] At the final "Okuku," or ceremony in memory of the departed, the most important feature is the sacrifice and eating of a male or female slave. The victim is bought after the chief's death, and is fattened and well treated, and is slain on the first day of the Ibo week, usually on market day. He or she is taken to the market place and made to eat and drink, and is beheaded at dawn on the following day in the burial room by the eldest son, and the body is shared by all present and eaten. In Nkwerri a woman is usually killed and buried with the chief in the belief that in this act the eyes of the departed soul, which were shut when he died, will be opened in spirit land.[4] In many cases three or four men are killed and buried with the deceased, with the object of raising him, *i.e.*, his soul, up by the head and feet when in the

[1] Kingsley, *Travels in West Africa*, p. 517.

[2] Hutchinson, *Ten Years' Wanderings among the Ethiopians*, 1861, pp. 123–129.

[3] A. G. Leonard, *The Lower Niger and its Tribes*, p. 160.

[4] *Ibid.*, p. 161.

grave. A number of slaves are also hung in the various rooms of the chief's house, and others in the roadway, besides those whom the chief has mentioned as being his hand, his foot, his face, or his skin. When the bodies are cut down they are decapitated. The Efik, Ibibio, and Ibo used to sacrifice virgins at the funeral of a chief, as well as the bearers of his snuff-box, sword, staff, and umbrella.[1]

Human sacrifices have been practised by all Yoruba peoples and other West African tribes, especially at periodic festivals and on other great occasions. The king of Dahomey, in 1664, is reported to have built a royal dead-house, the mortar of which had been mixed with human blood.[2] The headman of a Walungu chief is always killed on the death of his master and buried with him. All his wives also are killed and buried with him, except one, who is placed in a hole, just large enough to hold her, dug in the ground. She is then covered over, a small aperture being left for her to breathe through ; through this hole a spear passes which she holds in her right hand. If at the end of two days she is found to be alive, she is taken out, and permitted to live.[3]

MM. Bonnat and Kühne state that when Mensa Kuma died, the Odumfo, or executioners, rushed about everywhere seeking for victims. They ran upon man after man, pierced his cheeks with a knife, and then tied his hands behind him and drove him to the slaughter. Girls and pages were strangled on the spot, and a prince and several nobles were beheaded. In a war which took place between the tribes in 1873 about 136 chiefs were killed, and for each chief thirty slaves were sacrificed. At the funeral of an uncle of Kwoffi Kari-Kari, who died at the Ashanti town of Kokofu in November, 1871, 200 human beings were put to death. The ceremonies for King Kwamina, who died in 1797, were repeated weekly for three months, 200 slaves being sacrificed on each occasion. When the mother of Tutu

[1] *Ibid.*, pp. 444, 445.

[2] Dennett, *At the Back of the Black Man's Mind*, p. 262.

[3] Thomson, *To the Central African Lakes*, Vol. I, pp. 319, 320.

Kwamina died in 1816, 3,000 slaves and Fanti prisoners were put to death.[1]

In Ashanti, the king, as in ancient Egypt, slew prisoners with his own hand. In answer to a question put to a native, the German missionaries were told: "We slay five to ten a day, and on every day of the week except Friday."[2] A king of Oyo died in 1859, and only four men were sacrificed, but forty-two of his wives committed suicide. When the king of Ondo died twenty persons were sacrificed, and on the day of burial eight or ten more, with a cat, were either killed or buried alive with the body, and further victims fell during the three following months. When attempts were made to persuade the Oni of Ife to abolish human sacrifice, he objected, saying that the sacrifices were for the benefit of the whole human race, the white man not excepted; and that if the sacrifices made on his behalf were to be discontinued, his superior knowledge, and the arts derived therefrom, would depart from him.[3]

In Dahomey when a human sacrifice is made the head is placed upon the grave, and the body is buried with the master.[4] The Annual Customs cost 500 lives, and the Great Customs 1,000;[5] but according to Skertchley the numbers are only about 200 and 600 respectively.[6] The stories of the Customs which have been printed in England contain gross exaggerations, and they are only mentioned here to show that funeral murders are numerous and frequent in that country.

It may be thought by some who read the above statements that they refer to customs which were passing away even whilst they were being described; but a reference to George Grenfell's Diary proves that funeral murders were common in Congoland as recently as 1889 and 1894. Thus:—

July 5, 1889. A man and a woman have been killed to-day at Mungulu's to accompany his dead wife,

[1] Ellis, *The Tshi-speaking Peoples*, p. 162 ff.; see also Wilson, *Western Africa*, p. 219.

[2] Ramseyer and Kühne, *Four Years in Ashanti*, pp. 144, 297.

[3] Ellis, *The Yoruba-speaking Peoples*, p. 106.

[4] Burton, *A Mission to Gelele*, Vol. II, p. 164.

[5] *Ibid.*, p. 24.

[6] *Dahomey as It is*, p. 239.

Mbonjeka. In the entry for July 7 Grenfell describes how a man and a woman were buried alive.

April 13, 1890. Three people were killed to go with Manga yesterday, and four more are tied up ready for to-day.

June 17, 1890. Nine slaves were killed to go with the dead wife of one of Boyambula's men.

August 25, 1894. Mungulu died and was buried with several slaves, and possibly one or two wives.[1]

The above extracts prove beyond all doubt that all Nilotic people, and all the dwellers to the east and west of them, have in all times offered up from religious motives human sacrifices to their gods, kings, and chiefs, and there is good reason for believing that they will continue to do so for many years to come in all places where the British Administrator has no influence. The primitive Egyptians, so far as the indigenous African population is concerned, did the same in this respect as their countrymen in the Sûdân. At an early period, however, they substituted animals for men in their sacrificial ceremonies, but there is no doubt that they reverted promptly to the customs of their forefathers in times of public disaster, that for many centuries of the Dynastic Period they celebrated their victories, old and new, with human sacrifices, and that vanquished foes and strangers were not only slain, but eaten sacramentally.

[1] Johnston, *George Grenfell*, Vol. I, p. 386 ff.

CHAPTER VII.

Osiris and Dancing.

From Diodorus[1] we learn that when "Osiris passed "through Ethiopia, a company of satyrs were presented "to him, who, as it is said, were all hairy down to their "loins. For Osiris was a man given to mirth and jollity, "and took great pleasure in music and dancing. He "therefore carried along with him a train of musicians, "of whom nine were virgins, most excellent singers, and "expert in many other things (whom the Greeks call "Muses), of whom Apollo (*i.e.*, Horus) was the captain, "and was therefore called the Leader of the Muses. "Therefore the satyrs, who are naturally inclined to "skipping, dancing, singing, and all sorts of mirth, were "taken in as part of the army."

The information contained in the preceding paragraph is both interesting and valuable, for it not only describes the love of Osiris for music, and singing, and dancing, and the pleasure which he took in watching buffoons, whom Diodorus calls "satyrs," but it throws light on the cult of Osiris, and on one of the most important features of the African religion and the character of the African. All Nilotic peoples are greatly addicted to dancing, and they never seem able to perform any ceremony without dancing; they dance at weddings and they dance at funerals, and dancing among many tribes constitutes an act of worship of the highest and most solemn importance. We have, unfortunately, no description of the dances which were performed by the ancient Egyptians, but there is abundant evidence that they considered certain dances to be acts of worship. The earliest representation of dancing as an act of worship appears to be that given on the wooden plaque of Semti (Ḥesepti), a king of the Ist dynasty.[2] Here the king is seen

[1] Book I, Chap. 18.
[2] See above, p. 11.

wearing the crowns of the South and North, and in his right hand he holds his whip, and in his left a paddle. He is performing some dance which was connected with a festival, and the paddle probably symbolized the part which the ritual ordained him to take in it. The position of the king suggests that he is treading a measure to the accompaniment of some simple instrument of music, or perhaps to the clapping of the hands of his slaves. The

King Semti dancing before a god.
From an ebony plaque in the British Museum.

king wears a pair of short drawers, and apparently nothing else except his double crown. In the early dynasties both men and women wore only loin cloths or very short drawers, but the latter were fond of putting on ornaments, bracelets, bangles, etc. In later times the dancing women wore garments which reached to their ankles.

Passing to the period of the IVth dynasty, we learn that in the reign of King Àssȧ, a high official called Ba-ur-ṭeṭ brought from Punt a *ṭenḳ* (pygmy), who knew how to dance "the dance of the god,"[1] and was said to

1 .

come from the "Land of the Spirits."[1] Assȧ was so pleased with his officer that he bestowed great honours upon him, and we may assume that the pygmy was despatched to Memphis to dance before the king. In the text in the pyramid of Pepi I distinct mention is made of the "pygmy of the dances of the god, who "rejoiceth the heart of the god before his (*i.e.*, the god's) "great throne."[2] Thus it is clear that kings of ancient Egypt were very pleased to get possession of a pygmy who understood how to dance a particular kind of dance which was associated with "the god," who was probably Osiris, and that such pygmies were best obtained from Punt, and from the part of that country which was known as the "Land of the Spirits." The second extract shows that a king of Egypt considered that it would be an honour to him in the Other World if he could dance like a pygmy before Osiris, and proves clearly that the object of the dance of the god was to comfort, cheer, and strengthen the deity whose special dance he danced. The Egyptian bas-reliefs of all periods contain many illustrations of kings dancing before Osiris and other gods, and we may be sure that

Thothmes III dancing before the goddess Hathor, to whom he offers a bird.

1 

2 
 Pepi I, l. 401 = Mer-en-Rā, l. 573 = Pepi II, l. 1180.

the naturally conservative spirit of the people preserved faithfully all the essential characteristics of the dance which tradition had handed down to them. The following descriptions of the meaning and symbolism of dancing among the modern peoples of the Sûdân and West Africa, and the accounts of dances given by travellers, illustrate ancient Egyptian dancing, and throw much light on the subject, both as a religious exercise and a means of amusement.

In a description of his visit to Katchiba, chief of Obbo, Sir Samuel Baker says: "He came to meet us with several of his head men. He was an extraordinary looking man, about 58 or 60 years of age; but, far from possessing the dignity usually belonging to a grey head, he acted the buffoon for our amusement, and might have been a clown in a pantomine. The chief determined upon a grand dance, and soon the nogâras (drums) were beaten, pipes and flutes were soon heard gathering from all quarters, horns brayed, and men and women began to collect in crowds. About a hundred men formed a circle. Each man held in his left hand a small cup-shaped drum, formed of hollowed wood, one end only being perforated, and this was covered with the skin of the elephant's ear, tightly stretched. In the centre of the circle was the chief dancer, who wore, suspended from his shoulders, an immense drum, also covered with the elephant's ear. The dance commenced by all singing remarkably well a wild but agreeable tune in chorus, the big drum directing the time, and all the little drums striking at certain periods, with such admirable precision, that the effect was that of a single instrument. The dancing was most vigorous, and far superior to anything that I had seen among either Arabs or savages, the figures varying continuously, and ending with a 'grand galop' in double circles at a tremendous pace, the inner ring revolving in a contrary direction to the outer; the effect of this was excellent. Although the men wear a skin slung across their shoulders and loins, the women are almost naked, and instead of wearing the leather apron and tail of the Latûkas, they are contented with a slight fringe of leather shreds, about four inches long by two broad, suspended from a belt. The unmarried girls are entirely naked, or wear three or four strings of small white beads, about three inches in length, as a covering. The old ladies wear a string round the waist, in which is stuck a bunch of green leaves, the stalk uppermost."[1] Here we have a complete parallel with King Pepi, whose earnest desire was to dance before the god. Katchiba wished to please Baker, and so he acted the buffoon before him with such success that "he might have been a clown in a pantomine."

The god Bes playing a harp.

When Baker was talking with Kabba Rêga, and it "became necessary to change the conversation, a number of buffoons that were kept about the court for the amusement of the young king now came forward. The crowd was driven back, and an open space having been thus cleared, they performed a curious theatrical scene, followed by a general fight with clubs, until one man, having knocked down all the party, remained the victor. The scene terminated with an act of disgusting indecency, which created roars of laughter from the immense crowd, who evidently considered this was the great joke of the piece."[2]

After one of the many disputes which Speke had with Kamrasi, king of Unyoro, the latter sent a dwarf called Kimenya to visit him. Kimenya was a little old man, less than a yard high, and he came with a walking stick larger than himself. He made his salaam, sat down composedly, and then rose up and danced, singing

[1] Baker, *Albert N'yanza*, p. 197 f.
[2] Baker, *Ismailïa*, p. 313.

without invitation, and following it up with queer antics. Lastly, he performed the *tambŭra*, or charging march, in imitation of Wakungû, repeating the same words they use, and ending by a demand for simbi, or kauri shells. He was born in Chopi, and was sent for to come to court by Kamrasi,[1] much as King Pepi sent to Aswân to tell Her-khuf to send the pygmy in safe keeping to Memphis.

Another instance of the desire of African kings to attach pygmies to their court is recorded by Dr. Schweinfurth, who describes the pygmy Adimokoo, a member of the Akka nation, numbers of whom had settled down under the protection of the Mañbattû king. He was about 4 feet 10 inches high, and he was dressed like a Mañbattû, in a rokko-coat and plumed hat, and was armed with a miniature lance as well as with a bow and arrow. Although Dr. Schweinfurth had several times been astonished at witnessing the war-dances of the Niam-Niam, his amazement was greater than ever when he looked upon the exhibition which the pygmy afforded. In spite of his large bloated body and short bandy legs, in spite of his age, which by the way was considerable, Adimokoo's agility was perfectly marvellous, and one could not help wondering whether cranes would ever be likely to contend with such creatures. The little man's leaps and attitudes were accompanied by such lively and grotesque varieties of expression that the spectators shook again and held their sides with laughter.[2]

In October, 1902, Grenfell camped near the Nepoko River, and received a visit from a company of dwarfs. They are, he says, queer little folk, who live by their wits, and by their nimbleness as hunters. They are feared because of their cunning, and because they never fail to avenge any injury which they may receive. One of the groups was a sort of minstrel band, which, having played their music and danced before us, went later and performed in two other villages on the other side of the river. The music was only one degree less remarkable than the dancing. One refrain was like beautifully-toned

[1] Speke, *Journal*, p. 433 (Dent's reprint).
[2] *Heart of Africa*, Vol. II, p. 129.

bells in the distance. The second consisted of two chords only, and must have been copied from a bird's song in the woods. The third was a medley of hand-clacking and vocal tones that resembled nothing else so much as a troop of tropical frogs. The dancing was done by the headman, and is even more difficult to describe than the music. Azimbambuli, the dancer, was 4 feet 6½ inches in height.[1]

A witch-doctor's dance is thus described by Decle: The Mfumu first danced a *pas seul*, accompanied by five tom-toms, beaten with little sticks. He wore on his head a diadem made out of a zebra's mane; two bands of goatskin were arranged crosswise over his chest, and his arms were covered with the same. A piece of cloth hung down to his knees in front and to his ankles behind. He was also covered with anklets. He began by walking in a circle in front of the drums, then gradually increased his pace till he broke into a run. Then he stopped suddenly and began a jig, in the middle of which, heaving his chest vigorously, with his arms stretched out before him, he dropped to the ground. While dancing he sang a little solo of his own, accompanied by the spectators. Then he rose, and striking one of the drums two or three times, began another song, the whole company joining in the chorus, after which he went through the whole of the previous performance. This lasted all day and went on till late in the night. The large crowd was at times quite enthusiastic, and taking off ornaments, necklaces, bracelets and anklets, men and women threw them at his feet. These he picked up without speaking and deposited them in front of the orchestra of drums as he passed.

The Wakamba have three different dances. In the first men and women place themselves in two lines opposite to each other. Each man has a long drum, *i.e.*, a piece of wood hollowed out, about 5 feet long and 4 inches in diameter, with a handle at the top, and a skin stretched across the bottom; on the outside of the drum are rows of small bells. The men rush forward from time to time and each rubs his cheek against that of the girl opposite, singing and beating

[1] Johnston, *George Grenfell*, Vol. I, p. 331.

his drum on the ground. The men are naked for this dance. In the second dance the men and women in lines face each other. Big drums, which are placed behind the lines, are beaten. The men first walk up to the women, who stand with their hands on their breasts; then they retreat, then they rush forward and rub cheeks. This goes on for some time, and the men become more and more excited, and rush at the women in the maddest way, rubbing cheeks furiously, and singing all the while. The old women have a dance to themselves; drums are beaten, and they fling their arms about and sing slowly.[1]

The chief village of each Fân family has a huge idol, to the worship of which the whole family gathers at certain periods. This worship consists of rude dances and singing.[2] Another dance, which was performed at a ball given by King Bango, may be thus described: When the king gave the signal, all rose up, and beat a kind of tune or refrain to accompany the drums. Then six women stepped out and began to dance in the middle of the floor. Anyone who has seen a Spanish fandango, and can imagine its lascivious movements tenfold exaggerated, will have some faint conception of the postures of these black women. To attain the greatest possible indecency of attitude seemed to be the ambition of all six. These were relieved by another set of six in course of time, and so the ball went on for two hours, when the proceedings became extremely uproarious. Next, women came out, one at a time, and danced their best, before a closely critical audience, who, watching every motion with jealous eyes, were sure to applaud by audible murmurs of pleasure at every more than usually lewd *pas*.[3] One of the songs sung before the dance contained these words:—

> "When we are alive and well,
> "Let us be merry, sing, dance, and laugh;
> "For after life comes death;
> "Then the body rots, the worms eat it,
> "And all is done for ever."[4]

[1] Decle, *Three Years in Savage Africa*, pp. 356, 492.
[2] Du Chaillu, *Adventures*, p. 141.
[3] *Ibid.*, p. 141.
[4] Identical sentiments are expressed in the famous "Song of the Harper," which is written on the wall of a tomb at Thebes.

At a dance given in the open air, King Olenga-Yombi himself danced. "The excitement became "greatest when the king danced. His majesty was "pretty drunk, and his jumps were very highly "applauded. His wives bowed down to his feet while "he capered about, and showed him the deepest marks "of veneration, while the drums and kettles were "belaboured more furiously than ever."[1]

The traveller, Thomson, saw a dance performed in Masai-land without the help of musical instruments. The men had their hair rolled into strings, which hung like a mop over their heads. Small kidskin garments were flung over their shoulders or hung by their sides, and their bodies were plastered with grease and clay. The girls wore an under-girdle round the loins, and were loaded with beads, clay, and grease. A young man advances, holding a wand in his hand. His arms hang straight down. At first he hops forward like a bird, till, reaching the centre, he commences a series of leaps straight into the air, without bending his legs or moving his arms. From time to time he thrusts his head forward, bringing his long black hair over his face. After springing in this manner about a dozen times, he steps aside, and another takes his place, till all have gone through their paces. Then, with wilder movements, they trot round in a variety of evolutions, and so the dance ends, to be resumed in precisely the same manner.[2]

At the war dance at Miriali's, described by L. von Höhnel, some three hundred men assembled, most of them wearing feather collars on their shoulders, and Masai moran masks or monkeys' skins on their heads. Half of them carried guns, and the other half were armed with spears, shields, and swords. Their war mantles were made of red or other coloured stuff. The performers arranged themselves in a circle, and set up a really melodious chant, keeping time by striking their guns or spears with their clubs. The chant was sung softly in deep, vibrating chest tones. Slowly the circle of dancers moved round, whilst single performers,

[1] *Ibid.*, p. 202.
[2] *Through Masai Land*, p. 122.

generally six at a time, hopped into the centre, and, swinging their weapons to the time of the measure, sprang at regular intervals into the air. When Miriali had dressed himself in a gold-tinsel-covered cap, a general's red coat, a collar of vultures' feathers, a straw hat trimmed with bright red bendera, two long white ostrich feathers, knee ornaments made of colobus skin, and eleven yards of bendera, which he wound round his body, he came up, and the dance was gone through again. The guns were loaded almost to bursting with powder, and the dancers stepped out of the circle to fire, pointing their weapons to the ground, and reaching out as far as possible in front of them; as they pulled the triggers they sprang into the air. Then they started out as if on the warpath, going in skirmishing order, one or other of them rushing out of the line and uttering a terrible cry, and, having fired at an imaginary foe, he rushed back again.[1]

In Dahomey the king sings and dances in connection with the So-Sin Custom. According to Burton, he beat the drums with hooked sticks, and sang, and danced to the men's band and then to the women's. He then danced to six modes, and in one of them imitated the action of binding captives. Then he leaned upon his bard's staff, and sang whilst a "single cymbal made melancholy music." Then rising with uplifted staff, and turning towards the larger shed-tent, he adored, in silence, his father's ghost.[2] The Logun-sinsi, or "Tail-dancers," appear to be peculiar to Dahomey. They were about twenty in number, and wore pink skirts reaching down to the knee, and open-throated tunics of white calico embroidered with scarlet. Round their waists they wore broad scarlet sashes, to the back of which enormous bustles were attached. From the back of these proceeded a short stick, from which depended a long tail of alternate black and white horsehair, as thick as a man's arm, and just clearing the ground. They came in, and saluting the king, commenced their peculiar dance. Standing in a row, with their backs to

[1] L. von Höhnel, *Discovery of Lakes Rudolf and Stefanie*, Vol. I, pp. 179–181.

[2] Burton, *A Mission to Gelele*, Vol. I, p. 365.

the king, and their arms in the orthodox swimming position, they began a see-saw movement of the gluteus until their tails acquired sufficient momentum to swing completely round like a sling. They then commenced to walk in a circle, still keeping up the rotary movement of their tails, thereby eliciting thunders of applause from Amazons and warriors. A heavy *bakshîsh* (gift) followed their performance, and, wagging their curious appendages, they filed out of the presence.[1]

In the gorilla dance the principal incidents of a gorilla hunt are acted, as well as the death of the beast, and its performance is believed to ensure success to the hunters. Winwood Reade says the part of the animal was played by one Etia, whose left hand had been crippled by the teeth of a gorilla. Etia danced into the hut where three old men sat, with chalked faces, and playing a drum, a sounding log, and the one-stringed harp; as he danced he imitated the uncouth movements of the gorilla. Then an iron bell was rung, and Ombuiri was summoned to attend, and a hoarse rattle mingled with other sounds. A number of dancers then rushed in yelling and sprang into the air. There was a pause, broken only by the faint slow tinkling of the harp; then the measure grew quicker and quicker, and the drum was beaten, and the sticks thundered on the log. Etia then imitated the attitudes of the gorilla. He sat on the ground with a vacant expression on his face like that of the brute. Then he folded his arms on his forehead, and then, suddenly, he would raise his head, with prone ears and flaming eyes, while a loud shout of applause would prove how natural it was. In the chorus all the dancers assumed such postures as these, while Etia, climbing ape-like up the pole which supported the roof, towered above them all. In the third dance he acted the gorilla being attacked and killed. The man who played the hunter inimitably, acted terror and irresolution before he pulled the trigger of his imaginary gun. Etia, as gorilla, charged upon all-fours, and fell dead at the man's feet in the act of attempting to seize him with one hand.[2]

[1] Skertchley, *Dahomey as It is*, p. 263.
[2] Winwood Reade, *Savage Africa*, p. 194.

Mr. Dennett gives an interesting description of some West African dances which it is important to note. Lying on his camp bed he saw Ogugu standing before one of the altars in his house, dressed in what appeared to be a red hat and gown. Then a goat was held up so that he might sever its head from its body and sprinkle its blood on the altar. Six goats were killed, and all the altars within and without the house sprinkled with their blood, and all this was done in comparative quiet. Then Ogugu, a Nabori holding up one of his arms, and followed by his courtiers, danced before his people. Then followed the three great dances called Ukele, Ohogo, and Ugulu or Sakwadi. With these dances and further ceremonial, which does not concern us, did Ogugu celebrate the anniversary of the death of his father.[1]

The Ugulu was danced by one man only, who turned circles, keeping perfect time to the band of beaded calabashes and drums. The Ukele was danced by two men; the one held a fan, and the other had his hands clasped in front of him. The Ohogo was danced by fifteen men, three holding native bells, and the rest beaded calabashes. They were scantily dressed, and had bells and rattling seeds round their arms and ankles. Two men, one with a bell and the other with a beaded calabash, were surrounded by the other thirteen in a perfect circle. At a signal from their conductor the thirteen, singing in parts, ran round in a circle, while all beat their calabashes and bells; suddenly they stopped, turned towards each other in couples, and saluted each other. At a signal they then started off again, changing their step as it pleased their conductor, who seemed to have perfect control over their movements. Then at a signal all danced inwards towards the centre of the circle, and crowded themselves over their now crouching conductor and his companion. At a beat of his bell all withdrew and continued dancing in a circle.[2]

Among the Tshi-speaking peoples dancing is a special branch in the education of a priest or priestess. Priests must be very proficient in the art, and they are

[1] Dennett, *At the Back of the Black Man's Mind*, p. 207.
[2] *Ibid.*, p. 208.

taught privately by adepts for many months before they are allowed to perform in public. The dance is always performed to the sound of drums. When a priest enquires of a god on behalf of some one, he covers himself with white clay, puts on a white cloth, and carries a reed brush. Then he suddenly pretends to be convulsed, and the bystanders think that a god has taken possession of him. The drums strike up, and the priest commences his dance, leaping, bounding, and turning and twisting round and round, until he works himself into a real or simulated condition of frenzy, with foam dropping from the mouth and eyes wildly rolling. While thus dancing he lets fall from time to time certain remarks, which are regarded as the utterances of the god; and from them the person who sought his services forms his own conclusions.[1]

According to Sir Harry Johnston the Bantu Negroes have five dances: 1. The dance to celebrate the birth of twins; it is danced by men and women, and the gestures are obscene. 2. The death dance, which is danced by both sexes. 3. The dance of the sexual initiation ceremony, which is danced by both men and women. 4. The wedding dance, in which only women join. 5. The dance which takes place in seasons of drought to propitiate the good spirit and bring down rain. Among the Masai, Turkana, Sûk, Nandi, etc., the medicine man orders the people to go and dance under certain big trees on the hill tops. These dances are acts of worship to the deity, and are supposed to ensure good crops.[2]

Bentley quotes an instructive instance of dancing as an act of homage from a vassal chief to his overlord. The vassal was an old man, tall and thin, and stiff in his joints; he wore an old cocked hat and a soldier's red coat. When he came in sight of the king he stopped and began to sing, and he drew a long cavalry sword from its sheath, which he held in his left hand. He began to caper and dance about, and flourished the sword and its sheath alternately over his head. As he became excited he danced round and over his sword, twisting it in and out between his legs in a

[1] Ellis, *The Tshi-speaking Peoples*, pp. 121, 125.
[2] *Uganda Protectorate*, Vol. II, pp. 753, 883.

marvellous manner. As he became exhausted, the gyrations of the long sword lessened, and two trusty servants came and supported him by the elbows, whilst the aged body still jigged and wriggled about. Then he came to the king, and sank to the ground before him. Sitting cross-legged, he placed the sword and sheath on the ground, and made the usual obeisance, clapping, touching the ground with his third finger three times, and making marks with the dust on his temples; then, as he was of Zombo origin, he leaned forward, touched the ground with his shoulders, and then clapped.[1]

The subject of dancing among the peoples of Congoland has been treated in a general manner in the *Annales du Musée du Congo*, tom. I, fasc. I, and as the interesting remarks there made apply equally well to Nilotic peoples they may usefully be summarized here. The writer says: Dancing, singing, and the use of instruments of music are intimately related on the Congo; music is only considered as an accompaniment of dancing. Music and singing form an integral part of daily life. Dances begin with a slow rhythm. The step quickens under the influence of the singers' voices, and the sound of the tam-tam (tom-tom), pipe, and clapping of hands. The dancers put every muscle of the body in motion, from the neck to the feet. As the men and women dance, ever faster and faster, they utter shrill cries, seeking to drown the sounds of the drums, pipes, etc. They glide from their places in turn, twist themselves round, jump and leap, observing at the same time to keep their appointed places in the general scheme of the dance. After performing with incredible rapidity their whirlings and contortions and leapings, all accompanied by loud outcries, they fall exhausted on the ground, and their places are taken by others. Dances are usually performed at night, preferably at the new moon, to bring good luck to the new wine, or beer, or to any field enterprise, or to celebrate any event, or "pour passer le temps." Dances are performed at funerals, and frequently end in drunken orgies. Of the war-dances, which are becoming rarer, some are decidedly impressive. In dancing, the Ituri dwarfs merely leap into the air; this is the simple,

[1] Bentley, *Pioneering on the Congo*, Vol. I, p. 201.

primitive dance. The women of the Bongo dance very gracefully. Both men and women decorate themselves with great care for dances at new moon festivals, harvest festivals, and funerals.

Sir Harry Johnston notes that in Negro Africa dancing without singing is an impossibility; there must be songs, chants in chorus, rhythmic shrieks, shouts, yells, grunts, clapping of hands, stamping of feet, or a regular noise of some sort. The war-dances of the Western Tanganyika become sham fights. Dances for women only are connected with the birth of children, puberty, or the desire for good crops. Nothing like the European waltz or round dance is known. In Congo-land the natives (so Bentley) are addicted to the *danse du ventre*, as also are the Babangi. The shoulders, buttocks, stomach, and breasts, are all separately or simultaneously rotated, wagged, or otherwise set in motion[1]; there is, however, no indecency in this, or in any other dance of purely negro origin.[2] On the other hand, many dances are notoriously obscene.

Among the modern Egyptians, the most famous professional dancing women are the Ghawâzî, who used to perform unveiled in the streets. The chief characteristic is a very rapid vibrating motion of the hips from side to side. They begin decorously enough, but after a short time their gestures become characterized by lewdness, especially if their performance is not taking place in a private house. They are accompanied by women or men who play instruments of music, *i.e.*, tambourines or drums. The true Ghawâzî differ physically from the ordinary Egyptians, and it is possible that they may be descended from the professional singers and dancers who were attached to the courts of the ancient Egyptians. The better class of them dress well and

[1] This was one of the most popular dances in Egypt a few years ago. One of its principal homes was the town of Ḳenâ in Upper Egypt, from which troupes of dancers visited all parts of the country.

[2] "Africa, between the Zambesi and the northernmost limits of the "negro's domain, is freer from any public spectacle or behaviour (on the "part of the indigenes) which is likely to shock a normal sense of "decency than most parts of Europe and Asia."—*George Grenfell*, Vol. II, p. 717. But see also Torday and Joyce, *Notes on the Ethnography of the Ba-Huana*, *Jnl. Anth. Inst.*, Vol. XXXVI, p. 287.

even handsomely, and they will perform for a group of peasants as readily as for a Pâshâ, but they always expect to be paid, little or much, for their services. The modern Egyptian loves dancing, and a few taps on the well-known dancing drum in town or village will draw crowds instantly. One morning in 1899, the fast train from Cairo to the South, with an English railway official on board, was "held up" at Farshût for nearly forty minutes without any good reason. After a time the official stepped on to the platform and sought for the *Kumsarî*, or guard, to explain the delay, but he could not be found; the driver and stoker had also disappeared. At length the delinquents were found *outside* the station happily engaged in watching a party of dancing girls who were on tour, quite regardless of the facts that the engine was "blowing off," and that the working of the line was interrupted. The subsequent behaviour of the railway official was considered by the crowd to be extremely unsympathetic!

CHAPTER VIII.

Osiris and Sacrifice and Offerings, the Propitiation of Good and Evil Spirits by Offerings, Amulets, etc.

The ancient Egyptians worshipped their ancestral spirits and the gods, who, it seems, were developed from them, with sacrifices and offerings, with prayer, and, perhaps, by the wearing of amulets. For the sake of convenience we may consider the worship of the gods first. In every village of importance, and in every town, the local god had a house set apart for him called the "god-house" , which was tended and kept clean by a "slave of the god" , who in later days acquired the dignity and importance which we attach to the term "priest." If the god was considered to be a "great god," many "slaves of the god" would be attached to his house and its service; some would perform duties of a sacred character, and others would discharge the functions of mere cleaners and attendants. On the monument of a "slave of the god" called Seker-khā-baiu preserved in the museum in Cairo[1] we have a picture of an early temple of the god Set (Fig. 1), and another of the god Ȧnpu or Ȧp-uat (Fig. 2). The first of these is clearly an African hut, the sides of which are made of plaited reeds; the roof is made of some vegetable material which has been tied together, and consisted probably of a thick mat made of *salatik* similar to that which covered my *tukul* (hut) at Marawi (Abû Dôm) and other places in the Sûdân. The projections in front were, no doubt, the poles which formed the framework of the roof. The three curved lines in front represent

Fig. 1.

Fig. 2.

[1] See Mariette, *Les Mastabas*, p. 74.

the palings which are fixed before the tombs of great men all over the Sûdân. The second god-house is also made of plaited reeds or mats fastened to a rectangular framework, and its cornice is formed by a row of palm leaves set above the frame. Its front was provided with a door, whilst that of No. 1 was open. Another form of god-house is shown in Fig. 3. Here we see that the roof is curved, and that there is a door in the side.[1] The projections under the cornice may be the ends of the poles of the roof, or some ornament, or sticks placed for birds to alight on. The palings in front are as before. Other forms of this god-house are given in Figs. 4 and 5. Fig. 4 shows a projection at the back, and the whole building rests upon a platform similar to that on

FIG. 3.

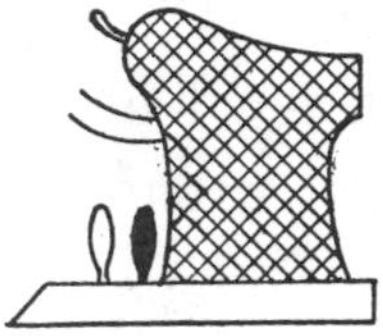
FIG. 4.

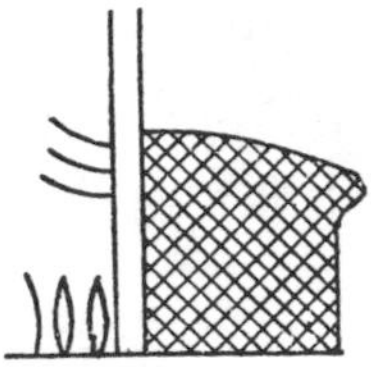
FIG. 5.

FIG. 6.

which the house of Osiris rests in later pictures.[2] In Fig. 5 we see the same building with two long poles placed in front;[3] these were no doubt flag posts, or supports for spirit emblems. Figure 6 is a god-house which rests upon a pedestal with four steps. The two pillars are in the form of lotus columns.[4] Now, all these god-houses were in use under the Ancient Empire, and in their essential features they resemble the houses in which modern Sûdânî peoples place the figures and statues of their ancestors.

Under the VIth dynasty certainly, and perhaps earlier, the Egyptians began to build massive stone temples for their gods, and, though it cannot be stated as a positive fact, there is good reason for thinking that internally the arrangement of courts, etc., was identical with that of

[1] Pyramid of Nefer-ka-Rā, line 107.
[2] Pyramid of Mer-en-Rā, l. 30.
[3] Pyramid of Tetȧ, l. 284.
[4] Pyramid of Unȧs, l. 604.

Osiris seated in his shrine at Abydos. Behind him stand the goddesses Isis, Åmentet, and Hathor.
Mariette, *Abydos*, Vol. I, Plate 17.

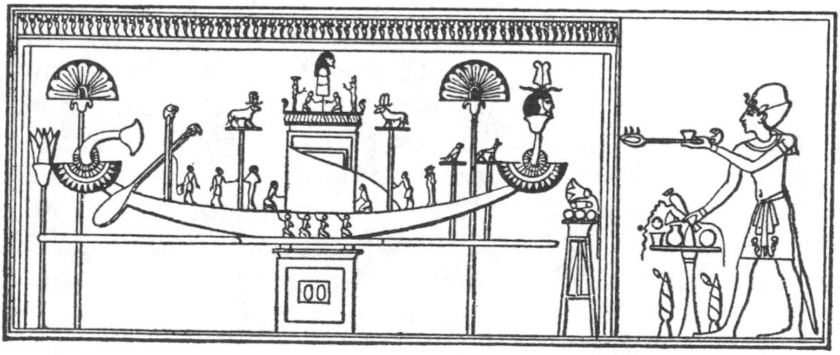

Seti I offering incense to the Boat of Osiris at Abydos.
Mariette, *Abydos*, Vol. I, p. 63.

the temples of the New Empire. The temple having been built, the first matter of importance was the selection of the place where the statue or spirit emblem of the god was to be established. It was not considered respectful to the god to set his figure or emblem where it could be seen by everyone as soon as he entered the temple, therefore the "slaves of the god" decided to set it, together with its house, at one end of the temple, where, by means of doors, it was concealed from the gaze of the vulgar. Meanwhile the god-house made of mat work was abolished, and a case made of wood was substituted, and later still the god-house, or shrine as we should call it, was made of fine, hard stone. The ancient shape was carefully preserved, for the Egyptians, in religious matters, were intensely conservative, and in one form or another they remembered every tradition, relinquishing nothing and forgetting nothing. The texts unfortunately reflect this characteristic, for they are full of views and traditions of all periods, many of which contradict each other absolutely. Under the XVIIIth dynasty the worship of the gods had assumed a complicated character, and its ritual was most elaborate. Of the ritual which belonged to the worship of many gods we know nothing, but most fortunately a copy of the service of the Divine Cult which was performed daily at Thebes in honour of Åmen-Rā has come down to us, and the following brief description of its contents will explain the principal facts about it.[1]

The priest begins by kindling a light in the sanctuary of the god, then taking the censer in his hand, and attaching to it the cup containing hot ashes, he throws incense into it; at each act he says the prescribed formulae. He then advances to the shrine, and breaks the cord which fastens the two doors, and also the seal, which he removes. He draws open the doors, and looks upon the god, and then prostrates himself flat on his stomach with his forehead resting on the ground. After the recital of a hymn of praise an offering of incense and honey is made. Then the priest advances to the shrine of the god, and stands at the foot of the steps, and then goes near the figure of the god and removes the decorations which he had placed on it the

[1] For the text see the publication of the Berlin Museum, *Rituale für den Kultus des Amon*, Fol. Leipzig, 1896–1901; also O. von Lemm, *Das Ritualbuch*, Leipzig, 1882; and the excellent work of Moret, *Le Rituel du Culte Divin*, Paris, 1902.

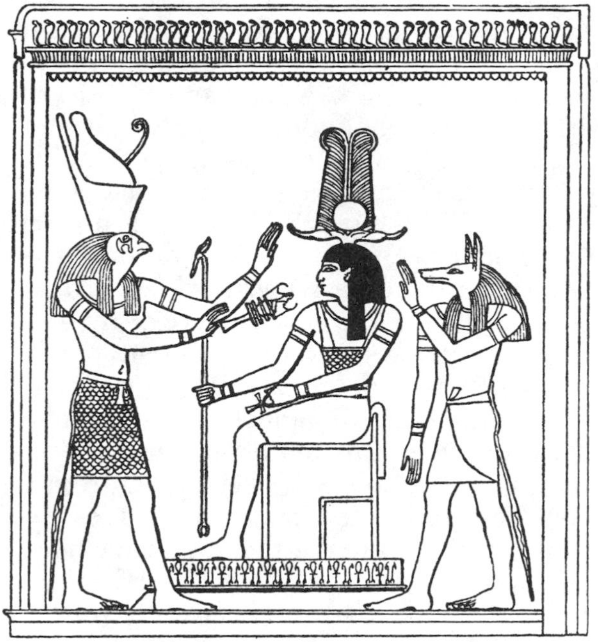

Horus presenting life and stability to Osiris-Seker.
Mariette, *Abydos*, Vol. I, Plate 27.

Thoth and Horus binding together the thrones of Osiris, Isis, and Nephthys.
Mariette, *Abydos*, Vol. I, Plate 31.

day before. Further ceremonies of purification with water and incense are performed, and the priest begins to dress the god for the day. He puts on him garments of various colours, red, white, and green, he anoints him with the seven holy oils, sprinkles perfume on him, smears his eyelids with eye-paint, puts anklets on his ankles and bracelets on his wrists, places the sceptre, crook, and whip in his hands, arranges the crown with feathers on his head, places a pectoral on his breast, and fastens a collar about his neck. The myrrh which had been burning during the performance of these ceremonies has filled the chapel with its pungent odour, and the space in which the shrine stands is ceremonially pure. The priest draws the doors of the shrine together, ties the bolts with a cord, affixes a seal, and utters a magical formula which shall keep all evil spirits from the shrine. He then descends the steps and leaves the chapel. Meanwhile other "slaves of the god" have been occupied in presenting the offerings of meat and drink, etc., which were brought to the chamber specially made to receive them, and the spirit of the god dwelling in the figure in the shrine partook of the spiritual portion of each offering, leaving the material parts for the "slaves of the god" and the other temple servants.

The above facts show that the "daily divine cult," from a merely material point of view, consisted of a series of acts of service such as the servants of a king or man of high rank would perform for their master each day; in fact, the god was treated like an Egyptian gentleman of wealth and position. His dwelling was cleansed and perfumed, a fire was kindled, his soiled garments were taken from him and removed, and when he had been washed, anointed, scented, and re-dressed in suitable apparel, and his jewellery and other ornaments placed on him, and the symbols of his authority put into his hands, he was supposed to partake of his meal, and then to pass the rest of the day as he pleased. Now if we compare some of the sections of this Daily Service which was in use in the XVIIIth dynasty with certain sections of the Book of Opening the Mouth and the Liturgy of Funerary Offerings, which were in use under the Vth and VIth dynasties, we shall find that they are identical. The two last-named works were, we know, recited, probably daily, for the benefit of dead kings

Seti I pouring out a libation to Osiris.
Mariette, *Abydos*, Vol. I, p. 37.

A priest pouring out a libation over Osiris.
Mariette, *Abydos*, Vol. I, p. 72.

Seti I offering incense and a libation to Osiris.
Mariette, *Abydos*, Vol. I, p. 58.

and men of high rank under the Ancient Empire, and the texts and ceremonies were intended to supply the spirits of the dead with everything which was necessary for their well-being in the Other World. The meat and drink offerings were scores in number, and each thing was presented with appropriate words, which had the effect of transmuting the food and of giving it such a nature that the deceased might feed upon it. Such food was offered to a figure, or statue, of the deceased king or noble, which was purified, anointed, scented, and dressed in garments which transferred to it magical powers, and made it to be a suitable dwelling place for his KA or "double."

Thus it is quite clear that a great portion of the Daily Service of the gods under the XVIIIth dynasty was a mere repetition of parts of the Daily Service which was performed daily for dead kings under the IVth, Vth, and VIth dynasties. And if we had copies of the Liturgy of Funerary Offerings and the Book of Opening the Mouth of the first three dynasties, we should undoubtedly find that they contained all the essential parts of those of the later periods which we now have. The only possible deduction which we can make from these facts is, it seems to me, that the god of the XVIIIth dynasty was to Egypt, to all intents and purposes, what the king was under the IVth, Vth, and VIth dynasties, in fact, that the god was only a somewhat glorified form of the ancestor whose descendants and subjects had exalted his spirit to the position of protector of his people. Ȧmen of Thebes, Horus of Edfu, Menthu of Hermonthis, Osiris of Abydos, Ḥeru-shefit of Herakleopolis, Ptaḥ of Memphis, Temu of Heliopolis, the goddess Bast of Bubastis, the goddess Neith of Saïs, etc., were all worshipped as the spirits of ancestors were worshipped, and all were, I believe, originally deified ancestors.

We have seen that, during the Daily Divine Service which was performed in the temple of Ȧmen-Rā at Thebes, offerings were presented in abundance. How these were procured, or by whom they were provided, need not concern us here, but it may be mentioned in passing that all temple endowments were supposed to be pious gifts made by the king. We may gain some idea of the vastness of the temple endowments from the information furnished by the famous Papyrus of Rameses III. According to this wonderful document the offerings to the temple of Åmen-Rā during the reign of this king included in one year 34 jars of incense, honey, and oil, 819 jars of

Seti I offering incense to Osiris.
Mariette, *Abydos*, Vol. I, p. 68.

Seti I offering incense to Osiris.
Mariette, *Abydos*, Vol. I, p. 60.

wine, 10,000 measures of grain, 795 bundles of vegetables, 2,064 bales of flax, 9,340 water-fowl, 28 cattle, and 24 geese.[1] And if we assume that the cultivable

[1] See the complete figures in Breasted, *Ancient Records*, Vol. IV, p. 102 ff.

area of Egypt is 5,000,000 acres (it was in 1902), the figures given by this papyrus show that the temples possessed about 14 per cent., or nearly one-seventh, of the whole.

Every formula which the priest said, and every hymn which he sang to Åmen-Rā during the Daily Divine Service contains allusions to the glory, splendour, and power of the god, and frequent acknowledgments of his creative power and he is acclaimed as the maker and preserver of heaven and the gods, and the earth and all things on it, and of everything that exists. From first to last, however, there is no confession of sin, no expression of desire for pardon for sins committed, and no petitions for grace and strength to lead a life of integrity and righteousness. Nowhere in the religious literature of Egypt do we find such things, and the fact that we do not proves that the Egyptian regarded sin from a standpoint which in its persistent intensity appears to be purely African. Every offence and sin which he committed he paid for by the gifts of sacrifice and offerings, and when he had made adequate gifts, he assumed that he had no further liability. The king discharged his obligations by making huge gifts to his god, and to the company of lesser gods who were associated with him. Strictly speaking, he was supposed to present them himself to the god, and to recite the Divine Daily Service each day, but as a matter of fact he only did these things on the most solemn festivals. On such occasions the touching and handling of the sacred apparel and ornaments of the god, and contact with the figure of the god, procured for him the spiritual essence and strength which resided in the figure and renewed his communion with his god, and gave him a new supply of that life which was believed to be the peculiar attribute of gods and the ancestral spirits from whom they had been developed. The king, or his vicar, felt no compunction about his sins, for the offerings which were made at the service to-day blotted out the sins of yesterday, and he had no doubt but that the ceremonial cleanliness of his body made him pure in every way, and fit to hold converse with his god.

Besides this, the offerings to the god served another

purpose. They fed the god, and so maintained his strength, and every man assumed that, when his offering had been accepted, the god was in honour bound to

Seti I offering incense to Osiris, behind whom stands Anubis.
Mariette, *Abydos*, Vol. I, p. 17.

Seti I offering incense to Osiris in his shrine.
Mariette, *Abydos*, Vol. I, p. 38.

bestow his friendship and protection on him. The praises which were heaped upon the god by his worshippers were supposed to please him and to cause benevolence towards them to arise in him, and the incense, sweet-smelling unguents, and fine apparel were believed to gratify feelings, the character of which they did not enquire into too closely. The wrath of the god was a thing to avoid at all costs, but in all periods the Egyptians believed that his fiercest anger could be turned away provided their sacrifices and offerings were sufficiently abundant, and that there was no sin which they could commit that could not be paid for, except personal insult to the god. The African god was always a "jealous god," and would tolerate no remissness in personal service to himself, no disrespect to the animal or object in which it pleased him to become incarnate, and no injury to his property. The god, like the ancestral spirit, had to be kept in a good temper, and the surest way of doing this was to praise and flatter him, to give him gifts, to keep his house clean and pure, to love his friends and to hate his enemies, to obey his least command, to anticipate his wishes, and to make him personally pleased and comfortable. If a man wished to enjoy the favour of his god he took good care to serve him faithfully, and true and loyal worship of the god of his town or tribe was of the first importance for his welfare in this world. Respect and toleration were shown to all gods, but these were not allowed to interfere with the worship of his own god, which was whole-hearted. Disrespect to a man's own god, or disloyalty, was not only an offence to the god, but to the man's own clan or tribe, and he who went after strange gods courted social and material disaster of every kind. This was true equally of king and peasant, for the whole of the social fabric of Egypt rested upon religious principles of the most absolute character; and the foundation of them all was the cult of the ancestral spirit, or ancestral god. The private citizen worshipped his god with the same scrupulous care as the king, and made gifts to his figure, which had an honourable place in his house, and adored him according to the custom of his people, and kept his festivals, and made the prescribed offerings at all the duly appointed seasons. We may now consider briefly the reports of travellers on the question of sacrifice and offerings among the modern peoples of Africa.

According to Count Gleichen, the Dinkas are "without any plan of prayer," and sacrifices constitute their only attempts at intercourse with God, Whom they regard as a destructive power, to be propitiated if possible. The Golos appease their god Umvili by sacrifices of chickens.[1] The Shilluks offer sacrifices

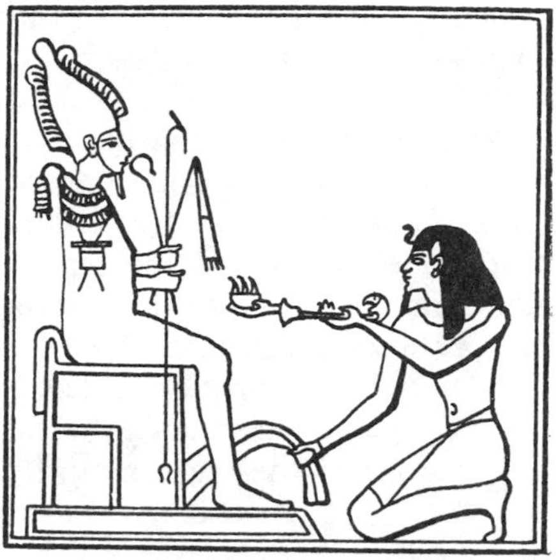

Seti I offering incense to Osiris.
Mariette, *Abydos*, Vol. I, p. 39.

Seti I pouring out a libation and offering incense to Osiris-Seker.
Mariette, *Abydos*, Vol. I, p. 36.

to the great deity Jo-uk once a year, at the beginning of the rainy season; the intermediary between Jo-uk and man is the demi-god Nyakang, whose mother was part woman, part crocodile. An animal is slain in each

[1] *The Anglo-Egyptian Sûdân*, p. 162.

village by the priest of the village, and the people cook and eat the flesh, assembling for the purpose at the house of Nyakang. The meal is followed by a dance and the drinking of merissa. The sacrifice and the dance are, "apparently, the sum of their worship." There is a house of Nyakang in each village, outside which all serious business is performed by the elders. In cases of illness, sacrifices are made to Nyakang.[1] The Matabele believe in a vast number of evil spirits, who are always ready to do harm, and chief among these are the ancestral spirits. They do not pray to them, or ask for their help, and they only offer sacrifices to them to appease them, when some evil has befallen the family.[2] The Batoka used to offer up prayer and sacrifices to the spirits (Barimo) at three places in the Cataract where they could hear the roar of the waters, and see the bows in the cloud.[3]

In most parts of Liberia the belief is current that the spirits of the dead can be attracted to the living by throwing down some sacrifice, a handful of beads, a strip of cloth, possibly a libation. Among the Kru peoples, fowls and oxen are sacrificed.[4] Mr. Isaac states that the Kamâsia people make the following offering to the Deity in time of trouble. Three holes are dug in the ground, and a portion of cooked food is buried in one hole by the oldest man, another portion is buried in another hole by the oldest woman, and a third portion is buried in the third hole by a child. The rest of the food is eaten by old men, whilst all the other people pray fervently. The buried food is believed to be eaten by the Deity and the ancestral spirits.[5] Among the tribes of the Lower Niger collective or general worship, with ritual and formulae, is not practised, except in the daily and weekly ancestral services and regular annual festivals, but individual prayer is offered in the form of a petition, always accompanied by an offering or sacrifice of fruit and meat, according to the nature of the

[1] *Ibid.*, p. 199.
[2] Decle, *Three Years in Savage Africa*, p. 153.
[3] Livingstone, *Missionary Travels*, p. 523.
[4] Johnston, *Liberia*, Vol. II, p. 1063.
[5] Johnston, *Uganda*, Vol. II, p. 884.

boon requested and the means of the worshipper; and, as a general rule, the adoration is one of propitiation, combined with a request.[1] After giving a list of Yoruba

Seti I offering two vases of unguents to Osiris, behind whom stands Isis.
Mariette, *Abydos*, Vol. I, p. 21.

Seti I anointing the face of Osiris.
Mariette, *Abydos*, Vol. I, p. 41.

sacrifices, Mr. Dennett says that they are chiefly atonement sacrifices, a fact which suggests that the Pagan Yorubas believed that sin and the anger of an offended god were the cause of the various ills incidental to human

[1] Leonard, *The Lower Niger and its Tribes*, p. 281.

life, and that to obtain blessings it was necessary to propitiate him with sacrifice and offering.[1]

In most villages will be found a low hut, sometimes not larger than a dog-kennel, in which, among all tribes, are hung charms, or by which is a growing plant. In some tribes a rudely carved human figure stands in that hut as an idol. That idol, charm, or plant, as the case may be, is believed for the time to be the residence of a spirit, which is to be placated by offerings of food of some kind—a dish of boiled plantains or a plate of fish. This food is not generally removed till it spoils. Sometimes, where the gift is a large one, a feast is made; people and spirit are supposed to join in the festival, and nothing is left to spoil. That it is of use to the spirit is fully believed, and some say that the "life" or essence of the food has been eaten by the spirit, only the material form remaining to be removed.[2]

The giving of offerings, regularly and unintermittently, to the spirits of the dead was carried out with scrupulous care by the worshippers of Osiris. The Africans have been in the habit of offering gifts of meat and drink to the souls of their ancestors from time immemorial, but the cult of Osiris developed the habit and made it obligatory on all who followed it. In the Dynastic Period a festival was celebrated in honour of the dead about every fifth day, on an average, and in the funerary chapels attached to the tombs of great kings service for the dead was said, and offerings were made to their spirits daily. The spirits of the dead were supposed to absorb the spirits of the meat and drink, and the priests and others ate the material parts. Early in the Dynastic Period the priests drew up an authoritative List of Offerings, which remained the standard authority down to and including the Roman Period. The ancient Egyptian, like the modern African, made offerings to the spirits of his ancestors with the view of keeping their help and protection by maintaining their existence, and he also did so in order to prevent them from being obliged to eat filth and drink polluted water.[3] Moreover,

[1] Dennett, *At the Back of the Black Man's Mind*, p. 260.
[2] Nassau, *Fetichism in West Africa*, p. 92.
[3] See Book of the Dead, Chapters CLXXVIII, LII and LIII.

by making offerings to the dead in this world, a man caused provision to be made for himself in the Other World when his time should come to depart thither. In

Seti I offering raiment to Osiris.
Mariette, *Abydos*, Vol. I, p. 50.

Seti I offering sceptres, etc., to Osiris.
Mariette, *Abydos*, Vol. I, p. 48.

other words, his offerings went before him to the Other World and awaited him there;[1] the offerings which he made to the gods also were as treasure laid up in heaven, and there became his own again, according to

[1] See the Book Åm-Ṭuat, Second Division.

some texts. As the offerings made to the gods brought the spirits of the gods to their statues to hold converse with the king and his high priest, so the offerings to the ancestral spirits brought them back to earth to hold communion with the living, and to take an active interest in their affairs. Eating and drinking with the spirits raised man's nature and "made divine his spirit," and destroyed the feeling of separation which came with the appearance of death. The character of the Egyptian offering is shown by the common word for offering "ḥetep," 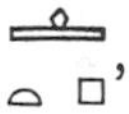, which means a gift of peace, or "propitiation." The stone or wooden tablet on which the offerings were laid is also called "ḥetep," 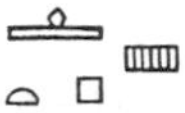, 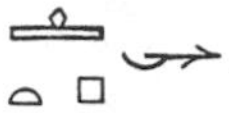. And it must always be remembered that the altar was believed to possess the power of transmuting the offerings which were laid upon it, and of turning them into spiritual entities of such a nature that they became suitable food for the god Osiris and his spirits. Funerary inscriptions of all periods are often introduced by the words "Suten ṭā ḥetep," 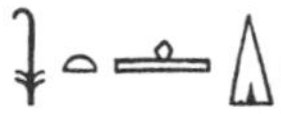, which must mean something like "the king hath given an offering," or "the king giveth an offering," or "may the king give an offering." These words take us back to a time when all Egypt and every man belonged to the king, and when the king made a gift, probably of food, for the funeral feast of such of his officers as he allowed to be buried with pomp and ceremony. In a comparatively short time this formula must have lost all significance, but the Egyptians nevertheless preserved it on their sepulchral stelae until the latest times.

Now the Egyptians were an eminently practical people in all matters which related to their personal welfare, both material and spiritual, present and future, and those who could not afford to pay for a constant supply of offerings to their ancestral spirits must have been sorely troubled. Though they had the words *suten ṭā ḥetep* cut in stone or wood, they knew that the king could not send gifts for the dead to every tomb in Egypt, and that the practical result of them was nothing.

They therefore deputed the duty of supplying meat, drink, and apparel to the gods Ȧnpu, Ḳeb (the Earth-god), and Osiris, believing that prayers addressed to

Seti I offering a breastplate and pectoral to Osiris.
Mariette, *Abydos*, Vol. I, p. 51.

Seti I offering fruit to Osiris, behind whom stands Thoth.
Mariette, *Abydos*, Vol. I, p. 74.

them would provide the dead with everything they required. These gods were in the Other World, and the dead were there with them and under their rule and care.

In some cases the Egyptians adopted another plan.

They prayed to the gods that offerings might be given to the dead, and they also entreated every visitor to a tomb to do likewise; as a reward for making this prayer visitors were assured that they should hand on their exalted positions and dignities to their children. The prayers they made were that "the king might give an offering," and that there might be for the deceased "*pert-er-kheru*,"[1] according to the saying of the ancestors, "like unto the *perrt*," *i.e.*, the things which came forth "from the mouth of the god." It will be remembered that, according to Egyptian views, the world and the things in it came into being as the result of the utterance of a word. The latter prayer alludes to this fact, and the writer wishes visitors to his tomb to pray for *pert-er-kheru*, *i.e.*, offerings, because he firmly believes that the mere mention of these words will result in the appearance of offerings, just as when the god who made the world uttered the word, the utterance of it was followed by the appearance of created things. It is only another example of the power of the word, or voice, which under certain circumstances was believed to be irresistible. The use of the words *suten ṭā ḥetep* and *pert-er-kheru* made it unnecessary to place offerings in the tomb, faith being greater than works.

Another point in connection with offerings must be mentioned. In the royal tombs, and those of men of wealth, tables for offerings, or altars, are commonly found. These are usually rectangular slabs of stone, with rectangular hollows in them which were intended to be used as receptacles for libations, etc.; on the upper edge a prayer for offerings is usually cut. Often the face of the slab is sculptured with the figures of offerings, geese, bull's heads, loaves of bread, vegetables, etc. Now similar tables for offerings are found in the tombs of men who were not rich, and whose relatives were not in a position to endow them with offerings in perpetuity. The explanation of their existence is this: the Egyptians believed that the prayer cut on the stone slab would cause the offerings to appear regularly, and that the figures of the offerings sculptured on the face of the slab

[1] . See Tylor, *Tomb of Paḥeri*, text, l. 42.

would suggest to the invisible beings who provided the funerary meals what offerings should be supplied. The slab, in fact, was regarded as a magical source for the

Seti I offering two bandlets to Osiris and receiving life from the god.
Mariette, *Abydos*, Vol. I, p. 53.

Seti I offering two bandlets to Osiris.
Mariette, *Abydos*, Vol. I, p. 52.

supply of offerings. That this was so is proved by the little models of altars which are found in tombs, and which are too small to have served the purpose of tables for offerings in the ordinary sense of the word. The custom of making offerings to ancestral spirits is so common among modern African peoples that only a few examples need be quoted.

In Anguru-land and on the Tanganyika plateau small shelters are erected for the spirits of the dead, and a daily allowance of food and drink is placed in each. The names of the dead are never mentioned under any circumstances whatsoever.[1] The Bavuma also make spirit houses, but they put neither meat nor drink in them. In times of distress an ancestor's spirit is called upon for help, and a goat is presented to it; the animal is dragged up to the house, but is then allowed to escape. The ancestor is also called upon to drive away the "bazimu" (devils), if their attacks become too frequent.[2] The Bakonjo also build houses for the spirits of their ancestors, each *kitwangani* (spirit house) being about 10 inches high, and open at each end. Small supplies of meat and drink are placed in them every two or three days.[3] The Basukuma sacrifice an animal to the spirit of a king in times of trouble.[4] The Lendu believe that the spirits of the dead remain on the earth for two months, and they build spirit shelters of grass for them, which they supply with meat and vegetables. At the end of two months the spirit goes to Waza, a place in the bowels of the earth, where the good and the wicked live together.[5] Whilst the body of a chief of the Makarakas is being smoke-dried, which operation takes about a year, food and a pot of beer are always provided for the spirit.[6] Over and near the graves of the rich in West Africa are built little huts where are laid the common articles used by them when alive. On one occasion Dr. Nassau observed tied to a tree a wooden trade-chest, five pitchers, and several fathoms of calico prints. The grave of a chief was near, and these articles were placed there as offerings to spirits to induce them to draw to the villages of his people the trade of passing merchant vessels.[7] The Bahima build a spirit house in

[1] Cunningham, *Uganda*, p. 12.
[2] *Ibid.*, p. 138.
[3] *Ibid.*, p. 260.
[4] *Ibid.*, p. 308.
[5] *Ibid.*, p. 337.
[6] Junker, *Travels in Africa*, Vol. I, p. 297.
[7] *Fetichism in West Africa*, p. 232.

every village, and a bundle of medicine is hung inside it. This house has often a hard clay floor, or roof with open sides, and on the floor are placed offerings of food and libations of beer. The worship of ancestral spirits

Seti I opening the door of the shrine of Osiris.
Mariette, *Abydos*, Vol. I, p. 59.

Seti I addressing Osiris-Seker in his shrine.
Mariette, *Abydos*, Vol. I, p. 44.

among the Bahima resembles that in use among the people of Unyoro. Many of the names of evilly-disposed ancestral spirits are identical with the names for diseases, and it seems as if certain diseases are believed to be sent by spirits whom the living have offended.[1]

[1] Johnston, *Uganda*, Vol. II, p. 631.

On the amulets worn in Abyssinia the persons for whom they were made pray to be delivered from a large number of fiends who are regarded as diseases personified, and who, probably, were ancestral spirits. The Christians of Abyssinia naturally condemn the belief in spirits of all kinds, and class them as things of evil. The people of Buvuma build tall, peaked fetish huts in which they place stones whereon offerings are to be laid. Such stones are the equivalents of the rectangular stone slabs, or tables for offerings, of the ancient Egyptians, which have already been described. A picture of such a hut and also of a "suspended grass extinguisher," with a libation slab below it, is given by Sir Harry Johnston.[1] The Wakamba in East Africa also offer sacrifices to spirits.[2]

The Bŭkalai believe that the evil spirits [of ancestors] walk among them at sunset. Du Chaillu says: At sunset every one of them retired within doors. The children ceased to play, and all became quiet in the camp. Then suddenly arose on the air one of those mournful, heart-piercing chants which you hear among all the tribes in this land. Tears rolled down the cheeks of the women, fright marked their faces and cowed their spirits. They sang:

Oh, you will never speak to us any more,
We cannot see your face any more;
You will never walk with us again,
You will never settle our palavers for us.[3]

According to the same authority, all the peoples of Equatorial Africa fear the spirits of the dead, and besides placing furniture, dress, and food at their newly-made graves, return from time to time with other supplies of food. During the season appointed for mourning, the deceased is remembered and feared; but when once his memory grows dim, the negro ceases to believe in the prolonged existence of the departed spirit. The fear of spirits of the departed seems an instinctive feeling for which they do not attempt to account to themselves, and about which they have formed no theory. They

[1] *Ibid.*, p. 717.
[2] Krapf, *Travels*, p. 356.
[3] Du Chaillu, *Adventures*, p. 72.

Seti I praying to Osiris. Before the god are the symbol of the bull's skin, and the ram containing his soul.
Mariette, *Abydos*, Vol. I, p. 61.

Seti I adoring Osiris-Seker in his shrine.
Mariette, *Abydos*, Vol. I, p. 75.

believe the spirit is near and about them; that it requires food and property; that it can and sometimes does harm them. They think of it as a vindictive thing, to be feared and to be conciliated. But as the memory of the departed grows dim, so does this fear of his spirit vanish. Ask a negro about the spirit of his brother who died yesterday, and he is full of terror; ask him about the spirit of one who died long ago, and he will tell you carelessly, "It is done"; that is to say, it has no existence.[1]

The native of Western Africa, in his kindness of heart, builds shelters for the spirits who have not yet been buried, and places in them beds which are so arranged that when the spirits are lying on them they face the villages. On the poles of one of these shelters, which was made for the ghost of a little girl, Miss Kingsley saw hanging the dolls and the little pincushions, etc., which a kind missionary had given her. Food is set out at these places and spirit poured over them from time to time, and sometimes, though not often, pieces of new cloth are laid on them. Many unburied spirits were believed to get away and haunt the villages, and the people of Creek Town, Calabar, used to clear them out every November. They did so by the following means. They set up large grotesque images called Nbakim in the houses, and placed food and spirits before them; strips of cloth and gewgaws were hung about them. The people gathered together and made a procession to every house, screaming, yelling, dancing, and beating tam-tams as they went. The wandering spirits were driven by the noise to the figures and took refuge in the strips of cloth, and the noise prevented them from venturing out again. When the noise had been prolonged for a certain time, and the strips of cloth were filled with spirits, the figures were taken and thrown into the river, and so the spirits were either drowned or driven away elsewhere.[2]

Livingstone found that the people of Chicova were accustomed to pray to departed chiefs and relatives, but the idea of praying to God (which, presumably, he suggested) was new.[3] They visit the graves of relations, making offerings of food and beer.[4] The people of Tette believe that many evil spirits live in the air, the

[1] *Ibid.*, pp. 335, 336.
[2] Kingsley, *Travels in West Africa*, p. 493 ff.
[3] Livingstone, *Travels*, p. 605.
[4] *Ibid.*, p. 641.

earth, the water. These invisible malicious beings are thought to inflict much suffering on the human race; but, as they have a weakness for beer and a craving for food, they may be propitiated from time to time by offerings of meat and drink. The spirits of their departed ancestors are all good, according to their ideas, and on special occasions aid them in their enterprise.[1] Livingstone heard some slaves who were fastened in the slave-sticks singing, and when he asked the cause of their mirth they replied that they were merry at the idea "of coming back after death, and haunting and killing those who had sold them."[2]

We have now to consider the use of amulets as a form of worship. The worship in which amulets play a large and important part is not that of God, but that of the "gods" and spirits of all kinds, nature spirits, ancestral spirits, and spirits which are supposed to live in common things. The Egyptian had a deeply rooted belief in the existence of God, Whom he regarded as the Creator of all things and the ultimate arbiter of the lives and destinies of all men; but, like the modern African, he also believed in spirits of all kinds. Benevolent spirits he did not fear, but of evil spirits he went in mortal terror all the days of his life, and he attempted to propitiate them and gain their good will by every means in his power. There were at all times in Egypt, it seems, men who served God and who put their whole trust in Him, and to whom the practices of magic of all kinds must have been an abomination. Still, the great mass of the people were firm believers in spirits and in the efficacy of magical figures, charms, spells, incantations, words and names of power, and these frequently appear in the most solemn texts and ceremonies from the earliest to the latest period. It would be idle to deny that among large masses of the population of Egypt the cult of spirits, or witchcraft, or fetishism, often took the place of the worship of the true God, and that even under the XVIIIth and XIXth dynasties the true and the false worship flourished side by side. The Egyptian appreciated at

[1] Livingstone, *The Zambesi*, p. 47.
[2] *Last Journals*, Vol. I, p. 306.

its true worth the beauty of the religion of Osiris and the high morality which it inculcated, and fixed his hope of immortality on the god who had been slain and had risen from the dead, but he was always haunted by the fear that he might suffer in the Other World if he neglected the rites and ceremonies and customs of his ancestors, and he could never deliver himself wholly from the idea that "there might be something after all" in these things.

We are justified in assuming that the gods and the sacred animals in which they became incarnate were at a very early period represented by statues in the temples, and also that figures or statues of great ancestors were made by their descendants in the earliest times. Thus gods and ancestral spirits possessed places in which to dwell, and they were believed to enter and leave their statues at will. The Egyptian next had to provide dwelling-places for spirits of all kinds, and with the production of such dwelling-places amulets came into being. Some may say that the use of amulets by the Egyptians was fetishism pure and simple, but such is not the case, and those who call it so will make the same mistake as the Portuguese made when they described as "fetishism" the cult of ancestral spirits which they saw being performed in West Africa. It would be equally wrong to call an Egyptian amulet either "fetish" or "juju." The first of these words is certainly not of African origin, for it comes from the Portuguese, and the latter is derived by some from the French. Fetish = "feitiço," the word used for "image," "saint," etc., and juju = joujou, a "toy" or "doll."[1] When the Portuguese explorers saw the Africans take a wooden image from the wall, blow on it, bespatter it, mutter to it, or give it food, they said: "This is witchcraft" (*feititto*). They looked on everything at home with the eyes of people believing in witchcraft and sorcery, for they believed in witches and sorcerers. "This feature of the Middle Ages brands them with the stamp of spiritual decadence."[2] The Portuguese did not

[1] According to Major Glyn Leonard "Juju" is derived from the native word "egugu," meaning "idol."—*Lower Niger*, p. 115.

[2] Frobenius, *Childhood of Man*, p. 182.

understand the cult of ancestors, and they confounded it with their own debased Christian idolatry. As a result of this, they wholly misrepresented the religion of the West African peoples, and caused them to be regarded by civilized nations with a contempt which they never deserved in the slightest degree.

Neither the Egyptian nor the modern African ever believed in the divinity of their amulets or fetishes, and they never considered them to represent deities. On this point the authority of Dr. Nassau is final. He says: "Fetich objects are simply local residences. "A spirit can live anywhere, and in anything. This "is bald fetichism. The thing itself, the material "itself, is not worshipped. The fetich worshipper "makes a clear distinction between the reverence "with which he regards a certain material object, "and the worship he renders to the spirit for the "time inhabiting it. For this reason nothing is too "mean, or too small, or too ridiculous, to be considered "fit for a spirit's *locum tenens*. For when for any "reason the spirit is supposed to have gone out of that "thing and definitely abandoned it, the thing itself is "no longer reverenced, and is thrown away as useless."[1] It is not true, as is asserted by some, in regard to these African tribes and their degraded form of religion, that they worship the actual material objects in which the spirits are supposed to be confined. Low as is fetishism, it nevertheless has its philosophy, a philosophy that is the same in kind as that of the higher forms of religion. A similar sense of need that sends the Christian to his knees before God to ask aid in time of trouble, and salvation temporal and spiritual, sends the fetish worshipper to offer his sacrifice and to ejaculate his prayer for help as he lays hold of his consecrated antelope horn, or as he looks on with abiding trust while it is safely tied to his body. His human necessity drives him to seek assistance. The difference between his act and the act of the Christian lies in the kind of salvation he seeks, the being to whom he appeals, and the reason for his appealing. The reason for his appeal is simply fear; there is no confession, no love, rarely thanks-

[1] *Fetichism in West Africa*, p. 76.

giving. It is not spiritual but physical, salvation that is sought.[1]

Everything that Dr. Nassau says about the modern African amulets applies exactly to those of the ancient Egyptians. Every Egyptian amulet that we know was made for the purpose of giving physical comfort, or relief, or pleasure in this world or the next; neither the maker nor the wearer expect an amulet to assist confession of sin, or love to God as Christian peoples understand it, or thanksgiving. Thus the Ṭeṭ 𓊽, or backbone of Osiris, made of gold and set in a plinth of sycamore wood, which had been steeped in *ānkham* flower water, gave the deceased the power to become a "perfect spirit," and enabled him to take his place among the followers of Osiris at the new-year festivals, when he would receive offerings of meat and drink in abundance.[2] The amulet 𓎬 conveyed to the wearer the virtue of the blood of Isis, and her strength and her words of power, and, if it were placed on the neck of a dead man, it was believed to cause Horus to view him with favour, and to give him access to every part of heaven.[3] What the object was, which the Egyptians represented by 𓎬, is not known, but it seems perfectly clear that it was not the "buckle," as it is usually said to have been. As the Book of the Dead connects it with the blood and strength of Isis, it must, I think, have represented some important organ of the body of Isis. The form of the 𓎬 as it appears in the Papyrus of Ani suggests that it represents the vagina and uterus, as seen when cut out of the body and laid on some flat surface, the flaps at the sides being the thick ligatures by which the uterus is attached to the pelvis, which have dropped from their normal position after death. I submitted this view to a medical authority, Dr. W. L. Nash, and he agrees with me in thinking that the

[1] *Ibid.*, p. 77.
[2] Book of the Dead, Chapter CLV (Rubric).
[3] *Ibid.*, Chapter CLVI.

amulet does represent the genital organs of Isis. And he thinks that the blood referred to in the Chapter of the Book of the Dead of which it forms the vignette may be the catamenial flow. We have seen that the Ṭeṭ represented the *sacrum* of Osiris, *i.e.*, the part of the back which is close to the sperm duct, and it is very easy to understand the importance which was attached to the amulet, for it symbolized the seed of the god Osiris. This being so it is only natural that the primitive Egyptians should make the picture of the genital organs of Isis a companion amulet, for by the two amulets the procreative powers of man and woman would be symbolized. The antiquity of these amulets is obviously very great. To the African, as to the ancient Hebrew, the blood represented the life, and therefore the spirit of the person to whom it belonged. And as blood carries with it protection, people, and even spirit-houses, and the gateways of villages are sprinkled with it by the modern Africans.[1] Livingstone mentions the fact of a woman cupping her child's temples for sore eyes, and then throwing the blood over the roof of her hut as a charm.[2]

The scarabaeus, or beetle, , which is one of the commonest of amulets, was buried with the dead in order to assist the restoration of their hearts. A Rubric to the LXIVth Chapter of the Book of the Dead directs that a green stone scarab, set in a gold frame, shall be anointed with myrrh, and then placed in the breast of the deceased where the heart would normally be. Before it was placed in the breast, and during the anointing with myrrh, a formula, which is now known as Chapter XXXB of the Book of the Dead, was said over it, and the effect of this on the deceased was to "open his mouth,"[3] *i.e.*, to reconstitute his jaws and mouth, and to enable him to eat, and drink, and breathe, and to perform the ordinary functions of a living man. Thus we see that the beetle was associated with the idea of

[1] Kingsley, *Travels in West Africa*, pp. 447, 454.
[2] *Last Journals*, Vol. I, p. 223.
[3] See the Rubric to Chapter LXIV of the Book of the Dead.

a renewal of vital power, and with new life generally. This idea is still extant in Africa as we may see from the following extracts. The beetle referred to in the Rubric is the large beetle which is generally known as *Goliathus Atlas*, and many models of it in green stone are to be seen in the British Museum. A specimen caught by Dr. Junker, who figured it two-thirds natural size in his book,[1] was 10 cm. long and $4\frac{1}{2}$ cm. wide. The wing-cases were brown, and on the black thorax there were broad white bands converging towards the head, while the sides of the abdomen and the legs were of a dark olive green colour. Sir Harry Johnston says that the natives give much attention to the various species of the *Ceratorrhina goliath*, and speaks of it being much used in native medicine and sorcery.[2] Mr. Torday also describes a magical ceremony in which the body of a goliath beetle plays a prominent part.[3] Baker, in an entry dated August 11, speaks of "immense beetles" which appear at this season and make balls of dung as large as small apples, which they roll away with their hind legs, while they walk backwards by means of their fore legs. They appear about the beginning of the wet season, and when the rains cease they disappear.[4] As in one of his forms Osiris was a River-god it is extremely probable, as Baker suggests, that the Egyptians associated the appearance of these beetles with the rise in the river level, and therefore with new life and fertility. The beetles deposit their eggs in the usual manner, and while the larvae are growing they feed upon the ball of dung until they are ready to begin the world for themselves.[5] That some tribes connect the beetle with ancestor-worship is proved by the fact that Livingstone saw a large beetle hung up before a figure in a spirit-house of a burnt and deserted village.[6] The modern Sûdânî women eat beetles and say that they make them prolific, and we may note in

[1] *Travels in Africa*, Vol. II, p. 450.
[2] *George Grenfell*, Vol. II, p. 944.
[3] Quoted by Johnston, *ibid.*, Vol. I, p. 405.
[4] *Albert N'yanza*, p. 240.
[5] Livingstone, *Missionary Travels*, p. 44.
[6] *Last Journals*, Vol. II, p. 27.

connection with the idea of new life which is associated with the beetle that the Egyptians used the shell of a beetle mixed with oil, etc., as a medicine to assist a woman in labour to give birth to her child.[1]

Another amulet of importance in connection with new life and new birth is the frog, small models of which have been found in tombs of all periods in Egypt. This amulet was supposed to hold the spirit of the Frog-goddess Ḥeqet, who is mentioned in the Pyramid Texts,[2] and whose cult dates from the earliest dynasties.

Seti I making an offering to the Frog-goddess Ḥeqet at Abydos.

She was present when Ruṭ-ṭeṭeṭ gave birth to three boys, who afterwards became Kings Userkaf, Saḥu-Rā, and Kakaa.[3] The cult of Ḥeqet was practised at Abydos under the XIXth dynasty, and on a bas-relief in the temple there we see a representation of Seti I offering two vessels of wine or unguents to her. She was present when Isis had union with Osiris after the death of the god, and she appears on a relief at Denderah[4] in the form of a frog seated on a pedestal at the foot of the bier of Osiris. In late times she was identified with Isis and Hathor and the

[1] *Ebers Papyrus*, Plate XCIV.
[2] Pepi I, l. 570.
[3] *Westcar Papyrus*, ed. Erman, Plate 9.
[4] Mariette, *Dendérah*, tom. IV, Plates 78–80.

great Mother-goddesses of fertility, generation, and birth. Tradition also gave to the four great primeval gods Ḥeḥ, Kek, Nāu, and Åmen the form of a frog. The Egyptian Christians also associated the frog with

Anubis, under the direction of Thoth, reconstituting the body of Osiris with the help of the Frog-goddess Ḥeqet. Nephthys sits at the head of the bier and Isis at the foot.

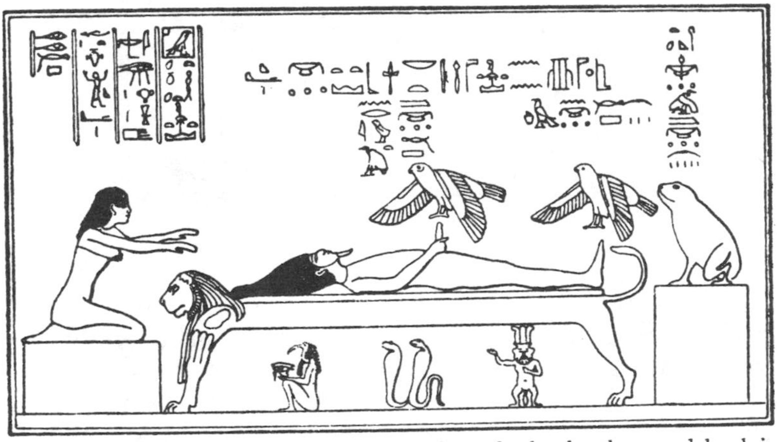

Osiris begetting Horus by Isis, who is in the form of a hawk; the second hawk is Nephthys. At the head of the bier sits Hathor and at the foot the Frog-goddess Ḥeqet.

new birth, and on a Christian lamp, described by Lanzone,[1] is a figure of a frog surrounded by the legend Ἐγώ εἶμι Ἀναστάσις, "I am the resurrection." It is not easy at first sight to understand why the frog should have been a symbol of new life to the Egyptians any more than the beetle, but when we read Livingstone's

[1] *Dizionario*, p. 853.

description of the frog called "matlamétlo"[1] the reason becomes apparent. This frog is $5\frac{1}{2}$ inches long, its head is 3 inches wide, its body $4\frac{1}{2}$ inches, and its forelegs and hindlegs are 3 inches and 6 inches long respectively. In the driest part of the desert after a thunderstorm the pools of water become filled immediately with loud-croaking frogs. The natives think they fall from the clouds, but this is not so. The matlamétlo hides itself in a hole at the root of a bush during the season of drought, and rushes out as soon as the rain begins to fall.[2] Thus the frog appears with the coming of the rain, just as the beetle appears with the rise of the Nile, and so the ideas of new life and fertility become associated with them. The inherent vitality[3] of the small tree-frog must have impressed the Egyptians, and it is probably this species that is represented by the little green-glazed steatite frogs which they wore suspended from necklaces, pectorals, etc.[4] The women of some tribes in Africa eat frogs, just as they eat the beetle, to make them prolific, but other tribes reject the frog because they think that if used as food it makes the eyes to bulge, like the frog's.[5]

In placing the amulet on the body, living or dead, the Egyptians usually recited a formula, the words of which sometimes had meaning, and sometimes had not. The recital of such a formula was supposed to give the wearer of the amulet the power of the spirit which dwelt in it. In the earliest times the formula and the amulet were probably distinct things, but in process of time they became associated, and later still the formula was cut on the amulet. Thus the wearer became doubly protected. The so-called "buckle" of Isis is often inscribed with the formula which in later times became a Chapter of the Book of the Dead, and such is the case

[1] The Pyxicephalus adspersus of Dr. Smith.

[2] Livingstone, *Missionary Travels*, pp. 42, 43.

[3] Note on p. 487 of the same work.

[4] "As I sat in the rain a little tree-frog, about half-an-inch long, leaped on to a grassy leaf, and began a tune as loud as that of many birds, and very sweet; it was surprising to hear so much music out of so small a musician."—Livingstone, *Last Journals*, Vol. II, p. 42.

[5] Johnston, *George Grenfell*, Vol. II, pp. 613, 615.

also with the amulet of the head-rest or pillow, the scarab, and many other amulets. For those who could not afford a properly made stone or metal amulet it was held to be sufficient if a man were protected by a drawing of the amulet and a written copy of the words which were associated with it. Thus in the Book of the Dead[1] we have pictures of several amulets, each accompanied by its formula, and in one exemplar in the possession of Mr. MacGregor a list of seventy-five amulets is given, together with drawings of them.[2] Originally the vignettes which adorn the fine copies of the Book of the Dead were simply magical pictures, or representations of what the deceased wished to happen, and the formulae attached were expected to enable him to realize his wishes. The little figures of the gods made in gold, silver, stone, etc., were nothing but amulets, or abodes for the spirits, or portions of the spirits of the gods, and the recital of "strong names," words of power, magical sentences, etc., was a prominent feature in the cult of them.

When we come to examine the use of amulets by modern African peoples, whether Christian, Muhammadan, or pagan, we find that the ideas which underlie it are identical with those of the Egyptians. The priest of the Christian, or the mullah of the Muslim, or the "medicine-man," or "rain-maker," or "witch-doctor" of the pagan is the equivalent of the kher-ḥeb priest of the Egyptians.[3] All these are supposed to be able to hold converse with spirits, and to be acquainted with means which will secure their favour for the petitioner. They use magic names, words of power, and some are supposed to have knowledge of spells and incantations which are of great antiquity, and which were revealed by the spirit-powers to certain medicine-men as a sign of signal favour. The Christian

[1] See Chapter CLVI ff.

[2] Described by Capart, *A.Z.*, Band XLV, 1908, p. 14 ff.

[3] The Egyptians distinguished between the "great Kher-ḥeb," , who was a great magician and performed the most important religious ceremonies, and the ordinary Kher-ḥeb who was not expected to possess any special magical power.

in Abyssinia wears parchment amulets inscribed with magical prayers which are intended to protect him against evil of all kinds, and against the spirits which cause diseases; women wear them to obtain children and to prevent miscarriage. The spirits invoked are the old spirits of the country, but the magical figures painted on them are effigies of St. George and other saints, and in all such amulets the picture of the Cross of Christ is regarded and used as a great fetish. The Cross typifies the Blood of Christ, and His Blood was His Life, and carries with it in the native mind the old African idea of the magical power of the Blood of God, and its invincible might. It is, in fact, to the native a blood fetish. The Muslim uses amulets likewise. These are pieces of paper or leather, on which are written extracts from the Ḳur'ân, *e.g.*, the first Surah, the Throne Verses, and the Declaration of the Unity of God, but side by side with these are placed magical numbers and letters arranged in squares, diamonds, triangles, etc., in which old pagan ideas survive in a remarkable degree. The Abyssinian Christian uses the Book of Psalms, the Adorations of the Virgin, or the complete New Testament as an amulet, and the Muslim uses the whole Ḳur'ân with the same object, and a copy of the Book of the Dead written on his tomb or coffin, or on a roll of papyrus, served the same purpose to the Egyptian. Among pagan tribes who cannot write, the magic doctor is called upon to supply the words which bring magical protection, and it is he who brings the spirit into the amulet or fetish, and utters the blessings which are so eagerly sought after. The amulet must pass through his hands before it can receive its spirit, just as the amulets of the Egyptians which were used in all sepulchral ceremonies must have passed through the hands of their priests before they were worn by the living or placed on the bodies of the dead.

African amulets consist of figures made of clay, wood, etc., sticks, stones of curious shapes, feathers of birds, strings, knotted cords, beads, shells of snails, horns of animals, bags of powder, seeds, etc.; nothing is too trivial to become the home of a spirit. Specially pre-prepared "medicine" to be put in a fetish horn contains ashes of certain medicinal plants, pieces of burnt bone, gums, spices, resins, filth, portions of human and animal bodies, *i.e.*, the brain, heart, gall-bladder, especially when belonging to ancestors, and eyeballs, those of a white man being much prized.[1] These ingredients are mixed in secret, whilst drums are beaten and dances are danced, and then the mixture is placed in a shell, or horn, or bone. If we look at the copies of the prescriptions given in the Ebers Medical Papyrus we shall find that the medicine-men of the Egyptians used similar ingredients in their medicines, and the ideas which were associated with them were the same, namely, that the spirits of the substances used as ingredients protected those who kept them by them, and healed them when they were sick. Thus we find used antelope excrement, the blood, fat, excrement, liver, milk, seed, ear, and teeth of the donkey, the blood of a bat, the intestines of the goose, the fat of the Nubian ibex, the case of the beetle, the hair, fat, excrement and uterus of the cat, the oil of a mouse, the fat, hide, hoofs, and oil of the hippopotamus, the shell of the tortoise, the gall of the ox, the eyes, blood, fat, gall, teeth, and excrement of the pig, the blood and excrement of wasps, etc. The reason why certain things are chosen as amulets is easy to see. Thus a part of a leopard or an elephant gives strength, a part of a gazelle gives cunning and agility, part of a heart gives courage, part of a human brain gives wisdom, and the claws, teeth, lips, and whiskers of lions and leopards protect their wearers in a country in which these animals abound. The bones of the legs of a tortoise are worn in the shape of anklets to give endurance, and the spine bones of serpents drive away backache.[2] But why the lower jaw of the tortoise is worn as a preventive of toothache, or why the blood and gall of a black ox bring rain, or why the possession of the liver and entrails of a crocodile enables a man to kill an enemy when he pleases is not clear.[3]

The modern African, like the ancient Egyptian, makes use of many amulets, and the following notes,

[1] Nassau, *Fetichism in West Africa*, p. 82.
[2] *Ibid.*, p. 84.
[3] Decle, *Three Years*, pp. 153, 154.

which are derived from Mr. R. G. Anderson's article[1] on the Superstitions of Kordofân, prove that the religious views of the people of this portion of Africa are the same now as ever. They believe in the Evil Eye, and ward it off by wearing a silver disk inscribed with a charm, by charms written on paper, etc. Diseases are caused by evil spirits of all kinds, whose names are well known. The most terrible spirit is a female called Umm al-Sebian, who destroys children, causes miscarriages, abortions, and still-birth, makes men impotent and women barren, lays waste the crops, and destroys people and things by her mere presence. Seven charms are known which are believed to counteract her evil acts, and these are claimed to be known by the Fiki, or magic doctor. These charms are written on paper and carried in small red leather cases, and consist of extracts from the Ḳur'ân, and magical arrangements of letters and figures, which vary in meaning according to the system of magic employed by the magic doctor. The water in which such texts have been soaked is considered to be the very best "medicine."[2] Besides these, the prayers and utterances of the late Mahdî are still copied on paper rolls and worn as charms. Roots of certain trees and plants are also used as amulets, and are worn to give protection from the "evil eye," and against spirits, scorpions, snake bites, etc. The root of the Abû Tamara prevents impotence, and gives success in love-making; small quantities of it are eaten as an aphrodisiac, and are believed to enable the eater to endure hardship and danger.

Certain stones also are worn as amulets. The opalescent stone *al-barad* guards a man's horse from sickness. The turquoise (*al-farûs*) prevents urinary retention. The stone is stirred in water, which is drunk as a medicine. The blood-stone (*al-hagar dam*) is worn on the neck, and prevents sunstroke, headache, and bleeding of the nose; a hard green stone, with the same properties, is also worn as an

[1] *Medical Practices and Superstitions amongst the People of Kordofan*, in *Third Report of the Wellcome Research Laboratories*, Khartûm, 1908, p. 282 ff.

[2] Schweinfurth, *Heart of Africa*, Vol. II, p. 325.

amulet. The white cat's eye stone (*al-hagar hurra*) is soaked in sour milk, which is given to a wife of doubtful fidelity by the husband before he leaves her to go on a journey. If she commits adultery there will be no offspring as the result. A stone from the grave of a holy person, if worn as an amulet, is believed to heal wounds, or give health, or give the barren woman a child, or confer personal holiness. Holy graves are greatly reverenced, and small offerings are made to them ; they are also used as places of safe deposit. Petherick says that an "old hag" who brought him some dust from the grave of Abû-Beshr, declared that it would enable him to pass through the Cataract of Wâdî al-Homâr in safety.[1] On another occasion a written prayer was nailed to the yard's end of his boat by Wâd Yûsuf, who was sure that all the previous accidents had happened because of the absence from the boat of such a charm.[2] In 1905, when Mr. Crowfoot and I were travelling in the Third Cataract, our captain nailed a little bag containing dust from the grave of Shêkh Idrîs at Kubbah Idrîs to the bow of our boat, and we made the journey in safety.

Women wear many amulets, which are suspended from the neck, and hang on a level with the breasts or hips ; these, of course, have a bearing on love. Men wear them above the bend of the elbow, or on the wrist, or attached to the rosary. The better class Arab wears them in a line over his left flank, suspended by a silk or leather cord which passes over his right shoulder. The written amulet is often fastened to a limb which is wounded, or round the waist for abdominal troubles, or round the temples for headache and toothache. To increase sexual vigour two are worn at the breasts and two at the hips. Three amulets prevent conception, and three render a person sterile, and in the latter case two are placed under the subject's bed, and another is deposited at night in a neighbouring grave. In childbirth many written amulets are worn by the sufferer. Strips of leather knotted are also worn as amulets, for knots play a prominent part in Kordofan magic as in that

[1] *Travels in Central Africa*, p. 53.
[2] *Ibid.*, p. 103.

of ancient Egypt. When the prayers of the written amulet are not considered to be effective, recourse is had to the magic doctor, who, for a consideration, recites special prayers, and utters formulae of a potent character. Such prayers usually contain a number of names, and words of power, and words which are formed of series of initials of magical names. The latter words are, of course, meaningless, but they are supposed to bring to the sufferer the help of all the spiritual beings from whose names the initial letters have been taken. A similar method was employed by the Gnostics in the second and third centuries of our era, for they made words of the initial letters of the names of the Angels and Powers and other emanations of God, and certain of these words were believed to be all-powerful. When such words and names are written upon paper and burnt, the sick man is thought to derive much benefit from the smoke of the burning paper, which thus takes the place of incense. Sometimes the written paper is steeped in water, which is either drunk by the sick man or poured over him, with salutary effect. The ceremonies which are performed whilst the prayers are being recited are often very old, and it is probable that many of them have been in constant use for centuries. The prayers likewise and the traditional amulets are often very old.

CHAPTER IX.

Osiris, the Ancestral Spirit and God.

If we examine a stele from a tomb of the Ancient Empire, or a "false door" from almost any maṣṭabah tomb, we shall find cut or painted upon it a figure of the person for whom the tomb was made. He is seated on a four-legged African stool, with a table before him, and about this are laid offerings of bread, beer, oil, wine, geese, legs of beef, etc.; sometimes his wife is seated by or opposite to him. When the tomb is a large one a series of supplementary reliefs represent the various members of his family and his slaves bringing offerings to his tomb for the funerary commemorative service which was held daily or at intervals of a few days. The deceased sits in state, and we see him venerated as an ancestor who has attained to the life of the gods; he is, in fact, a divine patron of his family to whom petitions for help can be addressed in time of need. Under the Middle Empire the figure of the deceased was still usually cut upon his sepulchral stele, but under the XIIth dynasty the custom arose of placing other figures in the place of honour on the stele. Thus on Stele No. 181, in the British Museum,[1] which was made for Ānkef, son of Tenȧuit, who flourished in the reign of Ȧmen-em-ḥāt III, there appear on the upper part the prenomen of the king, in a cartouche, and figures of the gods Khenti-Ȧmenti, and Ȧp-uat, one on each side of it. On the upper part of Stele No. 299 is a scene in which Isis and Horus are represented in the act of setting up a pole on which rests the box containing the head of Osiris; behind Horus stands the Cow-goddess Hathor, animal-headed. Behind Isis and behind Hathor are kneeling figures of the deceased, with his hands raised in adoration.[2] This scene represents the most

[1] Published in the *Guide to the Egyptian Collections*, p. 220.
[2] *Ibid.*, Plate VI.

important of all the ceremonies which were performed annually in November and December at Abydos, viz., the setting up of the Ṭeṭ, or backbone of the god, and the placing of his head upon it. Thus we find a scene connected with the cult of Osiris taking the place of the usual figure of the deceased.

Under the XVIIIth dynasty a further development took place, and a figure of the god Osiris is usually sculptured on the upper portion of the surface of the stele. Lower down a figure of the deceased sometimes appears, but in a subordinate position. The stele in this period has become as much a tablet of honour to Osiris as a monument to the deceased. Sometimes figures of Osiris and the jackal-headed god Åp-uat appear on the upper half of the stele, and then two figures of the deceased appear, one adoring Osiris and one adoring Åp-uat.[1] On the stele of Ḥeru and Sutui the gods are Osiris and Ånpu.[2] On a great many stelae of this period Osiris occupies the place of honour, and the figure of the deceased is relegated to a corner.[3] Under the XIXth dynasty a further development took place. Thus, on Stele No. 498 we see the deceased kneeling with his hands raised in adoration before Åmen-Rā Ka-mut-f, who has the form of the ithyphallic Menu; in the field are two large human ears.[4] On Stele No. 646 the figure of the deceased adoring the foreign goddess Āntåt is at the bottom, and all the upper half is occupied with figures of the goddess Kent standing on a lion, and Menu and Reshpu.[5] On other stelae we have figures of Åmen-Rā, Mut, and Khensu, and groups of gods, and on stelae of a later period are figures of the solar boats.

From the above facts it is clear that the figure of Osiris, or Osiris Khenti-Åmenti, usurped the place

[1] See *Guide to the Egyptian Galleries*, No. 377, p. 110.

[2] *Ibid.*, No. 475, p. 134.

[3] *E.g.*, the Stele of Thothmes, No. 460, p. 130.

[4] *Guide to the Egyptian Galleries*, p. 141.

[5] 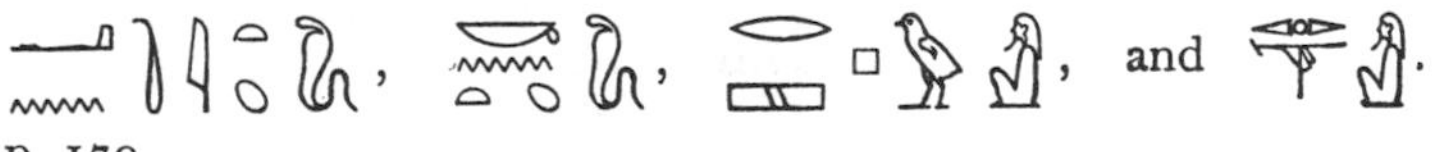

Ibid., p. 179.

occupied in stelae of the Ancient Empire by the deceased, and it seems to me that this was due to some modification which took place in the cult of Osiris under the Middle Empire, or to some change in the doctrine of his priests. Up to the time when the cult of Osiris spread throughout Egypt, the Egyptians, I believe, worshipped their ancestors, according to the custom of the African in most parts of the Sûdân, then and now. Everything about the figure of Osiris suggests that in one aspect at least he was an ancestor-god, probably at first of a comparatively small community. As the cult of the god spread, town and village communities all over Egypt adopted him as their ancestor-god, *par excellence*, and little by little he became the ancestor-god of the whole country. This, it seems, will account for the appearance of the figure of Osiris on stelae, especially on those which were found at Abydos, the central city of his cult in Upper Egypt. Devotees of other gods caused figures of them to be cut on stelae also, as we have seen above, but Khenti-Åmenti, Osiris, and Osiris Khenti-Åmenti are certainly the first to appear. The following examples will show how widespread is the cult of ancestors in the Sûdân, and will illustrate the similarity between the figures of ancestral gods and the figure of Osiris.

The Barotse worship chiefly the souls of their ancestors. When any misfortune happens, the witch-doctor divines with knuckle-bones whether the ancestor is displeased, and they go to the grave and offer up sacrifice of grain and honey.[1] "The essence of true "Negro religion is ancestor-worship, a belief in the "ghosts of the departed."[2] The Shilluks were in the habit of selecting a particular hero from among the dead, and they constituted him the ancestor of their tribe; when they needed rain or a good harvest they called upon him by name to provide it. They believe that the dead exist invisibly among the living, and they fear their anger and hatred. In many cases such ancestors attain to the position of gods, and in olden days the custom of sacrificing human beings to them was widespread.[3]

[1] Decle, *Three Years in Savage Africa*, p. 74.
[2] Johnston, *Liberia*, Vol. II, p. 1062.
[3] Frobenius, *Heiden-Neger*, p. 327.

Ancestor Worship in the Sûdân.

A prince offering incense to his father, who is seated within a shrine, holding his bow and spear in the right hand, and sceptre, mace and whip in the left. Osiris and Isis stand behind the seated king.

From a bas-relief in a pyramid chapel at Gebel Barkal.

In the middle of what seemed to be the principal street of Usimbi was a rude wooden figure of a bearded man, under a small conical-shaped roof, which was supported by nine ivory tusks, raised upon a platform of tamped clay, and carefully swept, showing that great care was bestowed upon it. Near the Aruwimi river was a large circular roof supported by thirty-three tusks of ivory, erected over a figure four feet high, painted with camwood dye a bright vermilion, with black eyes and beard and hair. The figure was very rude, still it was an unmistakable likeness of a man.[1]

The Lendu have no very clearly marked religion, though they have a distinct ancestor-worship, and are accustomed to remember the dead by placing roughly carved wooden dolls, which are supposed to represent the deceased person, in the abandoned hut where the dead lie buried.[2] A vague ancestor-worship exists among all the Bantu tribes, and they appear to have no actual religion, or belief in gods, as apart from ghosts and ancestral influences.[3] The Rev. A. B. Fisher says that among the Bantus the husband of the woman who has borne him a child brings his friends to help him to inspect the child three or four days after its birth. He then makes a present of bark-cloth to his wife, and that same night the child is presented with great solemnity to the Bachwezi, or ancestral spirits. The priest who understands the cult of these comes and prays aloud and intones songs or hymns to them, asking that the child may have long life, riches, no illness, and, above all, that it may be a faithful believer in the tribal and ancestral spirits. He accompanies each special request by spitting on the child's body and pinching it all over. The priest receives 108 kauri shells for his trouble, nine for each of the child's arms, and ninety for his whole body.[4] The greatest of the gods of Uganda was Mukasa, who seems to have been originally an ancestral spirit, and whose place of origin and principal temple were on the biggest of the Sese Islands. Later he became the Neptune of

[1] Stanley, *Through the Dark Continent*, Vol. II, pp. 260, 272.
[2] Johnston, *Uganda Protectorate*, Vol. II, p. 555.
[3] *Ibid.*, p. 578.
[4] *Ibid.*, p. 587.

Uganda, and the god of Lake Victoria.[1] The northern Kavirondo propitiate ancestral spirits, but worship two gods also, Awafwa, the chief of good spirits, and Ishishemi, a fiend. The Bantu Kavirondo set stones in the ground near their houses, and at intervals kill a goat, and pour out libations of goat's blood over these stones to the memory of the spirits of their ancestors. Some people also cut a small door at the back of their own dwelling with the idea that in some way it assists the passage in and out of the good ancestral spirits.[2]

In the country of Mambwe the people believe in a Supreme Being of a vague character, called Lesa, who has good and evil passions; but here, as everywhere else, the "Musimo," or spirits of the ancestors, are a leading feature in the beliefs. They are propitiated here as elsewhere by placing little heaps of stones about their favourite haunts.[3] Dr. Nassau states on the authority of Wilson that the people of Loango are more addicted to idol worship than any other people on the whole coast. They have a great many carved images which they set up in their fetish houses and in their private dwellings, and which they worship; but whether these images represent their forefathers, as is the case amongst the Mpongwe (at Gabun), is not known.[4] The religion of the Wanyamwezi is founded mainly on the worship and cult of spirits called "Musimo." Their ceremonies have but one object, the conciliation or propitiation of these spirits. They have no idea of one supreme power or God, personal or impersonal, governing the world and directing its destinies or those of individuals. They believe in the earthly visitation of spirits, especially to announce some great event, and more generally some big disaster . . . The dead in their turn become spirits, under the all-embracing name of Musimo. The Wanyamwezi hold these Musimo in great dread and veneration, as well as the houses, huts, or places where their bodies died. Every chief has near his hut a Musimo hut, in which the dead are supposed to dwell, and where

[1] *Ibid.*, p. 677.
[2] *Ibid.*, p. 752.
[3] Decle, *Three Years in Savage Africa*, p. 293.
[4] Nassau, *Fetichism in West Africa*, p. 49.

sacrifices and offerings must be made. Meat and flour are deposited in the Musimo huts, and are not, as with many other peoples, consumed afterwards. The common people have also their Musimo huts.[1] The Mfumu, or witch-doctor, obtains oracles from the spirits in this wise. He comes with his gourds full of "medicine," an instrument which opens and shuts like a concertina, and some tails of animals mounted on a stick. He kneels and prays to the spirits, bowing and bending to the ground from time to time. Next he rises and sings a hymn to the ancestors, and all the people about him join in the chorus. Then seizing his little gourds of medicine, he executes a *pas seul*, after which he begins to sing like one inspired. Suddenly he stops and recovers himself; except when chanting the spectators maintain a profound silence. After a brief interval of silence he proclaims the message from the spirits in mournful tones and with a dreary manner. The party then breaks up, and the proceedings end with a noisy dance. The hunter who succeeds in killing big game places the head of the beast he has killed before the hut, and inside it a little of the flesh. Mr. Decle adds: "This is a most remarkable fact, as I have never found in any other part of [savage] Africa the idea of a superior being whose help might be invoked."[2]

The Wanika of Rabbai Mpia ascribe a higher nature and power to the Koma, the spirit, or spirits, or shades, of the dead, but they have no image of them. The Koma, they say, is at one time in the grave, then above the earth, or in thunder or in lightning. It cannot, however, be seen, although it receives the gifts which are offered to it, and is appeased by them and rendered friendly to the living. The chief resting-place of the Koma is in or about the Kaya, the central point or chief town of the tribe, where a hut is erected for its habitation. As the Koma dwells by preference at the Kaya, the people often bring their dead from a great distance thither; and even disinter them in distant localities, and transport them to the graveyard at the Kaya, for reinterment, thinking that they find there greater repose.[3] The

[1] Decle, *op. cit.*, p. 344.
[2] *Three Years in Savage Africa*, pp. 343–346.
[3] Krapf, *Travels and Missionary Labours*, p. 176.

Jagga, too, pray to the souls of the dead, which they call Warumu ; but instead of rice and palm-wine, like the Wanika, they place milk on the graves.[1]

Du Chaillu saw the five most powerful "idols" on all the coast from Bansko to Mayombai ; they were placed in three little houses near the house of the king, who honoured them, and whom they protected. These "idols" were, of course, figures in which ancestral spirits had been induced to take up their abode. Pangeo (male) and Aleka (female) were in one house ; Makambi (male) and Abiala (female) were in the second house ; and Numba was in the third house.[2] Du Chaillu found that each head-man or chief of each family possessed a figure in which dwelt the ancestor spirit that was worshipped by that family. King Glass had one which was several generations old. Damagondai's figure was a female, with copper eyes, and a tongue made of a sharp piece of iron. She was dressed in Shekiani cloth. She cut to pieces those who offended her, she was said to speak, walk, and foretell events, and to come to people by night and tell them about the future. The family worshipped her by dancing round her, and singing her praises, and when they made petitions to her they offered her sugar-cane.[3] The ancestral-spirit figure of Npopo was a piece of ebony two feet high, with a man's face, with the nose and eyes of copper, and the body was covered with grass.[4] The ancestral-spirit figure of the clan to which Mbango belonged was a female, made of wood, nearly life-size, and with cloven feet. Her eyes were of copper, and one cheek was painted red and the other yellow. About her neck was a necklace of tigers' teeth. She was said to talk and to nod her head, and was very highly venerated by the people.[5] The large ancestral-spirit figure of a tribe or clan is kept in a house specially built, and to it come all its worshippers when they are about to hunt or make any important expedition. They present food to it, and then invoke its protection by dancing and singing

[1] *Ibid.*, p. 241.
[2] Du Chaillu, *Adventures*, p. 148.
[3] *Ibid.*, p. 238.
[4] *Ibid.*, p. 279.
[5] *Ibid.*, p. 293.

before it. Such figures are handed down from generation to generation and are much feared. They are believed to speak, walk about, and to eat and drink, in short to perform all, or nearly all, the functions of a man. It is remarkable that in many places such figures have no priests.[1]

The New Calabar people make images, called "Duen-fubara," of chiefs and men of importance, and perform very remarkable ceremonies in connection with them. The Duen-fubara image represents the head and shoulders of the deceased, and is carved in wood and painted. It is placed with images of two kinsfolk, sons or near relations of the deceased, on a wooden pedestal, which is placed in a recess. In front of the pedestal are made three mud altars, with a hole in each, wherein are thrown the offerings which the spirits eat and drink. On the eighth day after the installation of the figure, a great festival is made, and the son or successor of the deceased personally kills the goats and fowls, and throws or sprinkles the blood of each on the figure as he cuts each creature's throat. The sons of the deceased then go to the house in which the image has been deposited temporarily, and engage in a mimic fight with the men thereof, who attempt to keep possession of the figure. At length the blood-stained and consecrated image is permitted to be removed by the sons of the deceased, and a procession having been formed it is carried to the house which has been prepared for it, and placed in the hall or outer room. A watchman is appointed to take charge of it, and sweep and clean the house. The object of this ceremony is to secure the passage of the soul from the land of death to the land of the spirits, and to consecrate the released and sanctified spirit in his new position as spirit-father and mediator of the household, a position which entitles him to a daily adoration and a still more important weekly worship, accompanied by sacrifice.[2]

Major A. G. Leonard in his "Preliminary Survey" says that the entire basis of the whole natural conception of life, *i.e.*, of religion and philosophy, of the natives

[1] *Ibid.*, p. 337.
[2] Leonard, *The Lower Niger*, p. 164.

of Southern Nigeria is one of personal precedents and associations that are connected together in one long chain or existence of human generations, the links in which are purely and entirely ancestral.[1] Ancestral worship, or veneration of their fathers, was, he thinks, as natural to them as eating, drinking, etc., and it is quite evident that this primeval adoration of the father in the flesh, combining, as was subsequently the case, with a belief in the existence of the soul or spirit, developed first into the worship of the father in the spirit, and later on into that of certain deified ancestors. The patriarch became first the spirit-father, and then the ancestral deity, and thus in time a worship grew up around these shadow spirits, who exercised authority over their families, for good or for evil.[2] In the Warua villages a prominent feature are the numerous carved spirit figures which are set in small penthouses.[3] At Cabango a spirit figure, "consisting chiefly of feathers and beads," is paraded at a funeral.[4] The spirits of departed ancestors are all good, according to the ideas of the men of Tette, and on special occasions aid them in their enterprises.[5]

Among the Tshi-speaking peoples ancestor-worship prevails to a certain extent, and the assistance of deceased rulers is occasionally invoked. These *asrahmanfo*, or souls, still retain a certain amount of interest in the welfare of the tribe to which they belonged in life; and, when appealed to, they exercise such power as they possess for its protection. These souls are the "guardians of the tribe," and an eight-day festival is celebrated in August in their honour.[6]

According to Livingstone a "sort of idol" (*i.e.*, an ancestral-spirit figure) is found in every village in this part (Ujiji), and is made of wood with the features, markings, and fashion of the hair of the inhabitants; some have little huts built for them, others are in common houses. The Babemba call them "Nkisi"

[1] *Ibid.*, p. 63.
[2] *Ibid.*, pp. 68, 99, 106.
[3] Thomson, *To the Central African Lakes*, Vol. II, p. 153.
[4] Livingstone, *Missionary Travels*, p. 456.
[5] Livingstone, *The Zambesi*, p. 46.
[6] Ellis, *Tshi-speaking Peoples*, p. 167.

("Saucan" of the Arabs), and they present pombe, flour, bhang, tobacco, and light a fire for them to smoke by. They represent the departed father or mother, and it is supposed that they are pleased with the offerings made to their representatives, but all deny that they pray to them. Casembe has very many of these Nkisi; one with long hair, named Motombo, is carried in front when he takes the field; names of dead chiefs are sometimes given to them.[1]

The natives of Equatorial Africa worship also the spirits of their ancestors, a worship for which their minds are prepared by the veneration which they pay to old age. Young men never enter the presence of an aged person without curtseying, and passing in a stooping attitude, as if they were going under a low door. When seated in his presence, it is always at a humble distance. If they hand him a lighted pipe or a mug of water, they fall on one knee. The worship of their spirits follows the veneration of their relatives naturally enough. They believe that the shades of their ancestors exercise a beneficent influence over their lives and fortunes. They will send messages to their relatives by those who are dying. In times of peril or distress one may witness a very touching sight among these people. They will assemble in clans on the brink of some mountain brow or on the skirt of a dense forest, and, extending their arms to the sky, while the women are wailing and the very children weep, they will cry [for help] to the spirits of those who have passed away.[2]

The following is stated by Winwood Reade on the authority of one Mongilomba: When a dead person is tired of staying in the bush, his *obambo*, or ghost, will go to one of his former friends and say: I am tired of staying in the bush, please to build a little house for me in the town close to your house, and let there be singing and dancing. The next day the living man and his friends go to the grave of the ghost, and make a rude figure. They set it on the wooden frame on which the body was taken to the grave, and taking some of the grave dust they carry both figure and dust to a little

[1] *Last Journals*, Vol. I, p. 353.

[2] Winwood Reade, *Savage Africa*, p. 247 (Edit. 1864, p. 209).

hut which they build near the house of the friend of the ghost, and having placed them inside it they cover the door with a white cloth. They sing and dance whilst this ceremony is going on, and in the address which they make to the figure, or rather to the spirit in it, they say: "You are well dressed, but you have no canoe to go over to the other side."[1] The reference to the canoe is very interesting, for under the Ancient Empire the Egyptians believed that the souls of the dead were ferried over a large stream or river by a ferryman called Ḥer-f-ḥa-f , *i.e.*, "he whose face is behind him." We have a picture of this divine ferryman in the Papyrus of Ani,[2] and his face is literally turned behind him, the idea being, no doubt, that no unauthorized soul should be able to jump on to the end of the boat without the ferryman's knowledge whilst he was pushing off.

Finally, we may compare the "spirit-houses" of the kings of Dahomey with the building in which the god Osiris sits and which is usually called his shrine. The spirit-house of Tegbwesun was an oblong shed, the roof being supported on three sides by swish (mud) walls coloured red, white, and green. On the red stripe to the right there was a white globe, the sun, and on the left a crescent, the moon. The eaves were supported by tree logs, not very straight, and a little raised earthen step ran before the entrance. Within were the cloths which covered the fetish iron of Tegbwesun's spirit, with its custodians who beat off the devil with their besoms. In front of the house was a circular patch of chalked earth, in the centre of which an umbrella was stuck. On the left a circle of twenty-two skulls enclosed a similar whitened circle, with a single skull in the middle.

Three mud pillars supported the roof of the spirit-house of Mpengula, the end ones being whitewashed and decorated with blue horizontal lines upon their front. The centre ones, which were rudely fashioned into columns with capital and plinth, were also whitewashed

[1] *Ibid.*, p. 210.
[2] Plate XVII.

and ornamented with squares, diamonds, triangles, and other figures in blue, scarlet, and black distemper. The front of the raised floor was covered with white sand, and within the usual spirit-guardians surrounded the cloth-covered Asen (calapash).[1]

The facts quoted above seem to me to prove beyond all doubt that the Egyptians, like so many modern African peoples, worshipped the spirits of their ancestors, and that early in the Dynastic Period Osiris became the great ancestor of all Egypt, and was worshipped as such. The cult of the ancestor-spirit is common all over Africa, and its existence seems not to be incompatible with a belief in God, the Creator of the World and all in it. The Egyptians in very early times believed in the "Great God," 𓊹𓉻, and at the same time worshipped Osiris, whom they felt to be more sympathetic and more approachable by man than the Creator, Whom they regarded as remote from them and unknowable. The humanity of Osiris and the incidents of his life when upon earth, to say nothing of his murder, caused men to attach themselves to his cult and to worship him, and he became a father to them as well as a god. The thousands of figures of Osiris which have been found in Egypt are nothing more or less than figures of the great ancestor of the Egyptians, to whom men and women turned in times of difficulty and distress. Figures of the god were kept in houses, where honours were paid to them, they were placed in the tombs to keep away evil spirits, and they were laid among the wrappings of mummies to protect the body from all disaster and evil. The figure of Osiris brought with it the help, protection, and support of the Father-god, and it was to the Egyptian exactly what the ancestral-spirit figure is to the African to-day. There are in the British Museum no less than 300 figures of Osiris, little and big, made of bronze, wood, porcelain, and other materials; of no other god do there exist so many figures. The Egyptians were, even in theological matters, a very practical people, and unless these figures were believed to be of special importance for their physical and spiritual

[1] Skertchley, *Dahomey as It is*, pp. 404, 407.

well-being they would not have made them. Figures of Isis suckling Horus also exist in very large numbers, but this is not to be wondered at, seeing that she was the wife of Osiris, and if Osiris was the great father ancestor, she was, of necessity, the great mother ancestress.

The legends which exist in Egyptian texts tell us how the goddess, after she had conceived Horus, retired to the

The birth of Horus in the papyrus swamps.

swamps of the Delta, and how, being quite alone there, she brought him forth. In this, as in many other respects, tradition regarded Isis as an African woman, and preferably a woman from the Sûdân, for she brought forth her son as Sûdânî women bring forth their children. Piaggia says that the woman who is about to bring forth retires to the bush and is delivered there; sometimes she has an attendant, and sometimes she is quite alone. The husband and the witch-doctor stand in the hut waiting to learn if parturition has been successful. If successful the husband takes the wife back to the hut, and if she dies he leaves her there.[1] Mr. Hattersley also says that in Uganda children are born in the open air.[2] Sir H. Johnston says that among the Lendu women parturition takes place in a hut, to which, however, the husband may go, and the witch-doctor also if it be necessary. If there be difficulty in parturition, the witch-doctor makes a sacrifice of fowls and anoints the woman's forehead with the blood.[3] The pygmy women generally bring forth their children in the forest, severing the navel string with their teeth, and burying the placenta in the ground.[4]

Nekhebit and Ḥu presenting life and sovereignty to the son of Isis.

In the scene on p. 301, which is taken from a bas-relief at Philae, we have an attempt made to represent the parturition of Isis. The goddess is seated suckling her child Horus; round her are the lotus plants, which represent the "bush" into which the modern African woman retires when labour approaches. On one side of her stands Ȧmen-Rā, who assumes the paternity of the child and presents "life" to the face of Isis; on the other stands Thoth, who takes the place of the modern witch-doctor, grasping her right arm, and presenting to her "the protection of magic." The goddesses, standing one on each side, are Nekhebit and

[1] Mentre infatti la donna si reca colla sua compagna sul più vicino bosco onde deporre in mezzo alle erbe il proprio feto, il marito se ne sta nella capanna in consulta col profeta per sapere se o no il parto sarà felice.—Piaggia, *Viaggi nell' Africa Centrale*, p. 130.

[2] *The Baganda at Home*, p. 112.

[3] *Uganda Protectorate*, Vol. II, p. 553.

[4] *Ibid.*, p. 539.

Uatchit, and they present to the child the symbols of life, stability, serenity, long life, and the sovereignty of the Two Lands, *i.e.*, all Egypt. From the fact that Ȧmen-Rā and Thoth are present, these gods representing the husband and witch-doctor of modern days, we may assume that Isis suffered greatly, and that her

Uatchit and Sa presenting life and sovereignty to the son of Isis.

labour was "difficult." This assumption is supported by the description of the birth of Horus, given by Isis in her narrative on the Metternich Stele, in which her agony is insisted upon, as well as her loneliness. What objects the signs  and , which are in the hands of the gods, really represent is unknown, but I believe that the former was a "fetish," in which a spirit dwelt, and that the latter represented blood, which all over

Africa is thought to be "life." It is difficult not to think that these signs represent some internal organs of the body of Isis. The object on which Isis is seated suggests that during labour she sat on a stool,[1] as women do in West Africa, and did not kneel as do pygmy and Lendu women.[2]

[1] Winwood Reade, *Savage Africa*, p. 45.
[2] Johnston, *Uganda Protectorate*, Vol. II, p. 553.

CHAPTER X.

Osiris as Judge of the Dead.

We have already seen that, under the Ancient Empire, the god Osiris, the god who died, and who subsequently, because he rose from the dead, became the god of the dead, held his exalted position in the minds of the Egyptians because he was the great prototype and symbol of all dead men. Every man hoped to rise from the dead and to enjoy immortal life, because Osiris rose from the dead and enjoyed immortal life, which he had the power to bestow upon his followers. When these ideas were first developed, men believed greatly in magic, and they thought that it was only necessary to do for the dead man what Horus had done for Osiris in order to obtain his resurrection. The ceremonies which Horus performed on the body of Osiris, Anubis, the prototype of embalmers, helping him, and the formulae which Thoth recited during their performance, would, it was thought, if repeated, be followed by the same result as in the case of Osiris. Now, it was manifest to all that not every man was fit to be raised from the dead to life immortal, and at a very early period men felt that good and evil deeds of men ought to be taken into account somewhere by someone who had power to punish the wicked and to reward the just.

The views which the Egyptians held as to the qualifications which a man should possess before he ought to entertain the hope of immortality are well illustrated by the following: The judge, Ḥetep-ḥer-khut, who lived under the Vth dynasty, says: "I never took away any-"thing by force from any man, I never did an act of "oppression to any man,[1] [because] God loveth the thing

1 
. Mariette, *Mastabas*, p. 342; Sethe, *Urkunden*, I, p. 50.

"that is right."[1] The first sentence follows his statement that he made his tomb as a righteous possession, *i.e.*, that he acquired his tomb site by fair dealing. In the lines which follow, he says that he will "praise "greatly before God those who make offerings in his "tomb," and then comes the statement that he never oppressed any man or woman, followed by the words: "God loveth the thing that is right." He did not behave unjustly to his fellows, because he felt that God was a God of right and fair dealing, and it is impossible not to believe that he acted righteously to men because he feared the displeasure of his God. He gives no name to his God, and, even if we assume that Osiris is referred to, it does not alter the fact that he regarded him as a righteous God, who hated unrighteousness in man, and would punish the unjust. The allusion to offerings shows that he believed that his God would reward with an abundance of funerary offerings those who made offerings in the tomb of His servant.

In his tomb inscription, the high official Henqu, chief of the nome Ṭu-f, having decreed libations and offerings to Mateth and Ḥennu, says that he was beloved by fathers, and praised by mothers, and "buried" by the old men. He never wronged the daughter of any one of them. He gave bread to every hungry man in the nome, and he clothed the naked man therein. He even fed the jackals (or wolves) of the mountains, and the feathered fowl of heaven[2] with the carcases of sheep. He says: "I never stripped "any man of his possessions so as to cause him to "lay a charge against me on account of it before the "god of the city.[3] I was a speaker and a reporter of

1 

2 , l. 16.

3 , l. 20.

"what was good. No man feared the man who was "stronger than he, making a remonstrance because of it "to God. I speak no lie concerning this. Moreover, I "was beloved by my father, praised by my mother, "well-disposed towards my brother, sweet-tempered "with my sister. I possessed a perfect spirit."[1] . . . . Here we have a man who was chief of his nome, who fed the hungry, who clothed the naked, who wronged no maid, who fed the animals and birds sacred to the gods, who filched no man's goods, who protected the poor and weak, who lived on affectionate terms with the members of his family, and who was gracious to the aged. He strove to rule his nome in such a way as to incur no displeasure either from the "god of the city" or from God, and because he feared the god of the city and God he ruled justly. The inscription says also that he was overseer of the "grain of the South" in his nome, and it seems from the remarks which follow this statement that in his administration of this food supply he took care of the woman and the child. Such a man deserved "burial," and few in his nome would begrudge him his tomb.

In the two texts quoted above, the idea that Ḥetep-ḥer-Khut and Henqu ruled justly because they feared God is implied rather than definitely stated. In the following case the writer of the text makes very clear the motive of his benevolence and charitable works. He says: "I was one who spake good things, and reported "things which were fair. I never spake evil of any kind "to a man of power causing him to act against any man, "because I wished that I might obtain favour before the "Great God. I gave bread to the hungry man [and] "clothes to the naked man. I never gave a verdict in "a case between two brothers, with the result that a son "was dispossessed of his paternal inheritance. I was "loved by my father, praised by my mother, and beloved "by my brothers and sisters."[2] The official Àbà says: "I

[1] Sethe, *Urkunden*, pp. 76–79.

[2] 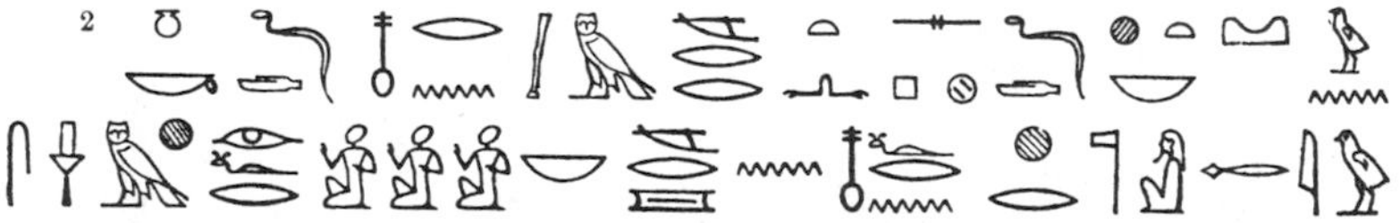

"was beloved by my father, praised by my mother, loyal "before the king, loyal before the god of the city."[1] The priest Åṭu records in his tomb that he settled a field upon his "beloved wife Ṭāsnek," and says that if anyone steals it from her he shall be [cursed] by the "Great God, the Lord of Heaven."[2] A little lower down he says: "If any "man shall steal this field from me the Great God shall "judge them."[3]

The above extracts from texts, all of which were written before the close of the VIth dynasty, prove beyond all doubt that the Egyptians believed that men who did what was right would find favour both with the "god of the city," and "God" or "the Great God," or "the Great God Lord of heaven," and that those who did evil would be cursed by the Great God, who would enter into judgment with them, and condemn them. Now in the pyramid text of Pepi I we read: "Pepi comes to thee, Osiris, thou givest him "life and serenity; Pepi comes to thee, O lord of "heaven."[4] Thus we see that in the VIth dynasty Osiris was called the "lord of heaven." In the inscription of Kaȧ Osiris is called "great god, lord of weighing of words" (*i.e.*, judge),[5] and in the text of Sabu Osiris is called "great god, lord of *Maāt*."[6] Putting these statements together we see that Osiris was the "great god, the lord of heaven, the judge, and the lord of *Maāt*."[7] By "lord of *Maāt*" is meant

---

 Sethe, *Urkunden*, I, p. 132.

1 *Ibid.*, p. 143.

2 

3  *Ibid.*, pp. 116, 117.

4 Line 188.

5  Mariette, *Mastabas*, p. 230.

6 *Ibid.* p. 375.

7 

"possessor of *Maāt*." The primary meaning of *Maāt* is "straight," and as far as we can see the same ideas which were attached to the Greek word *κανών* (*i.e.*, a straight rod, a mason's rule, and finally a rule, a law, a canon, which governs men and their actions) belong to the Egyptian word *Maāt*. The Egyptians used the word in a physical and moral sense, and thus it came to mean "right, true, truth, real, genuine, upright, righteous, just," etc. Thus in the Precepts of Ptaḥ-ḥetep it is said: "Great is truth (Maāt), the mighty and unalter-"able, and it hath never been broken since the time of "Osiris."[1] Ptaḥ-ḥetep exhorts his hearers "to make the truth (Maāt) permanent."[2] The just and upright man is *Maāt*,[3] and "God judgeth right."[4] When the Egyptian said that Osiris was the "lord of *Maāt*" he meant, clearly, that he was the "lord of justice," and a judge who "weighed words," or actions, with righteous impartiality: in fact, a just judge. Osiris was able to be the just judge when he sat in judgment on the souls of men, because he kept an account of all their deeds and words, which were duly written in books by "two scribe-"gods (Thoth and Sesheta) who made the entries in the "registers, and reckoned up the accounts on the tablets, "and kept the books carefully."[5] Every man's actions were known to him, nothing was hidden from him, and his verdict in each man's case was according to the evidence written in the Registers of Doom by Thoth and Sesheta.

Now, how had Osiris acquired this great reputation as a strictly impartial judge, and as a righteous god? The texts fortunately answer this question. From a number of passages, which have been already quoted, we learn that after the defeat of Set by Horus, the god of evil made infamous charges against Horus and

[1] P. 17, l. 5. [2] P. 18, l. 1. [3] 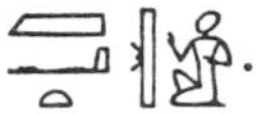.

[4] . Amélineau, *La Morale*, p. 138.

[5] Pepi I, l. 185, 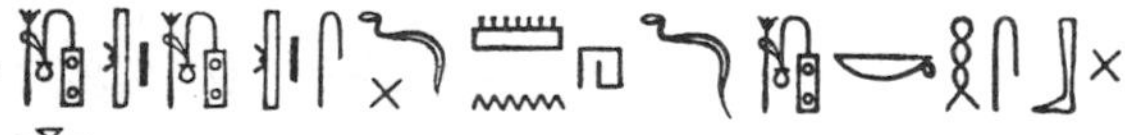

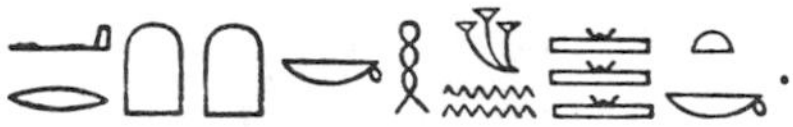.

Osiris in his closed shrine, accompanied by Isis and his four grandsons.
From the Papyrus of Ani.

against his father Osiris. Set, it is said, declared that Isis had played the harlot after the death of Osiris, that Horus was the child of her transgression, denying that he was the son of Osiris, who begot him after his death. Horus was therefore illegitimate and, of course, barred from succeeding Osiris on the throne of Egypt. The gods, who were greatly disturbed by these charges against the heir of Osiris, determined to enquire into the matter, and they assembled in the Great Hall of Heliopolis, where they heard the evidence of the accuser and of the accused. Their decision was that Set's charges were unfounded, and they determined to crown Horus king of Egypt on his father's throne. The coronation of Horus was carried out, and he was put in possession of all his father's kingdom. What the exact charge was which Set brought against Osiris is not known, but it was sufficiently grave to justify the gods in enquiring into it. This enquiry also took place in the Great Hall of Heliopolis, presumably immediately after the trial of Horus. Osiris did not plead his own cause, but Thoth appeared for him, and brought forward such evidence that the gods declared Osiris to be *maā kheru*, *i.e.*, "true of word, or voice," *i.e.*, not guilty. Thereupon Set was dragged into the Great Hall and thrown to the ground before Osiris, and Thoth led him to the place where Set was lying, and made Osiris to take his seat upon him as a sign of his triumph and of the victory of righteousness over evil. Thus Set failed to deprive Horus of his throne, and did not succeed in preventing the gods from acknowledging the sovereignty of Osiris in heaven, as men acknowledged his son's sovereignty on earth. The gods of Heliopolis had caused to be written a formal decree which confirmed their verdict in the case of Horus, and now they caused to be written another decree, which confirmed their verdict in the case of Osiris, and conferred upon him the kingdom of heaven.[1]

[1] Such a decree was written for Unȧs by Osiris, therefore one must have been written for Osiris himself. 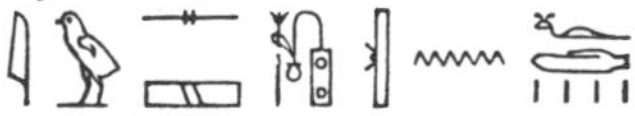
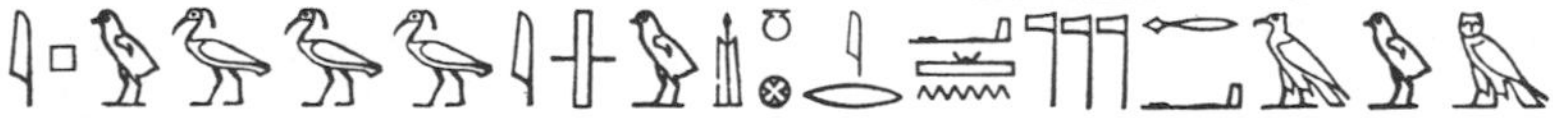
. Unȧs, l. 575.

They also ordered that Osiris was to take his seat on the chief throne in heaven, and, all the gods of the west, east, south, and north assisting him,[1] Osiris ascended into heaven, and was ever after the god and judge of the dead.

If we consider the facts stated above it becomes clear that the original conception of Osiris by the Egyptians developed considerably before the close of the VIth dynasty, and that from being the great ancestor god of a particular town or region, he had become the god and judge of all the dead of Egypt. As an ancestor god his power was very great, but as the judge of human conduct and morals it was practically illimitable. He rose from the dead by the help of Horus and Thoth, but he obtained the right to rule over the kingdom of heaven by virtue of his innocence and freedom from the defects of sinful human nature. The gods carefully scrutinized the charges which Set brought against him in his endeavour to prove that Osiris deserved the death of his body which was due to Set, and they decided that Osiris was innocent. They held, in fact, that an innocent being had been slain by the malefactor Set, who had made infamous accusations against him in order to hide his own guilt, and that he who had reigned blamelessly, and had lived a good and pure life on earth, had fallen a victim to evil and wickedness. Osiris suffered death because he was righteous, and because he had done good to all men. Osiris, being the son of a god, knew well the wickedness which was in Set, and the hatred which the personification of evil and his fiends bore to him, yet he did not seek to evade his murderous attack, but willingly met his death. There is nothing in the texts which justifies the assumption that Osiris knew that he would rise from the dead, and that he would become the king and judge of the dead, or that the Egyptians believed that Osiris died on their behalf and rose again in order that they also might rise from the dead. But from first to last the resurrection of Osiris is the great and distinguishing feature of the Egyptian religion, for Osiris was the firstfruits of the dead, and every worshipper of

[1] *Ibid.*, l. 572.

Osiris based his own hope of resurrection and immortality upon the fundamental fact of the resurrection of Osiris. It may be urged that, as the reconstitution of the body of Osiris was in primitive times effected by means of the magical ceremonies performed by Horus and the recital of the words of power by Thoth, who had himself composed them, it was only necessary to repeat these to arrive at the reconstitution of any person, and that the intervention of Osiris was, therefore, unnecessary, and that his assistance was not required. That the Egyptians themselves held this view at one time is very probable, but that time must have been exceedingly remote, certainly long before the VIth dynasty. It was one thing to reconstitute the body, but it was quite another thing to obtain for the spiritual body of the dead man admission into the kingdom of Osiris and life among the gods. Osiris only obtained the sovereignty of heaven and life among the gods because of his innocence of evil and his surpassing merit, and he who wished to enter that heaven must be innocent, just, and righteous. He must have done as Osiris did, "set right in the place of wrong,"[1] so far as the power in him lay, and his hand must have been purified by the "Maker of his seat" (*ȧri-ȧst-f*), *i.e.*, by Osiris.[2] A man must have lived in such a way that it could be said of him as was said of Osiris, "he hath done no evil,"[3] before he can enter the heaven of Osiris. In very early times the Egyptians believed that the dead were ferried over a stream or river to the Island of Osiris, by a ferryman called Ḥer-f-ḥa-f and Maa-f-ḥa-f.[4] This ferryman, however, would only ferry over the man who was innocent, or just, before heaven, and before earth, and before the

1  Unȧs, l. 394.

2  Unȧs, l. 393.

3  Pepi I, l. 455.

4  Unȧs, l. 489.

island of the earth.[1] Thus it is quite clear that truth and righteousness were required from his followers by Osiris, in very primitive times, and that without these qualifications no man could attain to everlasting life in his kingdom.

The standard of moral rectitude and well-doing demanded by the god was, clearly, beyond man's power of attainment, for of what human being who ever lived could it be said "he hath done no evil"? The Egyptians saw this difficulty and realized that, however great a man's righteousness might be, its measure must always fall short of that demanded by the god of truth and righteousness. Then they remembered that the god of truth was himself slain and his soul brought to judgment before the gods, and that his cause was pleaded for him by his advocate Thoth, who made clear the innocence of Osiris, and obtained a verdict of "not guilty" from them. Further, they thought, if it was necessary for Thoth to plead the cause of the innocent Osiris, who suffered death for his goodness, how much more is it necessary for us to have an advocate who will place our merits in the most favourable light, and plead extenuating circumstances for the sins which we have committed, and present our cases before Osiris in such a way that he will show us compassion and mercy, and induce him to accept us and hold us justified! The conception of a judgment of the dead marks a great development in the religious thought of the Egyptians. According to their original idea, sin was an insult to the god and a breach of the Law which could be adequately paid for by gifts and offerings, and this being so there was no necessity for a judgment. Later there came the consciousness of offences committed against the king, and the god of the city, and God, which was followed by the idea that these could not be atoned for by offerings and gifts, and that for these a man would be brought into judgment before Osiris. The Egyptians declared that Osiris was a just judge, and they knew that if he judged

1 
 . Pepi I, l. 400.

them with strict justice they must be condemned in the judgment, and that they could not be pronounced guiltless by the god unless he used his prerogative of mercy, and accepted such righteous intentions as they possessed, and their good works in respect of the obligations of the Law in full settlement of his claims upon them. They might fulfil the commandments of the Law, but it was only the mercy of Osiris which permitted them to enter his kingdom and to enjoy everlasting life. Osiris was not only a just judge, but he was also a merciful judge. His loyal followers placed their highest hopes in his mercy, for he had lived among men upon earth, had possessed a human nature like theirs, and understood all their weakness and strength, and could therefore make allowances for their sins and defects; finally he had suffered and died as men suffer and die. Though he had lived in the body of a man he lived sinlessly, and when he was judged by the whole company of the "gods" he was pronounced sinless. Those who wished to live with him in heaven were obliged to be sinless, and a measure of righteousness which had been accepted by the mercy of Osiris as complete was the only passport to his kingdom.

The conception of the judgment of Osiris is very, very old, but no representation of it older than the XVIIIth dynasty is extant. The Hall in which the judgment took place was, according to the Papyrus of Nebseni (Sheet 30), a long chamber which was called the "Hall of the Two Maāt Goddesses,"[1] *i.e.*, of the Two Goddesses of Truth, one goddess presiding over Upper, and the other over Lower, Egypt. They are also called the "Two Daughters Merti of the Lord of the city of Maāti,"[2] or the "Two daughters Merti, Eyes of Maāt (Truth)."[3] The door of the Hall was called "Khersek-Shu," and the

1 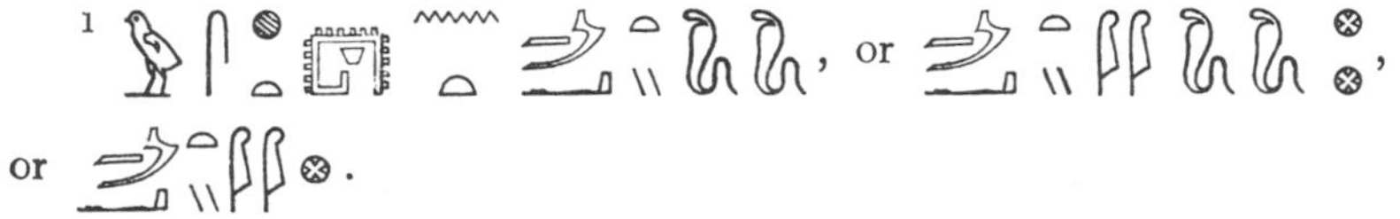

2  Papyrus of Nu.

3 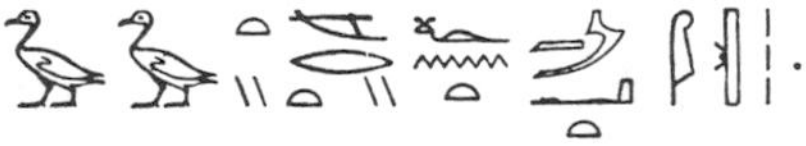 Papyrus of Nebseni.

upper leaf of the door "Neb-Maāt-ḥeri-reṭui-f," and the lower leaf "Neb-peḥti-thes-menmenet."[1] The Hall is, in fact, in the form of an elongated funerary coffer. Above the palm-leaf cornice is a frieze, and in the centre of this is the figure of a seated god with his hands extended over two pools (?), each of which contains an eye of Horus. These pools may have some connection with the two pools called "Millions of Years" and "Great Green Lake," which are mentioned in the XVIIth Chapter of the Book of the Dead (ll. 45, 46). On each side of this figure are:—1. An ape seated before a pair of scales. 2. Thirteen feathers of Maāt , and thirteen uraei , arranged alternately. 3. An ape seated before a pair of scales. The form of the scales is unusual. A forked upright supports a beam. At one end are attached two cords which hold the pan of the scales wherein is a square weight, and from the other hang two cords, which seem to be connected by cross cords or bars. What these signify or how these were used is not known. The ape represents Thoth, the inventor of numbers, and computer of time, and secretary of Osiris. By the side of one of the folding doors are seated the two Maāt Goddesses, each holding the sceptre of "serenity" in her right hand, and "life" in her left. On the head and sceptre of each is the feather , symbolic of "truth."

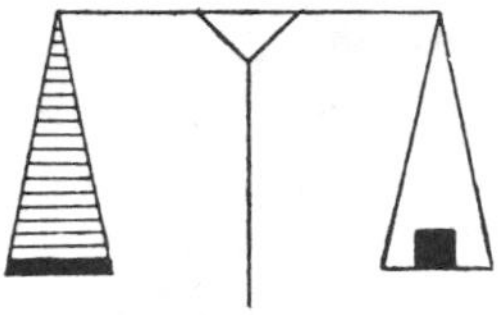

The Scales of Maāt (Truth).

Across the Hall is a row of mummied human forms, each wearing the feather of "truth" on his head. These represent a series of two-and-forty gods or spirits, whom the man to be judged is supposed to address individually by name, and to declare that he has not committed such and such a sin. It is possible that in the period anterior to the XVIIIth dynasty

1 

these gods were not addressed by the deceased, who, it seems, made his statement to Osiris, or Thoth, direct; for what they have to do with the judgment of Osiris or how they came to be associated with him as judge is not clear. On the other hand, they may, of course, represent a series of deified ancestral spirits who were addressed individually by the dead in very primitive times, and, if so, the statement made by the deceased, which includes their names, is older than that in which their names do not appear. We have already seen that the cult of Osiris took the place, little by little, of the cult of ancestors, and it is very probable that, when Osiris became the final god and judge of the dead, the deceased made his statement to him and also to the two-and-forty gods. Be this as it may, the two oldest XVIIIth dynasty copies of the Book of the Dead, viz., the Papyrus of Nebseni and the Papyrus of Nu, give the statement in two forms, one with the names of the two-and-forty gods and the other without. According to the information given to us by the latter form, the two-and-forty gods were beings "who made prisoners "of the wicked and devoured their blood on the day "when the characters of men were investigated[1] in the "presence of Unen-nefer" (*i.e.*, Osiris). The wicked were, of course, those who were condemned in the judgment of Osiris, and who were, in consequence, the enemies of these gods of punishment. The devouring of their blood is in agreement with the common and almost universal African custom of eating the bodies of dead enemies, and suggests that the conception of the existence of gods with cannibal tastes dates from primitive and pre-Osirian times. In this as in many other things, the inherent conservatism of the Egyptians caused them to retain the names of the two-and-forty gods in their religious works, long after all belief in their existence had disappeared from their minds.

Now, the vignette in the Papyrus of Nebseni, which represents the Judgment Hall of Osiris, gives us no idea

1 

of what was supposed to take place in it when the deceased was judged there beyond the fact that he made forty-two negative statements before forty-two gods, in the presence of the Maāti Goddesses and, presumably, of Osiris also. According to African custom we expect that the trial of the deceased followed his declarations that he had not committed such and such sins, just as at the present time when a man is about to undergo the ordeal of the "red-water" in West Africa, he makes a series of declarations of his innocence of certain crimes and offences, and then drinks the "red-water" which the magic-doctor gives him. The ordeal which the Egyptian went through was the weighing of his heart before Osiris. This is proved by the vignettes of the Judgment Scene in the papyri of the latter half of the XVIIIth and those of the XIXth dynasty. In the Papyrus of Nebseni in connection with Chapter XXXIXB we have this scene represented. Here we see the scribe seated in one pan of the scales, and the weight, which is in the form of a heart, resting in the other. The weighing is carried out by Thoth, "the lord of the Scales," in the presence of Osiris. In the *Papyrus of Iuáu* (Plate XXII) the heart of the deceased is being weighed against a weight in the presence of Thoth, in the form of a dog-headed ape, of Maāt, the daughter of Rā, and of Osiris. In the Papyrus of Ani the vignettes which appear inside the Hall of Maāti show us what was supposed to take place there when the deceased entered it to be judged. In the first are the Maāti Goddesses, as in the Papyrus of Nebseni. In the second the deceased is seen making offerings to and adoring Osiris. In the third Anubis is weighing the heart against the feather of "truth," and the composite monster Ām-mit stands by the scales ready to devour it if it be found light. In the fourth the god Thoth is seated and is painting a feather of Maāt (or "truth").

In the Papyrus of Ani, and in other finely painted papyri of a later date, we find that the small vignette has developed into a large Judgment Scene, the chief characteristics of which may be now described. Along the upper side of the scene, which is intended to represent the side of the Hall, is a row of gods who, in the Papyrus of Ani, are Rā-Harmakhis and Temu, Shu and Tefnut, Ḳeb and Nut, Isis and Nephthys, Horus Hathor, Ḥu, and Sa. All the members of the Company of Gods who are usually associated with Osiris are enumerated except Anubis, who stands in another part of the Hall and takes an active part in weighing the heart of the deceased. To this Company are added Rā-Harmakhis, Horus, Hathor, Ḥu, and Sa. In the Papyrus of Hunefer we have Rā, Temu, Shu, Tefnut Ḳeb, Nut, Horus, Isis, Nephthys, Ḥu, Sa, Uat-resu, Uat-meḥt, and Uat-Ȧmenti; Uat-Ȧbti has been inadvertently omitted. The names Uat-resu, Uat-meḥt, and Uat-Ȧmenti mean "Road of the South," "Road of the North," and "Road of the West" respectively, and it is interesting to note that personifications of the roads to the Hall are included among the gods who sit in judgment on the deceased, who was obliged to prove himself innocent before the roads, just as at an earlier period he was obliged to prove himself innocent before the Island of the Blessed itself. In the Papyrus of Ȧnhai two Companies of Gods are represented: (1) the Great Company of the Gods, the Lords of Khert-neter; and (2) the Little Company of the Gods, the Lords of Ȧmenti. In each case the gods represent, presumably, the group of gods who sat in judgment when Osiris was being tried in the Great Hall of Heliopolis. Among them are the grandparents, parents, sisters, and son of Osiris, and Set, his brother and murderer, is represented by his son Anubis, the nephew of Osiris.

At one end of the Hall, seated within a shrine, is the god Osiris, whose body is held up, or embraced, by the goddesses Isis and Nephthys. Thus these goddesses are shown twice in the Judgment, once among the gods who sit in judgment, and once here. The shrine is in the form of a funeral chest, the front side of which is removed so that the god, who is drawn in profile, may be seen. The roof or cover of the shrine is rounded, and upon it rests a hawk, with outspread wings; the head of the bird is clearly drawn, and on each side of it are six uraei. The cornice of the roof is ornamented with a row of uraei, each of which wears a disk; it is supported in front by two lotus pillars, with highly decorated capitals. The whole shrine rests upon a low pylon-shaped building with a palm-leaf cornice, and is reached by means of a short staircase, with a rectangular pillar on each side at the foot. The top of the low building was probably covered with a layer of sand before the shrine was placed upon it, or perhaps with a new grass mat. Osiris is seated upon a throne or chair, the side of which has doors with bolts, similar to those of a sepulchral shrine or coffer. This throne, as we shall see later, probably contained portions of the god's body, and was therefore made in the form of a funerary chest. Osiris wears the White Crown, to which are attached two feathers , one on each side. The White Crown was originally the crown of the god Khenti Åmenti, and when it was adopted as the head-covering of Osiris the two feathers were added to it to indicate Truth, which was his chief characteristic. It is possible that two feathers were placed on the ancestral figures with which Osiris was identified at a later period, and that they were merely transferred to the crown of Khenti Åmenti when Osiris was identified with him. What the original crown was made of cannot be said, but it was probably woven basketwork or white skin. The Bayanzi chiefs used to wear tall hats made of basket-work, and the Imbangala of the Middle Kwango used to wear striking head-dresses made of black and white Colobus monkey skin, as did also the Lomami, Lulongo-Maringo, Bangala, and Northern Ngombe.[1] Another crown often worn by Osiris in the Judgment scene is the "Atef," , which is the ordinary crown of the god with the addition of a pair of horns. This calls to mind the head-gear of the Alunda men, with their excrescent tufts and horns.[2] The picture of King Munza given opposite, after Schweinfurth, supplies a good typical example of the crowns which great African kings wore.

The feathers on the crown of Osiris are from

[1] Johnston, *George Grenfell*, Vol. II, p. 598.
[2] *Ibid.*, p. 599.

the ostrich,[1] presumably those of a male bird, but of which of the three great types, East African, South African, or North African, is not clear. Formerly the last-named type was found right across the Sahara from the Sûdân and Nigeria to Tunis and Algeria,

King Munza.

and from Senegal eastwards to Syria and Arabia.[2] One or more feathers were worn by many African peoples of the South with whom the Egyptians came in contact, and among the Egyptians "bearer of the feather" was a title of honour. Head-dresses made

[1] The Masai warriors wear ostrich feathers fastened to a frame of bamboo when they go to war. See Hollis, *The Masai*, pp. 320, 340.
[2] Johnston, *Uganda Protectorate*, Vol. II, p. 405.

of feathers are frequently worn by the peoples of the forest region between the west coast of Tanganyika and the Lualaba Congo at the present day.[1] A fine example of them, presented by Sir Harry Johnston, may be seen in the British Museum.[2]

On the face of the god are short side-whiskers, and from his chin hangs a long, plaited beard. The plaited beard is characteristic of several Central African peoples, among others of the Makarakas, many of whom have a well-developed beard, which is large enough to be arranged in plaits either artificially lengthened by introducing a little wooden rod, or else massed together by a copper band.[3] Kiteté, chief of Mpungu, was remarkable for his plaited beard, which was twenty inches long, and was decorated at the tips with a number of blue glass beads. His brother's beard was six inches long, and "there were half a dozen others with beards of three or four inches long."[4] The beard of Ndiayai, the king of the Fâng, was plaited in several plaits, which also contained white beads and stuck out stiffly from the face.[5] The men of the Lower Lulongo are frequently seen with beards, and the Batwa, or red dwarfs, who live between the main Congo and the Juapa, though they are not more than four feet six inches high, have big heads and beards. According to Lord Mountmorres these beards are black, and make their wearers remarkable in a region where almost all the people are clean shaved.[6] Among the Bayanzi on the Congo chiefs alone wear a beard, which is usually plaited.[7] The Mañbattu men grow an ample moustache, and a thick square beard.[8] The Bayaka grow a beard, and the Lunda and Luba chiefs endeavour to produce the beard in a long plaited plastered rod, growing from the middle of the chin, and artificially lengthened by

[1] *George Grenfell*, Vol. II, p. 597.

[2] See in the Ethnographical Gallery, Wall-case No. 109. Collection No. 1899—204.)

[3] Junker, *Travels in Africa*, Vol. I, p. 335.

[4] Stanley, *Through the Dark Continent*, Vol. II, p. 91.

[5] Du Chaillu, *Adventures in Equatorial Africa*, p. 74.

[6] Johnston, *George Grenfell*, Vol. I, pp. 138, 145, 504.

[7] *Ibid.*, p. 532.

[8] *Ibid.*, p. 534.

weaving black fibre into it.[1] Among the Bambala the beard grows on the point of the chin only, and it attains to a considerable length; it is bound up under the chin, and pieces of clay are often hidden in the knot to give it a more important appearance. The Babwende chiefs allow their beards to grow to a great length, and roll them up under the chin like a ball. Father Geens saw some beards that were one metre and a half long.[2]

Round his neck Osiris wears a deep collar or necklace composed of many rows of beads and other ornaments, and from that portion of it which lies on the nape of the neck hangs the *menȧt* , an amulet which signifies material happiness, physical well-being, bodily pleasure, and sexual delights. The tombs of Egypt have yielded untold thousands of beads of all kinds, which prove that the love of the Egyptians for beads, shells, teeth of animals and men, pendants, etc., which could be worn as necklaces, was as great as is that of modern nations of Africa.[3] The bead necklace or collar of Osiris was a most elaborate ornament, and the tradition of its form and shape was preserved down to the Roman Period. Perhaps the best copies of it are found on the brightly painted coffins and "mummy-boards" of the priests and priestesses of Ȧmen of the XVIIIth and XIXth dynasties. The objects strung with the beads were amulets which were intended to protect the god from injury of every kind, and they have their counterpart in the kauris, teeth, etc., which are found on the necklaces worn by men and women at the present day. The three objects,

[1] *Ibid.*, p. 579.

[2] *Ibid.*, p. 585.

[3] Necklaces formed of half-inch sections of the leg-bones of fowls were most affected in the old days. They were treasures indeed, and no slave-girl might wear them; death was the punishment of a slave-girl or slave-wife who wore them. The white china pipe-clay beads which Bentley brought were jewels. Anyone possessing them could load up his steamer with food. The women seemed to be insatiable in their greed for beads, and after a while long rows of free-born women would appear on great occasions to dance in caps of white beads, with anklets, bracelets and necklaces, 8 inches deep, their skins abundantly encrusted with powdered cam-wood and oil. The wealth and magnificence of Bopota had reached a climax undreamt of—inconceivable.—*Pioneering on the Congo*, Vol. II, p. 270.

the whip , or flail, and the two sceptres (?) , , were as much amulets as symbols of authority.

We next notice that the whole body of Osiris, from the neck to the soles of his feet, is covered with something which is commonly called "scale-work." It can hardly represent apparel, for we know of no Egyptian garment which covers the whole body, fitting it and the feet tightly, and I believe that this "scale-work" is intended to represent the design with which the whole body of Osiris was thought to be tattûed. Sir Samuel Baker notes that the Bari are tattûed upon the stomach, sides and back so closely that the design has the appearance of a broad belt of fish-scales, especially when they are rubbed with red ochre, which is the prevailing fashion.[1] That the body of Osiris is often painted white in the vignettes does not affect the identification of the scale-work with tattûing, for many tribes smear themselves with white earth or clay. The white colour may be symbolic of death, for among the Nilotic Negroes the women wear a black tail fringed with white strings for a month as a sign of mourning, and others smear themselves with white earth.[2] Another explanation of the scale-work is forthcoming. The Bantu Kavirondo smear portions of their bodies with white clay, on which a pattern is worked with a piece of stick; this removes the clay in places, and leaves the skin showing through.[3] It is possible that the whole body of Osiris may have been treated in this manner, but in view of the wide-spread custom of tattûing in the Sûdân, the scale-work is far more likely to represent tattû marks. If we examine the painted hollow wooden figure of Osiris which contained the Papyrus of Ȧnhai[4] in the British Museum, we see that the breast, arms, and shoulders are painted red, and that they are decorated with circular ornaments formed of dots, which resemble flowers in bloom. From the waist downwards the body is covered with painted scale-work, resembling that on Osiris in the Papyrus of Ani.

[1] Baker, *Albert N'yanza*, p. 59. The red ochre is mixed with grease.
[2] Johnston, *Uganda Protectorate*, Vol. II, p. 793.
[3] *Ibid.*, p. 730.
[4] Second Egyptian Room, No. 20,868.

So far back as 1866 Dr. Livingstone noted that the tattû, or tembo, of the Matambwé and Upper Makonde "very much resembles the drawing of the old Egyptians," and reproduced some of its marks in his *Last Journals*, Vol. I, p. 49. Among the Mittû the men tattû on a large scale, the lines usually radiating from the belly to the shoulders; the women have merely a couple of parallel rows of dotted lines upon the forehead.[1] Some Nandi girls tattû themselves by cutting three horizontal lines in their cheeks below the eyes, or, like the Kavirondo, by drawing one line down the forehead and nose, or, like the Masai, by making a pattern round the eyebrows and eyes.[2] Tattûing is well nigh universal on the Upper Congo.[3] All the Bantu-speaking forest folk between the slopes of Ruwenzori, the Shuliki River, and the Upper Congo, practice "cicatrization" to a remarkable extent; this takes the place of tattûing among other African peoples. Scores and weals of skin are raised either by burning or by cutting with a knife, and introducing the irritating juice of a plant into the wound. Sometimes these raised weals are so small that they produce almost the effect of tattûing. The Babira people of the forest near the Semliki River cicatrize their chests and stomachs.[4]

A third explanation of the markings on the body of Osiris is possible, for the scale-work may represent paint or colour only. George Grenfell, Father Geens, Mr. T. A. Joyce, and Sir Harry Johnston supply abundant proofs that many naked tribes of Africa paint their bodies, especially those who live between Stanley Pool and Stanley Falls, and between the Bantu border beyond the Northern Congo and the Lunda plateaux and the Zambesi watershed. Between Stanley Pool and the Albertine Rift Valley the naked tribes cover their bodies with a crimson paste made of camwood and palm oil. In the countries to the south the red pigment is made from iron rust, or

[1] Schweinfurth, *Heart of Africa*, Vol. I, p. 410.
[2] Hollis, *The Nandi*, p. 30; *The Masai*, p. 341.
[3] Bentley, *Pioneering on the Congo*, Vol. II, p. 270.
[4] Johnston, *George Grenfell*, Vol. II, p. 556, and see specially p. 564.

from the intensely red clay of decomposed granite, and is mixed with mutton fat and applied to the body; by the side of the camwood paste this colour is "hideous." White pigment is made from kaolin or ashes, yellow from clay or certain saps or seeds, blue-grey and mauve from wood ashes or clay, indigo, or certain saps or seeds. Some warriors seen by Grenfell were painted red, black and white. The Ikasa and Yalundi paint the face with some indigo dye in dots and geometrical figures, and the body is covered with a network of indigo lines. The Basoko use white as a war colour. Some of the northern Babati clans (Wele River) paint the body all over with grey clay, and then paint on top of this indigo spots and stripes with Randia sap. This is very effective. Some of the southern Ngombe paint the body red and the face black (with soot). The Azande paint blue stripes on their brown skins, paint themselves red for war, and blacken their foreheads with charcoal and oil. The Bangala paint themselves red and black as a protection against evil spirits. The Babwende use a great quantity of red and white in colouring their bodies.[1] The Ngombe men paint their bodies with four colours. Their ornamentation usually consists of parallel lines of blue-grey, yellow, red, and white, running along the two arms, and meeting over the shoulders in curved scrolls. The chest, abdomen, and lower limbs are also painted with parallel lines in these colours. According to Mr. Torday the Bambala ornaments his face with stripes of red, brown, orange, and violet. The Alunda either paint the whole body with white kaolin, or decorate their brown skins with white squares, dots, and crosses. The Ababua-Babati of the Wele district ornament their bodies with camwood paste, white clay, and charcoal paste. The Mañbattu women paint their bodies with black stripes, like those of a zebra, or with irregular spots. The above facts suggest that the scale-work on the body of Osiris represents a design made by tattûing, cicatrization, or painting.

In the shrine with Osiris we see close to one of the pillars a skin of an animal, which in this case appears to be certainly that of a pied bull, with the head cut off.

[1] Johnston, *George Grenfell on the Congo*, Vol. II, pp. 560–562.

Sometimes, as we see from the illustration on p. 328, the skin is that of some other animal. By the side of his feet there springs up the long stem of a lotus or lily, in full bloom, and upon it stand figures of the Four Sons of Horus, Ḳestȧ, Ḥāpi, Ṭuamutef, and Qebḥsenuf. The presence of the lily suggests water, and in the Papyrus of Hunefer the lily is seen to be growing out of a lake or stream, and figures of the Four Sons of Horus stand on the flower. This agrees with the old legend, which sets the throne of Osiris close to or above the fountain of water which flows from heaven, and is the source of the Nile upon earth.

Skin of the pied bull of Osiris.
From the Papyrus of Ȧnhai.

At the other end of the Hall of Judgment is the Balance in which the heart of the deceased is to be weighed. It consists of a stout upright pillar, set in a stand, from one side of which, near the top, projects a peg, made in the form of the ostrich feather typifying "truth." From this peg, suspended by a cord, hangs the beam of the Balance, with the two pans, each of which is suspended by two or more cords. The right pan usually holds the feather of Maāt, or the goddess Maāt, and the left the heart which is to be weighed. On the top of the pillar of the Balance is sometimes placed the head of the goddess Maāt, or the head of Anubis, or the head of the ibis, which was sacred to Thoth, or a figure of the dog-headed ape, which also was sacred to Thoth and was even called by this god's name. The actual weighing of the heart was usually performed by the jackal-headed god Anubis, the son of Set and Nephthys, who in dynastic times held in respect of the judgment of the dead the place which his father Set held in the great trial of Osiris before the gods who were assembled in the Hall of the Great Prince in Heliopolis. Set on that occasion was the accuser and calumniator of Osiris, and he brought charge after charge against the god with malicious pertinacity, until at length Thoth silenced him and made clear the innocence of Osiris. There is no proof that Anubis followed his father's example when he was present at the weighing of the heart of a deceased person, but the care which he displayed in scrutinizing the position of the pointer of the Balance, and his obvious anxiety lest the heart should gain any advantage to which it was not legally entitled, make it quite clear that the deceased could expect no favour from him.

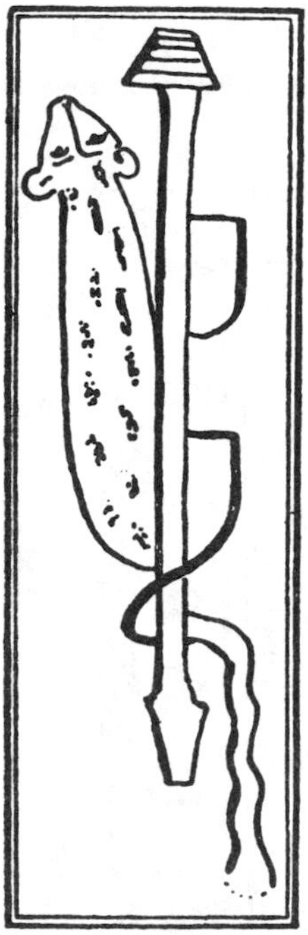

Skin of an animal sacred to Osiris.
From the Greenfeld Papyrus.

Close by the Balance, however, stood the ibis-headed god Thoth, holding his reed and palette, and he watched the weighing of the heart of the servant of Osiris as carefully as he watched the trial of Osiris himself. Near the Balance also sat or crouched the monster Ām-mit, , or  the awful "Eater of the Dead," a beast which had the head of a crocodile, the body of a lion, and the hind-quarters of a hippopotamus. This creature was believed to eat the hearts which were light in the Balance and were condemned in the judgment, or damned. In the Papyrus of Thena it is Horus, and not Anubis, who conducts the weighing of the heart, and Anubis presents the heart of the deceased to the two apes of Thoth which sit before

Osiris. In the Papyrus of Sutimes Anubis does not appear at the weighing of the heart, which takes place in the presence of the Maāti goddesses, whilst Thoth, in

the form of an ape, sits by the pillar of the balance. In the Papyrus of Neb-qeṭ the Balance stands immediately in front of Osiris, and neither Thoth nor Anubis appears. The monster Ām-mit is seen crouching by the side of a lake of boiling water or fire, at each corner of which is perched an ape. These are the four apes which are seen sitting, each with his Balance before him, on the cornice of the Great Hall of Osiris. To the prayer which the deceased made to them reference will be made later.

In the Papyrus of Māḥ[1] the weighing takes place in the presence of Rā, and Thoth appears in the form of an ape, and Anubis in the form of a being with an animal's head, who drags the deceased to the Balance and holds a knife in his hand. This being was, I believe, connected in some way in the artist's mind with the monster who appears in the vignette to Chapter XXVIII of the Book of the Dead in the Papyrus of Nefer-uben-f He has an animal's head with

a low forehead, a sort of short mane, a shaggy body, and a long tail which he grasps at the root with his left hand. In his right hand he holds a knife, with which he threatens

[1] See the vignettes printed by Naville, *Todtenbuch*, Band I, Bl. 136.

to cut out the heart of the deceased who kneels before him. The general appearance of this monster suggests that the artist who painted the figure must have heard a description of the great gorilla[1] of the African forest region, which had been brought down to Egypt from the Sûdân. It is true that the gorilla has no tail, and that he carries no knife, but in all other respects the monster painted on the papyrus closely resembles the drawing of the gorilla given by Du Chaillu on the plate facing p. 71 of his *Adventures in Equatorial Africa.* Some modern African tribes believe that gorillas of a certain kind, which are known to the initiated by peculiar signs, are the dwellings of spirits of departed negroes. Such gorillas, it is thought, can never be caught or killed, and they are said to possess more shrewdness than the common animal. Such "possessed beasts" unite the intelligence of man with the strength and ferocity of the beast. Du Chaillu repeats a native story to the effect that a party of gorillas were once found in a cane field tying up sugar-cane in regular bundles preparatory to carrying it away. "The "natives attacked them, but were routed, and several of "them were killed, while others were carried off "prisoners by the gorillas; but in a few days they "returned home uninjured, with this horrid exception: "the nails of their fingers and toes had been torn off by "their captors." Several of Du Chaillu's men mentioned the names of dead friends whose spirits were known to be dwelling in gorillas. No wonder the poor African dreads so terrible a being as his imagination thus conjures up.[2] The ancient Egyptian may have had similar ideas about the monster who ate hearts, and whom the artist painted on the papyrus, and if he had,

[1] On the Pongo (Mpungu) or gorilla, and the Engeco (Nsiku) or chimpanzi, see Pechuel-Loesche, *Loango Expedition*, Vol. III, p. 248. For Andrew Battell's description of the Pongo see his *Strange Adventures* (Hakluyt Society, 1901), p. 54. Battell lived in the second half of the sixteenth century. His reports were disbelieved by Burton and Du Chaillu.

[2] *Adventures in Equatorial Africa*, pp. 60, 61. Portions of the brain of the gorilla are used as fetishes, which are thought to give a man success in hunting and with women. On the other hand, pregnant women carefully avoid the sight of a gorilla, for they think that if when pregnant they see a gorilla they will have gorilla children.—*Ibid.*, pp. 260, 262.

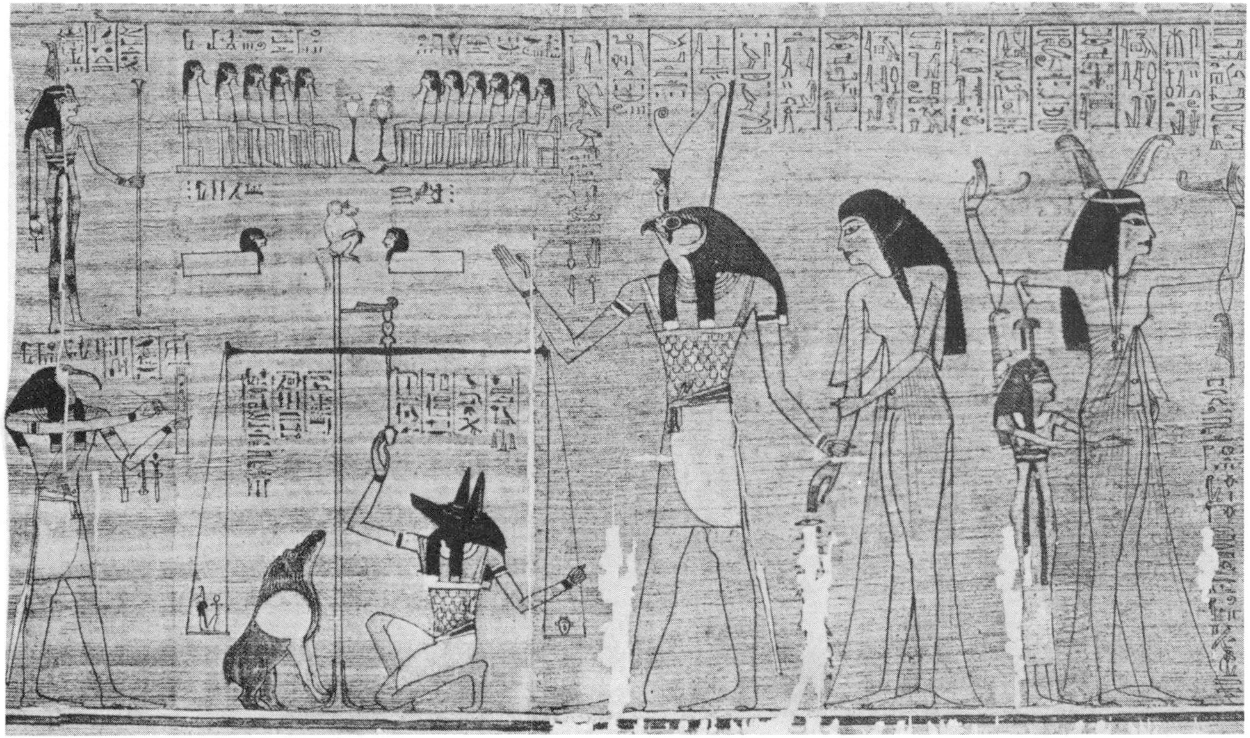

The Weighing of the Heart of the priestess Anhai in the presence of the Great and Little Companies of the Gods.

From the Papyrus of Ȧnhai, in the British Museum. (*No.* 10,472)

the creature's appearance in the Book of the Dead would be accounted for.[1]

Returning now to the Judgment Scene in the Papyrus of Ani, we see that the heart of the deceased is set in one pan of the Balance, and that Ani himself, accompanied by his wife, is looking on. His soul also, in the form of a man-headed bird, , stands upon a funerary building, and close by is a black rectangular object, with a human head, resting upon another funerary building. What this object is cannot be said exactly, but it may represent the box in which the umbilical cord of the deceased was placed when it was cut from him. It will be remembered that in the story of the birth of the kings as told in the Westcar Papyrus, the umbilical cord of each was cut off and placed in a stone box for preservation. (In the Papyrus of Ȧnhai two objects of this kind are represented, the one being called Shai and the other Renen; neither rests on a funerary building.) Close by the pillar of the Balance stands a male deity, wearing a tunic and a tail, who is called Shai ,

[1] For a scientific discussion of the gorilla see the Hon. Walter Rothschild's "Notes on Anthropoid Apes" in the *Proceedings of the Zoological Society* for 1904. For the extent of the gorilla country see Johnston, *George Grenfell on the Congo*, Vol. I, pp. 343–345. The Soko or chimpanzi is carefully described by Livingstone, who says that he is a "bandy-legged, pot-bellied villain, without a particle of the "gentleman in him . . . . . the soko, if large, would do well to "stand for a picture of the Devil. He takes away my appetite by his "disgusting bestiality of appearance. His light-yellow face shows off "his ugly whiskers and faint apology for a beard; the forehead, "villainously low, with high ears, is well in the background of the great "dog-mouth; the teeth are slightly human, but the canines show the "beast by their large development. The hands, or rather the fingers, "are like those of the natives. The flesh of the feet is yellow. . . . "The soko is so cunning, and has such sharp eyes, that no one can "stalk him in front without being seen, hence when shot it is always in "the back; when surrounded by men and nets, he is generally speared "in the back too, otherwise he is not a very formidable beast. . . . "Some Manyema think that their buried dead rise as sokos, and one "was killed with holes in his ears, as if he had been a man. He is "very strong, and fears guns, but not spears: he never catches women." —*Last Journals*, Vol. II, p. 52 ff.

and represents, perhaps, Ani's Luck or Destiny. A little behind him stand the two goddesses Renenit and Meskhenit; one of these presided over the chamber wherein Ani was born, and the other over his nursing and rearing. The Papyrus of Ani is the only Codex of the Book of the Dead which gives these three deities in the Judgment Scene, but what their exact functions were cannot be said. As they are ranged near Ani and his soul we may assume that they were believed to be friendly towards him, and that they appear at the weighing of his heart in order to speak in his favour, or to do something on his behalf. It is usual to regard Shai as Destiny, or Fate, or Luck, but it is difficult to see what part this abstract conception could play during the weighing of the heart. It seems to me that Shai, who is represented in the form of a god, is far more likely to be Ani's guardian spirit, perhaps even the spirit of his father, whose mere presence testifies to the gods that Ani is supported by the counsellor and protector of his family in spirit-land.[1] The fact that he is there shows that Ani has done nothing during his life to forfeit the good will and protection of his guardian spirit, and that he has done everything which it directed him to do, and that whilst living on earth he led a life which gained the approval of his father's spirit and of good spirits in general. Moreover, in a similar manner, the goddesses Meskhenit and Renenit testify by their presence that Ani has done nothing on earth to forfeit their good will and protection. Meskhenit was present at his birth, and allowed his soul to enter his body, and she now appears to give her help to deliver his soul from condemnation by Anubis, for it is pure in her sight. Renenit as the Nurse-goddess may or may not represent Ani's mother who suckled him, but she stands as his friend in spirit-land.

The speech which is put into the mouth of the deceased when in the Hall of Osiris during the weighing of his heart is the same in all the large illustrated copies of the Theban Recension of the Book of the Dead, and forms the section of that work which is commonly known

[1] See Major A. G. Leonard, *The Lower Niger and Its Tribes*, p. 190.

as Chapter XXXB. It is an address by the deceased to his heart, which he calls his "mother" and the seat of his being. He prays that nothing or no one may oppose him in judgment, and that there may be no opposition to him when he is in the presence of the Tchatcha, and that his heart may not be parted from him. The Tchatcha were the divine beings who assisted Thoth in keeping the registers of Osiris; they were, according to the Book of Gates, eight in number, and they kept a record of all men's lives, and worked in connection with the celestial timekeepers in the kingdom of Osiris. The deceased next addresses his heart, calling it his KA, *i.e.*, his double; he likens it to Khnemu, the Potter-god who fashioned man on his wheel. Thus the heart was regarded as the mother and the father of a man. The deceased then prays for his heart's happiness, that the Shenit, *i.e.*, the officials of the Court of Osiris, may not make his name to stink, that the weighing of his heart may result in a verdict of not guilty, and that no falsehood may be uttered against him. This prayer is very old, and is said in the Rubric to Chapter XXXB to date from the reign of Men-kau-Rā (Mycerinus). In the earliest times it was recited over a green stone scarab set in a silver-gold frame with a silver band over the back, but under the New Empire it was cut on the scarab itself. The scarab was placed inside the breast of the deceased, and it was believed to "open his mouth" for him, *i.e.*, give him back the power to eat, speak, think, remember, feel, and walk, which he had enjoyed upon earth. The prayer was used under the Middle Empire,[1] it was written on papyri of the Ptolemaïc and Roman Periods, and it was said by every follower of Osiris when in the Hall of Judgment for at least two thousand five hundred years. Few prayers in the world's history have had so long a life.

This prayer having been said by Ani, the god Anubis examined the pointer of the Balance, and finding that the beam was horizontal, and that the heart

[1] One of the oldest copies of the text is found in the transcript of the texts on the sarcophagus of Khnem-nefer, a wife of one of the Menthu-ḥetep kings (XIth dynasty); this transcript was made by Sir Gardner Wilkinson, and is now in the British Museum (No. 10,553).

of Ani exactly counterbalanced the feather of Maāt, he was unable to show reason why Ani should not be proclaimed innocent. Thereupon the god Thoth, the just judge, declared to the gods in the Hall of Osiris that the heart of Ani had been well and truly weighed, that his soul also had borne testimony concerning it, and that the Balance had proved that it was *Maāt*, or right and true. The weighing had discovered no wickedness in Ani. Thoth went on to say that Ani had not abused his position as treasurer of the sacred property of the gods, either by careless administration or robbery, and that he had neither done evil nor uttered evil while he lived upon earth. Thus Thoth was satisfied that in all his dealings with men, both as an official and as a private citizen, Ani was blameless. The gods then replied to Thoth, saying that they accepted his report concerning Ani and ratified it, and they declared that, so far as they were concerned, he had neither sinned against them, nor treated them lightly. Therefore they decree that the monster Ām-mit shall not have the mastery over him, that offerings of meat and drink shall be provided for him before Osiris, that he shall have an estate allotted to him in the Field of Peace (or, the Field of Offerings) for ever, and that he shall rank there with the gods of olden days who were called the "Followers of Horus." Thus Thoth and the Company of the Gods are satisfied as to the innocence of Ani, and it now remains for him to be presented to Osiris, so that the great god may receive him and admit him into his kingdom. The presentation is performed by Horus the son of Isis, who takes Ani by the hand, and leads him into the presence, saying, at the same time: "I come to thee, "Un-Nefer, I bring to thee the Osiris Ani. His "heart is righteous, it hath come forth from the "Balance. It hath not sinned against any god or any "goddess. Thoth weighed it in accordance with the "decree spoken to him by the Company of the Gods. "Great Truth hath testified [for him]. Let cakes and "beer be given to him [of] what appears before Osiris. "Let him be like the Followers of Horus for ever." In this speech Horus calls Ani Osiris, meaning that

Ani is as innocent as Osiris was; therefore he calls him Osiris. He then goes on to say that Ani has been through the ordeal which the gods decreed for every person who wished to enter into the kingdom of Osiris, and that he has come forth from it triumphant. Finally, he asks Osiris to let Ani live on the offerings which are made to him, and to let him take his place among the Followers of Horus. Thus Ani is innocent before the gods and goddesses; without this qualification of innocence he could not dwell with Osiris.

Ani then passed before Horus to the shrine of Osiris, and, kneeling by his table of offerings, which is the spirit-form of the offerings made by him to Osiris upon earth, he said: "Behold me, O Lord of Åmentet, I am in thy "presence. There is no sin in my body. I have not "uttered a lie wittingly. I have not done aught with "a false heart, *i.e.*, I have never practised fraud or "deceit. Grant thou that I may be like those unto "whom thou hast shown favour who are in thy following. "Let me be an Osiris who is greatly favoured by the "Beautiful God, for I am beloved of the Lord of the "Two Lands (*i.e.*, the king), the real royal scribe "who loveth him, Ani, innocent before Osiris." What answer Osiris made to his faithful servant is unknown, but it is assumed throughout the papyrus that he ratified the judgment of Thoth and the gods, and admitted Ani to his kingdom.

It may be noted that when Ani is seen coming forwards towards the Balance he is wearing a heavy black wig, and that when we see him kneeling before Osiris there is a small semi-circular object resting upon it. In the coloured facsimile of the Judgment Scene published by the British Museum we observe that his hair is whitened as if with powder. Various explanations of the object above the wig have been given, some regarding it as an ornament which was placed on the wig on state or ceremonial occasions, and others as an emblem of some rank or honour which had been conferred on the wearer of the object. It was worn by women as well as men, and the careful way in which it is drawn proves that it was some object of importance. The true explanation is probably supplied by the modern

Africans, many of whom place lumps of fat, or butter, on the tops of their heads, so that they may melt gradually and the grease run down on their bodies. Thus the people of Usikuma let their hair grow very long, and then they arrange it carefully in rolls. They next fasten a cloth round the head so closely that it flattens the hair, and on the following day they place on the top of the head a great lump of butter. This melts in the sun and runs down over their foreheads, necks, and arms, scenting them with the most delicious rancid odour.[1] The so-called "cone" on Ani's wig is, no doubt, some animal or vegetable substance either saturated with oil, or filled with grease, which melted through the heat of his head and ran down over his hair, or wig, and penetrated to his shoulders and body. The white colour on the wig represents the shining grease which is slowly running over it. The melting of the fat on the body fills both men and women with content and enjoyment.[2]

The short texts which are found in the Judgment Scene prove beyond all doubt that under the XVIIIth or XIXth dynasty the Egyptians considered that the whole duty of man consisted in worshipping the gods faithfully, in speaking the truth, and in acting the truth. The spiritual and moral conception underlying them is lofty, and illustrates the high standard of worship and morals which Osiris demanded of his followers before they could be considered fit to dwell with him. The pictorial form of the Judgment Scene cannot fail to strike us as belonging to a primitive period, when the Egyptians believed that hearts were actually weighed in a Balance before Osiris, while the words of the texts translated above suggest a development of ethics which we are accustomed to associate with the most civilized nations in the world. Some writers tell us that the Judgment Scene is just a magical picture which was painted on papyri with the view of compelling the Company of the

[1] Decle, *Three Years in Savage Africa*, p. 376.

[2] In the early days of the modern Egyptian Army I have often seen the soldiers on Friday mornings covered from head to foot with soft soap and sitting in the shallows of the Nile at Wâdî Ḥalfah, under a blazing sun, with the greatest content. As the soap ran off them friends on shore would fetch them tins of soap and anoint them afresh.

Gods and Osiris to make the result of the actual weighing of the heart to coincide with the result suggested by the picture, but this is a mere theory, for which there is no adequate support. The Rubric which follows the Third Section of Chapter CXXV orders a representation of the Hall of Maāti and what is done therein to be made upon a tile, made of earth on which no pig or other animal has trodden, but it makes no promise that the fulfilment of this order will be followed by the acquittal of the deceased in the Hall of Osiris. The true cause of the preservation of this Scene is the innate conservatism of the Egyptian, who forgot nothing connected with his religion, and abandoned nothing. The machinery of his religion, *i.e.*, the rites and ceremonies thereof, and several of the beliefs inculcated by it, were many centuries in arrear of his spiritual development, but still he clung to them, for, having served his fathers, they might, he thought, possibly still serve him. That he was content to regard as a satisfactory representation of the Last Judgment a picture in which a jackal-headed god and an ibis-headed god weighed his heart before a god who wore ostrich feathers in his crown, who held amulets in his hands, and who had his body painted in staring colours, or tattûed, or cicatrized, while a monster, part crocodile, part lion, and part hippopotamus, waited to eat up the heart, shows the lengths to which he allowed his conservatism to lead him.

The weighing of the heart, though a most important matter for the deceased, was not the only examination of his claim to be allowed to enter the kingdom of Osiris, which was made in the Hall of Maāti, and the declaration of his innocence of sin before Osiris was not the only one which he had to make. On this point the CXXVth Chapter of the Book of the Dead supplies much information, and the CXXVIth Chapter contains the prayer which the deceased made to the Four Apes who sat by the Lake of Fire near the throne of Osiris. When the deceased entered the Hall of Maāti he said:—
"Homage to thee, O great god, thou Lord of Truth. I "have come to thee, my Lord, and I have brought myself "hither that I may see thy beauties," *i.e.*, experience

thy gracious clemency. "I know thee, I know thy "name. I know the names of the Two-and-Forty gods "who live with thee in this Hall of Maāti, who keep "ward over those who have done evil, who feed upon "their blood on the day when the lives of men are "reckoned up in the presence of Un-Nefer (*i.e.*, Osiris). "In truth I have come to thee. I have brought Truth "to thee. I have destroyed wickedness for thee." These words are followed by a statement of the offences which he had not committed, the so-called "Negative Confession," and he says:—

1. I have not sinned against men.
2. I have not oppressed (or wronged) [my] kinsfolk.
3. I have not committed evil in the place of truth.
4. I have not known worthless men.
5. I have not committed acts of abomination.
6. I have not done daily works of supererogation (?).
7. I have not caused my name to appear for honours.
8. I have not domineered over slaves.
9. I have not thought scorn of the god (or, God).
10. I have not defrauded the poor man of his goods.
11. I have not done the things which the gods abominate.
12. I have not caused harm to be done to the slave by his master.
13. I have caused no man to suffer.
14. I have allowed no man to go hungry.
15. I have made no man weep.
16. I have slain no man.
17. I have not given the order for any man to be slain.
18. I have not caused pain to the multitude.
19. I have not filched the offerings in the temples.
20. I have not purloined the cakes of the gods.
21. I have not stolen the offerings of the spirits.
22. I have had no dealing with the paederast.
23. I have not defiled myself in the pure places of the god of my city.
24. I have not cheated in measuring of grain.
25. I have not filched land[1] or added thereto.
26. I have not encroached upon the fields of others.
27. I have not added to the weight of the balance.

[1] Literally, the land measure *stat*.

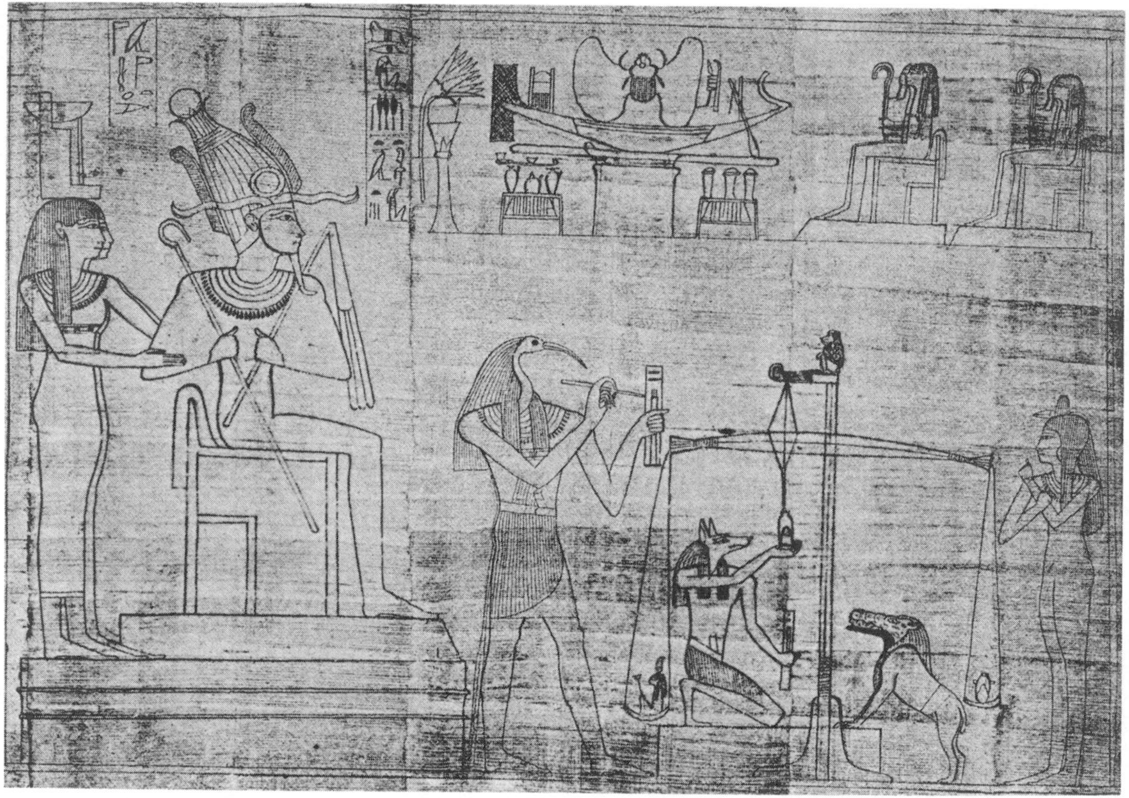

THE WEIGHING OF THE HEART OF PRINCESS NESI-TA-NEB-ASHER IN THE JUDGMENT HALL OF OSIRIS IN THE PRESENCE OF RĀ AND THE COMPANY OF THE GODS.

From the Greenfield Papyrus, in the British Museum (No. 10,554).

28. I have not cheated with the pointer of the scales.
29. I have not taken away the milk from the mouths of the babes.
30. I have not driven away the beasts from their pastures.
31. I have not netted the geese of the preserves of the gods.
32. I have not caught fish with bait of their bodies.
33. I have not obstructed water when it should run.
34. I have not cut a cutting in a canal of running water.
35. I have not extinguished a flame when it ought to burn.
36. I have not abrogated the days of offering the chosen offerings.
37. I have not turned off cattle from the property of the gods.
38. I have not repulsed the god in his manifestations. I am pure. I am pure. I am pure. I am pure.

The above series of statements was made by the deceased when he entered the Hall of Osiris, *i.e.*, before his heart had braved the ordeal of being weighed in the Balance, and it is interesting to note that among the Calabar tribes before a man undergoes the ordeal of drinking the great juju drink Mbiam, which is made of filth and blood,[1] he says :—

"If I have been guilty of this crime,
"If I have gone and sought the sick one's hurt,
"If I have sent another to seek the sick one's hurt,
"If I have employed any one to make charms, or to cook bush,
"Or to put anything in the road,
"Or to touch his cloth,
"Or to touch his yams,
"Or to touch his goats,
"Or to touch his fowl,
"Or to touch his children,
"If I have prayed for his hurt,
"If I have thought to hurt him in my heart,

[1] The Masai also drink blood at a trial by ordeal.—Hollis, *Masai*, p. 343.

"If I have any intention to hurt him,
"If I ever, at any time, do any of these things (recite in full),
"Or employ others to do these things (recite in full),
"Then, Mbiam! *thou* deal with me."[1]

The Egyptian acted exactly as does the modern African. The former made his declaration of innocence of a series of offences, and his heart was weighed by the gods to test the truth of his words; the latter makes his declaration of innocence, and the action of the juju drink tests the truth of his words.

We pass now to the second form of the "Negative Confession," in which the deceased addressed a series of Two and Forty gods by their names, one after the other, and asserted before each, that he had not committed a certain sin. These gods were the gods of the forty-two nomes of Upper and Lower Egypt. He had already told Osiris that he knew their names, and proceeded to prove it by saying the following:—

1. Hail, Usekh-nemmet, coming forth from Ȧnu (Heliopolis), I have not done iniquity.

2. Hail, Ḥept-shet, coming forth from Kher-āḥa,[2] I have not committed robbery.

3. Hail, Fenṭi, coming forth from Khemenu (Hermopolis), I have not stolen with violence.

4. Hail, Ām-khaibitu, coming forth from Qerrt,[3] I have not committed theft.

5. Hail, Neḥa-ḥāu, coming forth from Re-stau,[4] I have not killed men.

6. Hail, Lion and Lioness god, coming forth from heaven, I have not made light the bushel of corn.

7. Hail, Merti-f-em-ṭes, coming forth from Sekhem (Letopolis), I have not acted deceitfully.

8. Hail, Nebȧ, coming forth from Khetkhet (?), I have not robbed the property of the god.

[1] Kingsley, *Travels in West Africa*, p. 465; compare also, J. L. Wilson, *Western Africa*, p. 225.

[2] A large city which lay between Fusṭâṭ and Maṭarîyah.

[3] "The Circle," perhaps a place in the Other World.

[4] A region in the Other World of Memphis.

9. Hail, Seṭ-qesu, coming forth from Suten-ḥenen (Herakleopolis), I have not uttered falsehood.

10. Hail, Uatch-Nesert, coming forth from Ḥet-ka-Ptaḥ (Memphis), I have not stolen food.

11. Hail, Qerti, coming forth from Åment, I have not cursed.

12. Hail, Ḥetch-åbeḥu, coming forth from Ta-she (Fayyûm), I have not attacked any man.

13. Hail, Åm-senf, coming forth from the slaughter-house, I have not slain the cattle of the god.

14. Hail, Åm-besek, coming forth from Mābit, I have not used deceit (?).

15. Hail, Neb-Maāt, coming forth from Maāti, I have not stolen grain (?).

16. Hail, Thenemi, coming forth from Bast (Bubastis), I have not acted the part of the spy (or eavesdropper).

17. Hail, Āaṭi (or Ānṭi), coming forth from Ånu, I have not slandered.

18. Hail, Ṭuṭu-f, coming forth from Ati (?), I have not been angry without cause.

19. Hail, Uamemti, coming forth from the House of the Block, I have not lain with another man's wife.

20. Hail, Maa-ånuf, coming forth from Per-Menu, I have not abused myself.

21. Hail, Ḥeri-seru, coming forth from Nehatu, I have made no man to be afraid.

22. Hail, Khemi, coming forth from Aḥaui, I have attacked no man.

23. Hail, Sheṭ-kheru, coming forth from Urit, I have not been a man of wrath.

24. Hail, Nekhen, coming forth from Ḥeq-āt, I have not been deaf to the words of truth.

25. Hail, Ser-Kheru, coming forth from Unes, I have not stirred up strife.

26. Hail, Basti, coming forth from Shetait, I have made no one to weep.

27. Hail, Ḥer-f-ḥa-f,[1] coming forth from the place of sailing, I have neither acted impurely, nor lain with men.

[1] He was the ferryman of the Other World, but would only ferry over the souls that were righteous. He loved truth and hated sin, and because of his integrity became a leader of the gods.

28. Hail, Ta-reṭ, coming out of the night, I have not eaten my heart.

29. Hail, Kenemti, coming forth from Kenmet, I have not cursed any man.

30. Hail, Ȧn-ḥetep-f, coming forth from Sau, I have not done deeds of violence.

31. Hail, Neb-ḥeru, coming forth from Tchefet, I have not acted hastily.

32. Hail, Serekhi, coming forth from Unth, I have not . . . my skin, I have not . . . the god.

33. Hail, Neb-ābui, coming forth from Sauti, I have not made loud my voice in speaking.

34. Hail, Nefer-Tem, coming forth from Ḥet-ka-Ptaḥ (Memphis), I have not acted deceitfully, I have not acted wickedly.

35. Hail, Tem-sep, coming forth from Ṭeṭu, I have not cursed the king.

36. Hail, Ȧri-em-ȧb-f, coming forth from Tebti, I have not fouled water.

37. Hail, Ȧḥi . . ., coming forth from Nu, I have not made my voice loud.

38. Hail, Utu-rekhit, coming forth from thy house (?), I have not cursed the god.

39. Hail, Neḥeb-nefert, coming forth from . . ., I have not acted insolently.

40. Hail, Neḥeb-kau, coming forth from [thy] city, I have not worked for honours (?).

41. Hail, Tcheser-tep, coming forth from the cavern, I have not increased my possessions except through my own goods.

42. Hail, Ȧn-ā-f, coming forth from Ȧuḳer, I have not treated with contempt the god of my city.

The above form of the Negative Confession is very interesting, for it supplies us with the names of several spirits or gods who were worshipped in very early times, probably long before the cult of Osiris became general in Egypt. Among these were Ḥer-f-ḥa-f, the Egyptian Charon (see p. 341), and Tcheser-tep, both of whom are mentioned in early religious texts. Taken together these Forty-two gods represented at one period the spiritual masters of all Egypt, and he who succeeded in satisfying them of his innocence in the Hall of Judgment might well be proclaimed "just" or "true" before the whole country. It is not always clear why a certain sin is connected with a certain member of this company of Forty-two gods, but the traditional association of each god with a particular sin is very ancient, and if we knew all the facts we should probably realize that there was good reason for the association. We may wonder why the Egyptians continued to perpetuate these names after Osiris became the king and god of the dead, but here again we have a further instance of the religious conservatism of the Egyptians, who felt that any disregard of such an old and important text might be fraught with danger to their salvation. For us the second form of the Negative Confession, which is probably the older, is of special interest, for it shows that the idea of the Judgment is very old, and that the importance of a life of truth-doing and truth-speaking was recognized by the Egyptians, even while they believed in such a plurality of spirits or gods. The adoption of these into the Judgment system of Osiris was clearly the work of the priests of that god, who established his cult upon beliefs and traditions which were already old when they began their work.

The deceased then addressed the Forty-two gods in the following words: Homage to you, O gods who dwell in your Hall of Maāti. I indeed know you, I know your names. Let me not fall under your knives of slaughter, and bring ye not my wickedness before the god whom ye serve. Ye have no charge against me. Speak ye truth on my behalf before Neb-er-tcher, for I have worked righteousness in Ta-merȧ (Egypt), I have not cursed the god, and the king who reigned in his day had no charge [to bring] against me.

Homage to you, O gods, who dwell in your Hall of Maāti, who have no falseness in your bodies, who live on truth, who feed on truth, before Horus, who dwelleth in his Disk. Deliver ye me from the god Baba, who liveth upon the entrails of the mighty ones on the day of the Great Reckoning. Behold ye me! I have come before you. Without sin am I, without evil am I, without wickedness am I, without a witness (?)

am I. I have not done things against him. I live upon truth. I feed upon truth. I have performed the behests of men, and the things whereby the gods are gratified. I have propitiated the god with the things which he loveth. I have given bread to the hungry man, and water to the thirsty man, and apparel to the naked man, and a boat to him that was without one. I

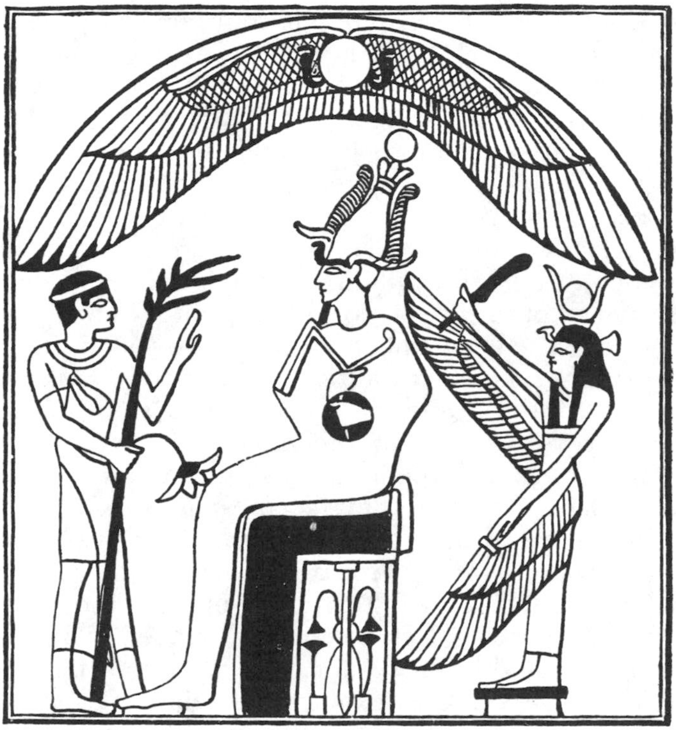

Osiris in the Meroïtic Period, A.D. 100–300.
From a bas-relief in a pyramid chapel at Meroë.

have made holy offerings to the gods, and sepulchral offerings to the Spirits. Be ye then my deliverers and protectors, and make ye no accusation against me before the Great God. I am clean of mouth and clean of hands. Therefore, let it be said unto me by those who shall behold me, "Come in peace! Come in peace!"

The deceased went on to enumerate before the Forty-two gods the various religious ceremonies at which he had assisted, and the festivals which he had attended.

THE JUDGMENT SCENE IN THE HALL (

From the Pyram

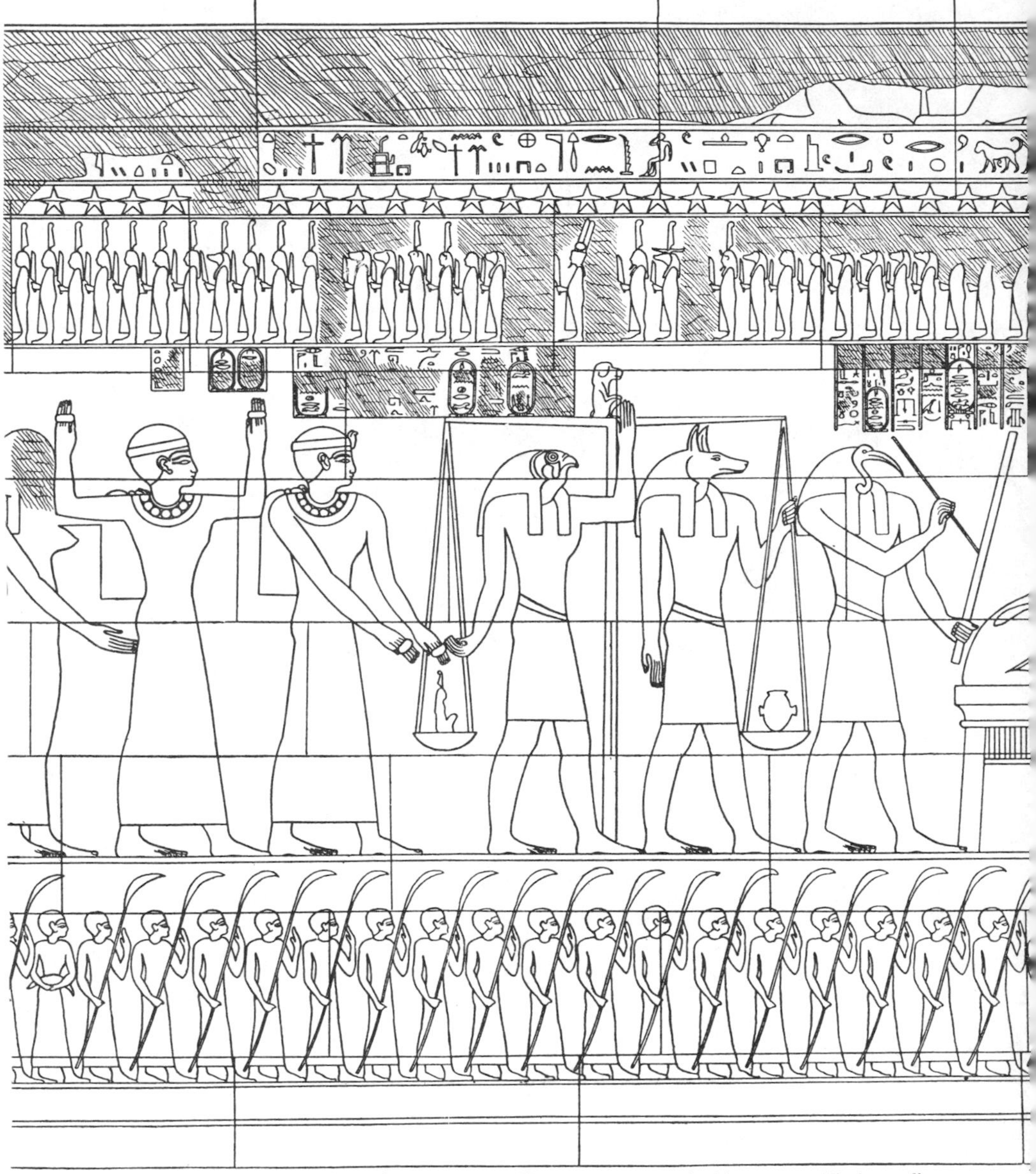

fe of the
:ceased.

The son of the deceased rejoicing at the result of the weighing of the heart.

The deceased king.

Horus.

Anubis.

Thoth recording the result of the weighing of the heart.

In the upper register are the Forty-two Assessors of the dead, and in the lower are servants bearing palm branches.

ɜIRIS IN THE MEROITIC PERIOD (A.D. 100—300).

Arkenkherel at Meroë.

ıe Eater of the dead,
ımed with two knives.

Table of
offerings.

Osiris Khenti Amenti,
Lord of Abydos, Lord of
Busiris, seated watching
the weighing of the
king's heart.

King Arkenkherel.

He had heard the "great word" which the Ass spoke to the Cat in the Temple of Ḥapṭ-re. He had given evidence before Ḥer-f-ḥa-f, the divine Ferryman who would allow no sinner to enter his boat. As this important god had regarded him as innocent of offence, and had spoken words of approval to him, the Forty-two gods, and even Osiris himself, must believe his declarations and receive the verdict of this just and stern god. The deceased had seen the Erica Tree of Re-stau, which covered the remains of Osiris; and he had borne true witness, and had helped to set up the Balance on its stand in Åuḳert. The deceased next addressed Osiris by his name of "Lord of Air," and proclaimed his righteous dealing to the god. "I am pure," he says, "back and front outside am I pure, and I am pure inside "also. There is no member of mine which lacketh "truth." He purified himself in the South, and he bathed in the North, and then he passed on to the olive tree where he saw the mystic leg and thigh. He received a flame of fire and a crystal sceptre; the former he extinguished, and the latter he broke and created a pool of water. These allusions are inexplicable at present, but the deceased clearly means that, before he came to the Hall of Maāti, he performed most solemn ceremonies in connection with the worship of Osiris. The bolts of the door, the door posts, the door step, the fastening of the door and its socket, the lintels, right and left, and the Porter, all asked the deceased to declare their mystic names, and when he had done so, they permitted him to pass through the doorway. Then the floor of the Hall of Maāti refused to be trodden by the feet of the deceased until he had declared to it the mystic names of his two feet; when he had done this he was permitted to stand on the floor. He was not, however, allowed to advance until he had repeated the mystic name of the Guardian of the Hall, who at once asked him the name of the "God in his hour." The deceased repeated his name, *i.e.*, "Māau-taui," and in answer to a further question said that this god was Thoth. Therefore the Guardian introduced him to Thoth, who asked him why he had come thither. He replied: "I have "come and I press forward so that [my name] may be "mentioned, for I am pure." Then Thoth promised to make mention of his name to the god Osiris, but before he did so he asked the deceased the question: "Who is "he whose heaven is of fire, whose walls are living "uraei, and the floor of whose house is a stream of "water?" The deceased replied: "Osiris." We may presume that his introduction to the god then took place, for Thoth said: "Advance, thou shalt be mentioned to him." The text ends with a promise that the bread and beer of the deceased shall be supplied from the Eye of Rā, and thus the continuance of his life and felicity was assured for ever.

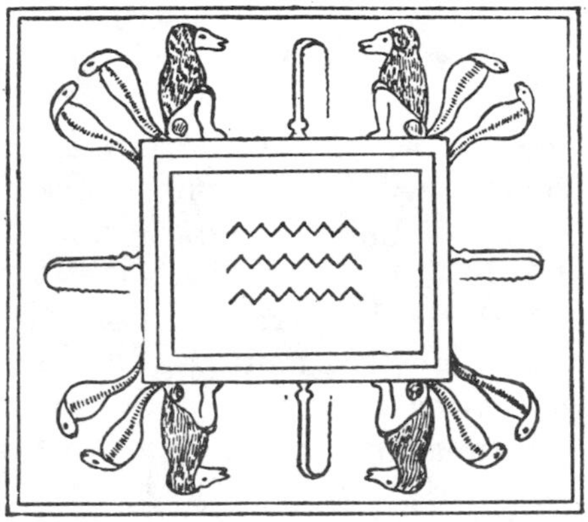

Closely connected with the Judgment Scene is the CXXVIth Chapter of the Book of the Dead, which contains the prayer of the deceased to the Four Apes who sit by the Lake of Fire near the throne of Osiris, and their answer. He says: "Hail, ye Four Apes, who "sit in the bows of the Boat of Rā, who convey truth to "Neb-er-tcher, who sit in judgment on my weakness "and my strength, who propitiate the gods by the flame "of your mouths, who make offerings to the gods, and "sepulchral meals to the Spirits, who feed upon truth, "who are without deceit and fraud, to whom wickedness "is an abomination, do away my evil deeds, put away my "sin, which merited stripes upon earth, destroy whatsoever evil is in me, and let there be nothing in me "which shall separate me from you. Let me pass "through the Ammehet, let me enter Re-stau, let me "pass through the pylons of Amentet, give me of the "bread, and beer, and dainty food which are given to "the living Spirits, and let me enter in and come forth "from Re-stau." The Four Apes say: "Advance, for "we have done away thy wickedness, and we have put "away thy sin, and thy sin committed upon earth, "which merited stripes, and we have destroyed all the "evil which appertained to thee upon earth. Enter, "therefore, into Re-stau, and pass through the secret "gates of Åmentet, and bread, and beer, and dainty "food shall be given unto thee, and thou shalt go in and "come forth at thy desire, even as do the Spirits who "are favoured of the god, and thou shalt be proclaimed "each day in the horizon." Thus the deceased, having satisfied the Forty-two gods and the Four Apes, and the Company of gods and goddesses who sat in the Hall of Maāt, and Thoth, the Recorder of the Two Lands, *i.e.*, all Egypt, is received by Osiris and is permitted to live in his kingdom henceforward.

The facts set forth above prove clearly that the ethical conceptions of the Egyptians under the XVIIIth dynasty were not those of a half-savage, barbarous African people, even though the phrases which they used to express them, and the pictures which they employed to represent them, are primitive. Enough has been said to show that these conceptions existed under the XIIth dynasty, and that the character of Osiris as the god of truth, and as a righteous and just judge, was well established at the period when the Pyramid Texts were written, under the Vth and VIth dynasties. The oldest remains of Egypt yield evidence of the great antiquity of the cult of Osiris, but there is no evidence to show when it began. It is, however, certain that the belief that Osiris was the impartial judge of men's deeds and words, who rewarded the righteous, and punished the wicked, and ruled over a heaven which contained only sinless beings, and that he possessed the power to do these things because he had lived on earth, and suffered death, and risen from the dead, is as old as dynastic civilization in Egypt, and that it grew and developed, and spread with ever-increasing power until it became the dominating religious influence throughout the country. Osiris was the symbol of the African conception of resurrection and immortality, and from first to last his worship was characterized by customs, and rites, and ceremonies which were purely African. How persistent and lasting these are is obvious to all who take the pains to study them in connection with the works of modern African travellers.

CHAPTER XI.

The African Belief in God and the Doctrine of Last Things.

Notwithstanding the comparatively large amount of religious Egyptian literature which has come down to us, our knowledge of what the Egyptians really thought about God is extremely small. So far as we know they wrote no treatises about Him, or if they did none has reached our hands, and what they imagined Him to be, or where they thought He dwelt, we can only deduce from the rare allusions to Him which we find in their moral and funerary works. Some years ago I stated[1] that the religious texts of Egypt, if studied, would convince the reader that the Egyptians believed in One God, who was self-existent, immortal, invisible, eternal, omniscient, almighty, and inscrutable; the maker of heaven, earth, and the Other World; the creator of men and women, animals, birds, and creeping things, trees and plants, and the incorporeal beings who were the messengers that fulfilled his wish and word. This statement was held up to ridicule by a reviewer, who regarded it as a serious misrepresentation of the Egyptian belief about God, and as a proof of the writer's incapacity to deal with the subject of the religion of Egypt. Since the time when that statement was written (1898) many valuable religious texts have been discovered and published with translations, in various languages, and the result of a study of these has further convinced me that the statement quoted above is true, and may be repeated here.

In spite of the numerous "gods" of Egypt with whom the texts make us acquainted, and the mixture of magic, black and white, in the Egyptian Religion, and the savage, crude ideas, which are the relics of a barbarous and half-savage period in Egyptian history, two fundamental, indigenous beliefs stand out in it clearly, namely, the

[1] *Egyptian Ideas of the Future Life*, p. 1.

belief in God, the Creator of the world and all in it, and the belief in a resurrection and in immortality. The student who views the Egyptian Religion from the lofty standpoint of spiritual Christianity only may say that it was gross polytheism or pantheism, that Egyptian rites were cruel, bloodthirsty, and savage, that the legends of the gods are childish, and are the outcome of debased minds and imaginations, that the story of the resurrection of Osiris is a farrago of nonsense in which absurd magical ceremonies play an impossible part, and that the heaven of the Egyptian was only an imagination of a people who always remained half savage. Nothing, however, can alter the fact that beneath such rites, and legends, and beliefs there lay the wonderful religious and moral conceptions which have been described in the preceding chapter, and the unchanging, persistent belief in the resurrection of the righteous and in immortality. It seems to be a mistake to estimate the Egyptian Religion from the standpoint of the highly civilized Asiatic, eastern or western, or European, for it is an African product, and can only be rightly appreciated and understood when considered in connection with what we know of modern African religion. There exists, fortunately, a great mass of information about the religion of the Sûdânî peoples, and the facts collected in the works of the serious travellers, who will be quoted later, are peculiarly valuable, because the writers set down what they saw and heard without bias and without prejudice. Travellers like Livingstone, Speke, Baker, and Junker recorded facts as they saw them, and having no special theories to support or problems to illustrate, their evidence is disinterested and their conclusions are honest. The facts collected by George Grenfell, Mr. Torday, Mr. Joyce of the British Museum, Sir Harry Johnston, Dr. Andrew Balfour of Khartûm and his colleagues, and the writers of the works issued by the Musée du Congo are specially valuable for the light which they throw on the ancient as well as on the modern religion of Africa, and the explanations which they supply of many of the beliefs and rites and ceremonies of the Egyptians.

The remains of the Archaïc Period of Egypt prove

that already under the first three dynasties the Egyptians believed in many gods, Osiris, Isis, Anubis, Nephthys, Horus, Set, Hathor, Shu, Tefnut, Apis, etc. Under the IVth dynasty, at least, they were in the habit of speaking of the "Great god," Osiris, probably, being referred to. The word for God and "god" is, from first to last, *neter*, , the original meaning of which is unknown. In the *Precepts of Kaqemna* (IVth dynasty) and the *Precepts of Ptaḥ-ḥetep*[1] (Vth dynasty) we find the following passages:—

1. "The things which God doeth are unknown (Plate II, l. 2).
2. "Thou shalt not terrify men; it is contrary to God'[s wish] (IV, line 8).
3. "Bread is eaten according to the providence of God (VII, l. 2).
4. "Art thou a farmer? Cultivate the field which God hath given thee (VII, l. 5).
5. "If thou wouldst be perfect, make thy son pleasing to God (VII, l. 11).
6. "Satisfy thy dependants; it is the duty of those favoured by God (XI, l. 1).
7. "Obedience God loveth; disobedience God hateth (XVI, l. 7).
8. "Behold, a well-doing son is the gift of God (XIX, l. 6)."

All the above extracts were written before 3000 B.C. The Being whose ways are inscrutable, who rules the world on a definite plan (*sekher* ), who confers possessions on man, who demands obedience from man, and expects him to bring up his children in the fear of him, and to deal kindly with his neighbours and dependants, can surely be no other than God. If the writers of the Precepts referred in their minds to any

[1] For the text see Prisse d'Avennes, *Fac-similé d'un Papyrus Égyptien*, Paris, 1847; Virey, *Études sur le Papyrus Prisse*, Paris, 1887; and for another version of the hieratic text see Maspero, *Recueil*, tom. XXXI, pp. 146; and Budge, *Egyptian Hieratic Papyri in the British Museum*, London, 1910, p. 17 ff.

of the "gods" of Egypt they would have added their names. The Being referred to cannot be Osiris, for in no text are such attributes ascribed to him. We must, it seems to me, conclude that only God, the Creator of All, could be spoken of in this manner.

From the so-called *Maxims of Ani*,[1] we quote the following :—

1. God magnifieth His name.
2. The sanctuary of God abominateth noisy speech. Make thy supplications with a loving heart, all the words of which are hidden. He will arrange thy affairs, He will hear thy words, and will accept thine offerings.
3. God is a righteous judge.
4. When thou makest thine offering to God, beware of offering what He abominateth. Consider His plans, adore His name. He giveth souls to millions of beings, He magnifieth him that magnifieth Him.
5. Thy mother carried thee for months, she suckled thee for three years, when thou wast at school she brought thee bread and beer each day. . . . cause not her to raise her hands to God in complaint of thee, for He will hear her prayers [and punish thee].
6. Commit thou thyself to God, take heed to thyself this day for the sake of God, [and] to-morrow shall be like unto to-day [to thee].

In these passages also the Being who loves silent prayer, and is a righteous judge, and the creator of souls, who brings to honour him that honoureth Him, and is tender to the cry of the mother who is afflicted by her son's harsh treatment, and demands daily devotion from His worshippers, can be no other than God. No attempt was made in any text to describe the form and likeness of this Being, who was regarded as invisible, and no artist or sculptor ever made any representation of Him. His inscrutability, omnipresence, and omniscience are assumed in the passages quoted, and when any "god," *e.g.*, Temu or Kheperȧ, is considered as his immediate representative, such "god" is always

[1] First published with a translation by Chabas in *L'Égyptologie*, Série I, tt. 1 and 2. See also Amélineau, *La Morale Égyptienne*, Paris, 1892.

described as self-produced *kheper tchesef*, 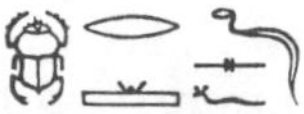, and is spoken of as if he had always existed, and always would exist, in fact, as the self-created and eternal God.

Side by side with this Being we have mentioned in all periods of Egyptian history a class of beings who were called *neteru*, 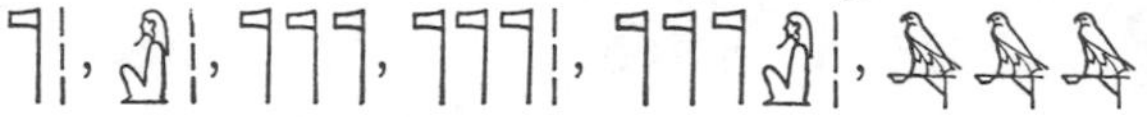, or , *i.e.*, "gods," some of whom are male and some female. These had many forms and shapes, and could appear on earth as men, women, animals, birds, reptiles, trees, plants, etc. They were stronger and more intelligent than men, but they had passions like men; they were credited with possessing some divine powers or characteristics, and yet they could suffer sickness and die. There is in no text any suggestion that God was passible, or that He could die; on the other hand, it was always taken for granted that the gods did sicken, grow old, and die. Thus the great god Rā, when bitten by the adder which Isis made, suffered violent pains in his body, and the sweat of agony rolled down his face, and he would have died if Isis had not treated him after he revealed to her his hidden name.[1] When he had become old anger seized him because of the slighting and contemptuous way in which men spoke of him; therefore he destroyed mankind.[2] The Pyramid Texts describe a hunting expedition of the deified King Unȧs in heaven, and tell us how he lassoed the "gods," and killed, and roasted and ate them.[3] King Thothmes III prays that he may not suffer corruption, and refers to the decay which the god Temu brings upon "every god and every goddess,"[4] and to the fact that they, as well as the animals and reptiles, perish when their souls have left them.[5] Most of the great "gods" had wives and offspring, and so triads came into being. Thus Mut was

[1] Pleyte and Rossi, *Papyrus de Turin*, Plates 31, 77, 131–138.
[2] Lefébure, *Tombeau de Seti I*, Part IV, Plates 15–18.
[3] Line 496 ff.
[4] .
[5] Book of the Dead, Chapter CLIV.

the wife of Åmen-Rā, and her child by him was Khensu. Sekhmet (Sekhet) was the wife of Ptaḥ, and her child by him was Nefer-Temu. The same anthropomorphic conception made Isis the wife of Osiris, and Nephthys the wife of Set, their children being Horus and Anubis.

The oldest triad was Temu, Shu, and Tefnut, the two latter gods springing directly from the body of Temu; these three "gods" were represented by the signs 𓊹𓊹𓊹, and by 𓊹𓊹𓊹 𓊹𓊹𓊹 𓊹𓊹𓊹, when their descendants were added to them. We also find , which represents *paut*, the primeval substance from which the gods were made, and *neteru* "gods"; the 𓊹𓊹𓊹 are perhaps only added as a determinative. The primeval god is called "Pauti,"[1] and it seems that this word represents a conception of deity which is older than that of *neter;* the meanings of *paut* and *neter* must be quite distinct. In the Pyramid Texts we find three "companies" or groups of gods, each of which contains at least three triads.[2] The above facts make it certain that the Egyptians distinguished clearly in their minds the difference which existed between God and the "gods," who were subservient to Him, and who were made by Him to assist in the work of administering heaven, earth, and the Other World. The Egyptian "gods" formed a sort of court or council of the God of the Egyptians, and they are the equivalents of the Archangels and the Orders of Angels which we find in other systems of religion. In some Oriental Christian systems

[1] .

[2] The Great Company 𓊹𓊹𓊹 𓊹𓊹𓊹 𓊹𓊹𓊹 , the Little Company, 𓊹𓊹𓊹 𓊹𓊹𓊹 𓊹𓊹𓊹 , and a third Company. The three Companies are the 𓊹𓊹𓊹 𓊹𓊹𓊹 𓊹𓊹𓊹 𓊹𓊹𓊹 𓊹𓊹𓊹 𓊹𓊹𓊹 𓊹𓊹𓊹 𓊹𓊹𓊹 𓊹𓊹𓊹, mentioned in the text of Tetȧ, l. 307.

the Prophets, Apostles, Martyrs, and many great Saints occupy in the celestial hierarchy positions identical with those of the "gods" in the Egyptian Religion.

Now, although the Egyptians wrote no treatise on God, or formally attempted to define His attributes, we must not assume, as some have done, that they were ignorant of conceptions of deity such as we find among other ancient civilized nations. In considering this matter, we must remember that in Egypt, as in the Sûdân to-day, each tribe, if nomad, and each community, if living in a town of any considerable size, had its own god or group of gods. The worshippers of each god or goddess regarded their town god as their all-powerful protector and friend, and little by little they ascribed to him, or to her, the attributes which modern peoples ascribe to God. This process went on all over Egypt, one proof of the fact being that the deceased had to make confession to Two-and Forty gods, one from each of the nomes of Egypt, in the Judgment Hall of Osiris, before he made his supplication to Osiris. Substantially each town was worshipping the same god, only under different names, and for all practical purposes the town god took the place of God. The form under which the town god was worshipped mattered not, for the object, whether animate or inanimate, was only regarded as the habitation in which it pleased the god to dwell, for a long or short time, as the case might be. Certain ancient gods, *e.g.*, Neith of Saïs, Bast of Bubastis, Temu, and the Mnevis Bull of Heliopolis, Apis and Ptaḥ of Memphis, Ḥeru-Shefit of Herakleopolis, Khenti-Åmenti and Ån-Ḥer of Abydos, Åmen of Thebes, Menu of Coptos, Menthu of Hermonthis, Khnemu of Elephantine, became for various reasons famous outside the towns in which their worship grew up, and they usurped the attributes of many gods of a totally different class and character, and very frequently the attributes of God Almighty were assigned to them.

Thus the theologians of Heliopolis, under the VIth dynasty, declared that the god "Father Tem" gave birth to King Pepi before heaven and earth existed, before men were made, before the gods were

The god Khnemu fashioning the body of one of the Ptolemies on his potter's wheel.

brought forth, and before death came into being.[1] The writer of this remarkable passage can hardly have intended his readers to understand him to mean that Pepi's physical body was created before the heavens and the earth were made, but there is no doubt that he meant them to believe that his existence was predestined, and his sovereignty fore-ordained by Tem. The "Father Tem," who existed in the beginning, "before ever the earth and the world were made," and who planned and fore-ordained the life of Pepi in this world, is no other than God, whom the priests of Heliopolis called "Tem." In a papyrus in the Egyptian Museum in Cairo[2] the following epithets and attributes are given to Åmen-Rā: "Sacred soul who came into being in "the beginning, great god who liveth by truth, primeval "god who gave birth to the two other primeval gods, "being in whom every god existeth, only One, creator "of things which were made in the beginning, whose "birth is secret, whose forms are manifold, whose "growth cannot be computed, who existed when "nothing else was. In the form of the Disk (*i.e.*, the "Sun) he shineth and lighteth all people. He traverseth "heaven untiringly, his vigour to-morrow will be as that "of to-day; growing old to-day he reneweth his youth "to-morrow. Having made himself he made heaven "and earth by his will (literally, heart). He was the "primeval water. He is the Disk of the Moon. Out "of his divine eyes men and women came, and out of "his mouth the gods. He is the lord of time and "traverser of eternity; of many eyes, many ears, the "lord of life, the King who maketh kings to reign, "governor of the world, the unknown, more hidden "than the gods. The Disk is his vicar. His decrees "are gracious and beneficent, and fulfil their purpose.

1 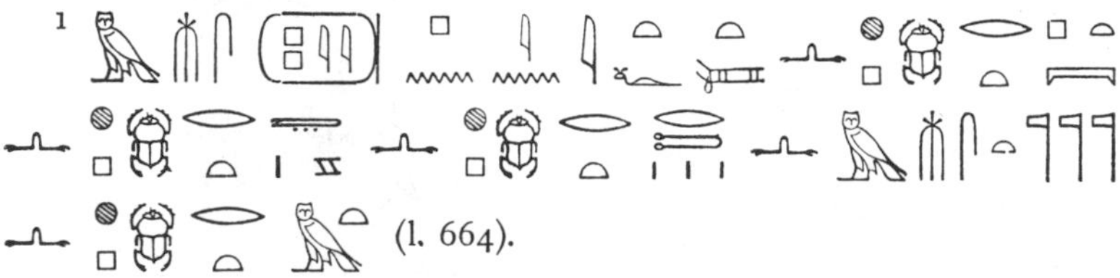 (l. 664).

2 See Maspero, *Mémoires Miss. Arch.*, tom. I, p. 594 ff.

"Giver of life and many years to his favoured ones, "protector of his chosen ones, maker of eternity and "everlastingness."

From a series of passages collected by Dr. H. Brugsch[1] may be quoted the following: "One and "Alone, without a second. One, the maker of all "things, the Spirit, the hidden spirit, the maker of "spirits. He existed in the beginning, when nothing "else was. What is he created after he came into "being. Father of beginnings, eternal, infinite, ever-"lasting. Hidden one, no man knoweth his form, or "can search out his likeness; he is hidden to gods "and men, and is a mystery to his creatures. No man "knoweth how to know him; his name is a mystery "and is hidden. His names are innumerable. He is "truth, he liveth on truth, he is the king of truth. "He is life, through him man liveth; he gave life to "man, he breathed life into his nostrils. He is father "and mother, the father of fathers, the mother of "mothers. He begetteth, but was not begotten; he "bringeth forth, but was not brought forth; he begat "himself and gave birth to himself. He created, but "was not created, he made his own form and body. "He himself is existence; he neither increaseth nor "diminisheth. He made the universe, the world, what "was, what is, and what shall be. What his heart "conceived came to pass forthwith; when he speaketh "what resulteth therefrom endureth for ever. He is "the father of the gods. He is merciful to his "worshipper, he heareth him who calleth on him, he "rewardeth his servants, those who acknowledge him "he knoweth, he protecteth his follower."

Among the epithets applied to Åmen-Rā is "Only One," or "One Alone" . This is not peculiar to hymns, etc., of the New Empire, but we find "One god" mentioned in the Pyramid Texts,[2] and "Only One" on a coffin which was made at the

[1] *Religion und Mythologie*, pp. 96–99.

[2] . Tetå, l. 247.

beginning of the Middle Empire.[1] It seems to me that the writer who called Åmen-Rā, or Rā, or any other god, "One," or "Only One," was applying the epithet which he knew to belong to God to his town god, who represented to him God Almighty.[2] The texts are full of allusions to the numerous names of God, whether He be called Temu, or Åmen, or Rā, and it is distinctly said that Temu, under the form of Rā, "created the names of his members, which took form as gods in his train."[3] Therefore the attributes which are ascribed to any god are ascribed to the "One," or "One God," or "One Alone," mentioned in the texts. The "oneness" ascribed to the self-created eternal creator of heaven and earth, and all therein, cannot, it seems to me, be explained by henotheism, for the texts show that their writers were, from many points of view, monotheists from very early times. On the other hand, the multiplicity of "gods" who are mentioned in the texts justifies the assertion made by many that the Egyptians were polytheists. Champollion le Jeune believed "the "Egyptian religion to be a pure monotheism, which "manifested itself externally by a symbolic polytheism."[4]

Professor Tiele, a very careful student of ancient religions, thought that the religion of Egypt was in the beginning polytheistic, but that it developed in two opposite directions; in the one direction gods were multiplied by the addition of local gods, and in the other the Egyptians drew nearer and nearer to monotheism.[5] Professor Naville considers the Egyptian religion to be a religion of nature, inclining to pantheism, in which nothing is fixed, nothing determined, without system, and without any closely reasoned logic to serve as a base for its philosophy, and full of contradictions and confusion.[6] Now, although he thinks that the Egyptian

[1] 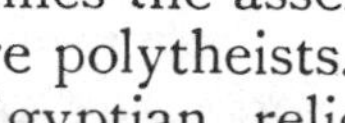. *Recueil*, tom. XXX, p. 187.

[2] See some fine hymns to Åmen-Rā in Moret, *Culte Divin*, p. 133 ff, and note the epithets applied to him.

[3] Book of the Dead, Chapter XVII, 9, 10.

[4] Champollion-Figeac, *L'Égypte*, Paris, 1839, p. 245, col. 1.

[5] *Geschiedenis van den Godsdienst in de Oudheid*, Amsterdam, 1893, p. 25.

[6] *La Religion*, p. 92.

religion began with pantheism, he hesitates to call it pantheism, and reserves that epithet for the "doctrine of Heliopolis, of the origin of which we know nothing."[1] Professor Maspero admits that the Egyptians called several gods "one god" and "only god," even when the god was associated with a goddess and a son, but he adds: "ce dieu un n'était jamais *dieu* tout court."[2] He continues: "The only god is the only god Åmon, the "only god Phtah, the only god Osiris, that is to say, a "being determinate, possessing a personality, name, "attributes, apparel, members, a family, a man infinitely "more perfect than men. He is a likeness of the kings "of this earth, and his power, like that of all kings, is "limited by the power of neighbouring kings. The "conception of his unity is geographical and political, at "least as much as it is religious; Rā, only god of "Heliopolis, is not the same as Amon only god of "Thebes. The Egyptian of Thebes proclaimed the "unity of Amon to the exclusion of Rā, the Egyptian "of Heliopolis proclaimed the unity of Rā to the "exclusion of Amon. . . . Each one god, conceived of "in this manner, is only the one god of the nome or of "the town, and not the one god of the nation recognized "as such throughout the country."

All this may be true under some circumstances, and so long as we are dealing with primitive Egyptians, when the figures of the town-gods or nome-gods were representatives of ancestors, and when the family, or tribe, to which each ancestor belonged naturally claimed the greatest possible power for him to the exclusion of all other ancestor gods. The equality of the gods may be explained by religious toleration, which was natural to the Egyptian, and by his conservatism, which was innate; anthropomorphism accounts for the rest. Assuming that Professor Maspero's view is correct, it does not make it impossible for the Egyptians to have possessed, even in the earliest period, a knowledge of the unity of God, and to have attributed this unity to "gods" which they well knew to be wholly different in nature from Him. They esteemed highly their local

[1] *Ibid.*, p. 116.
[2] *Histoire Ancienne*, Paris, 1904, p. 33.

gods, and the gods of great and ancient cities, *e.g.*, Temu of Heliopolis and Åmen-Rā of Thebes, so highly, in fact, that they lavished upon them the attributes of God the Creator. In the Negative Confession (l. 38) the deceased says: "I have not cursed the god," and in l. 42 he says: "I have not thought scorn of the god who dwells in my city." It is unlikely that "the god" and the "god of the city" are one and the same god, and it seems to me that "the god" refers either to God, or to Osiris, round whom the most exalted ethical conceptions of the Egyptians centred. Osiris was, as we have already seen, in the earliest times an ancestor god, and he certainly became the national god and judge of the dead. In the case of Åmen we have a god unlike any of the other gods of Egypt, for he symbolized the "hidden" power which is the source of the world and of all life in it. Had his priests been able to establish him as sovereign in the Other World in the place of Osiris, we might well regard him as the highest conception of deity which the Egyptians ever imagined. Taking all the facts into consideration, and making due allowance for the anthropomorphism of the Egyptians, and the contradictions and confusion which are found in their texts, it is impossible not to agree with the opinion expressed by de Rougé in 1860: "The unity of a "supreme and self-existent being, his eternity, his "almightiness, and eternal reproduction as God; the "attribution of the creation of the world and of all living "beings to this supreme God; the immortality of the "soul, completed by the dogma of punishments and "rewards; such is the sublime and persistent base "which, notwithstanding all deviations and all mytho-"logical embellishments, must secure for the beliefs of "the ancient Egyptians a most honourable place among "the religions of antiquity."[1]

The foregoing remarks and the diversity of the opinions on the Egyptian Religion held by great Egyptologists illustrate the difficulty of the subject, and show that several views of it are possible according to the standpoints taken by their writers. The same is the

[1] *Études sur le Rituel Funéraire* (in *Revue Arch.*, Paris, 1860, p. 12).

case with the religion of the modern peoples of the Sûdân. If, however, we examine the facts reported by serious travellers and students of it, we shall find that the fundamentals of the religion of the Sûdânî tribes are the same as those of the Egyptians before their conversions to Christianity and Islâm, and that the explanations of the whole group of modern beliefs given by men like Livingstone, Nassau, Dennett, Sir Harry Johnston, and others are most helpful in understanding the ancient beliefs of Egypt. It seems to me impossible that the religious beliefs of the Sûdânî folk of to-day can be derived from the Egyptians, or that they are survivals mysteriously preserved for nearly two thousand years after Egypt passed out of the hands of native kings.[1] All the evidence available suggests that Sûdânî beliefs are identical with those of the Egyptians, because the people who held them in Egypt were Africans, and those who now hold them in the Sûdân are Africans; what this evidence is we may now see.

I. Evidence against the African belief in God, immortality, etc.:—

Mr. Thomson says that the African appears to him to be practically a materialist. He has indeed a certain dim idea that there is a Supreme Being, but he cannot grasp the conception and lays it aside. His notion of immortality is a purely material one. The idea of a soul or a spirit, as we conceive it, is utterly beyond his mental calibre. The "phepo" or ghost is there, he says, but it is like the wind, we cannot see it. It feels pain, hunger, disease, cold, etc., as do living people.[2] According to Schweinfurth the Bongos have not the slightest conception of immortality, and they have no belief in the transmigration of souls. All religion as we know it is unknown to them. Their word for the Supreme Being is "Loma," which denotes equally luck and ill-luck.[3] They are in abject fear of spirits, devils, witches (bitaboh), and wood goblins (ronga). They know no Creator or ruling power above. They work magic by

[1] Egypt became a Roman province on the death of Cleopatra, 23 B.C.

[2] *To the Central African Lakes*, Vol. II, p. 87.

[3] See Piaggia, *Viaggi nell'Africa Centrale*, p. 129.

means of roots.[1] The Niam-Niam word for Divinity is "Gumbah," *i.e.*, "lightning." None of the natives of the Baḥr al-Ghazâl have "the faintest conception of true religion," but the Niam-Niam word "borru" means both prayer and augury, and this people have a sort of praying machine.[2] According to Johnston, the Pygmies have practically no religious belief, and no idea of immortality; when a man is dead he is done with, and "worn out."[3] The Latûka also have no religious conceptions.[4] Sir Samuel Baker says that the Obbo people have no idea of a Supreme Being, and that all bow down to sorcery; practical and useful magic is all that is esteemed by the savage. One Katchiba went so far as to place a spell on the door of Lady Baker's hut. The Kisoona have no Supreme Being and no object of worship, but they believe in magic like the Madi and Obbo.[5] In another work Baker says that the Bari reverence a large granite stone, but later on he adds: "the natives believed in nothing."[6] "The Wakamba have no religion, but recognize a well-"intentioned Supreme Being, called Ngae, to whom they "attribute good and evil. They neither worship their "ancestors nor believe in witchcraft.[7] However widely "spread and deeply engrained may be the belief in spirits, "it remains perfectly true that all the African tribes I "met with from the Zambesi to the Victoria N'yanza "are wholly lacking in any idea of a God. The "'musimo' (spirits) may be productive of evil: sacrifices "are offered to them to keep them in a good humour, "or to appease them when they are angry. But there "is no idea of a Creator or of a Supreme Cause pro-"ductive of good as well as evil."[8] Some of the natives of Southern Abyssinia have no god, no worship, and no rites, but they pay a sort of reverence to heaven, *Waḳ* ዋቅ፡.[9] He has no counterpart, is the Creator, and is lord

[1] *Heart of Africa*, Vol. I, p. 304.
[2] *Ibid.*, Vol. II, p. 31.
[3] *Tramps round the Mountains of the Moon*, p. 237.
[4] *Ibid.*, p. 451.
[5] *Albert N'yanza*, pp. 201–203, and p. 382.
[6] *Ismailia*, London, 1879, pp. 224, 446.
[7] Decle, *Three Years in Savage Africa*, p. 489.
[8] *Ibid.*, p. 514.
[9] Ludolf, *Historia*, I, 16.

of forty-four *ajana*, or spirits, good and bad, and of twenty secondary divinities. He has a black face, and his palace is set on a mountain.[1]

II. Evidence for the African belief in God, immortality, etc. :—

The Dokos, who live to the south of Shoa in East Africa, believe in a being called Yer. They pray to him with their head on the ground and their feet upright against a tree or stone; they are only four feet high, and they eat snakes.[2] The Supreme Being of the Gallas is Waku, or Malunga, who is associated with Oglie and Atetie, a female.[3] These three beings are a triad, and so the Gallas, like the Egyptians, had a god containing three persons. Their evil spirits are eighty-eight in number, one of great power being called Sar.[4] The god of Jagga country is Eruwa, *i.e.*, heaven.[5] The god of Wakuafi is called Engai.[6] The Makooa worship Ineb, *i.e.*, the sky.[7] Gugsa's tribe, the Edjou Gallas, believed in a Supreme Being and sacrificed men to him.[8] The bodies of these sacrifices were eaten, for cannibalism was customary with them, and when Mr. Gobat gave a dinner, he provided both roast meat and raw meat for his guests. Senhor Candido of Tete states that all the natives of this region have a clear idea of a Supreme Being, the maker and governor of all things. They call him "Morimo," "Molungo," "Reza," "Mpâmbe," according to the dialect; the Barotse name him "Nyâmpi," and the Balonda "Zambi." They also believe in immortality, they make offerings to the spirits of the dead, they hold up their hands to the Ruler of Heaven, as if appealing to him to assert their innocence; and they believe in the transmigration of souls.[9] The primitive African faith seems to be that there is one

[1] Paulitschke, *Ethnographie N. O. Afrika*, Vol. II, p. 21.

[2] Krapf, *Travels*, 1869, p. 52 f.

[3] *Ibid.*, pp. 80, 81.

[4] *Ibid.*, p. 77.

[5] *Ibid.*, p. 239.

[6] *Ibid.*, p. 359.

[7] Salt, *Voyage to Abyssinia*, p. 41.

[8] Gobat, *Journal of a Three Years' Residence in Abyssinia*, London, 1847, p. 63 f.

[9] Livingstone, *Missionary Travels*, p. 641.

Almighty Maker of heaven and earth. And we have found none in whom the belief in the Supreme Being was not found. He is so invariably referred to as the author of everything supernatural that, unless one is ignorant of their language, he cannot fail to notice this prominent feature of their faith. Everything not to be accounted for by common causes, whether of good or evil, is ascribed to the Deity.[1] The Matambwê believe in God and show great reverence for Him; when they pray they offer a little meal to Him. They admit that they know very little about Him, and Makochera told Livingstone that "He was not good, because He killed so many people."[2] The Manyema call God "Gulu"; He is a person, and men when they die go to Him.[3] The origin of the primitive faith in Africans and others seems to have been a divine influence persistent in all ages. One portion of this primitive belief, the continued existence of departed spirits, seems to have no connection whatever with dreams.[4]

Mr. Wilson says that there is no well-defined system of false religion in Western Africa which is generally received by the people. The belief in one great Supreme Being, who made and upholds all things, is universal. The impression is so deeply engraved upon their moral and mental nature that any system of atheism strikes them as too absurd and preposterous to require a denial. All the tribes met with by him have a name for God, but they have no correct idea of the character or attributes of the Deity; they think of Him as a being like themselves. On great occasions they invoke the name of God solemnly three times. The belief in a future state is equally prevalent, and the doctrine of transmigration is common. Fetishism and Demonolatry are undoubtedly the leading and prominent forms of religion among the pagan tribes of Africa. Many of the tribes speak of the son of God, who is called "Greh" by the Grebos, and "Sankombum" by the Amina.[5]

[1] Livingstone, *The Zambesi and Its Tributaries*, p. 521 f.
[2] *Last Journals*, Vol. I, p. 45.
[3] *Ibid.*, Vol. II, p. 149.
[4] *Ibid.*, Vol. II, p. 184.
[5] *Western Africa*, p. 209.

Among the Mpongwe the word for God is "Anyambia," which is said to mean "good spirits." They think of Him as a being like themselves, possessing their own characteristics, good and bad, only in a higher degree. They have a clearer and higher idea of his power and wisdom than of his other attributes . . . they have an idea of his goodness also, but this is never unmixed with notions of capriciousness and severity of character, especially in his dealings with men. Next to God come two spirits, Ombwiri and Onyambe, the former good and gentle, the latter hateful and wicked. Ombwiri represents a class or family of spirits, but he is regarded as a tutelary or guardian spirit. Almost every man has his own Ombwiri, for which he provides a small house near his own. Next to Ombwiri and Onyambe come two classes of spirits, the Abambo and the Inlâgâ; both represent the spirits of dead men. The Abambo are ancestral spirits, the Inlâgâ are the spirits of strangers who have come from a distance. The spirits are supposed to possess men and to cause illnesses, and they can only be driven out, and their evil actions stopped by series of magical ceremonies which take ten or fifteen days to perform. The Shekani and Bakĕle people have a great spirit whom they call "Mwetyi." He lives in the earth, but on occasions can be induced to dwell in a large, flat, wholly dark house in a village. Ancestor worship is a distinguishing characteristic of the religion of Southern Guinea. Images are used in ancestor worship, but they are seldom displayed to public view. They are kept in a corner and food and drink and a small share of any profit made by trade are offered to them. The bones of ancestors are carefully preserved, and thus a sort of "relic worship" exists.[1]

It is supposed by some that the black tribes and peoples of Western Africa worship animals and idols, and that they are acquainted with no higher Deity than the fetish which they carry on their breasts, or the serpent in their clay temple. This is a great mistake, for they possess the remnants of a noble and sublime religion, the precepts of which they have forgotten, and

[1] Wilson, *Western Africa*, p. 386 ff.

the ceremonies of which they have debased. They still retain their belief in God—the One, the Supreme, the Creator, who made the world and men, who thunders in the air, who destroys the wicked with his bolts, who rewards the good with long life, who gives the rain, the fruits of the earth, and all things that are good. Some speak of him with timidity, rarely utter his awful name, and pray to him only in their last extremity. Others think he loves to be supplicated, and pray to him like children. In some parts of Guinea the daily prayer is: "O God, I "know thee not, but thou knowest me; thy aid is "necessary to me. In some parts of Africa they believe in the existence of an Evil Power, and, courtiers even in religion, they pray to him. They also have a material religion of fetish; images, plants, trees, animals, etc., are to them symbols only, and are not regarded as gods.

Some stupid or ignorant people believe that such charms contain the spirit of the Deity, but this is a doctrine of transubstantiation which is not confined to Africa. The natives of the Gold Coast believe in a future life; the good will be wafted over a river to a land of happiness; the wicked will be drowned. The Ibo believe in transmigration and some in re-incarnation.[1] The Cabindas have two kinds of household gods: those of one kind have features of the Egyptian type, those of the other have Hottentot characteristics, and are steatopygous.[2]

The Masai believe in a god, or heaven, called Engai,[3] who placed a sort of demi-god called Neiterkop,[4] or Naiteru-kop, on Mount Kenya.[5] Masai women often pray twice daily, and when one of their number gives birth to a child they sing a prayer to Engai, of which the following is a translation by Mr. A. C. Hollis:—

[1] Winwood Reade, *Savage Africa*, p. 417 ff.
[2] *Ibid.*, p. 421.
[3] Thomson, *Through Masai Land*, p. 444.
[4] Krapf, *Travels*, p. 360.
[5] See Hollis, *The Masai*, pp. 270, 280.

My God, to thee alone I pray
That offspring may to me be given.
Thee only I invoke each day,
O morning star in highest heaven.
God of the thunder and the rain
Give ear unto my suppliant strain.
  Lord of the powers of the air
  To thee I raise my daily prayer.

My God, to thee alone I pray,
Whose savour is as passing sweet
As only choicest herbs display,
Thy blessing daily I entreat.
Thou hearest when I pray to thee,
And listenest in thy clemency.
  Lord of the powers of the air
  To thee I raise my daily prayer.[1]

According to Burton, the name for God in the Dahomey religion is "Mau."[2] Being incomprehensible the Supreme Being is thought to be too exalted to care for the low estate of man, and consequently is neither feared nor loved. He is regarded as the Cause of Causes, and the Source of Law, rather than as a local and personal fact. The Negro's Deity, if disassociated from physical objects, would almost represent the idea of the philosopher. The African holds that this dark, silent, eternal Deity can be influenced by intercessions animate and inanimate, human and bestial, and that the leopard and the crocodile control the inscrutable course of mundane law.

In the year 1700 the little kingdom of Whydah had three gods; Danh-gbwe, a serpent, Atin, a tree, and Hu, the ocean. To these some add Khevioso, the thunder-god.[3]

[1] The *Masai*, p. 346.

[2] The Male-Cat in the XVIIth Chapter of the Book of the Dead is called Màu, and the text contains a pun on his name.

[3] Lesser deities enumerated by Burton are: Afa, Bo (a priapus of clay), Legba (a priapus and Janus), Gûn (an iron fetish), Hoho (the twin fetish), Sapatan (small-pox), Takpwonun (the hippopotamus), Kpo (the leopard), Gbwe-ji (the great bush fetish), Kpate (a man-fetish), Kpase (a helper of Kpate), Nate (the storekeeper of the sea), Avrekete, Aizan (a street-god), Agasun (the old Makhi fetish), Li, Lisa (its messenger is the chameleon), Dohen, Nesu, Ajaruma (the white man's fetish), Tokpodun (the crocodile), Zo (the fire fetish), Aydowhedo, or

Mr. Skertchley considers that the religion of Dahomey consists of two parts, totally distinct from each other, viz., the belief in a Supreme Being, and the belief in a "whole host of minor deities." Mau, the Supreme Being, is of so exalted a nature that he cares very little for the circumstances of men, and his attention is only directed to them by some special invocation. He lives above the sky, and commits the affairs of earth to leopards, snakes, locusts, crocodiles, stones, rags, cowries, leaves of trees, etc. Mau must have mediators in dealing with him, hence the origin of fetishism. Mau has an assistant who keeps a record[1] of the good and evil deeds of every person by means of a stick, the good works being notched at one end, and the bad ones at the other. When a man dies, his body is judged by the balance struck between the two ends of the stick. If the good preponderates, it is permitted to join the spirit in Kutomen, or "Dead-land"; but if the evil outweighs the good, it is utterly destroyed, and a new body created for the use of the spirit.[2] The corporeal existence of the Deity is denied, but human passions are ascribed to him. The religion of Dahomey is not polytheism, for the people worship one God, Mau, who is propitiated through the fetishes,[3] who play the part played by Archangels and Angels in Christendom.

On the Congo the people are given up to fetishism, but everywhere the Bantu race has a name for God. Among the western Bantu we have "Nzambi," "Nyambi," "Anyambie," and the eastern Bantu speak of "Mulungu," or "Molongo," *i.e.*, the "Ancient One." In the central Congo basin the current names for God are "Ibanza," "Iyanza," or "Nzakomba." In the Bantu mind God is far removed from man, whose voice can never reach him; except his name, the natives in Bentley's time knew nothing about him.[4] Under the

---

Danh (the rainbow).—*A Mission to the King of Dahome*, Vol. II, p. 133 ff. See the list also given by Skertchley, *Dahomey as It is*, p. 466 ff.

[1] He seems to be the equivalent of Thoth in the Egyptian Religion.

[2] *Dahomey as It is*, p. 461.

[3] *Ibid.*, p. 465.

[4] Bentley, *Pioneering on the Congo*, Vol. I, p. 247 ff.

forms of Anyambe, Anyambie, Njambi, Nzambi, Anzam, Nyam, Ukuku, Suku, etc., the Western Africans know of a Being superior to themselves, whom they often declare to be the Maker and Father. Their knowledge of this Being is almost simply a theory, and though it is an accepted belief it rarely influences their lives. They say: "Yes, he made us; but, having made us, he "abandoned us, does not care for us; he is far from us. "Why should we care for him? He does not help nor "harm us. It is the spirits who can harm us whom we "fear and worship, and for whom we care."[1] According to the testimony of a native minister of Corisco who was born in "heathenism," his forefathers believed in a Supreme Being and many inferior agencies which were under his power; in times of need they appealed to the Supreme Being and prayed for his help. He made the world and all in it. There was in the earliest times a great man who merely spake words and things were made. Two eggs fell from heaven and broke on the ground, from one came a man, from the other a woman. A great chief warned men not to eat of the fruit of a certain tree, but he himself ate of it and died. A woman brought the fruit of a forbidden tree to her village, and to hide it she ate it; she became possessed of an evil spirit, which was the beginning of witchcraft. They had a tradition of a Flood; they knew they were sinners, but had no remedy for sin. Sacrifices were made to appease the spirits and to avert their anger. Most of the tribes were cannibals. They had a legend that a "Son" of God, Ilongo ja Anyambe, was to come and deliver mankind from trouble and make them happy, but as he had not come they had ceased to expect him. They believed in the immortality of the soul, but had no tradition of the resurrection of the body; those who kept God's law would go to a good place, and those who did not, to a bad place. They believed that some spirits were good, and others bad.[2] Mr. Nassau does not think that, when primitive man bowed down before a snake or a tree, he worshipped the objects themselves, and he believes that the assumption of a visible tangible

[1] Nassau, *Fetichism in West Africa*, pp. 36, 37.
[2] See the full statement in Nassau, *op. cit.*, pp. 40, 41.

object to represent or personify the Being or Beings is an after-thought added by human ingenuity.[1] The natives believe that away back in unknown time Paia-Njambi existed, and they say: "He was, He is," without having any definite idea about him.[2] The modern African has conceived the idea of "eternity," which he expresses in the words *pĕkĕ-na-jome*, "ever and beyond." The Egyptian word for illimitable time in the past is *pat*, , and the words *tcheta-neḥeḥ*, , mean illimitable time in the future.

The God of the Bantu tribes has many names—Nzambi, Nzam, Ukuku, Suku, etc., but Miss Kingsley found that the Nzam of the Fâns is practically identical with Suku, south of the Congo in the Bihe country, and so on. Though the Creator of all things, He is regarded as a "non-interfering, and therefore a negligible quantity." Not so, however, is it with the crowd of spirits with which the universe is peopled, for they interfere everywhere [usually with harmful effects], therefore the Bantu has developed a cult of spirits which we call witchcraft.[3]

Mr. Dennett, after a long study of the religion of many tribes in Western Africa, says that the Bavili conception of God is so spiritual, or abstract, that he fears the reader will think him mad to suppose that so evidently degenerate a race can have formed so logical an idea of God. He derives the name for God, "Nzambi," from *imbi* "personal essence," and *zia* or *za* "fours." The "fours" are the groups each of four powers called "Bakici Baci," which he describes. The group Nzambi consists of four parts: 1. Nzambi, the abstract idea, the cause. 2. Nzambi Mpungu, God Almighty, the father God. 3. Nzambici, God the essence, the God on earth. 4. Kici, the mysterious inherent quality in things that causes the Bavili to fear and respect.[4] The Tshi-speaking peoples divide their

[1] *Ibid.*, p. 48.
[2] *Ibid.*, p. 51.
[3] *Travels in West Africa*, p. 442.
[4] *At the Back of the Black Man's Mind*, p. 167.

"gods" into four groups: 1. Those worshipped by one or more tribes; these are few in number. 2. Local deities (*Bohsŭm*). 3. Family deities. 4. The tutelary deities of individuals (*Suhman*). The first group is too distant or too indifferent to interfere ordinarily in human affairs. Those of the second group were originally all malignant. They represent, according to Colonel Ellis, the original conceptions of the Negro in respect of God, and from them was developed the first group. The third and fourth groups are the product of priestcraft. With the Tshi-speaking peoples a "god" is a part of Nature, superhuman, but not supernatural. In speaking of these superhuman agents the following words are used generically:—1. Sunsum, *i.e.*, "spirit," or "shadow." 2. Srahman, "ghost," "goblin," or "lightning." 3. Abonsŭm, "evil spirit," "witchcraft," "magic." 4. Bohsŭm, *i.e.*, "occult," "mystic," "sacred." The people of each district worship their own local gods, and do not trouble about those at a distance.

The two great deities of the Gold Coast were Bobowissi and Tando. The name of the former means, perhaps, "rain-maker." He was worshipped with human sacrifices, and his statue and stool were worshipped with human blood. When the inhabitants became accustomed to Europeans they adopted the God of the Christians, whom they called Nana-Nyankupon, or "Lord of the Sky," and, later, many of the attributes of Bobowissi were ascribed to him. The natives believe that he has the body, senses, passions, and faculties of a man. Tando, the second of the old gods of the Gold Coast, has also a human form, and his disposition is malignant; the meaning of his name appears to be the "hater," and human sacrifices were offered to him, seven men and seven women at a time. Two most important deities are Srahmantin, *i.e.*, "tall spirit," and Sasabonsum, *i.e.*, "evil spirit" (or "evil spirits"). Sasabonsum is a monster of human shape and red colour, and lives either in or upon red earth; he is cruel and malevolent, and lives as far as possible upon human beings. His attributes are those of the Egyptian god Set and his "red fiends," and both he and Set were regarded as the makers of earthquakes, hurricanes, tempests, storms, and destruction and disorder of every kind.[1] Colonel Ellis quotes an interesting fact in connection with the worship of Brahfo, the "deputy" of Bobowissi, who was brought from Ashanti to Mankassim, which became his place of abode.[2] An interesting parallel to this among the ancient Egyptian gods is afforded by the legend of the Possessed Princess of Bekhten. To drive out the devil from this lady the priests of Thebes, at the request of the king of Bekhten, decided to send the statue of one of the forms of Khensu; but before they despatched the statue they took it into the temple of the great god Khensu, who transferred his power to it, and then the deputy god proceeded on his way.

Among the Yoruba tribes the word for a superhuman being or god is "orisha," which is used equally to express images and sacred objects, and also the idea of "holy": it corresponds exactly to the Tshi term *bohsum*. Their principal gods are: 1. OLORUN, the sky-god, who is the personification of the firmament; he is the equivalent of the Nyan-kupon of the Tshis, Nyonmo of the Gâs, and Mawu of the Ewes. The Egyptian equivalent was Pet, . The Yorubas, like the Egyptians, believed the sky to be a solid body, which curved over the earth so as to cover it like a vaulted roof. Compare the figure on stelae  Olorun is too distant, or too indifferent, to interfere in the affairs of this world. He has no images, symbols, priests or temples, and is only invoked in times of calamity when the lesser gods will not answer their worshippers. 2. OBATALA, who was made by Olorun, and manages the heavens and the earth for him. He is a sky-god with human attributes. He made the first man and woman out of clay, and his equivalent among the gods of Egypt is Ptaḥ, whom we see at Philae fashioning a king on a potter's wheel. As a judge he possesses some of the attributes of the Egyptian god Osiris. 3. ODUDUA, the wife of Obatala, is always represented as a seated woman nursing a child;

[1] Ellis, *Tshi-speaking Peoples*, pp. 1–36.
[2] *Ibid.*, p. 55.

in this respect she resembles the Egyptian goddess Isis, but as the patroness of love her Egyptian equivalent is Hathor. 4 and 5. Odudua bore her husband a boy and girl called AGANJU and YEMAJA, who represent Land and Water respectively. The brother and sister married, and their son was called ORUNGAN, *i.e.*, the Air. The following gods were the fruit of the unlawful intercourse of Orungan with his mother Yemaja: DADA, a vegetable god; SHANGO, lightning god; OGUN, god of iron and war; OLOKUN, sea-god; OLOSA, lagoon-god; OYA, Niger-god; OSHUN, river-god; OBA, river-god; ORISHA OKO, god of agriculture; OSHOSI, god of hunters; OKE, god of mountains; AJE SHALUGA, god of wealth; SHANKPANNA, smallpox-god; ORUN, the sun; and OSHU, the moon. OSHUMARE, the rainbow, is a servant of Shango, and his messenger ARA is the thunderclap; his slave is BIRI, the darkness. Shango hanged himself, but did not die, for he went into the earth and there became a god (*orisha*). 6. IFA, god of divination, who causes pregnancy, and presides over births. 7. ELEGBA, a phallic divinity; his symbol is a short knobbed club, which was originally intended to be a representation of the phallus. Circumcision and excision are connected with his worship. 8. OGUN, the war-god. The priests of Ogun take out the hearts of human victims, dry and powder them, mix them with rum, and sell them to people who wish to acquire great courage.[1]

Besides these "gods" the Yorubas worship several minor deities whose origin they cannot readily account for; these, of course, are not in any way related to the group headed by Olorun. It is important to note that this company of gods resembles in many respects the Egyptian company of gods of which Osiris was an important member. Olorun is the equivalent of Temu, Aganju of Keb, Yemaja of Nut and Tefnut, Orungan of Shu, Ȯbatala of Osiris, and Ododua of Isis, and the group of gods which were the offspring of Yemaja and Orungan may be compared to Nephthys, Set, Anubis, and the other gods of the cycle of Osiris. The Yoruba gods, other than those of Olorun's cycle, are represented by the chief local deities of Egypt, whose existence was

[1] Ellis, *Yoruba-speaking Peoples*, pp. 1–69.

taken for granted. The priests of the Yoruba gods are divided into grades, as were the priests of Egypt, and as intermediaries between gods and men they prepare and sell charms, amulets, etc.; this also did the priests of Egypt. In Yoruba and Egypt the office of priest was hereditary. The temple is called "Ile Orisha," *i.e.*, "house of the god"; in Egypt also the temple was called "house of the god," . The temple is a clay hut with a thatched roof, with the interior painted the colour sacred to the god, and the door, shutters, posts, etc., carved. The primitive temples of Egypt were probably of the same class. The spirits who enter the images of the Yoruba gods to receive the sacrifices and prayers of the faithful are worshipped, not the images themselves. Sacrifice is the most important part of ceremonial worship, and no god can be consulted without it. The Oni of Ife said that the sacrifice made at Ife was for the benefit of the whole human race, the white man not excepted.[1]

Sir Harry Johnston says that the negroes of all Congoland, and of nearly all pagan Africa, have imagined a Supreme Spirit of the Sky, a Jove, whose voice is the thunder, who gives or withholds the rain, and whose hand hurls the lightning. This is Nzambi, or Nzambi-ampungu, Nyambe, Nzakomba, Liyanza, Chambi, Kabezya-mpungu, Mfidi, Leza, Loula, Firie, Ruhanga, Namwanga, Ôri, Mböri, Eñketa, Ala, or Zaba, according to people and district. Even the Bambute Pygmies possess an original name for the Sky-god—Alidîda. The conception of the Sky-god is more or less anthropomorphic. "In the east and south-east of "Africa the conception of the Deity *may* be gradually "attained through steps of ancestor-worship; the mighty "chief, great-grandfather and founder of the tribe, may, "from haunting a cavern or tree, or living again in the "lion or elephant, gradually mount (in the imagination of "his descendants) to the cloud-world above, and in the "interests of his children's children take charge of the "thunder, lightning, and rain. But in the Congo basin

[1] Ellis, *op. cit.*, p. 106.

"God is rather imagined as the pre-existing Creator, who "has probably called man into existence, however "indifferent He may afterwards show Himself as to the "fate of each human being." Many of the Congo peoples believe that the Supreme God of the sky is too far off to care about humanity. The control of the world and all in it has, they think, passed into the hands of a host of spirits, or of a Devil, like the Moloki of the Bayaka, the Ngumba of the Nsakara, the Nkadi of the Eshi-Kongo, the Elemba of the Ababua, the Banda of the Basongomeno, and the Ngula of the Batabwa.[1] The spirits, or "gods," may dwell anywhere, and they are supposed to be able to locate their influence or power in trees and rock, and in substances of all kinds, in figures of wood, clay, or metal, in objects made of wood, stones, feathers, in parts of dead human beings, *e.g.*, fingers, skulls, etc., and of dead animals, and in living creatures. The object in which a spirit locates itself, or part of itself, or its influence, becomes what is commonly, but absurdly, called a "fetish." The intelligent African is far too shrewd a person to worship the objects in which the spirits abide, but large numbers of natives confuse the abode of the spirit with the spirit, just as many people do outside Africa, and give to the material thing the worship which should be given to the spirit.

The Dinkas, according to Count Gleichen, have a long list of gods and demi-gods. The head of these is Deng-dit, the Rain-giver, whose wife is Abôk, the daughter of the Devil (L'wâl Burrajôk). He has many forms and shapes. Deng-dit has three children, two sons and one daughter, whose names are Kûr Konga, Gurung-dit, and Ai-Yak respectively. Deng-dit is regarded as a malevolent being who must be propitiated by sacrifices, which represent the only intercourse which the people attempt to hold with him. The Golos worship Umvili and Barachi, who are said to have created man. They believe that the righteous will be rewarded with bliss, and the wicked punished by a spirit called Ma-ah, who is the servant rather than the enemy of Umvili. Like the Dinkas, they do not pray, and their worship is one of sacrifice. They associate good with the sky and

[1] Johnston, *George Grenfell*, Vol. II, p. 631.

evil with the bowels of the earth. "The natural human instinct for religion is probably as deeply rooted in the Baḥr al-Ghazâl as elsewhere, and manifests itself perhaps in the readiness with which its tribes embrace Islâm."[1] The priests of the Dinkas are called Tieit, and claim to possess the power of conversing with the dead.[2] The great god of the Shilluk country is called Jo-uk, the source of all life and of good and evil; he is everywhere, and when men die they go to him. He is feared and propitiated with animal sacrifices, *i.e.*, the priest of each village slays an animal with a holy spear on behalf of the people who assemble at the house of the Nyakang. The sacrifice is followed by a dance and drinking of much merissa; these acts appear to constitute Shilluk worship. The Shilluks believe in the existence of a series of semi-divine beings, male and female, who are descended from the great white Cow Deung Adok, which was created by Jo-uk and came up out of the Nile. This white Cow gave birth to a man-child called Kola (Kollo), and he begat Umak-Rā, or Omaro, who begat Makwa, or Wâd Maul, who begat Ukwa, who married Nikkieya and Ung-wâd, daughters of Ud Diljil, who was part man and part crocodile. These wives were part women and part crocodile. Ukwa subsequently married a third wife. His children were:—By Nikkieya two sons and three daughters, viz., Nyakang, Umoi, Ad Dui, Ari Umker, and Bun Yung; by Ung-wâd, one son, called Ju, or Bworo; by the third wife, a son, called Duwat. On the death of Ukwa, Nyakang and Duwat fought for the succession, and at length the former got wings and flew to the Sawbât country with his sisters, brother, and half-brother. Nyakang then created men and women out of the animals he found in the country, and from these the modern Shullas believe themselves to be descended.[3]

Before the conversion of Uganda to Christianity the common word for "god" was "Katonda," and "Kazoba" was the god of the firmament, or God. The religion of the people was derived from ancestor worship, but in its

[1] *The Anglo-Egyptian Sûdân*, Vol. I, p. 163.
[2] *Ibid.*, p. 145.
[3] Gleichen, *The Anglo-Egyptian Sûdân*, Vol. I, p. 197.

later form it became the worship of a long series of powers which were usually of a malevolent disposition. The chief god of the Banabuddu was Kitabumbuire, and other well-known spirits were Nkulo, who gave children, Kagole, Jero, the author of good fortune, Nuabulezi, who cursed people by request.[1] The Bators worship Ndahoro, Wamala, and Kyomya.[2] The great deity of Lake Victoria was Mukasa, a goddess of extraordinary power, who was said to control the Lake in all its moods. No one could cross it without her permission, and on one occasion it was "tied up" for three months, because King Mtesa had incurred her wrath. At length, Mtesa sent 100 slaves, 100 women, 100 cows, and 100 goats, and then Mukasa untied the Lake. The goddess Wanema had a temple at Bukasa, and was the mother of Mukasa. Kitinda was the god of Damba Island, Musisi of Fumvwe Island, and Nalwoga of Nsadzi Island.[3] Both Mr. Cunningham[4] and Sir Harry Johnston[5] record that the Bamandwa, or priests, made use of the sign of the cross in certain of their ceremonies long before the introduction of Christianity into Uganda.

From the above-stated facts it is quite clear that the majority of African travellers have come to the conclusion that the native believes in God as well as in the existence of a number of "gods" or "spirits," who practically rule the world for Him, and direct the affairs of men. And when we compare these facts with what is known about the God and "gods" of the Egyptians

[1] Cunningham, *Uganda*, p. 67.

[2] *Ibid.*, p. 56.

[3] *Ibid.*, p. 79 ff. The other great "gods" of Uganda were: Kibuka (the war-god), Musisi (the earthquake-god), Kaumpuli (the plague-god), Kawaga (the executioner of Kaumpuli), Mayanja (leopard-god), Musoki (the rainbow), Mwanga (god of divination), Wanema, a goddess), Kayindu (jumping-god), Kitinda (demon of man-eaters), Magobwi (snake-god), Nagodya (daughter of Mukasa), Lule (rain-god), Nagawonye (god of plenty), Nakayaga (storm-god), Kiwanka (thunder-bolt-god), Kizito (god of divination), Nalwoga, Waziba, Walusi (god of falling stars and red sky), Luisi (hyena-god), Lubanga (dancing-god), Mbajwe, Nabamba, Kagolo (god of thunder and lightning), Kigala (god of the deaf), Wamala, etc. *Ibid.*, p. 215. Besides the ancestral spirits and demi-gods the Baganda believed in the existence of elves or spirits whom they call "Ngogwe."—Johnston, *Uganda*, Vol. II, p. 677.

[4] *Op. cit.*, p. 216.

[5] *Op. cit.*, p. 678.

we find a resemblance which is too consistent and definite to be the result of accident or coincidence. The African of Egypt and the Sûdân has always believed in a God, almighty, omniscient, invisible, unknowable. Among the series of "gods" or "spirits" who are subordinate to Him there is one who unites the nature of man with a divine, or superhuman, nature, and special regard is always paid to him, for he is supposed to understand men's troubles and their needs. Originally he was, no doubt, an ancestral spirit, but as his cult developed the attributes of the great "gods," and even of God, were ascribed to him. Most of the African gods are credited with malevolent or evil dispositions, and among them is always one who is regarded as the personification of evil, and who is, in fact, the Devil. Like God he is immortal and indestructible. He is sometimes the servant of God, but at other times is His opponent; and he is assumed to pass his existence in subverting His plans, and in working destruction, and in overthrowing the powers of Nature. The ill-will of the "gods" may be set aside, and by means of gifts and sacrifices their influences and powers may be converted to the use of men; the Devil alone is implacable. The Egyptian god Set was in all respects the counterpart of the Devil of modern Africa. He was the personification of physical darkness and of moral wickedness, and he was the foe of physical and moral order of every kind. He waged war against the Sun-god Ḥeru-ur, and was defeated, but not slain, by the god of light. He was attacked by Horus, the son of Isis, who fought with him for three days, and though wounded he escaped with his life. He suffered sorely at the hands of Rā the Sun-god, but he was not slain. Though he daily attempted to prevent Rā from entering the sky, the Sun-god was content to cast a spell upon him, which made him powerless for evil, and to permit him to renew his evil actions on the following day. As Set was the everlasting foe of the gods, so was he the foe of every righteous man, and none could escape from him except by the help of Osiris and the gods who helped this god.

The groups into which the modern African has divided his gods closely resemble the "companies" of the gods of Egypt, and the ideas which underlie the worship of ancient and modern African gods are substantially the same. From first to last the view as to the importance and value of sacrifice has remained unchanged, and no substitute has yet been found for offerings which are as jealously regarded by the priesthoods of the Sûdân to-day as they were by the priesthood of Osiris at Abydos under the XVIIIth dynasty.

The modern African "witch-doctor," or "medicine man," plays a part in every important incident in the life of the modern Sûdânî, just as the *kher ḥeb* did in the life of the ancient Egyptian, and in each case the object in view is generally the same. In one particular the Egyptian enjoyed a great advantage over the modern peoples of Central Africa, *i.e.*, the blessing of a settled government for long periods at a time. Under the Ancient Empire Memphis and Heliopolis flourished, and the Pyramids of Mêdûm, Ṣaḳḳârah, Gîzah, etc., were built, to say nothing of the temples and maṣṭabah tombs. The cultured and the leisured classes had time to think about their religion and to observe its precepts, and to bury their dead with elaborate pomp and ceremony, and to celebrate their commemorative festivals. Under the Middle Empire Thebes became the capital, and what had been done at Ṣaḳḳârah was imitated, though on a less magnificent scale, at Ḳûrnah and Drah abû'l-Neḳḳah on the west bank of the Nile, by kings who were not only mighty warriors, but devoutly religious men. Under the XVIIIth dynasty, the kings of which extended the frontiers of Egypt from the Upper Euphrates on the north to Equatorial Africa on the south, the Egyptian religion reached its highest state of development, and the ethics of the greatest thinkers of the day were on a level with those preached by Solomon and Jesus the son of Sirach. The cult of the gods and the cult of the dead, as they were understood in Egypt, could only flourish there when the country was wealthy, and safe from the invasions of enemies. At no period were men more religious than under the XVIIIth dynasty, and at no period were the kings of Egypt greater or more successful conquerors. Towards the close of the New Empire a religious decline set in, and spiritual conceptions became obscured under a mass of confused legends, traditions, and contradictory opinions, which reflected themselves in the texts and inscriptions. In all this confusion, however, the great fundamental truths of the Egyptian religion are not lost, and the existence of God, and the doctrines of the resurrection and immortality, are proclaimed in the texts boldly and with conviction.

The reader will have observed that in the preceding pages which deal with the resemblances between Egyptian and modern African gods and god-groups, there is no mention of sun-worship. This may seem at first sight surprising, especially when we take into consideration the very important part which the Sun-god played in the religion of the dynastic Egyptians. The rise of the cult of Rā the great Sun-god as a dominant force in the religion of Egypt seems to date from the period when the king began to call himself "son of Rā," *i.e.*, about the end of the Vth dynasty. It is possible that the king adopted a "Son of Rā" name before this time, but it is unlikely, and as a matter of fact the earliest "son of Rā" name known to us is that of Åssȧ, a king of the Vth dynasty. The great home of the cult of the Sun-god was at that time Ȧnu (Heliopolis), and as the power of the priests of Rā increased they caused the worship of their god to spread rapidly, and under the VIth dynasty he was the greatest of the gods of Lower Egypt. As the religious writings of his priests were adopted by the priesthoods of great towns in Upper Egypt, and their doctrines became the foundation of the religious system which flourished at Thebes under the Middle and New Empires, and in Nubia from the XVIIIth dynasty onwards, the cult of the Sun is, of course, very ancient, and there is reason to believe that Heliopolis was one of its most ancient centres in Egypt, but there is no evidence to show that the Sun was the greatest god, or even one of the greatest of the gods, of the indigenous Egyptians. They certainly believed in the god of the firmament, whatever might be the name by which they called him, but the cult of the Sun as the greatest of the gods appears to be the product, in my opinion, of peoples who did not belong to their stock.

The Sun-worshippers may have numbered among their adherents the tribes of the Eastern Desert and Syria, and even seafaring folk and dwellers on the northern and southern shores of the Mediterranean Sea, who found it possible to merge their own phallic gods and war-gods in the person of the Sun-god. Heliopolis was always a very important station on the great trade route to the East, and of all the gods adored there the greatest would certainly be the deity who was reverenced by the greatest number of worshippers. The cult of the Sun seems to represent a higher order of civilization than that possessed by the primitive Egyptians, and its votaries were, if we accept the Legend of Horus of Beḥuṭet, *i.e.*, the great Sun-god of Edfû, their conquerors.

Among modern peoples of Africa the conception of God is little associated with the worship of the sun or moon, and little interest or superstition appears to be attached to these luminaries. This is certainly true of the peoples of the Congo basin.[1] Among the peoples visited by Miss Kingsley she found no trace of Sun-worship,[2] and Major A. G. Leonard says that among the tribes of the Lower Niger "there is no direct or pronounced adoration of the "celestial bodies, which, as subservient to the Creator, "are unconsciously included in their annual obeisance "to, their one great effort of recognition of, him."[3] Elsewhere[4] he speaks of the "entire absence of any "existing worship of those higher natural objects, such "as the sun, the moon, and the stars, or any ceremonial "connected with them," but he saw in many of the Juju houses in the Ibo interior rude clay images, purporting to be emblems of the sun, moon, rainbow, and stars.[5] This kind of adoration of natural objects he considers to be more specific than general. The purely negro races do not worship the sun.[6] Here and there, however, instances of a kind of Sun-worship appear. Thus the Ja-luo believe in a Supreme God whom they call "Chieng," which is also the name of the sun. When a

[1] Johnston, *George Grenfell*, Vol. II, p. 635.
[2] *Travels in West Africa*, p. 508.
[3] *The Lower Niger and Its Tribes*, p. 377.
[4] *Ibid.*, p. 133.
[5] *Ibid.*, p. 337.
[6] Johnston, *Liberia*, p. 1062.

man comes out of his house in the morning he spits towards the east, and in the evening he spits towards the west.[1] The Supreme Being of the Nandi is Asista, the sun, who dwells in the sky; he created man and beast, and the world belongs to him; men pray to him and make offerings to him.[2] The name of the Uganda god Kazoba has, according to Sir Harry Johnston, for its root—*zoba*, a variant of an old Bantu word for "sun," which is, however, sometimes applied to the sky in general.[3] Among some peoples the moon is regarded as the mother of the sun, but the sun and moon are also spoken of as brothers, or as brother and sister.[4] Mr. Torday says that the Bangala believe that the sun is in love with the moon. He pursues his beloved across the heavens, and when she receives his embraces, and the two lovers forget themselves in their passion, the sky becomes overcast, and darkness conceals their amours. This is the cause of an eclipse.[5] The stars are merely the slaves of the moon. When a solar halo appears the Congo peoples think it is a gathering of the heavenly notables, who have assembled to pass condemnation on some great but bad man.[6] Livingstone reports the explanation of a solar halo given to him by his chief boatman, who said: "It is the Barimo (gods, or departed "spirits) who have called a picho (council); don't you "see they have the Lord (sun) in the centre?"[7] The natives always look upon the halo with awe, and near the Victoria Falls it was called *motse oa barimo*, or "pestle of the gods."[8] The daily setting of the sun, and the phases of the moon, and the setting of the stars, must always give peoples who are at a low level in the scale of civilization, false ideas about the stability and permanence of these luminaries, and cause them to belittle their majesty and power. Their true functions were not understood by the primitive Egyptians any more than

[1] Johnston, *Uganda*, Vol. II, p. 791.
[2] Hollis, *The Nandi*, p. 40.
[3] *Uganda*, Vol. II, p. 677.
[4] Dennett, *At the Back of the Black Man's Mind*, p. 103.
[5] Quoted by Johnston, *George Grenfell*, Vol. II, p. 815.
[6] Bentley, *Pioneering on the Congo*, Vol. I, p. 169.
[7] *Missionary Travels*, p. 220.
[8] *Ibid.*, p. 524.

they are by many tribes of modern Africa, and as the great lights of heaven were, like the sky, remote and indifferent to the personal wants of men and their calamities, the African concerned himself principally with the natural objects, animate and inanimate, which were round about him.

CHAPTER XII.

OSIRIS AS A MOON-GOD.

THE facts quoted in the previous chapters prove that in the earliest times Osiris was believed to have been an African king of divine origin, who lived and reigned upon earth, and who after his death and mutilation assumed among the gods in the Other World the position of god and judge of the dead. It is certain, however, that just as at one time the star Orion was regarded as his abode in the sky, and Sothis that of Isis, so at one period Osiris was identified with the moon. This fact was well known to Plutarch, who says that on the new moon of the month of Phamenoth, which falls in the beginning of the spring, the Egyptians celebrate a festival which is expressly called by them "the Entrance of Osiris into the Moon."[1] He goes on to say that by Osiris are meant the power and influence of the moon, just as by Isis they understand the generative faculty which resides in it. This statement is supported by a passage in the Book of Making the Spirit of Osiris,[2] which reads :—

"Thou risest into the sky,
"Thou art united [thereto] like Rā.
"The sailors in [thy] boat give thee acclamations.
"The mouths of the gods of the horizon rejoice,
"Their throats (*i.e.*, cries) follow thee.
"The love of thee is in hearts, awe of thee is in breasts.
"As soon as thou enterest the Utchau,[3]
"And unitest thyself thereto,
"The beings on earth flourish (or, become fertile)."

[1] *De Iside*, Chapter 43.

[2] 

[3] 

The next few lines of the text are, unfortunately, mutilated, but enough remains to show that the moon is addressed as "bull, that groweth young in the heaven each day," and it is said: "at thy rising up into the sky wretchedness departs," and "when thou art seen in the sky on this day many conceptions take place."[1] There are also allusions to the female power of the moon,"[2] and to the "Power of Osiris, which is Thoth."[3] What exactly Thoth was supposed to do is not clear. The lines which follow add: "The Nile appeareth at thy "utterance, making men to live through the effluxes "which come forth from thy members, making all "cultivated lands to be green by thy coming, great "source (?) of things which bloom, sap of crops and "herbs, Lord of millions of years, sustainer of wild "animals, lord of cattle; the support of whatsoever is is "in thee, what is in earth is thine, what is in the "heavens is thine, what is in the waters is thine." Thus it is quite clear that Osiris was regarded as the Power of the moon, which produced the Nile-flood and therefore all the fertility in Egypt. There is also no possibility of identifying Osiris with Rā, for it is distinctly said Osiris in the moon unites himself to heaven like Rā. Also it is said in another passage "Rā seeth thee enter, love of thee is in his breast."[4] The identification of the moon with the power which produces vegetation on the earth is common among many peoples, as Mr. J. G. Frazer has shown,[5] and we should naturally expect Osiris at some time or other in the period of his cult to be considered a moon-god.

1 

2 

3  Ed. Pierret, *Études*, 1873, p. 29.

4 

5 *Golden Bough*, Vol. II, p. 154 ff.

It is nowhere so stated in the Egyptian texts, but Plutarch says that Osiris lived or reigned twenty-eight years, and thinks that the number twenty-eight manifestly alludes to the number of days in which the moon runs her course round the earth.[1] He also refers to the ceremony which is performed at the funeral of Osiris, when a tree trunk is made into the shape of a crescent, and assumes that this symbolizes the waning moon. And he records the views of certain investigators who stated that the death of Osiris took place at full moon, and that the number of pieces into which his body was torn—fourteen—marks the number of days of the waning moon.

Plutarch can hardly have invented these views, and it is probable that he is repeating the opinions of the learned which were current in Egypt in his day. In the matter of the number of pieces in which the body of Osiris was cut the Egyptian texts do not agree, and it seems as if the identification of the fourteen days of the waning moon with the fourteen members of the mutilated body of Osiris were an afterthought, though it must be admitted, a very ancient one. The Egyptian theologians received the tradition of the dismemberment of the dead from their primitive ancestors, and, in the period when the cult of Osiris under the form of a Moon-god was general, must have assumed that the number of pieces into which Set hacked his body was fourteen. A text at Denderah says that the figure of Seker-Osiris was made up of fourteen pieces,[2] but other texts mention sixteen.[3]

The sixteen members are: his head, feet, bones, arms, heart, interior, tongue, eye, fist, fingers, back, ears, loins, body, his head with a ram's face, and his hair. On the other hand, the Book of making the Spirit of Osiris[4] enumerates eighteen, thus :—

[1] *De Iside*, Chapter 42.

[2] See *A.Z.*, 1881, p. 90 ff.

[3] *Recueil de Travaux*, tom. III, p. 56; tom. IV, p. 23.

[4] Ed. Pierret, p. 27.

1. Head
2. Eyes
3. Ears
4. Nose
5. Mouth
6. Jawbones
7. Beard
8. Lips
9. Tongue
10. Body (breast)
11. Neck
12. Hands
13. Nails and ankles
14. Belly
15. Shoulders (?)
16. Genital organs
17. Backbone
18. Feet

This list is of great importance, for it mentions two portions of the body of Osiris which are ignored in the other lists, viz., the jaw-bones and the genital organs. Reference has already been made to the early text which speaks of the jawbones of a dead king of Egypt being restored to their proper place in his reconstituted body, and to the custom among the Baganda of cutting out the lower jawbones of their dead kings, and the above list proves beyond all doubt that the lower jawbone of Osiris was believed to have been removed from his body by Set when he dismembered him. Of the fate of the genital organs of the god no mention is made in the early rituals, or the Book of the Dead, and this fact no doubt gave rise to the tradition reported by Diodorus[1] and Plutarch[2] that Isis failed to find them, because they had been thrown into the river by Set, or Typhon, and had been eaten by the lepidotus, phagrus, and oxyrhynchus fishes. These writers add that the goddess was obliged to make models of the phallus of Osiris,

[1] Book I, Chapter 22.
[2] Chapter 18.

which she caused to be set up in the temples and to be "religiously adored." The above list, however, includes the organs, showing that, at the time it was written, the priestly authorities believed a tradition to the effect that they had been found; that they were in an effective state is clear from the words of the text.[1] As all the Egyptian books which contain addresses to Osiris by Isis and Nephthys, *e.g.*, "The Lamentations of Isis and Nephthys," and the "Festival Songs of Isis and Nephthys," assume that the body of the god was complete, we must believe that Plutarch and Diodorus repeated incorrect information, or confounded two traditions.

At what period exactly the Egyptians began to identify Osiris with the moon it is impossible to say, but, as there are evidences of the association of the cult of the god with the cult of the moon in the great religious texts of the Vth and VIth dynasties, we may assume that the identification was made in primitive times. In fact, it seems as if the identification of Osiris with the moon represents the fusion of the cult of the god with the very ancient African cult of the moon. Osiris the divine king was slain by Set, and it was Set who waged war against both Eyes of Horus, *i.e.*, the sun and the moon. The storms and eclipses which were caused by this god of evil blinded temporarily the Eyes of Horus, *i.e.*, the sun and the moon, and each month he destroyed piecemeal the moon, which was regarded from very early times as the abode of Osiris. It is possible that the moon was regarded as the home for the souls of the blessed, just as were the stars, but there is no evidence that the Egyptians ever believed that the souls of the dead found their heaven in the Sun. In the Hymn to Osiris in the Papyrus of Ani (Sheet 1, l. 17) the deceased prays that his KA "may "behold the disk of the Sun, and see the Moon-god "without ceasing." In the Book of the Dead (Chapter II) the deceased beseeches the "god who shines in (or,

1 
. Ed. Pierret, p. 27.

from) the Moon" to give him the power to wander about among the denizens of heaven, and to open his way for him through the Ṭuat. In Chapter VIII the deceased says that he shall live as Osiris lives, and then adds: "I am the Moon-god, the Dweller among the gods, I shall not perish." Chapter LXXX is a formula which was believed to give the deceased the power to transform himself into the "god who giveth light in the darkness," *i.e.*, the Moon. Chapter CXXXV was ordered to be recited at the new moon on the first day of the month, and the Rubric states that it caused the deceased to be a perfect spirit, and prevented him from dying a second time, and enabled him to "eat his food side by side with Osiris."

In the Lamentations of Isis and Nephthys[1] Isis addresses Osiris by the name of Ȧn , and says: "Thou risest for us in heaven every day, we cease "not to see thy rays. Thoth acteth as a protector "for thee, he maketh thy soul to stand up in the "Māāṭet Boat in thy name of Ȧāḥ (*i.e.*, Moon). I "come to see thy beauties in the Utcha[2] in thy name "of 'Lord of the Festival of the sixth day.' Thy "nobles are about thee, they depart not from thee. "Thou conquerest heaven by thine august majesty in "thy name of Prince of the Festival of the Fifteenth day. "Thou risest on us like Rā every day, thou shinest on "us like Ȧtem. . . . Thou comest to us as a child each "month.[3] Thy emanation glorifieth Saḥu (Orion) in "heaven in rising and setting every day. I am like "Sepṭet (Sothis) behind thee. I depart not from thee." In this passage we have a description of the glory of the moon at its first quarter, and at its full, and a direct identification of Osiris with the Moon-god Ȧāḥ. The star Orion is also said to derive its glory from Osiris, and Isis is made to identify herself with Sothis (the Dog-star) as in the older texts. The text goes on to say that the holy emanation which proceeds from Osiris

[1] Ed. De Horrack, Col. IV.
[2] One "Eye" of Horus, *i.e.*, the moon.
[3] 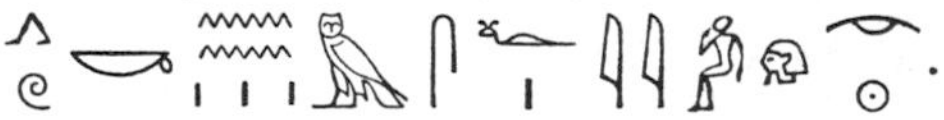

vivifies gods, men, cattle, and creeping things, and that in his season he flows forth from his cavern in order to "pour out the seed" of his soul, which produces offerings in abundance for his Ka, and vivifies both gods and men.[1] The exalted position which Osiris held in the minds of the Egyptians is proved by the words which follow: "No god who existeth is like unto thee."[2] The above-mentioned facts are sufficient to show that the identification of Osiris with the moon is certain.

The earliest lists of Egyptian festivals mention the fact that the first day of the month and the fifteenth were moon festivals, which were duly observed each month throughout the year.[3] These festivals must have been kept religiously by the Egyptians long before the Dynastic Period, and the following extracts prove that modern African tribes all over the Sûdân hold exactly the same views about the moon and its influence as did the Egyptians.

Clapperton, who was present during the feast of the New Moon at Coulfo, says that the people danced and sang to the moon. The hair of the women was plaited, and both hair and eyebrows were stained with indigo. Their eyelids were painted black with antimony, their lips were stained yellow, their teeth red, and their hands and feet were dyed with henna. On the great day of the feast they donned their gayest garments, with their glass beads, and bracelets made of brass, copper, steel, or silver.[4] Piaggia states that every new

1 

2 

3 See the allusion, , in the text of Tetà, l. 12, and in Pepi, l. 657, and Mer-en-Rā, ll. 763, 764.

4 *Great Explorers*, Vol. I, p. 143.

moon was welcomed with elaborate dances and joyful songs.[1]

Among the Barotse the new moon is the occasion of grand festivities. It is a general holiday; men of all ranks sing and dance, while the women assemble apart and give vent to strident howls of their own. They kill oxen, which they cook in the public places, and begin to eat with the appearance of the moon. Their most fashionable instrument of music is a kind of piano. On this they can really play airs, and that in four-time, not five-time like the Arabs; it consists of a square piece of wood hollowed out, on which are fixed a number of pieces of iron, and is played with both hands. To it are sung songs, pitched very high, through the nose.[2] For the new moon of the second month of the year, all the Matabele regiments assembled at Bulawayo, and King Lo Bengula was supposed to fast from food and drink. On the day of the new moon he abstained from all business, and held communication with the spirits of his ancestors. At the dance some 15,000 warriors formed in a semicircle, singing and dancing in time; numbers of women sang and danced too. When the king danced everyone had to dance too, and the witch-doctors went about with sticks beating all those who did not dance with sufficient vigour. After the dance a large number of cattle given by the king were slaughtered. The meat was not eaten that night, but was left for the spirits of the ancestors to come and partake of it; the following day the people ate it, and had a great feast. After the big dance the ceremony of firstfruits was performed. The people went and washed in the river, and then went home and prepared a dish of vegetables mixed with "medicine," prescribed by the witch-doctor, who took the food by handfuls and scattered it among the people. After this the men were allowed to eat any vegetable growing; the women took no part in the ceremony.[3] Among all the people from Nyasaland to

[1] *Viaggi di O Antinori E. C. Piaggia nell' Africa Centrale. Bolletino della Società Geografica Italiana*, Anno I, Firenze, 1868, p. 134.

[2] Decle, *Three Years in Savage Africa*, p. 86.

[3] *Ibid.*, p. 157.

Ujiji the first night of the new moon is a public festival. About Tanganyika it is celebrated by a dance in which the men alone take part.[1]

Du Chaillu noticed among the tribes which he visited an interesting custom. On the first night when the new moon was visible all the people in the village kept silent, and nobody spoke except in an undertone. In the course of the evening King Alapay came out of his house, and danced along the street, his face and body painted black, red, and white, and spotted all over with spots the size of a peach. In the dim twilight he had a frightful appearance, and when he was asked why he painted thus, he only answered by pointing to the moon, without speaking a word. There are other and varying ceremonies in use among different tribes for welcoming the new moon, but in all of them the men mark their bodies with charmed chalk or ochre.[2] In another section of his work[3] he says that a great effort was made by the people to ascertain the cause of their king's sufferings. Quengueza had sent a message to his people to consult Ilogo, a spirit who was said to live in the moon. To consult Ilogo the time must be near full moon. Early in the evening the women of the town assembled in front of Quengueza's house, and sang songs to and in praise of Ilogo, the spirit of Ogouayli (the moon), the latter name being often repeated. Meanwhile, a woman seated in the centre of the circle of the singers, who sang with them, looked steadfastly towards the moon. She was to be inspired by the spirit and to utter prophecies. Two women undertook this duty, but without success, then came a third, little, wiry, and nervous. As she seated herself the singing was redoubled in fury, drums were beaten, and the outsiders shouted madly. Then the woman began to tremble, her nerves twitched, her face was contorted, her muscles swelled, and at last her limbs straightened out, and she lay insensible. Meanwhile, the people besought Ilogo in the moon to tell them who had bewitched the king. When the woman recovered her senses she said she had seen Ilogo,

1 *Ibid.*, p. 295.
2 Du Chaillu, *Adventures*, p. 109.
3 *Ibid.*, p. 399.

who had told her that the king was not bewitched and that a certain plant medicine would cure him.

In the country of Sesheke the only stated day of rest is that which follows the appearance of the new moon. They watch eagerly for the first glimpse of it, and when they perceive the faint outline they utter a loud shout of "Kuā," and recite prayers to it in a loud voice. Livingstone's men called out: "Let our "journey with the white man be prosperous! Let our "enemies perish and the Children of Nake become "rich! May he have plenty of meat on this journey!"[1] On another occasion his men waited until they had seen the new moon to start on a journey.[2]

Rŭmanika, king of Karagŭé, held a New Moon Levée each month. He wore a tiara of beads, with a plume of red feathers over the forehead, and a large white beard set in a band of beads. Thirty-five drums were beaten, and then music was performed on smaller drums and pipes. Rŭmanika's officers then came up to him one by one, and swore an oath of fidelity and sincere devotion to him. A dance by the girls brought the levée to a close.[3] On the first appearance of the new moon each month, the king of the Wahŭma used to shut himself up, and arrange his magic horns for two or three days.[4] Of the king of Uganda Speke says: "The new moon seen last night kept the king engaged at home, paying his devotions with his magic horns or fetishes in the manner already described. The spirit of this religion, if such it can be called, is not so much adoration of a Being supreme and beneficent, as a tax to certain malignant furies, a propitiation, in fact, to prevent them bringing evil on the land, and to insure a fruitful harvest. It was rather ominous that hail fell with violence and lightning burnt down one of the palace huts, while the king was in the midst of his propitiatory devotions."[5] On the day after the appearance of the new moon, according to ancient

[1] *Missionary Travels*, p. 235.
[2] *Last Journals*, Vol. I, p. 298.
[3] Speke, *Journal*, p. 184.
[4] *Ibid.*, p. 213.
[5] *Ibid.*, p. 351.

custom, all the people about court, including the king, shaved their heads, the king, however, retaining his cockscomb, the pages their double cockades, and the other officers their single cockades on the back of the head, on either side, according to the official rank of each.[1]

The Mendis of the Hinterland of Sierra Leone, who reckon time by lunar months, but have not divided the month into weeks, hold a new moon festival, and abstain from all work on the day of the new moon, alleging that if they infringed this rule corn and rice would grow red, the new moon being a "day of blood." From this we may perhaps infer that it was at one time customary to offer human sacrifices to the new moon.[2]

The Tshi equivalent for "moon," *Bohsŭm*, is the name by which deities of the second and third classes are generally known, and from the etymology of that word it may be inferred that there was a time when the moon was reverenced, or regarded as a god. No such trace, however, of sun-worship can be discovered. The Tshi word for "sun" is *ehwia*, from *wia* (to creep, crawl, or move slowly), and its literal meaning is "the creeper," perhaps so named from its apparently slow progress across the heavens. From this it would seem that moon-worship takes precedence of sun-worship, and it certainly appears more probable that primitive man would be impressed by the, to him, erratic and varying phases of the moon, than by the constant and regular recurrence of the sun. But although he might thus at first regard the moon with awe, he would soon learn to know when its appearance might be expected; and then, finding himself neither obstructed nor thwarted by it, would cease to pay as much regard to it as to those sublunary powers which affected him more nearly.[3]

In the Bavili philosophy the moon is regarded as the mother of the sun and of the evening star (Nxienji); the full moon rises from her couch accompanied by this same star, her offspring, now her husband, and this star is then called "Ndongo," *i.e.*, the spirit of witchcraft. The sun

[1] *Ibid.*, p. 299.
[2] Ellis, *The Yoruba-speaking Peoples*, p. 146.
[3] Ellis, *The Tshi-speaking Peoples*, p. 117.

and moon are spoken of either as two Brothers, or two Sisters. The sun and moon are further spoken of as judges to whom certain palavers must be referred.[1] In Karague one night, during a partial eclipse of the moon, all the Wangŭana marched up and down from Rŭmanika's to Nnanaji's huts, singing and beating the tin cooking-pots to frighten off the spirit of the sun from consuming entirely the chief object of reverence, the moon.[2] The old chief at Eloby prayed to the spirit of the new moon, which he regarded as a representative of the higher elemental power, to prevent the evil lower-spirits from entering his town.[3]

The testimonies of travellers quoted above prove that veneration for the moon is universal among Nilotic and other peoples in the Sûdân, and show, moreover, that the spirit of the moon is regarded as the supreme power which presides over vegetation, crops, the harvest, etc. The rest-day which is observed in connection with the appearance of the new moon is fundamentally a religious festival and, as we have seen, kings and others have employed its hours in remembering their sins, and in offering up prayers to be defended from evil and from the attacks of evil spirits. The Egyptians held precisely the same views about the moon as the modern Africans, and they must have expressed their emotions on the days of the new moon and full moon much as they do. The new moons were constant and regular reminders that death was followed by renewed life, and when the full moon filled the sky with its flood of marvellous light, which was wholly free from the fierce, scorching heat of the sun, it produced in their minds the desire for existence after death in a region where reigned Osiris, the god of the moon, and for the refreshing of spirit which they associated with the life that they hoped to live with him.

Describing an entertainment at the court of King Munza Dr. Schweinfurth says: First of all a couple of hornblowers stepped forward and proceeded to execute solos on their instruments. These men were advanced proficients in their art, and brought forth sounds of such

[1] Dennett, *At the Back of the Black Man's Mind*, p. 103.
[2] Speke, *Journal*, p. 199.
[3] Kingsley, *Travels in West Africa*, pp. 110, 452.

power, compass, and flexibility that they could be modulated from sounds like the roar of a hungry lion, or the trumpeting of an infuriated elephant, down to tones which might be compared to the sighing of the breeze, or to a lover's whisper. One of them executed on an ivory horn, which was so large that he could scarcely hold it, rapid passages and shakes with as much neatness and decision as though he were performing on a flute. Next appeared a number of professional singers and jesters, and amongst them a little plump fellow, who acted the part of a pantomime clown, and jumped about and turned somersaults till his limbs looked like the arms of a windmill; he was covered from head to foot with bushy tufts and pigtails, and altogether his appearance was so excessively ludicrous that, to the inward delight of the king, I burst into a hearty fit of laughter . . . . His jokes and pranks seemed never-ending, and he was permitted to take liberties with every one, not excepting even Munza himself; and amongst other tricks he would approach the king with his right hand extended, and just as Munza had got hold of it, would start backwards and make off with a bound.[1]

[1] *Heart of Africa*, Vol. II, p. 50.

CHAPTER XIII.

Osiris as a Bull-god.

In a country like Egypt, the inhabitants of which have always been agriculturists, the bull, by reason of his great strength and virility, must always have been held in reverence, and regarded as the incarnation of a god. The kings of Egypt delighted to call themselves "Bulls," and one of the highest compliments the Court scribe could pay the king was to liken him to a "young bull," or a "mighty bull." Thothmes III describes himself as the "Mighty Bull, rising like the sun in Thebes," and the composer of the Hymn of Praise of him which is put into the mouth of the god Åmen-Rā, says: "I have made the people of Syria and Cyprus to "see thee as a young bull, of determined courage, with "horns ready to gore, indomitable." Again, Rameses II is described as a "Bull, fighting on his own field," the "Bull of Governors," the "Mighty Bull among the "people, thrusting his way through the hosts, destroying "the rebels on the mountains"; and on the Stele of Ḳubbân he is said to be the "Bull whose hoofs trample "down the Sûdânî folk, whose horns gore them, whose "renown is great in the Southern Sûdân, and the fame of "whose terror has reached Karei."[1] Among primitive folk, however, it was not the fighting qualities of the bull which won their regard and reverence, but his strength and usefulness in agricultural work.[2] Greek tradition asserts that the Bull-god Apis was held in the greatest honour in the time of Menes, the first historical king of Egypt,[3] but Manetho says that it was in the reign of Ka-kau,[4] a king of the IInd dynasty, that

[1] Compare a similar custom among modern African kings. The Barotse call their king *Namane Etauna*, *i.e.*, "Great Calf," and Lo Bengula was called "Great Black Calf." See Decle, *Three Years*, pp. 72, 145.

[2] See Diodorus, I, Chapter 21.

[3] Aelian, *De Natura Animalium*, XI, 10.

[4] .

Apis was appointed to be a god. The Stele of Palermo[1] mentions the first celebration of the festival of the "running round of Apis,"[2] but what this ceremony means is not known. Apis was a black bull, with a white blaze on his forehead ; on his back was the figure of an eagle, in his tail were double hairs, and on his tongue a beetle.[3] The bronze figures of the animal show that the blaze is triangular, not square, that vultures, with extended wings, are cut over the fore and hind legs, and that a diamond pattern is cut on the back.[4] The seat of the cult of Apis was Memphis. At Heliopolis the Bull-god Mnevis was worshipped, and the Bull-god Bacchis at Hermonthis, and Strabo says that there were many places both in the Delta and beyond it in which a sacred bull or cow was kept.[5] This statement is of interest, for it proves that in Strabo's time the cult of the bull was widespread.

The Egyptians connected Apis, both living and dead, with Osiris. He was the son of Osiris, as well as of Ptaḥ, and was the "living image of Osiris" ; he was said to have been begotten by a ray of light falling from the moon upon his dam.[6] After the death of his body, his soul was thought to go to heaven, where it joined itself to Osiris, and formed with him the dual-god Åsår-Ḥepi, or Osiris-Apis. Early in the Ptolemaïc Period the Greeks ascribed to this dual god the attributes of Pluto or Hades, and Graecized the Egyptian names under the form "Serapis," who henceforth became the principal object of worship of both Egyptians and Greeks.

The cult of the bull and the cult of Osiris were originally quite distinct, but at a very early period they became united, and worship was paid to the bull as the incarnation of Osiris. The primitive Egyptians imagined a heaven in which were fields of wheat and barley, and it followed, as a matter of course, that there were bulls,

[1] Ed. Schäfer, Berlin, 1902, p. 21.

[2] .

[3] Herodotus, III, 28.

[4] See the figures in the Third Egyptian Room, British Museum.

[5] Strabo, XVII, i, 22.

[6] Plutarch, *De Iside*, Chapter 43.

cows, and oxen there to plough up the ground, to tread in the seed when sown, and to tread out the grain on the threshing floor. The early texts mention the "four bulls of the god Temu," but there was one bull to whom the title "Bull of heaven" was given, and he was the master of all the fields of heaven and of all the cattle therein. With this bull Osiris was identified, and in the Theban Recension of the Book of the Dead we find such passages as these: "Homage to thee, Bull of Åmentet,"[1] "Hail, Bull of Åmentet,"[2] "Osiris, Bull of Åmentet,"[3] "Thou art raised up, O Bull of Åmentet."[4] As, according to one view, the Egyptians hoped to eat bull's flesh and to drink milk in the Other World, they assumed the existence in Sekhet-ḥetepet of a bull and seven cows, but to obtain the gifts of these creatures it was necessary for the deceased to know their names, which were supplied by the CXLVIIIth Chapter of the Book of the Dead. In the Papyrus of Nu it is said: "Homage to thee, O thou who shinest in thy disk, thou "living soul who comest forth from the horizon, Nu "knoweth thee, he knoweth thy name, he knoweth the "names of thy Seven Cows which are with their Bull." The bull, it is clear, was the "living soul" of a god, and of all animals he was held in the greatest honour. At a very early period the bull took the place of human beings in sacrifices to the dead, just as wine became a substitute for blood. And of the sacrifices which were offered up during the performance of the ceremonies for the "Opening of the Mouth" of the deceased, the most important were two bulls. The heart of the bull was cut out and whilst still warm was presented to the mouth of the deceased, or to that of a statue of the deceased, and, as the heart was the seat of the soul, the soul of the bull was transferred to the dead man by touching his lips with it. Now the bull was an incarnation of Osiris, whose son he was, so that the soul which was transferred to the deceased by this ceremony

1 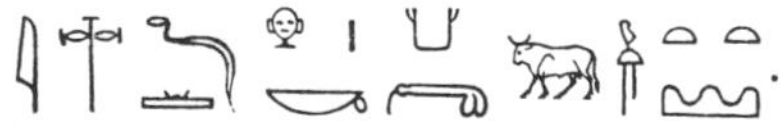. Chapter I, l. 4.

2 Chapter LXIIIA.

3 Chapter CLXXXII, l. 12.

4 *Ibid.*, l. 17.

was that of the son of Osiris, that is to say, Horus. Further, Osiris died and rose again by his own divine power because Horus transferred his soul to his dead father, and as by means of the bull's heart the soul of Horus, the son of Osiris, was transferred to the dead man, it followed that he too would rise again, like Osiris. In one of the ceremonies of the "Opening of the Mouth" the deceased was temporarily placed in a bull's skin, which was probably that of one of the bulls which were offered up during the celebration of the service. From this skin the deceased obtained further power, and his emergence from it was the visible symbol of his resurrection and of his entrance into everlasting life, endowed with all the strength of Osiris and Horus. The ideas which are associated with the skin and the heart of the bull are not peculiar to the Egyptians, and the following passages show that the cult of the bull is widespread among modern African peoples, many of whom sacrifice the animal in funeral ceremonies, and wrap the dead in its skin.

According to Schweinfurth, every thought and idea of the Dinka people is how to acquire and maintain cattle; a kind of reverence seems to be paid to them. Their dung, which is burnt to ashes for sleeping in and for smearing their persons, and the urine, which is used for washing and as a substitute for salt, are their daily requisites. These customs, which exist among most of the pastoral tribes of Africa, may perhaps be the remnant of an exploded cattle worship. The great amusement of the children is to mould goats and bullocks out of clay.[1] Though the Baḳḳârah (*i.e.*, cattlemen) derive their name from cattle, they are more often robbers than neat-herds.[2] The Niam-Niam brought a fine white bullock to Petherick as a peace-offering, and it was slaughtered with great ceremony, and its blood sprinkled over the tents.[3] The Jûr tribes place bull's horns over their graves,[4] and at the burial of a Moro chief a bull is slain and eaten.[5]

[1] *Heart of Africa*, Vol. I, pp. 163, 166.
[2] *Ibid.*, p. 66.
[3] *Travels in Central Africa*, Vol. I, p. 196.
[4] *Ibid.*, p. 256.
[5] *Ibid.*, p. 270.

The Nuba who are not Muslims venerate a bull. The animal chosen as the object of their worship is a piebald

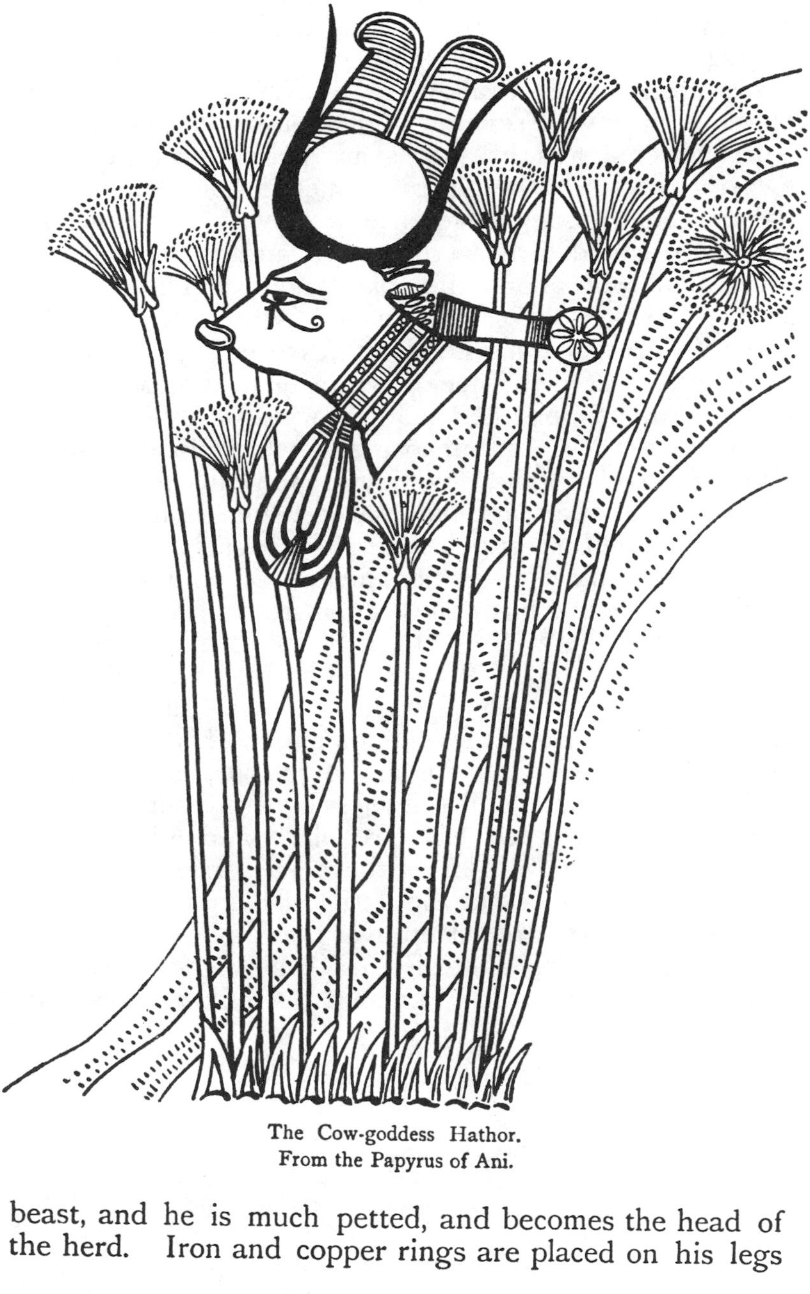

The Cow-goddess Hathor.
From the Papyrus of Ani.

beast, and he is much petted, and becomes the head of the herd. Iron and copper rings are placed on his legs and ankles, and tails of cows and giraffes are suspended from the tips of his long horns. Songs are composed and sung in his praise, he is invested with supernatural powers in the minds of the natives, and in times of danger his help is invoked. This kind of worship extends over a vast portion of Central Africa. When dead, the bull is buried with great ceremony, and when his master dies he is slaughtered and his horns are placed over his dead owner's grave.[1] When a Bari chief is buried a bull is slain.[2] The Busoga reverence bulls with white spots.[3] They are regarded as sacred cattle, and are allowed to wander at will about the plantations. The Nilotic negroes lay a new ox-hide at the bottom of a chief's grave.[4] The Amara, who lived near the N'yanza, when killing a cow, used to kneel down in an attitude of prayer, with both hands together, held palms upwards, and utter the word "Zŭ."[5] On one occasion when Speke visited Mtesa, king of Uganda, he found him sitting in state, with the head of a black bull placed before him.[6]

Du Chaillu mentions that his friend Quengueza believed that many generations before, one of the women of his family gave birth to a calf instead of a child, and that therefore he would not eat bull's flesh,[7] which was "roondah" or "tabû" to him. The Masai bleed their bulls and drink the blood warm, believing that thereby they obtain the strength of the animal and his undaunted courage in battle.[8] The Andorobo not only eat the meat of the ox raw, and whilst it is still warm, but, like the Masai, they bleed their cattle regularly and either drink the hot blood or mix it with their porridge.[9] The Shilluks kill a bullock at the burial of a man of importance, and its horns are set up over the grave. According to Shilluk mythology the Great Creator Jo-uk created a great white cow which came up out of the Nile, and

[1] *Ibid.*, Vol. II, p. 10 ff.
[2] Cunningham, *Uganda*, p. 360.
[3] Johnston, *Uganda*, Vol. II, p. 720.
[4] *Ibid.*, p. 794.
[5] Speke, *Journal*, p. 191.
[6] *Ibid.*, p. 241.
[7] *Adventures in Equatorial Africa*, p. 308.
[8] Thomson, *Through Masai Land*, p. 430.
[9] Johnston, *Uganda*, Vol. II, p. 871.

was called Deung Adok, and this cow gave birth to a man-child, who was the great ancestor of all the Shilluk kings.[1] Mr. Türstig describes an interesting ceremony connected with making enquiries of the dead concerning a sick man. The priest, *Tieit*, sat on his cow-hide seat near a tree from which the branches had been lopped, and to which a number of cows' horns had been fastened. Near the tree a bull was tied. The priest sat with his legs crossed, supporting his head with one hand, whilst with the other he rattled a bottle-shaped gourd half full of lubia beans. After much shaking and rattling of the beans he asked questions on behalf of the sick man, and gave the answer to the relatives in a deep guttural tone, his eyes being meanwhile rigidly fixed on the ground, his voice sounding as though it were not his own. The ceremony lasted from 5 P.M. to 10 P.M., and a good deal of dancing was performed by women, who were decked in fantastic fashion with ostrich feathers, etc. A woman anointed with liquid butter the necks of those who were present and the whole of the body of the bull, after which it was sacrificed. The priest received the ribs of the animal as his share, but in this case no one partook of any of the flesh until 5 A.M. the following morning. During the night it was supposed that the ancestral spirit or god ate the spirit of the bull. Mr. Türstig does not regard the Dinkas who perform ceremonies of this kind as a particularly superstitious race.[2]

Among the Kytch tribes every herd of cattle has a sacred bull, which is supposed to exert an influence over the prosperity of the flocks; his horns are ornamented with tufts of feathers, and frequently with small bells, and he invariably leads the great herd to pasture. On starting in the morning from the cattle krall, the natives address the bull, telling him "to watch "over the herd; to keep the cows from straying; and to "lead them to the sweetest pastures, so that they shall "give abundance of milk."[3] The Egyptians credited bulls and oxen with powers of speech, for in the Tale of

[1] Gleichen, *Anglo-Egyptian Sûdân*, p. 197.
[2] Gleichen, *op. cit.*, p. 146.
[3] Baker, *Albert N'yanza*, p. 49.

the Two Brothers the ox warns the younger brother that his elder brother is lying in wait behind the door with a knife ready to kill him. And the bull in which Bata the younger brother had become incarnate reproached the unfaithful wife of his elder brother, and was slain in consequence of his words to her.[1]

[1] See my *Egyptian Reading Book*, p. xxv.

A CATALOG OF SELECTED

DOVER BOOKS

IN ALL FIELDS OF INTEREST